Environmental Communication and the Extinction Vortex

Technology as Denial of Death

Communication, Comparative Cultures, and Civilizations

Eric M. Kramer, *Series Editor*

Environmental Communication and the Extinction Vortex

Technology as Denial of Death

Eric M. Kramer

University of Oklahoma

Gabriel Adkins

Arkansas Tech University

Sang Ho Kim

Kyoungpook National University, Korea

Greg Miller

University of California, Berkeley

 HAMPTON PRESS, INC.
NEW YORK, NEW YORK

Printed in the United States of America

Library of Congress Cataloging-in-Publication Data

Kramer, Eric Mark.
  Environmental communication and the extinction vortex : technology as denial of death / Eric M. Kramer, University of Oklahoma; Gabriel Adkins, Arkansas Tech University; Sang Ho Kim, Kyoungpook National University; Greg Miller, University of California, Berkeley.
     pages cm. -- (Communication, comparative cultures, and civilizations)
  Includes bibliographical references and index.
  ISBN 978-1-61289-138-5 (hardbound) -- ISBN 978-1-61289-139-2 (paperbound)
  1. Nature--Effect of human beings on. 2. Technology--Environmental aspects.
3. Technology and civilizations. 4. Extinction (biology). 5. Human ecology.
I. Title.
  GF75.K73 2014
  304.2--dc23
                              2014009040

Hampton Press, Inc.
307 Seventh Avenue
New York, NY 10001

Contents

Tables and Figures

Preface

HUBRIS ON A GLOBAL SCALE

Welcome to the Anthropic Reality

Perhaps the most prominent proponent of the link between culture and the environment is the Harvard evolutionary biologist and conservationist Edward O. Wilson. However, it was of course Darwin who decentered the human being by insisting that we are animals like all the rest. Yet this idea has been resisted and rejected, and even for those who accept Darwin, we still act as though we are worthy of privilege. The consequence has been nothing short of cataclysmic for many other species who share the Earth with us.

Wilson (2013) estimates that 27,000 species of all kinds go extinct per year. An early promoter of coevolution theory, Wilson recently laid out the relationship between culture and ecology in *The Social Conquest of the Earth* (2012). In a similar approach to what Kramer (2000b, 2003, 2008, 2012, 2013; Kramer, Callahan, & Zuckerman, 2013) call the pan-evolutionary web of biotic and abiotic factors, Wilson observes a domino effect emerging. To give but one example, since 2007, bee colonies have increasingly devolved into an inexplicable disorganization that leads to what is called "colony collapse disorder." As described by Newitz (2013), "Worker bees would fly away, never to return; adolescent bees wandered aimlessly in the hive; and the daily jobs in the colony were left undone until honey production stopped and eggs died of neglect" (p. 1). Due to complex pan-evolutionary interconnections, this disorganization is not just bad for bees but for everything they pollinate and everything that feeds on what they pollinate, including humans (Kramer, 2000b, 2008, 2012, 2013; Kramer, Callahan, & Zuckerman, 2013).

Due to this recent modern Western cultural propensity for dominion and technological power, we are seeing a whole new epoch on Earth. Consequently, in 2000, Eugene Stoermer and Paul Crutzen began to forcefully lobby the geological societies of London and the United States to adopt a new nomenclature to include the Anthropocene Epoch. In 2008, the Stratigraphy Commission of the Geological Society of London proposed a new epochal division to include Anthropocene. In 2011, the Geological Society of America titled its annual meeting, "Archean to Anthropocene: The Past Is the Key to the Future."

In short, scientists are beginning to recognize that human technological activity beginning with the agricultural revolution about 12,000 years ago, which initiated a growing human influence on ecosystems but absolutely exploded in the last few centuries, has reached global proportions, drastically affecting biodiversity and species extinction. Many ecologists such as Charles Sutherland Elton, John Beard, John Muir, Aldo Leopold, Rachel Carson, and Paul Ehrlich already recognized the growing problem. Of course the great colonial ambitions of the seventeenth and eighteenth centuries set the stage for various efforts to form international institutions. And as Crutzen (2002) reminded us, in 1873, Antonio Stoppani had already named our era the "anthropozoic era" to acknowledge the increasing power and effect of humanity on the Earth's systems.

But the concept of a single, vast global suprasystem of interconnections was not fully conceptualized until the 1970s by environmentalist James Lovelock (1973) and microbiologist Lynn Margulis (1974) with the publication and explanation of the Gaia hypothesis, which sees the entire Earth as a self-regulating system by which homeostasis occurs. The human species appears to be violating the overall homeostatic quality of the Earth's suprasystem. In other words, human activity is destabilizing the Earth's equilibrium.

In December 2012, a group of scientists and scholars launched the Cambridge University Project for Existential Risk. In the spring of 2013, they issued a warning about potential planetary risk due to anthropic bias. The anthropic bias involves observation effects based on perspectivism—specifically, a sort of ego-centric bias on a species scale. Even in our attempts to grapple with the current mass collapse of bio- and cultural diversity, this bias is so obvious. For instance, as is discussed shortly, many futurists are suggesting massive geoengineering of the planet to keep it safe for humans but without really addressing the root causes of problems such as pollution, water degradation, overpopulation, atmospheric warming, and the like. In this book, we reprise the work of Emmanuel Levinas to elucidate and suggest a more integral need for identification with and appreciation of other life on Earth (Kramer, 2013).

The Project for Existential Risk notes that we are in the midst of a human-caused Sixth Great Extinction or "Great Dying." Their efforts are mirrored in many ways by the Future of Humanity Institute at Oxford and publications sponsored by the institute, such as *Existential Risk Reduction as the Most important Task for Humanity* by Nick Bostrom (2011). The previous five extinction events were natural. The one we are currently witnessing is the product of human activity. According to esteemed virologist Frank Fenner, who was instrumental in eradicating Small Pox, humans are part of the ecosystem. He predicts that we may fail to survive the Sixth Event, which essentially makes us suicidal on not just a species level but on a trans-species level (Fenner, quoted by Jones, June 16, 2010).

A founding member of the Cambridge project, Astronomer Royal Martin Rees (2009), has warned that, due to our technological ambitions, humanity may well be in its "final hour." Many scholars such as microbiologists Frank Fenner, Stephen Boyden, and Simon Ross of the Optimum Population Trust claim that an inevitable collapse of human population will occur within the next century or two. In 2013, the director of the Natural Environment Research Council's Centre for Population Biology at Imperial College, Georgina Mace, and her co-investigator Drew Purves, who is head of the computational Ecology and Environmental Science Group at Cambridge, concurred (Predicts, 2013).

Some of course see technology coming to the rescue by means of geo-engineering the atmosphere and oceans. Examples are Tim Kruger, the head of the Oxford Martin School, who suggests geoengineering the oceans by adding huge amounts of lime to lower acidification and capture increased amounts of carbon dioxide. In his book *Sustainable Energy—Without the Hot Air*, David MacKay (2009), a Cambridge physicist, suggests pulverizing a massive amount of rock and leaving it exposed to absorb the carbon dioxide that is overheating the Earth. MacKay also suggests spreading magnesium silicate dust (talcum powder) over a vast area, which could include the ocean. But too much could plunge the planet into a new ice age. MacKay's engineering and instrumentality are emphasized at the beginning of the book, where he has a section on "how to operate" this book.

Other fantasy writers (literally) and "futurists" who suggest we geo-engineer our way out of trouble include Jamais Cascio (2010), who is also a proponent of artificial intelligence in his article, "The Singularity Needs You: Artificial Intelligence, Information Technology, and Virtual Reality Will Radically Change Human Existence," and Annalee Newitz (2013).

Their suggestion for how to "survive extinction" involves space travel and massive geoengineering projects to cool down the climate. No serious scientist considers such solutions remotely feasible. Even if such projects made any sense, they are offered with no context. Such solutions do not address the causes of the problem, such as overpopulation, deforestation, overfishing, and a plethora of other problems. Furthermore, even Cascio concedes that it may be possible that attempts to reengineer the Earth on a global scale could hasten extinction not prevent it. The problem with such suggestions is that they are part of the problem. They present a technological fix for technology. The mindset that we can manipulate our way to utopia by simply magnifying the size of our efforts to technologically alter the most encompassing environmental processes on the planet is illogical. It is the height of hubris. It is like trying to put out a fire by pouring more gas on it.

But some researchers have given it serous consideration. Their conclusions are not promising. Atmospheric scientists have run a number of computer simulations of the sulfate-particle injection process that has been suggested to lower global temperatures. Even if the project could be implemented on a scale large enough to make a difference, the outcome could backfire. Robock, Oman, and Stenchikov (2008) warn that deploying a huge flotilla of ships to emit sulfur into the atmosphere could destroy familiar weather patterns, erode the ozone layer, and hasten the process of ocean acidification, a major cause of extinctions. Unintended warming and acidification are two other possibilities. Also, geoengineering could shut down monsoons (Driscoll et al., 2012). Conveniently left out of the context of such massive projects are the likely socioeconomic impacts that could threaten world peace (Spring & Brauch, 2011). Which part of the globe, for instance, the northern or southern hemispheres, would get the fix would become an issue of the haves and have-nots.

Power and Control

The notion of using technology to our advantage begs two questions. Who is represented by "our"? Therefore, who or what in the larger ecosphere is disadvantaged by "our" relative increase in power and control? Who or what are we gaining advantage over? What are the long-term consequences of this increasingly lopsided ideology of survival of the fittest taken to absurd levels? The notion that technology is power and that it gives advantage is fundamental to the modern notion of technology, and it is a problem when Others, including other species that we have co-evolved with, are dominated and even exterminated.

Positivistic technophiles and the authors of this book part ways on two points. First, without a larger systemic understanding, we are failing to understand the definition of "desirable" outcomes. For instance, eliminating barrier islands and mangrove marshes may, in one economic context with one particular set of interests, seem desirable, until a hurricane comes and its unabated storm surge wipes out the city within which those same people live who initially promoted the destruction of the barrier islands. Second, even when we just concern ourselves with human interests in a naïve and narrow sense, an informed reading of human history demonstrates there is no reason to believe that technology will be used strictly for desirable human ends posited by technology advocates—the history of technological development supports the argument that technological power is developed by the wealthy, closely guarded by those with power, and used to exploit and control societal forces and individuals in society. The powerful technologies that technology advocates foresee are at least as likely to be used for sinister means, such as control and exploitation of social forces and others, including human beings and the Earth in general, as they are to be used for the creation of a techno-utopian society.

The more technology is conceived to serve individualistic ends, the more communities are fragmented and humanity fractures into groups and generation gaps, where one generation uses up resources with no concern for future generations, economic stratification and subcultural groupings and self-segregation intensifies, and so forth. The automobile is a good example. Individuals ride around in massive machines dissociated from the environment and each other to such an extent that their psychology even changes, with normally agreeable and polite people suddenly feeling empowered to express road rage. This empowerment of the individual and devaluation of community by technology occurs not just on actual roads but on the virtual Internet "super highway," where individuals act toward others in more aggressive fashion than in face-to-face interactions. Insofar as power is seen not as a collective quality but as a trait belonging to individuals, technology conceived to service and multiply individual power will facilitate social dissociation, fragmentation, and competition.

Personal status is increasingly expressed by the gadgets one can buy and command—by what one consumes rather than what one produces. Such things belong to our collections of private property; for private use only. The intensification of individualism that marks Western (and Westernizing) modernity is reflected in the technologies this culture is building. The mass society is the flipside of modern individualism. Via things like the Sony Walkman and Apple I-Pod and smartphones, people increasingly inhabit small bubbles or personal spheres of information that dissociate them from others who are sitting right next to them or who are travelling the same thoroughfare. It has only been recently in human history that you could avoid salutations when passing another on a path or trail. Speeds were slower and traffic much less dense. When traveling a route by foot or horse, it was not unusual for people to strike up an acquaintance along the way and share a campfire, stories, and a meal or barter along the way. The journey was not so individuated and dissociated from the destination as it is today. Today we seek faster and faster means to traverse the world, to in effect eliminate the journey altogether as we seek to kill time, which is life itself. Today, whether riding in a car by oneself and listening to one's favorite tunes or on a subway using headphones, technologies increasingly optionalize our lives, enhancing social, psychological, and even cultural distances. Anonymity is thus enhanced even as crowding increases in our burgeoning urban world. Perhaps our narcissistic turn inward is a warning sign that we are overpopulating the world. But as Desmond Morris (1969) warns, living in an increasingly anonymous mass of aggregated individuals leads to less and less empathy and sympathy, traits vital to human cooperation.

From fire making to spear points and more advanced products of "missile envy" (Caldicott, 1986), technology has been around since the beginning of humanity, but today it is reflecting our cultural imperatives, which are individualism and competition over community and cooperation. Our particularly intense externalizing of our wills and imaginations may actually define us as a species. The words *machine*, which shares the Indo-European root *mag(h)* with other modern words, including magic, make, might, and macho, and *engine*, which originally meant a movable tower for assaulting city walls, a means of converting energy and will into mechanical force, manifest the most advanced technological ambitions of our species. Our species is marked by its ability to multiply our will-power-drive by external means, an ability that has expanded spectacularly in the last two centuries to a global ambition to make the world in the image of our own vision, a world of artificial ecosystems, while organic ones face mass extinction. Such power is not such a problem when it is limited. But when our vision, which is limited to our perspective, our narrow view of interests, gains such power, things become unbalanced and distorted.

Unless and until we transcend the dominant individualism that is celebrated in modernity, unless we can integrate our narcissism with the needs of the entire super- and hypersystems that we belong to and that sustain us, we are endangering everything. Reciprocity within a holistic understanding can sustain feedback and adjustment that in some contexts may be similar to empathy, sympathy, and the hermeneutic principle taken from Aristotle of *phronesis* or prudence. We must listen to the feedback the rest of the planet is giving us and care about it.

Technological prowess tends to see all things as rational. But the idea of rationality in modern individualism becomes extremely truncated. Techno-rationality is defined as the most efficient means to achieve a narrow goal— my interest or a small group's "special interests." Under these conditions, a rational course of action is simply the most efficient way to get what I want. This constitutes a sort of Baconian hedonic calculus or cost/benefit analysis that embodies positivistic epistemological criteria and is terribly truncated and premised upon narcissism. It not only lacks empathy for the Other, be it another human group, the American Bison, the Dodo bird, or entire forests and fish stocks, but techno-rationality defines such feelings as irrational and delusional—as backward compared with forward progressive thinking. As a result, in recent history, we have countless examples of mass destruction seen as irrelevant "collateral" damage in the proper, progressive pursuit of interests.

For example, there was the heartbreaking spectacle of millions of giant salmon on their prehistoric migration routes suddenly depleted by modern industrial scale fishing and then blocked completely on all the great rivers by dams such as the Bonneville Dam that flooded the Cascades Rapids on the Columbia River and the Shasta Dam on the Sacramento River. Native peoples who had netted salmon in rapids such as Celilo and Kettle Falls and Priest Rapids on the Columbia, the former of which was flooded by the Dalles Dam, stood by in horror and watched millions of the spirit/fish flounder and perish in the backwash at the base of the new technological marvels. Thus, we have the modern clash between cognition versus affect, objective truth versus subjective sentimentalism. But we claim that such adumbrations of the basic dualism that marks modernity from Descartes on are merely the expression of one particular ideology—modern positivism.

According to this modernist worldview, technological prowess can be defined as majority expression. All else is defined as resource base, as pools of raw resources and labor meant to be converted/organized into power guided by particular interests. Applied elite "special interests" give directionality and purpose, and that is often taken for rationality itself. To question what the most rational or efficient course of action is presumes a final goal, and such goals are defined and given by elites within society. Their narcissistic interests become society's standard of reason. With a postulated goal, progress toward it can commence and be measured. And the goal of the modern elite is to accumulate ever more power to define the direction of society. It is a vortex of power for power's sake. The goal and purpose is to amass more power that will enable one to amass yet more power in an endless cycle of acquisition, what Lewis Mumford called the Leviathan on wheels—the will to ever more will. This force of ordination for a single purpose is described by Mumford (2010):

> From Descartes' platform it was easy to take the next step; and that was to outline a set of principles favorable to a political order that would deliberately turn men into machines, whose spontaneous acts could be regulated and brought under control, and whose natural functions and the moral choices would all be channeled through a single responsible center—the sovereign ruler or, in the bureaucratic jargon of our own day, the Decision Maker. (p. 98)

Thus, Mumford agrees with Max Weber that the technicization of life extends to the ordination of human comportment in ever-greater detail. The more we link into the systems of technic, the more we are regulated. Millions if not billions of pages of laws, regulations, and policies proliferate. Regimentation thus expands from militaries and religious orders into everyday life and for the same purpose—control. Communication technologies increasingly enable this purpose via feedback. Efficiency of regulation becomes the last and only moral standard.

As the old saying of robber baron industrialists goes, the best way to predict the future is to make it. Such daring, such hubris and narcissistic exuberance exists at the core of the motives, beliefs, and values of modern individualism. It has a vitalizing force that liberates individual innovation, but without reflection and prudence it becomes destructive of other agendas, including those that exist in nature. This devolves into the modern survival of the most willful, the Hobbesian war of all against all. Those who guide the design of new technological systems and who own and control them—the "decision makers"—are the power elite. Thus, technology cannot be dissociated from political-economic aspects of reality.

The natural world, the world as given, is seen as inadequate to our wants and needs. The wild must be domesticated. Civilization must spread. It must be conquered and eliminated. It must be manipulated and improved. The current state of affairs involving mass extinction of both flora and fauna and also entire cultures highlights the fact that our species has been exercising great ambition to construct a made world without philosophical reflection, a world that is literally dying even as we attempt to achieve immortality. This reveals our situation as demonstrably narrowing to the vanishing point of a single positive reality that claims, absurdly, universal validity. Is this our vision? If it is not, then our pursuit of the considerable technicization of the world as the means to extend our existence and will beyond our mortal limitations has run horribly amuck. Vital and robust life proliferates forms. It does not contract to a single permanent form.

This ambition for control and immortality is essentially personal. It lacks the altruism that lies at the core of tolerance of diversity. Positivistic logic dictates that every problem has solutions and that among those solutions there is one best way. Cultures present abundant ways of living and solutions to survival problems. But according to positivism, there is only one "best" way. This is hypertrophic individuation that institutes one perspective and then applies it to all. This is the essential relationship between the modern individual and the modern mass, the standardized, average individual where a single size, a single life agenda such as the accumulation of wealth, that logically/naturally should—and this is the moral imperative of a judgment that claims for itself objective status—fit all. Objectivity, rationality, and naturalism are thus exploited as inoculating myths of modernity that justify the status quo as inevitable (Kramer, 1997). We masses on the normal curve all aspire and work to acquire our personal computers, smart phones, automobiles, collections of music, and mass-produced stuff, our trophies as a "natural" condition long recognized by social scientists and observers of the modern condition (Gans, 1991; Lippmann, 1955/1989; Packard, 1972). Our death-defying delusion is expressed through status developed by being higher than others as measured through wealth and consumption (Packard, 1964, 1969). Every year the measure of narcissism increases.

The modern individual believes that she has a divine right to be free to pursue whatever makes her happy, and structured paths are presented to her by her sociocultural and psychoeconomic environments (Postman, 1985). Postman (1985) put the confluence of technology and culture this way: "The introduction into a culture of a technique such as writing or a clock is not merely an extension of man's power to bind time but a transformation of his way of thinking—and, of course, of the content of his culture" (p. 13). Culture, as Ernst Becker (1973, 1997) points out, is the socially constructed (objectified) set of "appropriate" alternatives to status.

Self-esteem and status emerge from our ability to buy happiness. This is the role of modern consumer culture. It is to present ways of being satisfied—of being a meaningful and valued member of something bigger than oneself. Entertainment (happiness), self-esteem, and status are measures of the manifest consumption capacity of the individual. Increasingly such roles involve producing and consuming technology. This is a new form of status and structure for gaining status via organized opportunities offered through post-World War II organizational culture, which spread throughout society and highly orchestrated campaigns promoting consumerism of consumer technology (Whyte, 1956/2002). From this emerged the modern and massive cult of youth and its impact on cultural products from film to music and on an individual's mortality salience and self-esteem. The very perception of aging changed dramatically for consumption, requiring ever-changing product lines. And the idea and valuation of technical obsolescence was transferred to human beings. Thus, planned obsolescence, first described in 1960 by Vance Packard in the book *The Waste Makers*, makes waste out of a growing graying population across the industrialized world. Everything becomes disposable in an increasingly commercialized and technicized world, including temp workers and other forms of humans caught up in the modern time condition variously described as temporal anxiety or a chronic sense of urgency (Kramer, 1997, 2003). Humans are increasingly described as mechanical parts within a larger structural functional system. They are seen as having "skill sets," "capacities," and "competencies," the variable demand for which is transforming education into an increasingly vocational orientation. It is time, we are told, to "get real." Thus, culture is changed.

The manifestation of this ambition is to transcend the personal into the public sphere, where all can see one's productive prowess as an industrious person—as an objective, demonstrable fact and score-board of "visibility." Look what I have built? It is built to last, to outlast me, and therefore, absurdly, to extend *me*, my *personal* ambition, into a transcending *objective* field. Thus, Facebook pages, resumes, and vitae endure and continue to communicate in cyberspace, in a strange twilight existence long after the person has died. People continue to visit deceased people's Facebook pages to "see each other." The modern individual cries out from beyond the grave, "I have created an object of lasting power/value that yells 'me' forever." This absurdity of objectifying the subjective self via one's products, including a record of one's productivity, is rooted in the philosophical justification for modernism; namely, positivism as the dominant and founding ideology of modernity. We seek a permanent and accurate record of all that has expired and transpired. This includes the political, philosophical, ethical, and epistemological dimensions of positivism. Hyper-individualism is modern objectivism.

Positivism is an absurd philosophy that denies the existence of philosophy as not being an object, and it grounds knowledge in empirical, which is to say direct personal observation as the source of objectivity. Simply piling up personal observations and averaging them does not guarantee truth. In fact it may institutionalize a fallacy as a mere consensus of error. But what is popular, what sells, has become truth in the modern world, a world that has armies of professional sales persons who eventually climb the corporate pyramids to become leaders of our societies and cultures, strongly suggesting, persuading us what is natural, just, and moral, what we as free individuals deserve, and what we should want and need from gadgets to wars (Henry, 1963; Packard, 1957/2007; Riesman, Glazer, & Denney, 1969/2001). The reason that "modern progress" is killing the planet is because of the fundamental absurdity of positivistic modernity (Lerner, 1965). It is progress without a goal, the fundamental flaw of absurd utopianism. While we have noted that this is the will to more will, it is also called progress for its own sake. Because we don't know what our goal is, we cannot measure progress rationally, and it therefore becomes a permanent state of being—what J. Hillis Miller (2009) calls a kind of moronic perpetual happy positivism. Because no final goal is defined, we can never arrive and stop our endless machinations to conquer nature and be happy.

This enormous will-to-power via the engine, the means of converting will and energy into material mechanical force, separates humans from other members of the Earth community, a separation that marks the split in the so-called cosmic egg of primordial unity between nature and culture. Culture is, by definition, that which is not nature. Culture is material technology and behavior, but it is also the motives and values that guide what is to be made. Thus, the denial of values as unreal unhinges our ability to critically assess what kind of world we are making. The ideology at the core of this out-of-control expression of will-power-drive is positivism. Positivism as first articulated by two French social activists, Claude Saint-Simon and Auguste Comte, celebrates the application of instrumental reason to industry as the solution to all problems. It also inoculates itself from criticism by first denying any use-value to philosophical critical reflection regarding values and motives, and second by claiming to establish once and for all the one and only valid version of reality. The industrialist thus monopolizes the most powerful discourse, which is the definition of use-value and reality itself.

This book argues that positivistic modernity expresses everything, including technology, in a particularly extreme and myopic fashion, suggesting a second absurd condition whereby progress has no final goal but has become a permanent justification for all sorts of manipulation of the material world. A third absurdity is that the philosophy that denies the reality of values named itself after a value position—namely, positivism as opposed to negativism.

Technology is materially manifested instrumental reason. Instrumental reason is perspectival judgment—expressed desire, motive, and ambition. It defines the usefulness of a value orientation from a particular perspective, but then, because technology can "prove" that it works, it inflates that singular perspective to be the only true and real one. Technology embodies particular desires. It is perspectival, meaning that instrumental reason is an expression of *egocentric interests*. While technology can publically, "objectively," demonstrate its prowess, it is in fact an expression of a particular interest. It is conceived and executed to manipulate and exploit resources in a *particular* way and for a particular goal by grasping/interpreting the environment including human beings as means to those specific ends. This process involves transforming all Others into tools in the service of the self. This "objective" and "objectifying" process is the *good* in itself. Technicization and the metaphysical presumption of materialism constitute a blatant value judgment that inoculates itself against reflective examination by proving, empirically/materially, that it *works*. Technicization is thus beyond criticism. It becomes positive, good—progress. Technicization of the world is the penultimate utopian expression of modernity and the age of ideology. It involves hubris on what Jean Gebser (1949 Ger./1985 Eng.) has called a hypertrophic or, by historical standards, an extremely exaggerated level.

Manifested by this egocentric attitude is a particularly individualistic concept of value. In this worldview, if a thing, animal, or person cannot be exploited for or by me, *according to my interest*, then it has no value at all. This is so because material technology and ordination (organization), as a metaphysical bias (that absurdly denies the existence of metaphysics) denies the very existence of inherent rights, value, or dignity. Modern ego-hypertrophy opens the door to extreme relativism. Rather, modernity and late or "post-modernity" admits no such thing as inherent meaning or value. That thing, animal, or person has value only from my perspective and only insofar as they can be exploited. Thus, the wielder of technology becomes more responsible for technological influences because technology is a means of amplifying power. If this is not the case, then we must admit to living in an entirely meaningless world of randomly jostling material bits, where such phenomena as caring and empathy are pure nonsense—where brute power, including technology, is the only real thing, in which case any ethics of technology, though begged, is delusional. We take a different position.

Our stance in this book contends that, first, technology is quintessentially a human activity/product, and, as such, is steeped in ethical issues and demands self-reflection. It is as much an issue for the humanities and social sciences as it is for material engineering.

Second (and made even more disturbing when the previous arguments are considered), we disagree with the implications of the "intermarriage" of ourselves with our technologies. While we have no opposition to utilizing technology to advance (for example) medical treatments with the hope of eliminating diseases and disabilities, the implications of merging physically with our technologies is another matter altogether. But even here, some medical professionals have confessed that their ability to save infants with serious birth defects who, in a previous era would have died, has had the unintended consequence of proliferating and amplifying those genetic predispositions in subsequent generations.

Bottom line, technology is the expression of human perspective, an individual's or group's ideology onto nature. Technology is hardly value-free. To the contrary, technology is a bold expression of value as expressed by goal orientation and means. Values, expectations, motivations, and beliefs are thus transforming nature. There is a darker side to the human-technology exchange that pro-technologists fail to address; this dark side includes disturbing implications for social structures, species viability, individual protection from intrusion and control, and individual susceptibility to technological failures. An example is the increasing proliferation of "superbugs," which are bacterial agents such as Methicillin-resistant *Staphylococcus aureus* (MRSA) and carbapenem-resistant *Klebsiella pneumonia* (CRKP).

From this position, we seek in this book to offer not a warning about technology but rather a warning about the uses of it. We have seen in the course of human history that technology utilization frequently has unintended negative consequences. Too often societies and individuals have adopted technology based on utopian hopes rather than a careful consideration of all the existing evidence while also failing to examine how that technology may either fail or be utilized by those who are ignorant or have sinister or hidden intentions. It is apparent that society is susceptible to the music of the "pied pipers" as far as technology is concerned—the tendency is to rush to follow those with a positive view of technology (many with vested financial interests) without carefully considering where we are going or what we are doing, or who will benefit from adopting the technology being promoted. Unfortunately, we can no longer afford to follow blindly the path we are on (while certainly paved with promise) because it could indeed be a rocky future for both individuals and society as a whole. Promise, a wonderful paving material for dreams, is not the same thing as factual outcomes. This book is a message of "caution" for humanity: The path to the technological utopia that supposedly lies ahead may prove to be missing a bridge or two.

Introduction

Welcome to the Grand Modern Accomplishment—The Extinction Vortex

TECHNO-NARCISSISM AND THE EXTINCTION VORTEX

Do not expect spectacular geysers of fire and brimstone, dark skies, the bellowing roar of a demonic being, the Earth spinning in the wrong direction, the oceans turning to blood, the four horsemen of the Apocalypse and other such dramatic imaginings of fantasy writers of antiquity or today. Nonetheless, the world is in decline—not stock markets or property values but life on Earth.

Thanks to its Goldilocks fortune, the Earth sails almost friction-free through a complete orbital path that is 584 million miles or 940 million kilometers long. It does so once every 365 times it rotates. In the last 24 hours, we, all of us—plants, animals, and people—traveled roughly 1,600,000 miles along our orbital path at a speed of about 66666.6666666 miles per hour (on average). If this number bothers you, you can convert it to different units. Measurements are all relative and arbitrary anyway. A thing is not reducible to its measures. Measures measure something other than themselves, and that something has inherent qualities that measurements describe such as weight. Scales are arbitrary. They are simply semiotic markers that allow us to discern relationships. The relationships between numbers give meaning. As the Nobel-winning physicist Richard Feynman (2005) said, "You can know the name of a bird in all the languages of the world, but when you're finished, you'll know absolutely nothing whatever about the bird. . . . So let's look at the bird and see what it's doing—that's what counts" (p. x).

Two kinds of dualism often get confused. One we should never ignore, and that is the difference between words and deeds. The second one is a false dualism between empirical objects as real and logic as not. That is a false dualism that we should ignore. Both are real.

No matter what I say or believe, I can be wrong. I can be empirically mistaken or illogical. Reality is not simply what I say it is. And those who deny the impact of human activity on the environment and climate are demonstrably wrong. The "linguistic turn" aside, every philosopher has understood that there is an important difference between knowing the name of something and knowing something. Ironically, when the old joker Feynman told his bird story, he made up fake Japanese, Chinese, and other words to denote a "thrush" to underscore the difference between arbitrarily naming something like a bird and actually knowing it.

Now for the second dualism: Something like a measurement, which is not an empirical object (I cannot visit the number 3 on vacation, and it makes no sense to ask how much mathematics weighs), cannot be good or evil because it is arbitrary. The key here is to understand that while all organisms function on the basis of sensory input from the environment, only humans can know by means of logic, which has no texture, length, color, weight, or other empirical qualities. Only humans do science. Despite the true fact that neither logic nor science has color or extension in space, they are not only real, but they also constitute the higher order cognitive ability that characterizes human beings as unique on the planet. The dualism, which denies the existence of things that are not empirical, must be avoided lest we become absurd and reject our own logical accomplishments, our own special capacity to think beyond the immediate here and now (Husserl, 1913 Ger./1982 Eng.).

It may be that those who are attacking intellectualism and science these days are people who simply do not understand how higher order thinking works. Seeing something with your own eyes is empirical but also merely anecdotal. Anecdote does not meet the standards to be called knowledge. Knowledge requires more than empirical input. It requires constant comparison of repeated observations (reliability) and the application of logical, analytical method.

There are realities that may be very inconvenient, realities that we do not like. Yet they cannot be linguistically manipulated or "converted" to make them disappear as we can 66666 mph by simply transforming it into 107288.527 kph. Such realities that are more than mere arbitrary words can be judged as "warning signs," as accurate indicators of things to come—as omens no matter what language or unit of measure you use to describe them.

All mythological whimsy about the good and evil of particular numbers aside, the reality that the Earth is in the "Goldilocks zone" (or whatever you wish to name it) around its star is actually very good luck for all of us. The set of relationships so nicknamed makes this planet ripe for life. This said, it is a bit of a fad these days to speak of the imminent extinction of humans. Perhaps. But we argue that that is unlikely. And for life in general? The Earth will endure what we do to it, and life is very likely to continue for a long time, quite probably long after humans are gone. *However, life as we know it really is in trouble*, no matter how you measure it and despite the rhetorical denials of "conservative" anti-environmentalists. And furthermore, all ideology and talk aside, it is demonstrable that the environment is in trouble because of the negligence and even malice of our species. Malice?

We have never knowingly witnessed the birth of a new species in nature. But we have knowingly witnessed the death of entire species. Countless examples can be offered to make the case, from the ruthless extermination of the Carolina parakeet to the annihilation of what was once the most numerous bird in North American, the passenger pigeon. The last free Carolina parakeet was deliberately killed in a swamp in Florida in 1904. On February 21, 1918, Incas, the last Carolina parakeet in existence died in the Cincinnati Zoo. Incas perished in the same aviary cage where Martha, the last known passenger pigeon, had died four years earlier on September 1, 1914. In both of these cases, we knowingly watched the very last of a species live out its days and perish as scientists and naturalists searched in vain for mates. These are examples of wanton environmental destruction.

A more contemporary example occurred in 1991. In that year, Iraqi forces in Kuwait deliberately opened the taps on an offshore terminal and several oil tankers spilling between 400 and 520 million gallons of oil into the Persian Gulf, the largest oil spill in history, an amount much higher than initially estimated (Khordagui & Al-Ajmi, 1993; *New York Times*, March 18, 1993; Zielinski, 2010). This resulted in "considerable damage to wildlife" in the Persian Gulf (Bultmann, 2001). For the sake of comparison, as famous and disastrous as it truly was and continues to be, the 1989 *Exxon-Valdez* does not even make the top 10 list of the largest oil spills in history.

Another uniquely human trait, not high-order logic but careless greed, has marked the Earth. And the problem is not limited to one culture, linguistic community, ideology, religion, economic class, or political persuasion. But it does mark the rise of a single civilizational structure we call perspectival modernity (Gebser, 1949 Ger./1985 Eng.; Kramer, 1992, 1997, 2003a, 2013). The word *perspectival* delineates the modern style of hypertrophic individualism that characterizes the modern human being. And this type of human who tends to elevate her own little perspective to the status of truth (the egocentric fallacy) is spreading across the globe. The valorization of individualism and its egocentrism constitutes the essence of what it means to be a modern Westernized person. Also we confront the spread of the single civilizational form as monoculture, for the globalization of modernity begs the question whether it is even possible to modernize without Westernizing. Modern hypertrophic individualism, which is valorized as the greatest accomplishment of humanity, worth defending at all costs, is, thanks to globalization, no longer limited to Western Europe and the United States. This has led to new expectations about personal liberty, rights, wealth, and comfort. This increase in life expectations has inspired the "march of progress." This march has spread out along the historical expansion of Western colonialism, science, and technology, which are all integral to conquest. Adoption of this civilizational structure, which emphasizes technological culture, has defused into cultures and places across the globe. It has infiltrated places that, left to their own indigenous "devices," did not and may not have ever created technological culture as we have it today.

For instance, the first offshore oil drilling occurred not in Western Europe but in the Caspian Sea in 1873. Since then the Caspian (the largest enclosed inland body of water on Earth) and the Aral Seas have been devastated by greedy practices including overfishing, water diversion (theft from the lake), and local oil production—all directly linked to the adoption of a culture that stresses individual, private wealth accumulation and modern technological culture to make it possible. Since the 1960s when Soviet engineers rerouted the rivers that fed the Aral, which was formerly one of the four largest lakes on Earth, it, like the Salton Sea in California, which was also drained for irrigation purposes, dried up. Peter the Great's legacy was not simply a Russian version of Western enlightenment culture but also the technological ambition that was the material proof of its superiority.

The political ideology of nation-states does not matter. Modernity, with its intense industrial scale operations directed by the "fathers of progress," positivistic entrepreneurs and/or dictators, is the essential factor in explaining our technological activities and their consequences today. Progress is a spatial-linear concept. It is an essential expectation of the modern human. Progress means to move away from past practices, expectations, motivations, and values. It presumes that the past had no methods and therefore no valid knowledge or adequate–satisfactory solutions. Progress means "better." Positivism is the grand value judgment of modernity. Anything that challenges it is seen as negative. Progress has many consequences. One is the deliberate and methodical eradication of traditional societies, including their ways of relating to the environment—specifically to encourage them to start to see it as a resource base in need of development. Western notions of progress also encourage traditional peoples to see themselves as backward and in need of development into a new modern form of human being. If they conform, they too, like their environment, can become a valuable or productive resource, which demonstrates advancement. As noted, progress has many consequences and one is to exterminate the past so that difference can emerge. Progress means change—change in a "good" way.

Only one tenth of the Aral remains today, leaving layers of highly salt-ed sand. When we drain away traditional values, beliefs, motives, expecta-tions, and ways of living, what is left? The impact of modernization always involves Westernization, including irreversible changes in both watersheds and communities, in both eco- and ethnospheres, even in what people con-sider right and wrong; wise leadership versus foolish or obsolete council (Davis, 2007, 2009, 2010; Kramer, 1992, 1997, 2003a, 2013).

Some efforts by Iran to restore the Aral have been made but they are limited, and the sea will never be as it once was. In the Caspian, like so many places across the Earth, thanks to more technologically efficient methods, overfishing along with pollution and insecticide runoff have caused a "dra-matic" decrease in fish populations. For instance, the sturgeon population crashed "from 30,000 tons in 1985 to only 5,672 tons in 1995," leading to an attempt to regulate the harvest, but unfortunately "a quota system, intro-duced together with a temporary ban on pelagic fishing, does not appear to have been effective in reviving the dwindling fish populations" (Caspian Environment Programme, 2013, p. 1). Regulations work only if they are enforced. Entire seas have been absolutely decimated by modern human activity. Meanwhile on land, the Caspian tiger (*Panthera tigris virgate*), which roamed forest corridors from Turkey to China for countless cen-turies, became extinct in the wild in 1973. Today, there are no individual Caspian tigers left even in captivity (Seidensticker, Christie, & Jackson, 1999).

Wide-scale environmental degradation in China is equally disturbing and by all accounts rapidly escalating (Day, 2005; Economy, 2010; Shapiro, 2012; Tilt, 2009). From Muslim Indonesia to Catholic Brazil, from Hindu India to Madagascar, where a large percentage of the population practices a religion of traditional ancestor worship, wide-scale deforestation has been devastating. The problem transcends religion, politics, even economics. Is it only kleptocratic atheistic Communist dictators and Christian capitalistic managers of massive industrial operations who are destroying the environ-ment? The answer, sadly, is no. That would be simple and fairly easy to address. Rather the problem is culture—the globalizing spread of modern expectations, values, and motivations. Culture is total. Because everyone expects more and more wealth and convenience, the scale of production/ consumption has exploded. The issue involves us all.

For instance, who would think to lump pot growers with oil magnates? But this problem of highly technologized large-scale activities extends to marijuana growers in rural California. "There are people coming from all over America to grow marijuana. They're here to get in on the action—the so-called Green Rush" (biologist Scott Bauer quoted by Mozingo, 2012, p. 1). They are rushing to "cash in" on the burgeoning medical marijuana indus-try. The unregulated and illegal operations are destroying the environment.

State scientists, grappling with an explosion of marijuana growing on the North Coast, recently studied aerial imagery of a small tributary of the Eel River, spawning grounds for endangered coho salmon and other threatened fish. In the remote, 37-square-mile patch of forest, they counted 281 outdoor pot farms and 286 greenhouses, containing an estimated 20,000 plants—mostly fed by water diverted from creeks or a fork of the Eel. The scientists determined the farms were siphoning roughly 18 million gallons from the watershed every year, largely at the time when the salmon most need it. (Mozingo, 2012, p. 1)

And that is just "one small watershed." Scott Bauer, the state scientist in charge of coho recovery on the North Coast for the Department of Fish and Game, lamented that if you extrapolate from that one sample to all the other tributaries, the impact is widespread and occurring just as millions of dollars in investment to bring back the coho after decades of logging was beginning to show signs of recovery. This is bad. But the impact of modern large-scale marijuana production is not limited to damage to streams and rivers. Researchers from the University of California Davis found 58 rare mink-like fishers in Humboldt County near Yosemite killed by rat poison used by pot farmers to stop the animals from chewing on their plants. Mark Higley, a biologist who works on the Hoopa Indian Reservation, was "incredulous over the poisons that growers are bringing in. He and other scientists have found black bears poisoned by Carbofuran, which the growers mix with tuna and sardines to poison the bears to keep them from raiding their camps. It is just one in a litany of pollutants seeping into the watershed from the pot farms: fertilizers, soil amendments, miticides, rodenticides, fungicides, plant hormones, diesel fuel, human waste" (Mozingo, 2012, p. 1). Scientists have also found the anticoagulant d-Con, which the growers spread around in the deep forest to protect their plants from wood rats, in dead endangered spotted owls (scientist Mourad Gabriel quoted by Barringer, 2013, p. 1).

The problem involves everyone who is rushing to modernize/ Westernize/technologize everything for the sake of efficiency in order to satisfy a hypertrophic form of selfish individualism (Gebser, 1949 Ger./1985 Eng.; Kramer, 1992, 1997, 2003a, 2013). Pot makes me feel good. I want my pot. Anyone, communist or capitalist, banker or "hippie farmer," anyone doing anything on an industrial level, as Ernest Friedrich Schumacher (1973) explained to us long ago in his landmark book, *Small Is Beautiful: Economics as if People Mattered*, creates huge amounts of wealth in a short period of time but also profound ethno- and eco-environmental degradation. In this book, we modify Schumacher's sentiments to include all living things, not just people—as if all life mattered.

How can we be so careless, even malicious? What is happening? As dissociation increases in the modern world, we identify less and less with Others—other things, people, plants, and animals (Kramer, 1992, 1997,

2003a, 2013). Over centuries, our view of the universe has been changing. The universe has been emptying out, expanding to infinity, and dying. As it expands, we contract into individual monads with personal perspectives and interests. Once our own little "light cone" perspective of the world is all that is left, we exalt it to the status of truth. Careless arrogance is the result. Traditional human communities believed in animism, that everything was alive, finished, perfect, unchanging, finite, and that there was no such thing as empty space. Because everything was alive and watching us, we had to be careful lest we offend something. Most ritual had to do with giving thanks and asking permission. Care and appreciation are the operant terms here. We had to show respect for the Other because it shared identity with us as either a totem animal or a sacred place. Because of this attitude, large-scale manipulation of the environment was deemed both unnecessary, as the universe is perfect and finished, and potentially offensive to other beings. But once the universe changed into a dead void, we could proceed to pursue our own desires with impunity (liberty). Urban empire arose, and the world of the Neolithic and Mesolithic hamlet and clan began to wane. Almost none still exists today.

As dissociation increased, the innumerable and intermingling spirits coalesced into pantheons of distinct gods who were increasingly distant (spatial) and anthropomorphic. The amorphous spirits we perceived became increasingly anthropomorphic because we were becoming increasingly self-centered. Over time, pantheons collapsed into a single god. And finally that last god, which tolerated no Others, vanished into an infinite void universe containing a little bit (by spatial proportion) of dead vibrating matter devoid of life and spirit. The new dead and empty universe does not know or care that we are here. And this is a projection of our own state of being. In our anxiety, we search not for the last passenger pigeon but for some other sign of life "out there" in the vast reaches of space.

As our meaning and identity shrank, the universe expanded and meaning evaporated along with care and appreciation. We suggest that this state of affairs has created the famed "existential angst" and alienation that plagues the modern individual, and that this has made the Modern frantic to accumulate as fast as possible as much as possible—for only material things are real. But the comfort they afford is qualitatively limited. At the same time the universe was expanding and dying, the idea that all humans shared a common bond with all of the cosmos faded. Our extended sense of self collapsed. Our cosmic community shrank to a common blood identity with only but also all other true human beings. There were other human-like beings around, perhaps in a valley beyond the mountains, but they were not true humans. Then as dissociation continued to increase, human identity dwindled further to include only tribal identity/caring, and that then decreased to extended clan identity. As dissociation intensified extended clan identity contracted, limiting our care and identity to those in our modern nuclear family. Finally, our identity shrank down to the hypertrophic modern individual I, who has no inherent meaning or identity—for there is nothing else to be identical with. The sins of the father no longer are the sins of the son. My wealth is mine, not my brother's. I share nothing.

The modern I is a monad, which the Enlightenment modern philosophers such as Hegel, Kant, and Leibniz described. The modern individual has meaning only as a function of relative difference from the Other, not communal identity with the Other-which-is-me. His fortune is not my fortune. What I am is nothing but the fact that I am *not* you. I am nothing but a negative linguistic function within an arbitrary semantic field. As dissociation increases, meaning, identification with other things, and care evaporate. Inherency is deemed a fiction. And so we find ourselves in a peculiar situation that is absurdly suicidal and nihilistic yet resolutely narcissistic.

Late modernity is increasingly looking like a psychopathic culture. Our leaders are shameless, and voters are either apathetic or sycophantic followers of what Plato (1998a, 1998b) called "evil lovers," public speakers who do not seek to speak the truth and free their beloved audience members to make independent judgments but instead lie and seek to enslave their audiences, making them dependent. The evil lover is a degenerate cult leader who censors what her followers can hear and see and demands they terminate all ties with all other possible influences, such as family, friends, and other sources of information. Often evil lovers are gifted at twisting words such as "conservative" to mean an attitude in opposition to all efforts at prudent "conservation" and preservation, especially when such efforts impede any and all expressions of individual free will, desire, and impulse. A perfect spokesperson for this modern hypertrophic individual is Ayn Rand.

We have become more individualistic and narcissistic at the same time that we have become massive in numbers. Scholars including Karl Marx, Ferdinand Tönnies, Max Weber, Sigmund Freud, George Simmel, and many others even argued that one causes the other—that once our populations grew beyond the reach of interpersonal and kinship relationships, we became indifferent to each other, capable of inflicting great cruelty, and then by habit beyond each other to everything within our reach (Gebser, 1949 Ger./1985 Eng.; Kramer, 2003a, 2013; Morris, 1969; Packard, 1972; Putnam, 2000; Riesman, Glazer, & Denney, 1950). The anonymity of my neighbor and social isolation breed indifference. Once we knew all things and animals were familiar to us. We lived with other animals and had appreciation for their strength, intelligence, and dedication to parenting; we identified with them. We admired them. As industrialization and urbanization has distanced us from other organisms, except our few pets, we have become ignorant of their ways and disinterested in their plight. This transformation of the human lifeworld, this new set of relationships along with the modern economic structure, population growth, fragmenting kinship, and widespread alienation, inspired the formation of the social sciences. The initial question that motivated social scientists was what was happening in the nineteenth and twentieth centuries and why (Kramer, 1992, 1997, 2003a). Today we observe the continued global spread of that cultural revolution.

Modern society is mass culture—an aggregate of competing individuals as opposed to traditional organic community among extended kin in traditional villages and hamlets. And modernity is spreading rapidly, leaving almost no traditional communities or ecosystems untouched. As you read this, enormous and unprecedented internal changes to the ecosphere and ethnosphere are unfolding concurrently (Davis, 2007, 2009, 2010; Kramer, 1992, 1997, 2003a, 2013). In this book, we see the fragmentation of the ecosphere from the ethnosphere, as conceived by Wade Davis (2009, 2010), as a barrier to understanding how and why both are in decline. For the way we conceive of nature is a cultural construct. Today we moderns apprehend nature differently than our ancestors. And this is the essential, necessary condition for the form and impact of modern technology. Today the variety of both species and cultures is in utter collapse. This book seeks to answer why now.

PART I

THE ORIGIN OF OUR ANTHROPIC EPOCH

1

Narcissistic Culture

The Made World and the Valuable in Itself

THE MADE WORLD AND THE VALUABLE IN ITSELF

In recent centuries we have been changing from a tribal species to a super-tribal species (Morris, 1969). A major consequence is that relations are increasingly anonymous, impersonal, and disinterestedly objective. The universe is emptying out and dying (Kramer, 1997a, 2003a, 2013). The vacuum that has replaced the thick association of spirit-beings, the space between things is clearly creating dissociation, a lack of empathy. When nothing is watching, we do not take care.

As humanity has moved from animism to pantheism to monotheism and finally the void, as "the people" have fragmented and shrunk to one tribe among many, down to the clan, down to the extended family, down to the nuclear family, down to the hyper-defensive individual who has to find him or herself, identity has become a major concern—at the same time cultures and species are vanishing. Difference is dwindling and monoculture is ascendant (Kramer, 2003a). Today Shanghai looks more like New York City in 1930 than Shanghai in 1930. More people in China speak English than people in the United States.

This process of homogenizing convergence, of modernization/westernization liberates us from associations and obligations (caring) and enhances material efficiency enabling us to perceive everything as essentially the same, as assemblages of proverbial "building blocks of nature" available to us for manipulation at will. The age of transcendentalism means that history, the plan, subsumes us all. We either conform or are seen as insane. This trend is now on the verge of reducing subjectivity out of existence, of "liberating" us from our uniqueness, our parochial selves (Marcel, 1950-1951 Ger./2001 Eng.; Fromm, 1976/2013, 1968/2010; Jaspers, 1931 Ger./2009 Eng., 1938 Ger./1971 Eng.). We have become an aggregate of competing individualists. The irony is that that is the grand modern ideology that encourages us all to pursue the same end—hypertrophic individualism.

This situation is absurd. As difference is eliminated so too is meaning. Our condition constitutes a hypertrophic humanism wiping out humans in order to advance humanity. Hypertrophy is the current obsession. On the one hand we have extreme positivism that, in its profound immodesty demands that only one interpretation of reality be allowed and on the other an equally dogmatic insistence that all interpretations are equally valid, that validity itself is not real (Kramer, 1988).

Standardization and technology have exploded. One scale rules the world, mechanical clock time. Other scales such as currencies are slowly converging. Humanity has achieved great power especially in organizational regimentation. But it also makes for a very lonely existence verging on nihilism. For those who are able, consuming can offer some satisfaction. But nothing can replace meaningful human relationships. They are different from having a fetish for electronics, a house, car, or boat.

Standing alone with all else at our feet, humans have no equals, no companions within the ecosphere. Cultures too are hierarchized as first, second, third, and fourth worlds. Philosophies, where they are still recognized at all, are hierarchized with positivism reigning in this era of unchecked power. As Gabriel Marcel (1950-1951 Ger./2001 Eng.) argued, and we agree, everyone has a philosophy, a perspective but only critical self-reflection can make that apparent to us. On the one hand, when reduced to material bits governed by the inviolable laws of physics, human free will and dignity are eliminated. On the other hand, the drive to transcend ourselves also threatens human dignity and unfettered freedom demands that we become more responsible for ourselves. Independence is taking a profound toll.

Increasingly we even regard ourselves as nothing more than objects in space available for arbitrary self-manipulation at the levels of overt social engineering and genetics. Eugenics is one example.

Such dissociation (objective disinterest) involves all relationships, including those between people, and between humans and the rest of nature (Kramer, 1995, 1997a, 2003a, 2013). Relationships become increasingly engineered and litigious. Because we are strangers to one another we have difficulty forming bonds. And time-pressure is all pervasive leading to phenomena such as speed dating—by the regulating stopwatch. Normative regulation of behavior has given way to institutional and script-based conflict resolution administered by professionals—the legal sphere. And the power-distance between people and between people and other animals has expanded enormously. We share less and less with the Other. In the magic tribal world for instance, shame and glory, joy and sadness, used to be shared among all of the clan, but today the sins of the father are not of the son and my money is mine, not my brother's. Decisions and consequences become increasingly egocentric. Significant portions of a society can be depressed while other sectors blissfully ignore the situation because they are dissociated and distantiated from one another. Walls and distance or tele-surveillance proliferate. Incarceration is a growth industry. Personal security has become a fashion. Since we can no longer assume that we will come to each other's aid, carrying handguns is not only thinkable but also increasingly commonplace. Welfare, the wellbeing of each one of us is increasingly privatized.

Spatial thinking dominates the modern mind. Alienation is the modern plague. It is rooted in geographic, economic, social and psychological mobility, and isolation—individualism premised on the modern sense of spatial thinking. We even think of time in spatial terms. To progress in personal growth means to leave the past ^ along with most if not all who populate it. The individual craves stimulation. And yet we are so overwhelmed that we cannot focus on just one thing and do it well, which better suits our evolutionary psychology. We have not evolved to multitask (Williams, 2012; Ophir, Nass, & Wagner, 2009).

We can trace the shift from the mythic to the modern perspectival worldview. While Socrates' method was comprised of group discussions and dialogue, Plato began to write for personal reading albeit in dialogical form which was often performed by students. Then Aristotle, the first true modern wrote analytical prose for individual silent consumption (Kramer, 1997a). Writing would become essential to the conceptual stability and indifference of policy-driven action in the modern urban empire (Innis, 1951; Ong, 1982).

After the midwives of the rebirth of ancient modernity, with Dante and other humanists reviving literature of a highly personal nature such as his love poems to Beatrice, we finally arrive at James Joyce's characters as interior soliloquies. Joyce's work is late modern. It is the full expression of minds isolated from each other in emotional space even as they live together. From the rise of existentialism and the economics of alienation to Ernest Hemingway's 1933 short story, "A Clean, Well-Lighted Place"; from Mishima's character Masaru in "Death in Midsummer," who sits in utter emotional isolation surrounded on a crowded train on his way to the coastal scene of his sister's and children's drowning, realizing that no one around him has a clue to his personal tragedy; to Munch's four versions of *Shrik* (*The Scream*, 1893-1910), the arts as well as the social sciences and humanities have recognized and embodied the problem.

In the span of a century we see the rage of Karl Marx literally watching his wife and children starve to death in London and the angst in Friedrich Nietzsche's breakdown at the sight of a horse being beaten in the streets of Turin. We also see the Dadaist response to the horrors of the first mechanized war and Franz Kafka's and Max Weber's critiques of nonsensical colonial bureaucracies that fostered unfathomable faith in inaccessible and nonresponsive authority, what Antonio Gramsci (1952 It./2011 Eng.) wrestled with in his attempt to understand the subaltern's submission in the face of official disregard for his or her plight—the dissociative psychopathology of objective administrative reason. Where Charles Dickens described simple and comprehensible greed and industrial oppression in his tales, Kafka described something far more ominous, that the faceless madness of bureaucracy in fact has a method—a discipline—a rationale but one that remains cryptic. The Right Hegelian Nazis and the Left Hegelian Stalinists proved that order and efficiency could serve oppression as much as liberation and even amplify its scope and impact. Modern bureaucracy in its complexity mystifies the modern citizen as much as the fog of superstition did the medieval serf. When trying to cope with inquiries that the lowly employee cannot explain he or she instinctively retreats to the fatalistic adage that "that is what the computer says."

At the same time these and others such as William Blake were outspoken witnesses to the dawn of a new machine age and its effects on humanity. Walt Whitman, John James Audubon, John Muir, Charles Jesse "Buffalo" Jones (who initiated the effort to save the North American Bison), Jack London, Upton Sinclair, and others were sounding the alarm that industrial progress was eliminating entire ecosystems. Dystopian urbanscapes are in vogue for a reason. The late-modern lexicon has shifted from expressions of positivism to speak in Orwellian and Kafkaesque terms. The official picture presented by corporate World's Fairs, conquest of the moon, the nuclear arms race, and other theotechnic expressions acted as facades hiding deep conflicts and alienation "down in the streets," while extending the in-group/out-group mentality by ignoring pleas to design a new flag to represent all of humanity and instead planting the flag of one nation on the moon. Jean-Paul Sartre (1943 Fr./1984 Eng.) noted that we have figured everything out except how to live. The virtue of efficiency was proven by the biggest bang for the buck.

We are increasingly distanced from the rest of nature. Other animals that we once regarded as brothers, even as awesomely superior to ourselves, we now regard as collectible arrangements of DNA that we kill for fun and/or breed in mass misery. The great whales nearly went extinct, boiled down to oil to light the first assembly lines that began to run around the clock. Bowhead whales, the second heaviest animal to live after the blue whale, were particularly easy and profitable targets. They have the most blubber of any animal on earth and being trusting animals, whalers could easily pull along side and kill them. Recently, efforts to study a population that has retreated to the farthest north finds them unusually hard to approach. Their skittish behavior has been explained by the fact that they live to be over 200 years old and that they probably remember the trauma-tizing hunts that decimated their species (Rozell, 2001). How do we know this? Because studies have found some surviving bowheads with stone har-poon heads embedded in their blubber, harpoon heads that are well over 100 years old (Rozell, 2001). Few bowheads are so old because few survived the ordeal. Zoologists from the Scripps Institution of Oceanography have deter-mined one individual taken in 1997 at Savoonga by the Alaska Eskimo Whaling Commission to be 211 years of age (George et al., 1999). To put that in perspective, it was "alive during the term of President Clinton [and] was also gliding slowly and gracefully through the Bering, Chukchi and Beaufort seas when Thomas Jefferson was president" (Rozell, 2001, p. 1).

The great whale hunt, like so much else, was pulled along in the moti-vational wake left by the desire for mass manufacturing which was motivat-ed by accelerated profit-taking in the new industrial economy. Their oil lit-erally greased the skids of a modern-style industry that never rested, work-ing by the light of oil-filled lamps. Labor became dissociated from its own products and also time—the seasons, day and night. Work became perpetu-al. The modern city was unique among human habitats because it never slept. The modern clock culture collided with the whale and every other species, including the one that invented it.

Increasingly we are stressed for time and so we do not linger in the wilderness and observe things as they show themselves. Boredom extends time—our lives but it also requires imagination. So we escape into streams of stimuli and seek to extend our lives through other means. At the same time we segregate and warehouse both unproductive human individuals in highly institutionalized settings such as daycares, nursing homes, and pris-ons, and productive individuals in high-rise office complexes, schools, and industrial parks; all self-managed domestic spaces organized by mechanical clock time, what Desmond Morris (1969) calls the human zoo. Landscapes that initially defy exploitation surrender to economic imperatives offered as natural laws; rivers are dammed, swamps and lakes drained, prairies tilled, forests felled. Meanwhile deviants are corrected. Modern efficiency demands regimented conformity. In the world of mass production, a hand-wrought artifact is considered a work of art, a rare heirloom. And perhaps that is appropriate. A handwritten letter seems more satisfying than an e-mail.

Jean Gebser (1949 Ger./1985 Eng.) calls this modern attitude the men-tality of the sector or zoning—it manifests hypertrophic perspectivism and temporal anxiety—ratio order, reason perceived as discipline—knowledge is power while wisdom is supportive (caring understanding). This modern divisive mode of thinking, knowledge defined as the ability to identify things as categorically separate, results in the fragmenting separation of aspects of what was once a holistic life; culture from nature, work from play, education from home, generations from each other (gaps), and other forms of segregation as interests narrow along with concentrated attention and magnified effort. Knowledge in the three-dimensional modern mentality came to mean focus and depth. Knowledge fragmented into disciplines that pursued more and more knowledge about less and less—specialization and strict research agendas. Anything outside our cone of attention literally does not exist to us (Chabris & Simons, 2010; Mack & Rock, 1992).

As the urban world increases the stimulation in our experience cognitive tunneling increasingly blinds us. One example is being over-stimulated with distress calls from other humans and animals all over the world via global media networks and our resulting emotional fatigue, which we cope with by dissociation and desensitization. We feel smaller and smaller, having less and less control over our world. Communication falters and relationships and identity become problematic and so new disciplines are launched to study the problems. As physical and emotional space expands we shrink into defensive egotistic and egoistic postures (the former connoting boastful arrogance and the latter self-centered moral judgment). We regard only our own interests as we look out for number one. This is very different from the slow-paced village life and extended kinship we evolved within for millennia. Our cognitive and emotional evolution has not prepared us for the modern world. At the same time, as our special standing in the universe has eroded our psychological defenses have intensified. The absurd position of egotistic transhumanism is one conclusion.

TO BE . . . POSTHUMAN

Our narcissism has reached a self-destructive level where transhumanists such as Nikolai Fyodorov, John Haldane, Julian Huxley (Aldous Huxley's brother), Marvin Minski, Hans Moravec, Ken Hayworth, and others advocate a form of self-engineered evolution dictated by and limited to our own imaginations—total self-domestication. Transhumanists (the word coined by J. Huxley in 1927) campaign for the transformation of humanity into posthuman machine beings (Huxley, 1927). In an interview with the *Chronicle of Higher Education* Hayworth is clear,

> "The human race is on a beeline to mind uploading: We will preserve a brain, slice it up, simulate it on a computer, and hook it up to a robot body." He [Hayworth] wants that brain to be his brain. He wants his 100 billion neurons and more than 100 trillion synapses to be encased in

a block of transparent, amber-colored resin—before he dies of natural causes. Why? Ken Hayworth believes that he can live forever. (Goldstein, July 2012)

According to the grand ought of the hedonistic imperative at the core of transhumanism we should willfully separate from our own biological bodies in order to achieve immortality (More & Vita-More, 2013). Technical problems such as avoiding ice crystals forming between brain cells or distortion due to dehydration aside, is this self-destructive hyper-narcissism? And if I destroy my brain by slicing it up so that it can be electromicroscopically imaged then digitized have I really preserved my unique identity as Hayworth (2012b, 2013) claims?

Molecular tickertapes and other technologies copy me but do not preserve the atoms and molecules that form my neuroanatomy. And as György Lukács (1957 Ger./1963 Eng.) reminds us, realism, no matter how careful the mimesis, how high resolution and high definition the imaging is, remains a genre of fiction. Even when experts have difficulty identifying a copy from an original work of art, one is still a forgery. Only one was actually touched by the artist. The virtual is the opposite of the actual. I may enjoy the forgery just the same but it is not identical with the original. They may be equally real but they inhabit different spatio-temporal coordinates. This is especially significant with the connectome, because while the genome never changes, neural connections in the living brain are constantly changing because of experience/time. This is what Sebastian Seung (2012) means when he argues that the brain is where nature and nurture not only meet but also are utterly intertwined. The physical brain, let alone the mind, is a socio-cultural product that is never finished (Kramer, 1992, 1993b, 1997a, 2013). Mapping is a spatial phenomenon, a snapshot that manifestly articulates the modernist ideology/mythology of realism (Kramer, 1993c). In the case of the brain, it is an attempt to get control of consciousness itself at its origin.

We are not among those who protest this effort because we believe there is something unfathomable about consciousness. We tend to agree that the mind is an epiphenomenon of neuronal circuitry—that the structure of neural connectivity is not merely correlated with, but is a functional necessity for awareness to exist. Nor do we believe that consciousness or the soul is inviolate. Rather we think that even if it is possible to preserve a human brain, be it through plastinating chemical or vitrifying cryogenic means, and then to cut it into very thin slices, scan it with an electron microscope to render countless high resolution images of the neural circuitry and the trillions upon trillions of synapses that make up a person's memories and personality (the connectome), which many such as Narayanan Kasthuri and Jeff Lichtman (2010) do not, and then upload that into a computer that would have the storage capacity for all that data (about one trillion gigabytes worth), even if all that is possible, we believe the idea of living forever in a computer has other problems. We are not saying that such research, which in the past decade has received literally billions of dollars in funding, is not worthless. We hope it will be useful in combating problems such as autism and Alzheimer's.

Our problem is with the effort to cure death by escaping into a robot body as promoted by transhumanists such as Hayworth (2012a). In fact, if this is ever accomplished, we predict that those beings would soon enough wonder about and wish to be able to reverse the process, to once again extend their minds through living tissues to feel petting a cat and sunshine, smelling rain, tasting chocolate, balance, and other aspects of organic being. Living inside computers would render the world abandoned because there would be no point in maintaining amusement parks or cities or even homes for instance, because riding on a rollercoaster or splashing on a beach would be senseless if you cannot feel the sensations we take for granted as incarnate conscious beings. And what possible horror might unfold if you awoke inside a computer, utterly disembodied? There may be profound wisdom in Einstein's unheeded plea to let his brain rest with his body (Paterniti, 2001).

Two issues arise. First is the hypertrophic egocentrism of such a dream. In this case, getting what you wish for could be catastrophic beyond words. Second is the equation of virtue with our own technical prowess. We address each here.

First, the drive to achieve immortality is rooted in the desire to own everything including the future. Why do this? Hayworth, a champion of brain preservation to "cure death" wants to replicate his brain because he "wants to see the future" (Hayworth quoted on *Through the Wormhole with Morgan Freeman*, July, 2012a). Transhumanists make this desire quite explicit as they explain their efforts to solve the "problem" of death. Traditionally the future was left to our offspring. But as we live longer we are having fewer and fewer offspring. If we "live" in computers, it will be quite impossible to reproduce anyway. The fact remains that humans who wish to live forever must first live. Before you can digitize my brain I have to have one, which requires that I begin as a biologically based phenomena. Once we are all in computers that will mark the end of the human species as a biological process. There will be no more new minds.

Some advocates of the transhumanist movement may argue that my negative assessment of this goal of prolonging life is based on pure conjecture about what *might* happen. But this is false. We can already see how this dream of immortality is affecting the world. The world is aging. Antibiotics and other modern innovations in medicine and hygiene have suddenly and on a massive scale lengthened the average lifespan of humans. As this has occurred many important consequences have followed. One is the greatest threat to human quality of life and to ecosystems, the population explosion.

Second is a dramatic drop in fertility rates in the most advanced industrial nations.

The desire to live as long as possible is driving both trends. In many of the wealthiest countries the population is dropping dramatically affecting every aspect of life. For instance, social welfare systems for retirement are going bankrupt because people are living much longer than presumed by the original policy calculations and the concurrent drop in fertility means that fewer and fewer people of working age are supporting more and more retirees. Another problem is that as nations age and workers are not replacing themselves with their own offspring, the largest migration of humans in history is taking place as people from differing ethnic groups and poorer nations are moving to richer nations to fulfill the demand for labor. This has led to profound changes in the ethnic makeup of many nations and serious problems in interethnic relations. The consequences of a very sudden and worldwide extension in human life expectancy are many and profound. These problems would only be amplified if suddenly no one died.

Second, the equation of virtue with immortality achieved by escaping the biological basis of our lives via technology is open to debate.

This reduction of evolution to human technical achievement such as genetic engineering, digitizing our brains, and nanotechnology applied to everything including our children, promises to make new forms of life and a new form of human being and civilization rather than living life naturally (Drexler, 1985, 2013; Seung, 2013). Slicing our brains up for digitization and moving the resulting information into robotic bodies will be our "final invention" (Barrat, 2013). This is a sort of material teleology not unlike when Ludwig Feuerbach "stood Hegel on his head" (Marx & Engels, 1845/1932 Ger./2004 Eng.). Regardless of the metaphysical bias, idealism or materialism, the temporal structure of a fatalistic mechanical chain of causation, or spirit comprised of evolutionary stages leading to a final solution remains the same.

Such a dream is not new. It articulates a faith in the *non plus ultra* of positive achievement—suicide. As for nature we put what is left into "preserves," seed banks, and genetic "arks." The notion of a genetic ark is instructive because Noah was expecting the end of the world. Biodiversity is plummeting in proportion with our narrow-mindedness. A preserved or duplicate sample is not the same as a whole organic ecosystem. For instance, attempting to rebuild large stocks of bison from a handful of individuals can be done but the result is a much less diverse, less robust genome.

Regarding the transhumanist promise of duplicating myself as a computer program, the problem is that whatever consciousness is duplicated, it is not me. This is a basic hermeneutic truth. It is not a form of immorality. The instant you switch on my duplicate, it will see the world from a different perspective and that will require that all previous "facts" be reinterpreted in the light of new information—the new existential condition. Nature and nurture combine in the temporality of the brain. Its identity will be that of a duplicate having a completely different origin from me, and a different future. Facts are never final. No matter how precisely we copy information, it is nothing more than a duplicate. If we did manage to duplicate my consciousness, the duplicate would diverge quickly and profoundly from who I am. I may marvel at the copy I have made of myself but it is still not me. And would he/it marvel at himself as a copy? And what would he think of me (deceased or not)? Perhaps the young Mary Shelley (1818, 2013) understood who the real monster is better than many transhumanists do today. What transhumanists want is to be everything, both creator and creation at once.

Referring to a different technology transhumanists appeal to for inspiration, the biotechnology of cloning, it too fails to escape the same hermeneutic principle of constant integration/interpretation of the past in light of the present and vice versa. Biocentric constant integration has been proven. Even cows have perspectival consciousness, which is unexpectedly complex (Lanza & Berman, 2010). When one makes an entire herd of genetically identical cattle, they form dominance hierarchies and very unique personalities, proving the veracity of environmental influences and consciousness as temporal and spatial perspective (Cibelli, Wilmut, Jaenisch, Gurdon, Lanza et al., 2013). Their lifespans vary also.

Gebser (1949 Ger./1985 Eng.) argued that conscious awareness has an efficient perspective as well as a deficient one that is self-destructive. Deficient perspectivism is self-destructive hubris. It confuses what it knows with all that is. Thus, we tend to describe ourselves in terms of our latest technology and so many transhumanists see our minds as "computers," or as a "connectome" storage device for information that can be transferred to artificial storage machines and thus become immortal (Kurzweil, 2013; Seung, 2012). This understanding of the mind is limited (Changeux & Ricoeur, 2002; Lakoff & Núñez, 2001; Nagel, 2012). This limitation, this tunnel vision is what is so dangerous about efforts to engineer everything in terms of our own measly imaginations. It means to discard what is obsolete in favor of an idealistic mysterious and techno-romantic ought. Discovery is the power of reality to surprise us. Transhumanism sees no value in discovery, but only invention. It marvels at our own limited abilities missing the world that sustains us while we pursue our projects. As the old saying goes, life is what is happening while we are busy making plans. If the plan includes abandoning life itself, we have a problem.

The ultimate absurdity is a perspective that erases itself in order to enhance itself. What we have with transhumanistic idealism is a basic ontological error. No matter how detailed a map is it is still ontologically different from the terrain it references. Realism is a genre of fiction. No matter how detailed your copy of the terrain you still end up with two different realities, each existing in a unique set of spatial and temporal relationships, including to each other. The old becomes old only vis-à-vis the new. And when we discuss duplicating minds, rather than landscapes, we have to recognize the completely different emotional and historical coordinates each mind inhabits.

If this mind replication were to take place, when the original meets the duplicate, they would have very different perspectives. It is not unlike looking at old pictures of oneself and feeling a nostalgia that that person in the photo cannot share. What would you say to yourself if you could talk with yourself as a teenager? It would not be what the teenager would say to you. As Edmund Husserl (1905–1910 Ger./1964 Eng.) demonstrated, consciousness is *essentially*, inescapably time/difference, an aporia that Jacques Derrida appreciated but did not fully comprehend (Kramer, 1988).

Instead of promoting the maintenance of the natural origin of life, transhumanism is the ultimate delusion of escapist ideology; one Francis Fukuyama (2004) has called one of the worlds' most dangerous ideologies, an idea that poses a greater threat to humanity than any other. The Frankensteinian motive is to escape death by eliminating biologically-based humanity as we know it—to escape our own biological existence by fabricating new vessels out of inanimate matter for our artificially enhanced consciousnesses (Kramer, 2000a, 2004; Bostrom, 2005). How do you escape dying? Do not live. According to this ideology our children will be our greatest artifactual legacy. This will-power-drive takes modernity to its logical conclusion. It is the tightest hairpin turn of cybernetic feedback control (Kramer, 1997a). Nothing will be left to chance or discovery, which are aspects of life. The risk of death will be eliminated. But since everything will unfold as engineered, everything will become redundantly meaningless. To the Late Modern, uncertainty only yields anxiety, not an opportunity for what Roland Barthes (1973 Fr./1975 Eng.) calls the ecstasy of the unexpected. Life is worth living only when you do not already know how every story ends.

The transhumanist dream is that robots will inherit the earth, replacing our children, our species—because, as the champion of artificial intelligence, Marvin Minsky declares, *they will be our children* (Minsky, 1994; also see Kurzweil, 2000). This "evolution" to a non-biological form has even been ironically called by transhumanists our destiny, our natural impulse for liberation—the ultimate good and most natural of drives (Bailey, 2004). The irony here is that they appeal to naturalism to outrun potential criticism for only insane people attempt to defy the laws of nature. In this sense eugenics, transhumanism, and cyborgism share a common ideological core (Gelles, 2009). They claim that other futures are inferior and "unnatural." And they share a common essential dream of idealistic total control, which is the political side of positivism. Whereas Eugenics selected traits from one group and encouraged the eradication of other groups and "unnatural" beliefs and behaviors, transhumanism selects immortality. And since no group is immortal they must all be eliminated.

Such equality makes the suggestion seem amoral. But this is not at all the case because the transhumanist is making a judgment, which is that organic humanity in its entirety needs to be eliminated to facilitate evolution in a direction deemed to be more advanced—good. Cyborgism means that we become machines in order to improve the human condition (Hughes, 2004). The human condition is thus improved by abandoning it altogether for the posthuman future (Ettinger, 1972; Minsky, 1994; Moravec, 1988). It is akin to solving problems of intercultural and interethnic misunderstanding by eliminating cultures and ethnicities as assimilationists suggest—throwing the baby out with the bath water (Kramer, 1993b, 1995, 2000a, 2000b, 2003a, 2008, 2011).

The ability to manufacture the self as cyborg requires reductionism and precision down to the molecular, if not atomic level (Drexler, 1985). Precision, which is fragmenting disambiguation (definitive segregation of objects, species, types of people, etc.), is a hallmark of the modern mind. It is not a universal truth but a dream of a specific place and time. It is a form of awareness that is essentially spatial thus enabling individuation as a modality of thought—the separation of things, concepts, ideas, and also time spatialized as a punctuated line—a measure. Life is divided up into enumerated units on the clock face and on the calendar, each of which is subdivided into hours and minutes, what Robert Levine (1989) calls "time rooms" dedicated to just one activity at a time. Precision thinking means mutual exclusivity, the fragmentation of a gear, for example, into more and more, smaller and smaller teeth, incremental reckoning that enables greater control. At the same time, greater control is enhanced by public uniformity enabled by synchronization of large populations orchestrated via master clocks and their time signals that are broadcast across the land.

One result of this precise cybernetic feedback and control is the industrial age organization human who wastes no time but instead suffers from "time famine" (Johnson, 1978), a perpetual sense of time shortage experienced as a chronic sense of urgency (Braverman, 1974; Whyte, 1956). Most software suites are designed for business applications to accelerate productivity and extend organized productive activity to every population on earth and into every hour and minute of the day.

Aristotle, arguably the first full-blown Modern, stressed digital thinking with its essential logic of the excluded middle. It is the intolerance of either/orism that clarifies modern thinking and which is essential for precise analytics (Kramer, 1997a, 1997b). Either you got things done on time or you did not. Aristotle equated knowing a thing, time, place, or idea to knowing what it is not, and so knowledge itself became a matter of abstractly defining identities and categorically labeling them as mutually exclusive. For instance, to know something is to know if it is a mineral, plant, *or* animal, a nomenclatural form of thinking, which was expanded during the European Enlightenment by Linnaeus in the eighteenth century. Clock time, likely the most influential invention of the modern technological world clearly fragments and demarcates moments, functions enabling reliable (consistent) measurements, the virtues of control and efficiency, and the prevention of simultaneity. Combined with motion, we have the linear modern industrial mentality—the assembly line.

With this new *zeitgeist*, everything became methodical, a step-by-step pre-engineered process. This mechanical form of time and production is utterly unnatural. While each day sees different lengths of light and dark through the seasons, the clock assures 24 identical hours. Stability, uniformity, and equilibrium are thus guaranteed. The virtue of predictability and consistent operation made quantification the new elite language. Pacing, in all its monotony and forms becomes the modern mode of existence. A good example is the use of bells in churches, mosques, schools, and factories to chime on the hour, synchronizing life reduced to habitual, predictable functions. The Benedictine Catholic Order formalized the idea of a daily routine regulated by mechanical clock-time (Boorstin, 1993). Ordination moved from the monastic disciplines to all of society. Increasingly in Western art and literature the angel of death holds a ticking clock and we wear the machines on our bodies. Computers, geo-positioning satellites, and cellular phones are essentially forms of the clock. Speed is essential for the Modern. Time is of the essence.

So the modern human increasingly excludes (dissociated) itself from the rest of nature as being essentially different from all other forms of life. This exclusivity is mirrored in the rise of universal scales, commandments/laws, and monotheistic religions that reject animism and polytheism as absolutely untrue and profane. Humans privilege themselves as the only bearers of souls. The insistence that there can be only one truth, the essence of Modern Western positivism, is the grandchild of Western monotheism. This threatens "primitive" altruism for no alternative truth can exist. There is only one correct way to reckon time, and the more consistent the reckoning the better.

The emphasis on spatial thinking is a fundamental characteristic of the modern Western style of thinking. It is often expressed through visual metaphors. As George Hegel (1820 Ger./2002 Eng.), the great Aristotelian argued in the preface to his *The Philosophy of Right*, "the owl of Minerva begins its flight only with the falling of dusk" (p. 10). After all facts have become clear, after the debacle of the pathetic contingent subjectivity of raw humanity can no longer be ignored, logic clarifies and allows one to see in the dark. Am-bi-guity means things touch each other, they overlap, get entangled, share space, time, and meaning. Things are unclear and confused. The effort of analytical disambiguation is to disentangle meanings, to be definitive and resolve objects, meanings, and things clearly—to maximize definition. We answer the question "what is it" when we strain to see something in dim light, by resolving the question through definition, by resolving its outlines that make it distinct from adjacent but separate objects.

THE TRANSHUMANISTIC DRIVE FOR PERFECTION AND SELF-HATE

We must pause for a moment to appreciate what this all means. Aristotle equated knowledge with power. The concept mind and the verb "to think" are derived from the Proto-Indo-European *ménos*, from *men-*.

> The first word of the first verse of the first canto of the first major work of the Western world, the *Iliad*, is *menin*, which is the accusative of menis. *Menis* means "wrath" and "courage." It is derived from the Proto-Indo-European *menos* meaning "resolve," "power," "conviction." The Latin *mens* means "intent," "anger," thinking, and "thought." From the ancient Greek *menin* is derived "man." "As expressed in the *Iliad*, the classical Greek world unfolded as an image of action that was directed, causal, and willfully ordered. Having and giving direction(s), such as a chain of command from first cause on "down" presumes a perspective, distance, inequality—separation. *Menos* is the root of men(tal). (Kramer, 1997a, p. 80)

Analytical, dialectical thinking is disputative—aggressive and to know is definitive. It targets problems in need of resolution. In taking aim at human mortality, which is an essential part of being, transhumanism is turning its guns on humanity as flawed. The fact that Hayworth wants his own brain preserved and digitized is proof of the self-objectifying hairpin turn of hyper-cybernetics. Positivism holds that facts are things already done. Established fact marks the end of discussion. The origin of the modern Western mentality presents an attitude that is goal oriented, which promotes measuring progress and regress, and it is masculine. Manipulation is the modus of modernity. It equates the good with resoluteness of purpose. Process, hesitation, discourse, and compromise are suspect modes of being. They are perceived as such from what Paul Ricoeur (1965 Fr./1970 Eng., 1969 Fr./1974 Eng.) calls the hermeneutics of suspicion, the sense that what is given should be doubted because it clouds perception via an ambiguity that cloaks the true motive of the Other, as for instance, the patriarchal notion that woman, the wild, and other Others are mysteries and dangers that can derail the accomplishment of the straight and narrow mission of civilization.

The conflict of interpretations must be resolved once and for all for the sake of truth, the whole truth and nothing but. If that requires that I crush the Other in refereed combat, proving their beliefs false, their values impractical, so be it. The relationship with the Other is not as important as the objective truth. Skepticism means to trust only what one can verify for oneself. Trust is the opposite. Trusting faith is thus regarded as a potentially fatal flaw to knowledge. To be inoculated from sentimental subjectivity and other siren-like forces one must remain "true" to oneself (not "go native"), and ruthlessly unmask the truth by presuming that the words of the Other are camouflage for their real intent. Interrogation and cross-examination are in order. To do so one must not sympathize, empathize, or identify with the Other. Strategic dissociation and Occam's razor parses and pares away surplus meaning. Parsimony displaces harmony.

Menos means mind but also purpose, anger, power, man, and violence. Thinking, analytical mechanical imperative is inconsiderate. It is the meaning of mind as that which invalidates collective myth. Here we have the origin of the notion of thinking and knowing as being spatial, directional and intolerant. Either you do or you do not know the truth. Analytics excludes the middle maybe that may lead to ambiguity and ambivalence. Modern three-dimensional directional thinking abandons mythic two-dimensional perception, which shifts often effortlessly between literal and figural understanding. Analytical thinking becomes methodical. Computers can do it. And so the modern defines the mind as a computer. Unlike all other animals, the human has a destiny and a purpose. And it is pursued with a vengeance. Precise thinking abhors ambiguity.

Menin appears in the *Iliad* as Achilles' anger toward Agamemnon because the king will not return Achilles' war prize, Chyrseis. Achilles' feelings are hurt. Thus he refuses to fight, an unprecedented selfish act that confuses and frightens the Greek host of warriors. Achilles' pouting costs his best friend Patroclus's life because Patroclus wears Achilles' armor into battle and Hector kills him. Ajax is especially perplexed and disturbed by Achilles' self-centered behavior. This disturbance in the order of things is Achilles' selfish attitude. Both Agamemnon and Achilles manifest the first expression of modern individualism in literature. According to Gebser (1949 Ger./1985 Eng.), the story marks the eruption of the modern ego and its disruption of a fundamentally collectivistic milieu. It is demanding and intolerant—narcissistic. It is about this time when the Greeks invented the amphitheater, a lens that focuses attention on a few while fragmenting the tribe into those who dance and those who watch. Song fragments into chorus and audience. Ritual ceremony thus enters time—secular humanism. Performers become celebrities that their clan members passively watch, launching an ideal vicarious regard for the human condition—the human condition as spectacle—drama (Kramer, 1997a). And then we have the Olympics, which fragments play into competition with clear winners and losers. Sculpture begins to mimic the actual faces of individuals. Precision, such as knowing precisely will lead to quantification. Fragmenting the psyche has been the path to clarity based on separation and isolation. From thenceforth play becomes a form of evaluative measure that renders winners and losers. The arts of freedom, the liberal arts decline in status compared to to competitive sports and the drive to engineer.

This shift toward individualism with its tendency to demand things is expressed in the tales of the times. In the battle between the amorphous primeval forces Gaia (Earth) and Uranus (Sky) and their rebellious off-spring, which marks the divisive origin of modernity, Sky is cut to pieces by his titanic son Kronos. In turn the titans will be overwhelmed and subdivided more by their offspring, the anthropomorphic gods. Unity is thus sliced into segments, reduced to more controllable subunits.

This is the cultural origin of a compulsion that reaches its logical con-clusion in the doctrine of transhumanism. Thus transhumanists believe they are pursuing hyper-enlightenment by abandoning the subjective temporal body that ages and is fraught with mortal difference/variance, its patheti-cally flawed contingency. Time is the enemy. Everlasting life is the goal. According to the hypertrophic selfishness of the transhumanists, humanism, which was of this temporal world, secular, must be abandoned. Subjectivity is inconsistent. We must advance. Mortal humans are invalid, baseless, and infirm. As such we are all invalids. Criminal time must be transcended or at least arrested (Kramer, 1997a, 2000a, 2004a).

So why is this "the most dangerous idea in the world?" (Fukuyama, 2004). Because this drive to be free of time and space, this absolute teleologi-cal dream, fully articulated by Hegel, means suicide. The human race must abandon itself in order not to merely evolve, for evolution is random, but to advance in a specific and preconceived direction—beyond death. Conquest continues. The effort to escape all limitations including death itself can only be eliminated if we cease to be born. Humanity must be sacrificed for the sake of absolute narcissism. It is a tautological absurdity for the objective is to become an object. The goal of perfecting human beings has a horrendous history. The effort to conform to a virtual ideal always causes suffering for actual people.

One measure of the progress of knowledge is an ever-more precise pars-ing and defining categorization of classes and subclasses of cases. Quantification has linguistically enhanced this push to tighten up loose tol-erances. Clarifying power-distance is one way to define one's own and an Other's place vis-à-vis each other (the spatial metaphor is self-evident) be they animal, supernatural being, or other human being within a hierarchy of being. Power-distance is the normative sense of how much inequality is appropriate. It is a defining measure of cultures (Hofstede, 1991).[1]

---

[1]Unfortunately, Hofstede (1991) refers to such normative interpretations as "soft-ware of the mind" (p. 3), failing to recognize the profound differences between a human mind and a primitive binary computer. But following from Talcott Parsons' 1950s work he did make famous the useful variable of power-distance.

Some cultures are relatively high power-distance, seeing inequality as normal and natural, others are relatively low power-distance. Power-distance is the antithesis of identity. To be identified with an Other or to be identical with it means to regard it as an equal, as not separate from it. Archaic peoples identify with their environments rather than see the environment as an Other with which to conflict. They do not see themselves as against the environment but one with it. While archaic pre-spatial cultures are very collectivistic and exhibit very low power-distance, modern mass society is marked by individuation/separation—inequality (Kramer, 1997a, 2013). Lewis Mumford (2010), Morris (1969), and others argue that this rise in distance between people and groups begins with urbanization and the rise of empires. As the Neolithic and Paleolithic hamlet gives way to the city, we have the invention of "the stranger." We all become strangers to each other.

The Modern sees identity not as an inherent fullness that is shared but as the empty difference between myself and the Other. I am not you. That is who I am. I am a negation. This is the essence of modern dissociative systems thinking. Insofar as it rejects inherency, it is mechanistic, structural nihilism. Everything is thus reducible first to component parts and then the ratios between them until the sense of what once was has evaporated. We become nothing but the sum of our measures and how variables fact-or. You add a "y" and you have factory where the future is made, not inherited (shared inherency). For positivists, facts are self-evident. They stand alone. Technical proof dominates what can legitimately be called real. If it works, if I win, I am the truth.

Rather recently in the history of human evolution, the rise of imperial urban powers all over the world exhibit extreme power-distance with living god-kings and subhuman slaves existing simultaneously within societies (Morris, 1969). By contrast, within clan-based tribal communities no such enormous power-distance exists. In the latter, the chief typically lives within the village and may often play with his nieces and nephews and walk among and speak with all other members of the tribe—his or her kin. In today's super-tribal nation-states, their "fellow citizens" typically know leaders only as video images. A fading residual magic consciousness is evident in nationalism and language-use as, for instance, when we speak of our "founding fathers."

In imperial societies the equestrian class literally rides above and over the pedestrian class. To be pedestrian is to be plain, common, numerous, and uninterestingly redundant. Today that distinction has been increased via technology with the weak riding bicycles and public buses and subways, while the powerful use limousines and private aircraft moving far above the masses, the "riff raff" the ancient Greeks called the *hoi polloi* and the Romans the plebeians (as distinguished from the elevated patrician class) (Kramer & Kim, 2009).

The size of personal space, the ability to travel at will, the determination of who will wait to see whom, personal access to resources, private entourages to keep others at a distance; privatization marks status in the modern world. Today the elite are literally buying slots to one day go into outer space and achieve the ultimate high ground and vista that will encompass all of us. It is a form of possession, a beholding of all there is. It involves the observed and the observer via panoptic technology and an attendant attitude so that many submit their resumes, for example, to be appraised while the resume of the appraiser remains hidden. The transcending panoptic attitude, a voyeuristic way of regarding the Other, characterizes the mode of communication between people and between humans and the rest of the universe. The relationship modern humans have with nature is essentially instrumental.

Instrumental technical regard apprehends the other as not equal but rather as subaltern (Gramsci, 1952 It./2011 Eng.). It is a transcendent way of seeing nature and other entities as naturally inferior and subordinate—available for uncaring (disinterested) analytical gaze (Levinas, 1948 Fr./1987 Eng., 1961 Fr./1969 Eng.). This modality is not universal to all human groups. It is essential to the engineering process. It enables a form of dissociated manipulation. We can watch in high definition, slow motion, from intimate angles, freeze frame at will, and at our pleasure and convenience— we have the power of how the Other is beheld (Kramer, 1993a, 1993c, 1994b, 2004a).

This is the operationalization of Hegel's master/slave logic. It is the slave and the robot lover/laborer for our pleasure. But this is a bias. We thus limit our own perception of the sense of the Other. We are limited because we learn nothing when we only hear ourselves talk. Our truncated sense of the world is a consequence of having no Other to challenge our control of the way we regard things. It is like being a rock star who destroys himself because no one can challenge anything he wants to do. Too much self-indulgence is suicidal.

Power-distance is a measure of how appropriate it is for the subaltern to look back and frame and behold the superordinate in evaluative regard (Levinas, 1972 Fr./2005 Eng.). When only the superordinate's view is empowered and operationalized, then the sense of things that most commoners have, the common sense, is delegitimized via power-distance. Hence the distortion of the Luddites' interpretation of automation by their employers as being simply anti-technology and anti-progress when in fact it was a rational and prophetic concern about concentration of power, losing control over the production process, and job loss. To be lively is to be happy, buoyant, vivacious, and proactive. To lose one's livelihood is a profound blow to any human, often de-animating them. They no longer float but sink emotionally and spiritually. Their vibrancy stills. Such concentration of power began with the first urban centers and in the last two centuries it has become global in scope. It segregates members of community from decision making and participation. They lose their voice and become unsound. The widespread alienation that resulted from the rise of mass society inspired the establishment of the social sciences as a genre of inquiry (Kramer, 1997a). Globally, mass monoculture is rapidly expanding and displacing the great diversity of traditional communities with all their differing ways to regard things (Kramer, 2003a). From Søren Kiekegaard and Karl Marx to Émile Durkheim and Sigmund Freud, from Ferdinand Tönnies and Max Weber to Kurt Goldstein and Marcel Mauss, from Friedrich Nietzsche and Bronislaw Malinowski to Thorstein Veblen and Abraham Maslow, and many others, recognition of the incredibly rapid change in social relations and institutions spurred critical analyses. And among the heralds of the new positivist secular religion, Hegel, Claude Saint-Simon, Auguste Comte, Herbert Spencer, Francis Galton, and later structural functionalists such as George Homans and Talcott Parsons, the charge was to determine how to enhance stability by eliminating difference, by socially engineering a singular new modern human who could competently fit within the singular milieu of the new industrial system that promoted one true reality, one political-economic system, and one definition of a good human. Everything became engineered and equilibrium became the watchword.

Magic initially created culture and nature simultaneously as humans began to separate from and exert their will on natural processes such as fertility. In this way nature and culture became two increasingly opposing spheres of existence. As dissociation continued and segregation intensified, in the modern world culture itself came to be instrumental. It came to be what happens to people, and how it can be manipulated and managed. It came to be how people are overtly assimilated, socialized, acculturated, trained, and programmed rather than culture being what humans share organically. Culture became an industry and a form of social engineering from above. The spatial dualism of culture from above and nature as resource base below has had profound consequences.

One example is the invention of the mechanical clock and the subsequent temporal anxiety that has swept the globe, teaching people the meaning of speed. Extension transference is a process whereby in physical culture, an artifact is made by a human or small group for a specific utilitarian purpose, and then it comes to transcend, dominate, and measure/evaluate the very people who invented it (Hall, 1959, 1983). Today we time everything from testing how fast our children should do math to how long wars last. Scheduling and logistics are fundamental to "scientific management" and rational organization. Society is more machine-like than organic. It is good when things work "like clockwork." We are all evaluated according to pre-established production targets. Goals and expectations dominate our thoughts. We strive to be objective while we seek to reach our objectives. Nothing is personal. This is the essence of the modern mass society. But it is made up of individuals even as they are regarded as social atoms.

Careless and narcissistic human activity is behind the great extinction wave. So too is an apparent contradiction which Gebser (1949 Ger./1985 Eng.) addressed. Modern mass society has resulted in billions being motivated by and valuing the same individualistic goals, mostly personal liberty. Wealth is regarded as a means to personal autonomy and autonomy has become equated with freedom. Ironically, this singular value system has become a mass ideology. An ideology promoting conformity to doctrines of personal growth has become dominant. So we have a situation where individualism has become hypertrophic on a mass scale. The result is a deficient, destructive aggregation of "objective" individuals facing a level of anonymity never before experienced.

Modern society is marked by a level of dissociative anonymity our species has never dealt with before. It is characterized by a loss of identity and belongingness. Many such as Tönnies (1887 Ger./2001 Eng.), Durkheim (1893 Fr./1997 Eng., 1897 Fr./1979 Eng.), Mauss (1925 Fr./1990 Eng., 1934 Fr./2006 Eng.), David Riesman, Nathan Glazer, and Reuel Denney (1950, 2001), William Whyte (1956/2002), Morris (1969), Kramer (1992, 1994a, 1997a), Robert Putnam (2000), Robert Bellah and Richard Madsen (2007), and others have pointed out a loss of traditional community and a rise in global monoculture (Kramer, 2003a). They are correct. Kramer and Hsieh (2012) note that nearly all the victims of the great heat wave that struck Europe in 2003, and the Tohoku earthquake and tsunami that struck Japan in 2011, were elderly people who had been left alone without extended family support. Stéphane Mantion, an official with the French Red Cross, explained the situation in Paris: "These thousands of elderly victims didn't die from a heat wave as such, but from the isolation and insufficient assistance they lived with day in and out, and which almost any crisis situation could render fatal" (Mantion quoted by Kramer & Hsieh, 2012, p. 135). These were not natural disasters. They were human-made disasters.

Jeremy Rifkin (2004) noted the fallacy that privacy and money will save you. In fact it can be a trap because we are raised to believe that to be secure is to be self-sufficient, financially autonomous (Rifkin, 2004). This makes sense only in a world where being left alone means being secure—the world of survivalists, recluses, feral children, and places such as North Korea. It is a delusion. Human beings outside of social support and interdependence do not survive well or long.

As bureaucratization, managerialism, careerism, and organizational complexity increase, we become progressively competitive and isolated, mostly for the sake of ever more efficient production/consumption. Paths of promotion are designed by others for us and they are linked to productivity. Our self-esteem is involved. These structures appeal to our greed for money and liberation. We seek free time and space. We are eager for power and position (status) and so we are driven to become a "more effective person today!" (Covey, 1990, p. 2). The delusion is that we can "take control," that we are invulnerable and free. While organic community is like nature, simply there, finished, and perfect, we moderns believe everything is changeable according to our wills. Community is something to build and manage. An entire industry of community organizers and builders now exists. We suffer from hurry sickness while we enjoy our privacy, until we need help. As the old saying goes, we love to see the plumber come as soon as possible, and we love to see him go as soon as possible. We want relationships on our own terms. Society is fragmented, zoned. We rarely kill what we eat. We rarely visit a nursing home until we have to go to one. We rarely see birth and the dead and dying.

Globalizing monoculture means that across the globe, the same cultural structures are being adopted and the old duality separating culture from nature is proving to be false. Everything from fish stocks and forests to people and carbon pollution are perceived as markets (Greider, 1997). The more we impact the environment the more we experience cybernetic feedback. What we sow we reap.

Because we are all increasingly trained in similar ways to do the same tasks, believe the same things, value the same things (even to speak a single common language), we are interchangeable—general issue (GI). Whyte (1956, 2002) referred to this as the rise in "practical curriculum" (p. 78) and the administration of "tests of conformity" (p. 182). While in his early writings Marshall McLuhan (1964) celebrated the emergence of the global village, Zbigniew Brzezinski (1970) noted that a better metaphor would be the rise of the global city, which has a very different set of connotations. While the village suggests cooperative slow-paced community, the city suggests fast-paced, competitive, anonymous society. In the mass city we wear mass manufactured clothes and cosmetics, eat mass produced food, listen to mass produced music, and live in mass produced enclosures. By comparison, the Paleolithic and Neolithic tribal member can be identified by his or her headband or cloak. Everything is handmade and unique. Blankets, rugs, baskets, baby carriers, bows, everything is carefully crafted with recognizable style and skill. Individual expression was more common than moderns think.

The slow-pace of traditional community was not perceived as slow until the accelerated life of the modern city appeared. Knowing was analogical, not digital. The shift in how we claim to know something or someone is a function of massification and its attendant reliance on disinterested quantification. Sampling saves time. We like convenient samples. Knowing used to mean to be familiar with something or someone. Now to know something or someone, how we regard them, means to possess quantitative data about certain variables identifying overt behavior patterns—the particulars about something or someone. Fragmentation in the modern world is the method for precision and precise knowing.

Knowledge today tends to be digital rather than analogical, fragmented rather than holistic. After years of practice, indigenous hunters have holistic knowledge of the animals they stalk and eat. Today people will seriously argue that they can know more about a country and people like Russia, for instance, by reading statistical data about them than actually going there and living there. This is the consequence of the modern value of minimalism, of the vaunted Occam's razor. It is not disinterested. Quite the contrary, it is the imposition of very narrow interests defined as the valuable in it. It also involves impatience. I want to know now. Just cut to the chase—to the quick. This is dissociation—abstraction. It presumes *a priori* that much information such as how the food smells and tastes, how people express happiness, how they raise their children, pay their bills, make their money, argue, care for each other, and so forth, is useless. Today we know actually very little about how our environment works. When we ask our students how electricity is made and how it gets to the switch in the wall, most do not know *or care*.

Human beings and other beings are increasingly conceived as measurable objects, as being reduced to the sum of their measures. And what is measured exposes interest. We measure everything today in terms of productivity further reduced to profitability as rationality itself. To be rational and realistic is to realize the profit margin on any and all relationships seen as transactions. Thus to be selfish is to be rational.

Economic metaphors have always been borrowed. Paul in the *Bible* spoke to shopkeepers in Greece and told them that The Christ had paid their "debt" of sin for them. Modernity is increasingly reducible to economic thinking. The founder of behavioral sociology, George Homans, called all human behavior social exchange. Altruism is thus impossible. Even "sacrifice" would not exist unless individuals felt that they were getting something out of it, such as the admiration of a hero's status. According to Homans (1958), all behavior is very simple. One will continue a marriage, a business partnership, a friendship, and so forth, only so long as one perceives a net profit from the interaction. Psychology jumped on the bandwagon launching *transactional* psychology to explain all human behavior. This is very Western and modern, although, as is typical of positivism, modern social scientists who ignore subjective culture believe that their explanation is not "modern," but instead universal. This actually betrays their cultural/ideological propensities.

Value and worth have become equated with quantifiable exploitability. If I cannot find a way to exploit a piece of land, a horse, or my neighbor, they have little value to me. In the new positive polity, human beings have been redefined by economic calculus as units of production—consumption. Quantification, literally counting people, presumes that for our purposes, everyone is essentially identical, like dollar bills or individual digits in an endless sequence. And statistical representations of samples of aggregate human behavior dominate the social sciences. Anonymity liberates the individual from social obligations as well as social support, which was normal in the hamlets and villages we evolved in for millions of years. We have shifted interest from each other to the virtual average person. This dissociative trend has also objectified everything in our environment, reducing plants, animals, and minerals to measurable resource bases. This enables them to become data and input for formulaic manipulation and prediction. At the same time in modern mass society each individual presumes an inalienable right to all things, and so we have the Hobbsian war of all against all in a race to accumulate as much of finite resources as possible as fast as possible. Hence the modern truism, I am unique, just like everyone else. With the elimination of traditional culture, the sacred and the profane evaporate, abandoned as subjective nonsense. As a result, we have come to believe that nothing is sacred, that everything has a simple contingent price tag, that the rarer the more expensive, and that we have a right to whatever we can afford (Eliade, 1957 Ger./1987 Eng.; Campbell & Moyers, 1988; Kramer, 1997a, 2013). Just name your price. The result has been disastrous.

2

Cybernetic Narcissism

The previous chapter outlined the history and impact of a growing narcissism concluding with the economic reality that today people take whatever they can afford. This disregard for context, for anything other than satisfying the self, was described as having "disastrous" consequences.

Take, for example, shark-fin soup. No organization, including the United Nations, has been able to count the number of sharks killed every year for their fins. But as Krista Mahr (2010), writing for *Time Magazine*, notes,

> Last week, as millions of viewers in the U.S. tuned in to Discovery Channel's *Shark Week*, probably nearly 1.5 million sharks were killed in the shark-fin industry—just like the weeks before. All told, up to 70 million sharks are culled annually for the trade, despite the fact that 30% of shark species are threatened with extinction. Indonesia, India, Taiwan, Spain and Mexico land the most sharks, according to a recent survey of global shark populations conducted by the Pew Environment Group. "Sharks have made it through multiple mass extinctions on our planet," says Matt Rand, director of Pew's Global Shark Conservation division. Now many species are going to go the way of the dinosaur—for a bowl of soup. (p. 2)

Since Mahr's report in 2010, the number has increased to an estimated 80,000,000 sharks killed every year, and some put the number much higher

(IUCN, 2013). These numbers do not count "ghost fishing," whereby discarded nets that drift for years in the open oceans snag turtles, seals, and sharks (and other species) too large to fit through the mesh. Unlike other fish species, sharks reproduce very slowly. Most sharks taken are too young to have reached reproductive age. The most popular sharks, such as the oceanic Whitetip and certain subspecies of hammerheads, have declined by 90 percent, and some, such as the Great White, are endangered (IUCN, 2013). The IUCN's Shark Specialist Group has stated, "Over three quarters of the large ocean shark and ray species have a heightened risk of extinction" (Dulvy et al., 2007). Once taken, because of their slow reproductive rates, the populations do not rebound. Richard Fitzpatrick, a marine biologist who has been studying shark behavior at Australia's Great Barrier Reef for decades, says, "The shark stock on the Great Barrier Reef was hit hard when fishing started in earnest here 30 years ago, and it hasn't recovered at all" (National Geographic, 2013).

On November 11, 2011, the Union of Conservation of Nature, the species survival commission of the largest conservation network on the planet, officially pronounced the West African Black Rhino extinct. Observers had not seen one for more than 5 years, since 2006. The same day, the IUCN reclassified a type of yew tree (*Taxus contorta*), which is used to produce Taxol, a chemotherapy drug, and the Coco de Mer, a palm tree that produces the largest fruit in the world and is found in the Seychelles, "endangered." Nearly every day, more bad news about the environment comes to light. Writing for *Scientific American*, John Platt (2012), in his column, "Countdown to Extinction," noted that the Japanese River Otter, *Lutra lutra whiteleyi* (a subspecies of the Eurasian Otter), as well as the Least Horseshoe Bat, *Rhinolophus pumilus miyakonis*, were both officially designated extinct in Japan in 2012. The IUCN has issued a report on the worldwide decline in the world's oldest and largest species, the conifers, including the Sequoia (Coastal Redwood or *Sequoia sempervirens*). In July 2013, after the publication of the first global assessment of cone-bearing cedars, firs, cypresses, and other conifer species since 1998, it was determined that 34 percent are threatened with extinction, including California's Monterey Pine (*Pinus radiata*) and the Atlas Cedar (*Cedrus atlantica*), which is native to the Atlas Mountains of North Africa.

While the largest living organisms on land and megafauna such as rhinos capture our imagination, insects are in trouble too. Because massive use of insecticides has wiped out the wild bee population, nearly all cultivated agricultural products now grown in the developed world are pollinated by domestic bee colonies, and bee keepers report that those bees too are dying out even though they try to use them at times when insecticides are mostly dissipated. Writing for *The Economist* magazine, science and technology correspondent Tim Cross and Geoffrey Carr, Science Editor for *The*

Economist (2012), reported, "In the winter of 2006 beekeepers in America noticed something odd—lots of their hives were dying for no obvious reason. As the months passed, reports of similar phenomena began coming in from their European counterparts. Mystified scientists coined the label 'colony collapse disorder' (CCD) to describe what was happening. Since then, much brow-sweat has been expended trying to work out just what CCD really is" (p. 1). The answer has been found in imidacloprid, the most widely used insecticide in the world. It is a type of neonicotinoid that acts as a neurotoxin on insects (Lu, Warchol, & Callahan, 2012; Whitehorn, O'Connor, Wackers, & Goulson, 2012). Wide-scale use of this type of insecticide began in the mid- to late 1990s. Today, millions of tons of the poison are sprayed all over the world, wiping out honey and bumble bee colonies and proving to be somewhat toxic for birds and highly toxic for aquatic animals, especially invertebrates. As bees become poisoned, they either die outright because they become disoriented and cannot find their way back to their hives or are weakened and become susceptible to other dangers such as climate change, fungal infections, and parasitic infestation.

From all subspecies of sawfish and tuna to several subspecies of seals, from rhinos to Charles Darwin's Frog (*Thinoderma rufum*), from the Florida Cougar and all subspecies of tiger, to the Fraser Fir and Koai'a trees, thousands of plants, animals, birds, insects, and fish species all over the Earth are in steep decline (less than 15 percent of population left), including many that have just been discovered by science (see the United Nations Environment Programme and the World Conservation Monitoring Centre on biodiversity and extinctions). The distribution of megafauna, especially but certainly not exclusively apex predators such as the giant flightless birds, is shrinking at such a rate that from a historical perspective, we are witnessing a mass extinction event. Some argue that this is not the first such extinction event caused by humans. Many argue that the end-Pleistocene and Holocene megafaunal extinctions are linked to the arrival of human beings in different parts of the world (Martin, 2007). Even if this controversial theory about the disappearance of Pleistocene and Holocene megafauna is true, what is happening today is different. All flora and fauna are under tremendous stress due to many magnitudes greater of human population, and the impact is magnified by modern technology. The human track, the human footprint, has grown enormous and continues to expand.

For instance, from Russia and India to Nepal and Sumatra, the largest feline species, the tiger, is vanishing overnight. The tiger population has collapsed from about 100,000 in 1900 to fewer than 3,000 in 2013 (Walston et al., 2010). This decline is due to an expanding human population and more powerful vehicles of transportation, including helicopters, more powerful weapons, siting scopes, all-weather technologies such as Gortex clothing, GPS, freeze-dried food, carbon fiber tent parts, and, of course, an expanding network of communications and transportation that makes it feasible for tiger parts to find their way to global markets. According to the best and most recent estimate available at this writing, there are about 2,126 mature breeding-age wild tigers in the world (Walston et al., 2010). Of the nine sub-species of tiger based on morphology (six by molecular markers according to Luo et al., 2004), three, the Bali, Caspian, and Javan, are already extinct, with the Siberian (Amur), Indochinese, Bengal, South Chinese, Malayan, and Sumatran subspecies dwindling below sustainable populations.

To offer just one specific example of recent extinction of megafauna, it was reported in June 2012 that the Formosan Clouded Leopard endemic to Taiwan is extinct (China News Agency/*Taipei Times*, 2012). This report was not made in haste. The mid-sized feline was thought to be extinct for decades, but hope remained. So in 2000, a team of zoologists from Taiwan and the United States launched a last-ditch effort to find one. Unfortunately, after 13 years of searching, they announced in June 2012 that they had given up hope. For more than a decade, zoologists Chiang Po-jen and Pei Jai-chyi led teams that used 377 infrared cameras and 232 hair snare stations in the last of Taiwan's diminished forests, but they came up with no evidence of the cat's existence. The last known siting was in 1983. Habitat destruction depleted the prey of Taiwan's top predator. Finally, the zoologists conclud-ed that the last individuals were probably poached to extinction for their popular pelts (China News Agency/*Taipei Times*, 2012). The only one left is a stuffed specimen on display in the Taiwan National Museum. A pair of leopards is kept at the Taipei Zoo, but they are a different subspecies import-ed from Southeast Asia.

As dense human populations expand into wilderness, species are being destroyed, and as wealth explodes and technology makes transportation and communication more pervasive around the world, demand for the last scrap of whatever is left is funding poaching and over-fishing worldwide.

For instance, since China's economic takeoff, the tiger population in that country was exterminated for use in traditional medicines. Consequently, newly wealthy Chinese who demand the best medicines for themselves have begun importing tiger parts from Vietnam, Laos, Cambodia, Bangladesh, Nepal—in short, from anywhere tigers are left. Between 1989 and 1991, dur-ing the initial stages of the economic boom in China, one third of breeding-age female tigers were lost. In August 2005, the largest single seizure of tiger bone was made in Kaohsiung, Taiwan, one of the (if not the largest) transit points for rare animal parts such as sea turtles, tigers, shark fins, and rhino parts. During this operation, authorities seized 140 kilograms (308 pounds) of tiger bones, including 24 skulls from Indonesia (along with rare pangolin parts) (TRAFFIC, 2005). One tiger has about 21 pounds of bones. This trade probably contributed to the extinction of the three subspecies once found in Malaysia and Indonesia. Taiwan is a signatory to the Foreign Trade Act and

CITES international agreement to protect endangered species. What are these illegal animal parts worth? In 2007, two Bengal tiger pelts were seized in Qingdao in Shandong Province, China, worth about $135,000 (China.Org.CN, 2007). As the animals become more rare, the prices soar, motivating more poaching to feed demand and making possession more of a status symbol for the narcissistic owner.

Two principles if not truths inform this book. First, we must remember from the ancient Greek story that narcissism is suicidal. While we obsess on ourselves and ignore our environment, we are approaching a tipping point that will plunge us into self-destruction. Second, narcissism at the ego- and species-centric levels is a form of positivism. While other authors have discussed the "epidemic of narcissism" (Twenge, 2007; Twenge & Campbell, 2010), they have not touched on the global spread of this personality disorder and how it is related to the larger ideology of modern positivism. Positivism is a form of epistemology, and the self-evident and quantifiable truth of wealth "proves" the rich to be "better"—what the cultural anthropologist Jules Henry (1963), who studied normative (naturalistic–realistic) behavior in modern society, called "pecuniary truth." As positivism has spread across the globe, forming the basis of development ideology, it presumes to define how humans should evolve, advance, progress—in short, develop into modern style individualistic consumers. Narcissism is the most pronounced trait of the new human. It accentuates and valorizes individualism, greed, competition, and personal will-to-power without external regulation. It has become a culture, arguably the dominant culture initiated with colonial hubris.

The key to understanding this situation is to understand that we are not in a "postcolonial" era but rather in a continuation of an older globalization that has reached hypertrophic proportions, whereby people all over the world have said, if you can't beat them, join them. And so all over the world, the lower classes do not fight the culture of colonial elites but seek to join them with the promise that every man will be a king and every woman a queen sitting in their castle with a car in the garage and a plethora of *private* property and *personal* communications devices at their control. The triumph of the culture of narcissism is that it no longer has to convince anyone of its truth and value, but rather everyone has become made in its image.

Our personalities have been programmed. Everywhere modern urbanizing individuals are rushing forward in a chronic state of urgency to achieve personal actualization defined as personal liberty from obligations and traditional expectations. Status is no longer measured by the stature one holds within a community or what one builds and accomplishes but increasingly by how much one has and consumes. Standard of living indexes that rank-order nations, assigning levels of relative development and economic maturity, are based on this definition of wealth.

But the thing about progress is that it has become a meaningless concept. In order to meaningfully speak of or measure progress, one must first posit a goal so that relative movement toward or away from the goal can be ascertained. That would imply that once we achieve the goal, progress stops, and we have arrived at utopia or whatever. This was the founding belief system behind modern Enlightenment thinking that spurred colonial ambitions. But as one after another utopian project was deemed irrational during the twentieth century, the idea of a final solution or goal was abandoned, but not the motive force of progress. Consequently, we are perpetually pushing for progress toward no end. Progress has become a logical absurdity. Progress is never ending. And so we have a system of ambition without external criteria that can guide us or limit our chronic aspirations to more, ever more. As a result, we now simply compete against each other for the relatively biggest carbon footprint. This is why we cannot achieve satisfaction and happiness. Our endless striving toward happiness makes us miserable. And now, our mania for progress as domination is grossly affecting all other life on the planet.

Narcissism deploys rhetoric that convinces us that all is well, that progress is not only continuing but that more of the same is the solution, not the problem. Positivism is optimistic, good, and happy. According to this ideology, self-confidence and aggressive dominance are virtues. This system of beliefs forms a complex of denial. It insists that everything is okay and getting better, that development and markets are progressing; to propagate this positivism, we have "conservative" media personalities, business leaders, and politicians denying the science behind the current collapse of life on Earth. Why? Because they are self-deluded. We believe we are exceptional organisms. We believe we are miraculous, that humans can transcend the laws of nature including the balance between life and death and achieve immortality and unlimited hedonism. These are the twin tails of our delusion, rooted as it is in our self-centered attitude that has only grown more hypertrophic in recent centuries (Gebser, 1949 Ger./1985 Eng.; Kramer, 1992, 1995, 1997, 2003a, 2013).

Contrary to the tendency of writers to jump on bandwagons, we are not in a postcolonial world at all. Colonization of every niche of the world is rushing forward with ever-greater slickness and seduction. This is the age of the third sophistic (Dalton & Kramer, 2012; Kramer, 1997). Sophistry is the art of delusion, of deceit and persuasion. The First Sophistic was met by the rise of logic to combat it in ancient Greece. The Second Sophistic occurred with the fall of Rome and the rise of religious dogma as the most powerful force. Today we are in the Third Sophistic. Billions of dollars are spent on campaigns of mass persuasion. It is an age of institutions dedicated to persuasion over conquest. This new form of colonialism (not post-colonialism) offers a velvet touch. We wage wars for "hearts and minds." Positivism is spreading in various discursive guises presented as truisms, such as the unquestionable greatness of market capitalism, the unquestionable fatalism of social Darwinism, and the inevitable conquest of all by greed.

Proof of our dominance and uniqueness is expressed in our technology. Who is "we" and "our"? First, this undeniable truth was demonstrated by Western colonial powers conquering all Others before them. Now, after assimilating most Other cultures, those conquered peoples have accepted the premises of progress and development presented to them by colonial masters, and they are rushing to urbanize, grow markets, increase production/consumption, and "develop" into the best kind of human possible—the modern private individual.

Indeed, just as Narcissus was undeniably handsome, so too the seduction of freedom from obligation, the promise of status mobility and dominance, and the acceptance of hedonism as good and rational are powerful enticements. But therein lies the hook of our delusion. Although we tame rivers and continents and genetically alter plants and animals, still they affect us. As systems theory based in hermeneutics has maintained, what goes around comes around, and we cannot not communicate (Watzlawick, Beavin, & Jackson, 1967/2011). As explained in greater detail below, we are literally drinking each other's urine, ingesting hundreds of pharmaceuticals now found in our drinking water. What you reach out and touch, touches you back. Communication means reciprocity. There is inescapable feedback from what we do. It comes back to affect us. What we do to other things, we do to ourselves.

The essence of our power-delusion is that we believe we can act on other things without them having the power to act on us. Our grand delusion is that we are all-powerful and that every problem can be solved by more technology, including, as is discussed below, proposals for climate engineering.

What is the number one problem we are working to eliminate? Mortality and any friction we encounter in the exercise of our wills. We cannot exercise will-to-power unless we exist, and so our deepest drive is to conquer death. Death is the great thief. It takes away all we have and all we might have had. Religion has not been satisfying enough. Our devotions, prayers, and pleas are not heeded, the dead do not rise again, and we are of little faith about a spiritual life everlasting that we have no direct experience of. And so we are driven to conquer death itself. We have managed to extend our lifespans, and now science and technology hold out the ultimate prize— the ability to stop aging by manipulating the telomeres at the ends of our chromosomal genetic material. When we run out of telomeres that serve to buffer chromosomes at the end of our chains of DNA, then with each subsequent replication valuable genetic material necessary for optimal cell replication is destroyed. Telomeres are called "trash genetic material" that does not contain information essential to cell replication. Telomeres are discarded each time a cell divides without effect thus protecting the operant genetic information. However, when all the telomeres have been used up vital chromosomal information becomes vulnerable to degradation. Aging occurs when the genetic information necessary for optimal cell division is exposed and begins to be lost with each cycle of cell division. If we can preserve the telomeres, we stop aging. Elizabeth Blackburn, Carol Greider, and Jack Szostak were awarded the Nobel Prize in Physiology and Medicine in 2009 for their discovery of enzyme telomerase, the process by which "junk DNA" or telomeres act as buffers to protect DNA higher up the strand that is necessary for normal reproduction. Immortality is becoming feasible.

We are mesmerized by our own technological achievements. They are material proof that we are right and powerful. When we believe we are right, then we insist that doing more of the same makes us more correct. This is the thought pattern behind all conservatism from the argument that guns are good and right and therefore what we need is more of them to be more good and right to the idea that you cannot be too rich, too thin, too normal, or too young.

Since might is good and right, we need more might. One cannot be too powerful. Our culture has reached a point where power alone is not enough. We are marshaling all our might to become evermore mighty. This is will-power-drive dedicated to more will power. Positivists call it predetermination based on inherent personality traits—to be always already determined, to know with devotion and commitment. And so they stubbornly stick to positions on issues no matter how things change. They are staunch absolutists and fear evil relativism. But everyone knows that if you have a 20-year-old biology textbook, you are very out-of-date. According to the dialectical deliberative movement of knowledge, science is always getting truer because it never stops testing itself. This is a form of humility. Scientists are loath to make categorical claims because they know they cannot be absolutely positive once and for all about anything. Conservative, old-fashioned positivists take advantage of this humility all the time as when they claim that the theory of evolution is no better than the theory of creationism.

Humility, pausing for self-reflection and assessment, doubt, and the ability to transvaluate one's own values and reality are all seen as weakness. The modern positivist is masculine and certain. The modern is resolved to resolve all issues and obstacles. This is the fascist culture clearly articulated in Martin Heidegger's (1927 Ger./1962 Eng.) "resoluteness toward death" and exposed by the one-time leader of the logical positivist movement himself, Ludwig Wittgenstein, who, very much *unlike* Heidegger, abandoned his own early work for further investigations and self-correction in later works such as *Philosophical Investigations* (1953) and *On Certainty* (1969). Ironically, Heidegger, the philosopher who gave us a cogent critique of technological attitude, also valorized resoluteness as the crowning virtue, a fact that the great Nietzsche scholar, Walter Kaufmann (1975, 1992), points out as he exposes Heidegger's neo-Hegelian narcissism and his obsession with dominance display and Being.

The selfish attitude of total resoluteness onto death manifests as we marvel at our own products including ourselves as bootstrap creator/creations. The Modern hails himself as the self-made man. The Modern has trouble seeing that neither he nor his technology are the end all and be all.

In this book, we acknowledge the obvious fact of human industry and ingenuity and will-power-drive, but we also argue herein that technology and technique (including in art production) is not all that is. It is but one small aspect of being. To reduce human culture to technology is to live a tautology. It is akin to reducing everything to measurements. But as noted before, measurements are measurements of something that is not itself a measurement. So too, culture is not identical with technology and within it exists the ability to transcend and control technology. So long as we concentrate only on technological marvels and solutions, and not the feedback that their existence creates within the larger nontechnical context, we are missing the vast ocean that will swallow us without a ripple as if we had never existed.

The sources of many extinction events are directly linked to modern human activity, including the transportation of invasive species, pathogens, habitat fragmentation, and destruction such as deforestation on a massive scale for unregulated charcoal production and agricultural expansion, and widespread water quality degradation. For instance, we offer just one small case, the Powder Blue Damselfly, *Arabicnemis caerulea*, which is native to southern Arabia, Yemen, and Oman. It is disappearing due to pollution of its aquatic habitat and over-extraction of water.

Other causes of extinction include over-hunting and over-harvesting, species persecution, widespread use of insecticides and other chemical toxins, and climate change. Animals and plants that have co-existed with us and have existed since long before the emergence of the human species, such as the Siamese Crocodile, *Crocodylus siamensis*, the Sulawesi Crested Black Macaque, *Macaca nigra*, the Yangtze River finless porpoise, *Neophocaena phocaenoides*, the Orangutans, and countless less famous organisms are crashing mostly due to massive conversion of wilderness lands into agricultural domestication. We are harnessing the world for our interests and in the process killing it. Deforestation is but one example. We are transforming rainforests into ranches, farms, and plantations that produce beef and other commodities such as palm seed oil used in cosmetics, mechanics, and biodiesel. And we are now farming trees on a massive scale, producing "forests" that profoundly lack biodiversity. Per narcissism, value has been reduced to personal use value. If I cannot exploit a person or thing, it has no value to me. If I cannot transform something into instrumental use value, then, to the modern ego, it is a taunting experience. That which resists transformation denies me power over it and hedonic satisfaction of using it at will. So I double my resolve to conquest.

Positivism as a philosophy and an ideology is rooted in the very concept of culture. Culture, to cultivate, to civilize, to "advance," "prosper," "progress," is marching across the globe, and it is a particular culture that is virulently aggressive, spatial-linear, and self-confident—a culture that equates knowing with disinterested observation and technological might—it is Western positivistic modernity—industrial culture. It is self-certain, arrogant, and robust. This culture, positivism, completes a hairpin turn of self-recognition, consciously and explicitly seeing itself as a culture, as a choice, and also as the *non plus ultra* of human development (Gebser, 1949 Ger./1985 Eng.). According to its own criteria of evolutionary progress through stages of civilization, no other culture can compare. Arrogance is one facet of narcissism.

Are we naïve hippies? Are we ignorant alarmists? We have company. We agree with the various reports put out by the Club of Rome beginning in the 1970s and many others, including the British Astronomer Royal Sir Martin Rees's (2003) book *Our Final Hour*, Ronald Wright's (2005) *A Short History of Progress*, and Jared Diamond's (2004) *Collapse: How Societies Choose to Fail or Succeed*. Human technology has become nothing short of a "disaster" for the planet. Even Raymond Kurzweil (2005), in his book *The Singularity Is Near*, agrees with this assessment, but his Frankensteinian "solution" is to abandon the planet, indeed to abandon life, and store intelligence on machines that will allow "humanity" to transcend biology. Kurzweil's solution is a form of absurd hyper-positivism. His proposal is to solve the problem of technology with super-technology. We believe that such a position, and not our own, is naïve.

In this book, we do not agree with many doomsayers who, in our opinion, overly dramatize the timetable for human extinction. We do not believe that humanity will go extinct or migrate into computer chips anytime soon. But this is not to say that we are optimistic. Humans are crafty and tenacious, although not wise. To paraphrase Darwin, it is not the strongest or the smartest who will endure but those who can tolerate change the most. We can get used to practically anything. We are flexible. This is the source of both our strength and our horror. No, we will not die out soon but endure. However, this is not a blessing. Our species is more likely to endure for centuries in an increasingly uninhabitable world, spiraling toward extinction through spasms of wars over disappearing resources and a darkening twilight of banal narcissistic self-destruction. If we are to endure with dignity and in a world rich in diversity, we must transvaluate our values, remaking not the world but ourselves. To do this, we must first understand that this is possible. This is the goal of philosophy because philosophy is about producing change but not easy change. It is about specifically knowing and changing ourselves.

In this book, we aim to explain what has driven recent human behavior toward the ultimate contradiction, suicidal tendencies in the search for immortality. We argue that we are caught in a profound self-contradiction. In our quest to never die, we are killing everything, including ourselves. In part we argue that we are not choosing to do this but rather we are caught up in what Hans-Georg Gadamer (1960 Ger./1975 Eng.) calls "blind preju-dice," which is an essential aspect of hegemonic identification with an ideol-ogy and culture, and which it is the role of philosophy to combat. The call is for another phenomenon on the brink of extinction, philosophy. We des-perately need culture critique because it is only through a thorough and honest self-reflection that we can hope to break out of our own suicidal worldview and see it as contingent and available for critical modification if not abandonment. This book is in a sense an attempt to grasp our dominant version of reality, to see it as just that, a version of what can be, and to grasp it with the same sort of ambition that drives technology. We need to grasp our sense of reality with a mind toward transforming it, to see our world-view as a human artifact that is available for change, to get the horse back in front of the cart, to start to build our own consciousness structure with a principle based on the preservation of life rather than blindly rushing along with the cultural currents that are ultimately self-annihilating.

ENGINEERING THE CULTURE OF ENGINEERING: SELF-CYBERNETICS

An obvious question is why are we so determined, so dedicated to the cur-rent course of action? Insofar as we are making our environment and then adapting to it, we are caught up in a cybernetic loop tightening-down toler-ances and limiting creativity to our own imaginations, or more narrowly to the imaginations of a dominating few. This is ultimately environmental fas-cism. To choose to be self-made is the height of hubris for it suggests that no other imagination or set of random factors could conceive of a future form as wonderful as our own. And yet, while we admire our own brainpower and the technologies we have created, we have to admit that we came out of nature. Natural processes must therefore have value we can appreciate. But as dissociation increases, we forget where we come from and hyper-value our own singularly self-centered interpretation of things. We want to take credit for the good but not the bad. For instance, so far as global warming is bad, we choose to claim we are not the cause.

A perspective, by definition, never encompasses or knows everything. To believe otherwise is to manifest hypertrophic egocentrism, which limits us to our own perspective, uncritically presuming that it is all that there is or should be—really, naturally. If it does not affect me, what does it matter any-way? But that presumes that we know everything about process and system.

For the sake of rhetorical convenience we tend to vacillate between organic reality and instrumentality. The ambiguity is strategic. What results is a grand contradiction for this rhetoric and bias which is patently, intrinsically, a cultural phenomenon, working to inoculate itself from cross-examination by claiming to be natural and therefore beyond reasonable deliberation. And here we have the problem of freedom and determinism. We are told that we are free to do what we will, by nature. We cannot escape freedom. We *must* be self-made and then adapt to what we have created.

Naturalizing claims are ideological forms of apologetics. They are forms of myth-making according to Husserl (1913 Ger./1982 Eng.) and Roland Barthes (1957 Fr./1972 Eng.). The human-made world is, by definition, a cultural artifact, not a naturally occurring phenomenon. It is a construct held together through social interaction, which Alfred Schutz (1945 Ger./1970 Eng.), along with Gebser (1949 Ger./1985 Eng.) and Morris (1969) agree, is becoming a world increasingly mediated and characterized by anonymity. For example, increasingly we no longer make music together but instead listen alone to a machine (Benjamin, 1936, 1961 Ger./1969 Eng.).

This problem of mass conformity to a human conceived world pretending to be natural and therefore beyond reflection and choice (predetermination) is not new. And the current modern version caters to individualism, including private property. Individualism and selfishness can overlap. Rather this idea that socio-cultural reality is natural and naturally Darwinian is a historical derivation. It allows the dominating power to argue, "Hey don't blame me, it's just how it is—naturally." So should one take personal pride in being self-made or not? Should we accept things because they are?

During the height of Victorian colonialism, colonial imperialists were utterly convinced that they were naturally and demonstrably superior to all Others they encountered including subordinates in their home countries. And their ideology of positivism reinforced this delusion. They insisted that all Others should freely conform. All Others should seek to conform to their superior, more evolved values, beliefs, motivations, expectations, and ways of doing things in order to advance and become civilized—evolved. Subordinates should know and accept their natural place. This ideology lives on even today. Gudykunst and Kim (2003) clearly state that civilizational and personal advancement means to manifest "plasticity and adaptability" (p. 380), to willingly accept such "conformity pressure" (p. 371), "coercive pressure" (p. 360) from the "majority," which they define as a simple numerical advantage, the "size of the population sharing a given stranger's [their word for the Other] original culture" (p. 360). In other words, one should seek to conform (which Gudykunst and Kim strategically and incorrectly equate with "adapt") to the mainstream majority just because they are the majority and can affect your life in negative ways because "they [the majority] control the daily survival and function of strangers [presenting] a coercive pressure on them to adapt" (p. 360).

This is base pragmatism without any consideration of power as defining majority/minority identities, for in many societies "majority" is not a numerical value but an issue of power and control of resources. This notion of conformity as good also fails to take into consideration higher-order human considerations such as issues of social justice. This view also fails to recognize that "strangers," nonconformists, deviants, innovators, immigrants, refugees, and others are always already a part of the system, that one immigrant family moving into a community and opening an ethnic restaurant changes choices for the entire community. Furthermore, the existence of the Other need not be next door to impact our lives because the system is global and so the existence of cheap labor in China effects workers in Ohio. In short, the simple existence of the minority affects the entire system, unless they can be eliminated by assimilation or other means assuring the status quo. Gudykunst and Kim (2003), like all political positivists presume a highly dissociated and simplistic view of reality—one that is biased in favor of the dominant power regardless of justice or the reality of globalization.

Gudykunst and Kim (2003) equate compliance by the Other with "adaptation" and "upward-forward" (p. 382) "psychic evolution" (p. 384), "mental health" (pp. 372, 376, 381), and "maturity" (p. 381) toward functional fitness and "operational skills" (p. 364). This is how current Spencerians such as Gudykunst and Kim (2003) define a competent person who is "fit to live in the company of others" (p. 358). But conformity is not the same thing as adaptation. Conformity is a closed system. The real world is open and exhibits evolution, which includes adaptations and random mutations of all sorts that diverge from past forms, opening up new paths for life. Mutation is discontinuity. Learning, adaptation does not mean simply mimicking what has been.

According to Gudykunst and Kim (2003), to become "competent" includes accepting "appropriate motivations" (pp. 275-276) and "accepted modes of experience" (p. 378), as defined by the majority coercive power, enabling the assimilator to "work effectively with others. . . . Effectiveness is a function of professional expertise" (p. 274). Any deviance or friction is defined by Gudykunst and Kim (2003), the spokespersons for the dominant majority, as not merely unprofessional and incompetent, but as "immature" (p. 369), "cynical" (p. 380), "self-deceptive" (p. 380), "maladjusted" (pp. 366, 372), "unbalanced" (p. 383), "counterproductive" (p. 380), and exhibiting "extreme mental illness" (pp. 365, 372-373, 381-383).

According to Gudykunst and Kim (2003), nonconformists are in "need of psychotherapy" (p. 382). Resistant personalities, they claim, are rooted in "personality dispositions," and "attributes" as well as "ethnicity" (Gudykunst & Kim, 2003, pp. 368-369). This is a complete rehash of the functional positivism put forth at the height of European (and we might add

Japanese) imperialism. As Gudykunst and Kim (2003) see it, deviance is not a necessary condition for evolution, but instead conformity is the way "upward and forward" (p. 382), which somehow leads to psychic and societal "growth" and advancement, while "unlearning" leads to greater "cognitive complexity" (pp. 380-383). This runs completely counter to the logic of evolutionary divergence but such expert-sounding language serves the persuasive interests of the dominant and coercive mainstream group (Kramer, 1995, 1997a, 2000a, 2000b, 2000c, 2003a, 2003b; Kramer, Callahan, & Zuckerman, 2013). Spencerians and St. Simonians offer social scientific justification for assimilation leading to a more efficient world.

According to Gudykunst and Kim (2003), the minority opinion must "undergo fundamental psychic transformation" (p. 376) by "systematic forces" (p. 380) in the mainstream culture in order to conform and properly fit. The minority must have their "nervous systems" "reprogrammed" (pp. 358, 376-377) in order to be psychologically "balanced" (p. 383) and become "realistic" (p. 369). According to Gudykunst and Kim (2003), this remolding of the immigrant's and/or minority's psyche by the "coercive forces" (p. 360) of the "appropriate" (pp. 363, 376) and simple numerical majority (p. 360) is for the immigrant's own good. Per Gudykunst and Kim, (2003), learning and "growth" via a remolding conformity process they call "becoming intercultural" (pp. 384-385) via total "assimilation" (p. 360) requires a complete psychic disintegration (pp. 380, 381) of the immigrant/minority. They define this process as deculturation, which they explain as "unlearning" one's original culture and identity (pp. 380-384), which otherwise retards adaptive success. Their concept of personal evolution and growth is not growth at all but rather a zero-sum process whereby one can learn something new in direct proportion to how much one "unlearns" older information. In short, for Gudykunst and Kim (2003) there can be no accumulation of new repertoires of foods, fashions, languages, ideas, but instead only a replacing of old foods and ideas with new ones. They argue that for the minority to succeed, they must willfully forget all aspects of the self, comprised of how one thinks, feels, and behaves, including abandoning one's traditional foods, music, media content, religion, language, sense of aesthetics; everything. Failure to unlearn one' self will stop one from becoming "functionally fit" (pp. 360, 380-383). According to Gudykunst and Kim (2003), such willing psychic disintegration is the only way to save the minority and/or immigrant from mental and emotional "disturbance" (p. 378), and enable them to have a "leap forward" (p. 384), meaning losing the original cultural self and becoming one with the mainstream..

Now, how does this reprogramming occur? Gudykunst and Kim (2003) go into some detail about the need for the minority to undergo "psychic disintegration" (pp. 380, 381) so that they can achieve "psychic evolution" (reprogramming) (p. 384). If successful, the minority will become one with the majority and become competent, operationally skilled mature and sane persons.

The goal of acculturation can be achieved only to the extent that a person "unlearns" their original identity, is "deculturized" (pp. 359-360, 380-383). The goal is to become a highly malleable "universal person" (p. 384). Hence we have the perfect global worker who is skilled and who will never rock the boat. Such an ideal person belongs nowhere, or to put it another way, can work anywhere. They are someone who has no identity or perspective of their own, who has no "interests" (p. 384). This universal worker should achieve an "absolute point of view" (p. 385) that Gudykunst and Kim (2003) define as a "transcendental perspective" with "optimal communication competence" (p. 384), because they have "a greater capacity to overcome cultural parochialism and develop a wider circle of identification, approaching the limit of many cultures and ultimately of humanity itself. . . . As we reach the mountaintop, we see that all paths below ultimately lead to the same summit . . ." (p. 385). The perfect person belongs nowhere and everywhere. They are not even human, as we know it.

Two problems immediately appear. First, to belong nowhere is what has been widely recognized as diaspora, a condition which causes great anxiety and psychological stress until and unless one finds a new home. Incidentally both William Gudykunst and Young Kim, the authors of this theory of "universal person" who has no "belongingness" (p. 384), were both very much entrenched in academic networks and members of professional associations and cultures and were proud to be identifiable as such. Second, while they promote this liberation from identity because "intellectual distinctions" (p. 385) constitute "emotional defilements" (p. 385), they do so on the same page where they discuss the essential cognitive ability of the universal person to "exhibit greater cognitive differentiation" (p. 384). And, they point out, this great goal of evolving beyond cultural parochialism, beyond cultural identity, is inspired by a specific and distinctly "eastern philosophical tradition" (p. 385). Contradictions abound because to be consistent would mean to recognize basic hermeneutic tenets of identity, memory, communication and meaning making, and social cohesion.

This recipe for socially engineering the perfect universal person is a fusion of Hegelian absolutism with one particular eastern doctrine of self-annihilation for the sake of self-liberation from the wheel of suffering, what Kramer has called "contemptus mundi," a hatred of being itself (Kramer, 2000a, 2000b, 2000c). The engineering solution to intercultural communication offered by Gudykunst and Kim (2003) is the elimination of cultural differences in lieu of a single positive perspective. Once difference and distinction is eliminated then there is no meaning to misinterpret and no perspectives to differ. They are correct to state that were this state of affairs to occur there would be no humans left. Just as the claim that the average American family consists of 1.8 persons and .6 dogs is unreal, so too is Hegel's utopia. Responding to Hegel's positive utopia, Kierkegaard (1843 Danish/2006 Eng.) pronounced it dead and "unfit for human habitation" (p. 46). Likewise

Nietzsche (1887 Ger./1989 Eng.) correctly identified such rhetoric as self-serving justification for administrative nihilism, a neo-Hegelian nightmare about a positivistic monoculture with logic like iron clamps and all of its own internal contradictions. Systems engineering, not systems theory, which tries to understand natural systems, but systems engineering that believes we can do better than nature has with a billion years of absolutely objective experimentation, is producing a world unfit for habitation.

What social and systems engineers Gudykunst and Kim (2003) offer is this conflation of Hegelian hubris with pop notions of absolute mystical enlightenment. It is pure dissociation from confounding existential reality where misunderstandings and inefficiencies exist — *contemptus mundi*. But such inefficiencies may not be bad when more perspectives are privileged. Initially we thought that many species were pests and deserved to be eliminated only to discover that they had important functions within the environment. This structuralist ideal of a purified (Pure Land) properly organized world-as-accomplishment or world-as-artifact is actually very egocentric. It is what Professor Detelf Ingo Lauf of the Carl Jung Institute in Geneva, an authority on western interpretations of eastern spiritual traditions has called "beatnik-zen" (Lauf, 1981, personal conversation).

On the one hand positivism promises a contradiction, a new objective subject (human) who has no point-of-view, no obligations, no interest, nor identity, and is therefore very plastic — useful — good. But on the other hand the progressive evolutionary process concludes with an absolute singularity of perspective that unifies all people in their values, beliefs, ways of thinking, feeling and behaving — a cosmopolitan "transcultural identity" forming an all "inclusive whole" (Gudykunst & Kim, 2003, pp. 384-385). To these authors, this version of positivism is clearly inspired by a specifically naïve western youth cultural version of smatterings of eastern mysticism. An ironically, counter-culture novice interpretation of mysticism that was pervasive on every academic campus from Heidelberg to the University of Hawaii from about 1960 to 1980. This was the heyday of beat Zen that bore little resemblance to actual Chan and Zen Buddhist cultural and monastic discipline as practiced and maintained for hundreds of years in the orient.

Here is the grand irony. The Zenish rhetoric totally contradicts the social engineering philosophy that claims to be inspired by it. The real consequence for such an assimilationist ideology is that deviance and contrary points-of-view can never be good. A monk setting himself on fire in Saigon is regarded as merely maladjusted. Resistance to mainstream majority culture can never be appropriate, just, right, or true. The stranger, is, by definition, confused and neurotic. The mainstream culture and its trajectory can never be wrong. Any alternate perspective is thus preemptively, by definition, delegitimized as unrealistic and, ironically, unnatural.

This is the problem of positivism, even when offered a mystical façade to make it more sexy. And this is what this book refuses to accept. The idea that there is one reality and not multiple interpretations is Hegel's Absolute Reason. Nietzsche (1887 Ger./1974 Eng.) responds to this saying that such an interpretation, that excludes all other interpretations, is "one of the *most stupid* of all possible interpretations of the world, meaning that it would be one of the poorest in meaning. This thought is intended for the ears and consciences of our mechanists [and their] essentially mechanical world, an essentially *meaningless* world" (p. 335). Nietzsche is challenging the increasingly dominant and seductive techno-rationality of his and our time, the ratio of gearing and calculation equated with creation itself and the reduction of the human being to fragments (cognition, affect, behavior) that lend themselves to social engineering—reprogramming. The great chain of positive causation leaves no freedom between cause and effect—on to infinity. This is what Nietzsche (1887 Ger./1974 Eng.) says, "is streaming around all these positivistic systems, the vapor of a certain pessimistic gloom, something that smells of weariness, fatalism" (p. 288), which leaves nothing but coursework for the true believers. The great chain of positive causation would make all tomorrows predictable and as such utterly redundant and meaningless. Hope, creativity, invention, and discovery would all be snuffed out as alternatives are closed-off. Progress becomes a permanent condition, which is absurd, and creativity becomes programmed, which is also absurd.

In the positive religion we see the self-privileging narcissism and egoism of the absolute perspective that refuses to see itself as just that, a perspective among others. Nietzsche (1887 Ger./1974 Eng.) finds positivism to be nihilistic and a "ridiculous immodesty" (p. 336) that permits only one interpretation of the world, the one from my "corner" (p. 336). Rather he argues for an infinite world of countless interpretations. He does not say they are all equally meaningful, interesting, or . . . useful. In this book we encourage us all to try to take a much broader perspective on things, a global perspective that appreciates the interests of many species and cultures. W. E. B. Dubois can help us appreciate the Other.

Exactly one century prior to Gudykunst and Kim's (2003) solution to intercultural miscommunication by eliminating cultural difference through convergence and assimilation toward a single cultural form, in 1903, W. E. B. Dubois published *The Souls of Black Folk*. In this classic sociological text he points out that one cannot deculturize and unlearn oneself. Over half a century later Milton Rokeach (1968, 1973) experimentally proved that core values last a lifetime and are the basis for all our interpretations of things. This is why Kramer (1997, 2000a, 2000b, 2000c, 2003a, 2008, 2013) and Kramer, Callahan, and Zuckerman (2013) have argued that what occurs is real growth, that one need not unlearn or deculturize oneself to learn something new. Rather cultural fusion occurs as one adopts new styles of thinking and doing

(Kramer, 2000b, 2000c, 2003a, 2008, 2011, 2013). Growth is not a zero-sum game. The mind is not finite. As we experience life our horizons expand and we acquire new repertoires of doing things and thinking. I can learn a new dance or language without first erasing my memory of an old one.

Dubois asks, what if in the process of internalizing and assimilating completely to the majority worldview you are forced to see yourself as inherently inferior and unworthy of full citizenship and human dignity. Can you really willfully forget who you are as Gudykunst and Kim (2003) claim? Dubois says no. He writes, "It is a peculiar sensation, this double-consciousness, this sense of always looking at one's self through the eyes of others, of measuring one's soul by the tape of a world that looks on in amused contempt and pity" (Dubois, 2013, p. 1). And how could one conform if that means changing one's race? Religious conversion may be possible but I cannot change my phenotype and efforts to do so are widely received with pity, if not contempt even by people you are trying to emulate. Dubois is talking about a profound dissonance that accompanies an effort to join a club that hates you. So even if you as an individual can pass, you will soon find yourself confronting a discourse in the club that denigrates your mother and father, sister and brother. This dissonance is what Dubois called double-consciousness. It has been long established in experimental psychology that forced assimilation/conformity does not make a person satisfied, balanced, well-adjusted, and/or identical with the mainstream majority (Festinger & Carlsmith, 1959). In fact, if one tries hard to conform to their expectations, that is almost never what mainstream majorities expect. If you really conform to their values, expectations, and beliefs you will stay in your place. But many believe they belong to groups such as the economic middle class when they do not. We falsely believe in unanimity of interests—namely the consistency of the trajectory we are taking known as the equilibrium or consistent stability of things—*status quo.*

How is it that we agree with, conform to, and even defend policies and actions that are destroying our world, the world we all share—our habitus? Perhaps it is a massive form of groupthink, which involves unquestioned belief in the morality of one's group, self-censorship, the illusion of unanimity among group members, and, most perilous of all, a delusion of invulnerability (Janis, 1968, 1972). Such group dynamics lead members to fail to accurately assess the risks of their actions, to fail to seek out information about their situation, and when doing so to exhibit strong selection bias as they cherry pick facts that fit the scenario they want to believe in. It also involves a failure to create any contingency plans or survey alternative solutions that other cultures may offer. Such irrational decision-making processes have been long recognized (Koestler, 1940 Ger./1984 Eng.; Orwell, 1949; Sherif & Hovland, 1981; Whyte, 1952). Many, such as Kurt Lewin (1943/1997), explored the problem of collectivistic group cohesion and morale leading to groupthink and the role of individuals and critical divergence.

Unfortunately, much of this work has not been applied to our current situation or not on the global scale. We have high agreement across the globe that profit-driven individualism is the answer to all questions and even natural. The collapse of the Soviet system is often given as proof of the inviolability of western economic culture—often conveniently ignoring the periodic boom and bust history of the system and internal conflicts among economists themselves about the best course of action. But what if this conformity, this unanimity, cohesion, and agreement on a single course of action is leading us over a cliff? The consensus theory of truth demonstrates that such a basis as mere popularity of a claim has nothing to do with reality. Just because a majority believes that Jews are evil, that the world is flat, that global warming is not real does not make it so.

Efforts to insist that the best way forward is to promote a global monoculture of industrial technological prowess, to even socially engineer more compliant people using public education systems and the mass media, as Gudykunst and Kim do (2003, p. 389), is an effort to create a homogeneity of ideology that insulates itself from alternative interpretations and options. This is when dissent is labeled by writers such as Gudykunst and Kim (2003) as "mental illness" (p. 381) defined as being maladjusted and unfit cognitively, affectively, and behaviorally. It is a temporary phase of "immaturity" (p. 381), a sign of "positive disintegration" (p. 381) of the original self on the way to reprogramming. And effort to hang on to one's original identity, any resistance to the positive process of conforming to mainstream "conformity pressure" (p. 371) is defined by Gudykunst and Kim (2003) as irrational "hostility and aggression toward the dominant mainstream host environment" (p. 372). Thus, alternative voices are discredited, even criminalized for being merely different—alternative.

This is a tautological trap where one is marginalized for being marginal. If the Other internalizes this ideology, then they are lost and their alternative voice is lost to all of us. Irving Janis (1968, 1972), Carl Hovland and others (1953; Hovland, Janis, & Kelley, 1953), have demonstrated that this drive for coherent homogeneity for the sake of "smooth and effective dealings" (Gudykunst & Kim, 2003, p. 373) leads to muting options and dangerous self-delusion. This process of assimilation means silencing the Other by eliminating it, be it nature or other cultures.

The mainstream is the true, the beautiful, and the right. And so, whatever it says about itself is impervious to challenge except by wrong, ugly, and immoral people. The mainstream dominant path is thus impervious to rational critique. Any criticism whatsoever is defined *a priori* as irrational and unbalanced. The mainstream dominant set of beliefs, thought patterns, and behaviors are promoted as being reality itself, as beyond rational deliberation—invulnerable. This is a discursive strategy of self-inoculation. But existentialists have shown that there is always an opening, a place for deviance and therefore real change and what might sometimes be called progress.

The absurdity of assimilationists is that they argue that progress, "growth," "upward-forwards" or in whatever direction one claims, comes from conformity when in fact progress requires deviance and that is what evolution is. Evolution is a series of differences, of mutations of life forms, modes of thinking, values, motives, and so forth, some of which prove robust and enduring. Assimilationism, even when misnamed "adaptation" for rhetorical purposes, is an ideology for lemmings. And we are in fact heading over a cliff.

Such claims that one can and should undergo "psychic disintegration" so that one can become a new better person are not new (Gudykunst & Kim, 2003, p. 380). While the terminology may sound more "scientific" or impressive than in Spencer's day, the goal of social engineering for compliance gaining is exactly the same as it was over 100 years ago. And already back then it was confronted as unworkable and as immoral. It has repeatedly been demonstrated experimentally and historically that this recipe for social engineering how people think, feel, and behave, that forced compliance is not persuasive. Rather it breeds not only dissonance but also a drop in motivation and commitment and even resistance (Carlsmith, Collins, & Helmrich, 1966; Festinger & Carlsmith, 1959; Nuttin, 1969).

Bottom line, forced conformity does not lead to assimilative identification and attitude change. Rather as Nuttin (1996) conclusively showed after summarizing 30 years of evidence, forced attitude change is an illusion. There are ample historical examples as well. European populations have maintained their languages and cultures for millennia even as they exist side-by-side and Jews have endured even longer, resisting assimilative deculturation and disintegration. Assimilation is not the same thing as adaptation (Kramer, 1997, 2000a, 2000b, 2003a). Under duress or reward, a person might comply behaviorally and temporarily but never accept what they do not want to, nor can they willfully "unlearn" their own identity and culture as Gudykunst and Kim (2003, p. 380) claim they should for their own psychic evolution, growth, sanity, and competence.

Such pseudo-scientific advice first hit its stride with Herbert Spencer, who was the great British apologist for this ethnocentric and class-justifying and reifying positive faith. The solution continues to be the same one that Spencer offered. Gudykunst and Kim (2003) state that the overall goal for the advancement of operational efficiency and competence is for the minority person to "develop increasingly refined and positive views of their relationships with the host [which they define as the coercive majority]" (p. 382). So let us look at the origin of this positive faith that argues that we should all simply accept things as they are without reflection, to strive to make our "internal subjective world" the same as the "external objective reality" (Gudykunst & Kim, 2003, pp. 378, 380), to comply with "accepted modes of experience" (p. 378) as defined by the mainstream dominant group, because to question "what is real, what is true, what is right, what is beautiful, and what is good" is to be functionally unfit, immature, and mentally ill (Gudykunst & Kim, 2003, p. 376). In fact Gudykunst and Kim (2003) note that "maladjusted" and "cynical" individuals who pathetically see themselves as "victims of circumstances" are in danger of becoming "disagreeable" and even "hostile" in their "aggressive self-assertion and promotion of their identity" (pp. 371-372). But this is exactly what all the research about forced compliance and coerced conformity predicts. And insofar as "reality" is human made, we are responsible for it. And furthermore, if what is emerging is a disaster, it is our moral and practical obligation to argue against the forces that are promoting it.

Today we are beyond the turning point. Already many species and ethnic and linguistic communities have gone extinct and thousands more are on the brink. So we must address the origin of this apologetics for assimilative destruction. The core of the problem is cultural. We must look at the culture, the dominant ideology to understand how it is dominating and driving our world into extinction.

In conventional positivistic style, Spencer was a leader of the priestly class of social scientists for the new positive religion so named by August Comte in his influential texts—most importantly his six volume work *Course on Positive Philosophy* (1830-1842 Fr./1853 Eng.), his four volume work *System of Positive Polity: Treatise on Sociology Instituting the Religion of Humanity* (1851–1854 Fr./1875-1877 Eng.), and his *The Catechism of Positive Religion* (1852 Fr./2012 Eng.). Hence a new absolute dogma was launched that aspired to be as totalitarian as the Catholicism it purported to replace. The new religion of humanity put the human being at the center of all things and the industrialist at the top of the human hierarchy. A limited notion of instrumental rationality was to dictate all human activity and it remains the justification of mathematical economics to this day—what many are now calling "autistic economics" because of its intense dissociation/ abstraction and uncaring attitude toward those impacted by its policies (on this issue see the works of the Nobel Economist Joseph Stigliz, 2003; Stigliz et al, 2010).

Already by 1887 Friedrich Nietzsche had exposed two fundamental problems with the theology of the new positive religion. Being narrow minded is a danger to the mind that is self-constricting and also to Others around it. Both nature and less aggressive cultures were, and continue to be, threatened by this self-certain worldview that places itself at the apex of evolutionary achievement—the final stage of human growth that cannot see any possible future beyond its own perfection.

Nietzsche slammed Spencerian morality clearly exposing the two basic flaws with Spencer's colonial ideology masquerading as social science. First

Nietzsche (1887 Ger./1989 Eng.) points out that Spencer's ultimate value is nothing more than typical British ethnocentric racism and utilitarianism and that what is utility to Spencer is pliable, uncomplaining workers. Eric Kramer (2000b) has pointed out that the robot is the final solution for the positivist because it is designed for its function and therefore it is Spencer's dream worker—functionally fit. Slaves by comparison tire, age, and sometimes get sick and/or revolt. But absent the presence of robots and slaves, subject workers have proven effective in amassing great wealth for their employers. They are perceived as part of the natural resource base available for programming, the new euphemism for socializing and acculturating workers for compliant exploitation (Postman & Weingartner, 1969). Today millions go deep into personal debt to acquire degrees and competencies they hope employers will find financially beneficial to their enterprises.

The value of a degree, of education in general, is increasingly marked by exploitability within worldwide markets of competing laborers. Personal growth and an informed citizenry capable of critical thinking skills have become quaint notions if not threats to progress. Managerialism, including the inoculating power of elite "expert knowledge," mutes populations who do not have access to technical systems. This is the application of the new positive religion to social control (Lyotard, 1979 Fr./1984 Eng.). The anonymous few who do breech the barricades, such as hackers and others like Julian Assange, create profound dissonance. Insofar as we integrate into the system, we cannot make up our minds if such efforts at militant transparency are literally heroic or criminal terrorism (Assange & Appelbaum, 2012; Leigh & Harding, 2011; Mitnic, 2012; Olson, 2013). We are assured that it is best for us "regular people" to leave decision making to the experts. Complexity is dumbed-down for us in the media, especially the so-called conservative media that one might assume would encourage classical education, but which attacks educators as dangers to their version of positive polity.

Gebser (1949 Ger./1985 Eng.) draws a distinction between efficient ego and rationality and hypertrophic or deficient ego and rationality reduced to instrumentality. A deficient state is one that has become self-destructive. Gebser is drawing on Nietzsche. Nietzsche does not denigrate the ego or will as a problem but rather the Western colonial request of all Others to be "unegoistic," to deculturize themselves via "self-abnegation, self-sacrifice" as "value-in-itself," the "dead stop" of a "retroactive weariness" (Nietzsche, 1887 Ger./1989 Eng., p. 19).

As conceived by Saint Simon and Comte, enlightened colonial Europe presented a unified front of industrial leaders and intellectuals who justified and valorized their enterprise as the march of civilization. It was the job of the intellectual to convince all who might resist their advance to come to their senses, to give up and to do so for their own good. Rather than bring hope, this message sowed the seeds of chaos and hopelessness. The stories of many resistance leaders including Gandhi in India and Sun Yet Sen in China reveal the struggle to find indigenous vitality to confront the Western hypertrophic drive and its powerful industrial technologies. But from the point-of-view of the Darwinian West, no resistance could ever be rational, practical, or mature. The surrender-for-one's-own-good colonial argument was characterized as being the good-in-itself, as wise because it is useful, practical—sane. Nietzsche (1887 Ger./1989 Eng.) sums up the core message of colonial positivism thus: "According to this theory, that which has always proved itself useful is good: therefore it may claim to be 'valuable in the highest degree,' 'valuable in itself'" (p. 27).

But like rationality, what is useful becomes truncated in deficient modernity. It becomes a matter of narrow perspective and therefore conflict ensues. Such limited perspectives become inflated to mean all of reality itself. Consequently, when a perspective is challenged it is defended to the death. So what is rational, sane, good, sacred, and even beautiful become nodes of fear and violence. To avoid difference, to sidestep problems in intercultural contexts, some such as Gudykunst and Kim (2003) argue we should simply eliminate difference. Everyone should assimilate to a common, "mainstream" culture. The unegoistic worker is good and valuable and that is because such a person or animal conforms to the master's will, which brings us to the second problem of Hegelian, which is to say fatalistic positivism as an ontology and morality—as the inevitable march of reason to the Absolute final solution.

For those who would evolve and grow in the eyes of the colonial master, it requires what Nietzsche called the "atrophy" of the spirit and of one's self, a surrender to mechanistic inevitability (Nietzsche, 1887 Ger./1998 Eng., p. 78). Many who still uphold the Spencerian faith consistently argue that human evolution in an "upward-forward progression accompanying an increased level of functional fitness (greater adaptation) and of psychological health" (Gudykunst & Kim, 2003, p. 382). And unlike the biological notion of evolutionary adaptation that sees a proliferation of differing life forms presenting millions of viable solutions to assure survival, contemporary Spencerians equate adaptation with a collapse of diversity to a single mainstream culture. They literally equate adaptation with assimilation; "Cross-cultural adaptation process involves a continuous interplay of deculturation and acculturation that brings about change in strangers in the direction of assimilation, the highest degree of adaptation theoretically conceivable" (Gudykunst & Kim, 2003, p. 360). A stranger is an outsider such as an immigrant or a person whose country has been conquered by a coercive imperialistic cultural force.

According to this doctrine of adaptation/assimilation, the direction of advancement requires the "maturing" minority human to deculturize and unlearn himself in exact proportion to how much, how well he adapts to the inevitable final solution—"equilibrium" or total identity with the objective external and *real* mainstream culture (Gudykunst & Kim, 2003, pp. 361). Those who surrender to reality, which is the will of the majority (literally the numerical majority according to Gudykunst and Kim), are smart, competent, mentally healthy, satisfied, good, productive, and even, and most importantly, enlightened minorities (Gudykunst & Kim, 2003, p. 359). According to Gudykunst and Kim (2003), such adaptable people, who we are told have inherent "personality attributes" (p. 368) that give them "profoundly plastic" (p. 380) personalities effecting an "adaptive predisposition" (p. 370), are useful and as such good in themselves. They are the obedient ones who strive to identify with the master's will and even internalize the master's every value and belief conforming as much as possible "cognitively, affectively, and behaviorally" (Gudykunst & Kim, 2003, p. 354). The magnitude of this supposed truism offered by social scientists is total and itself forms part of the coercive force of the mainstream assimilationist ideology.

To contemporary Spencerians who see a tripartite human composed of an affective part, a cognitive part, and a behavioral part, the old adage of when in Rome, do as the Romans do, is not enough. To be truly useful, good, and well-adjusted, a minority person must think and feel as the majority does, and if that means to see herself or himself and evaluate herself or himself through the master's eyes and therefore to see herself and her culture as immature, backward, incompetent, and even deluded because her culture has not developed powerful technologies to transform the environment, so be it. Gudykunst and Kim (2003) argue that this is the positive truth of things and such complete conformity will assure "competent communication" (p. 360) promoting efficient, "smooth and effective dealings" (pp. 372-373) with the dominating "external" "objective" (p. 378) reality ensuring the unhindered advancement of world markets defined as civilization itself. So Spencer and his followers counsel all that it is time to get with the program, to become "functionally fit to live" (p. 358), to become realistic, to erase one's self and conform to "objective circumstances" (Gudykunst & Kim, 2003, p. 378).

This positivistic fatalism backed up by technological and economic power renders the self, the subject a shame (Nietzsche, 1887 Ger./1998 Eng., p. 67). Values and valuation are "internal" subjective nonsense. The objective external *status quo* is what counts and what determines what is appropriate thinking, feeling, and behaving. Instituted values take on a life of their own, and so Spencer's "administrative nihilism" rules hegemonically, by habit—by routinized dependency. "Equilibrium" and psychological balance are achieved if and only if one internalizes the master's agenda. And so the subjects of masters accept their place and forfeit their right to make and assert values of their own.

In this book we reject the notion that there is nothing that can be done about our current trajectory. And we dare to insist that the values behind current trends need to be transvaluated.

Colonial rhetoric can be seen as such. And in the moment of reframing an opening in our episteme, in our worldview, appears. Colonial rhetoric, which permeates the global semantic field at home and abroad, promotes conformity, even equates disintegration of the self with "emancipation" (Gudykunst & Kim, 2003, p. 382). Spencerians equate such willingness to be self-erasing, to strive for "psychic disintegration," to be "flexible" and "adaptable" with "liberation" (Gudykunst & Kim, 2003, p. 385). Any attempt to resist such disintegration of one's way of thinking, feeling, and behaving is defined by Spencerians as "immature" (p. 381) "self-deception" (p. 380). Gudykunst and Kim (2003) suggest that deviants are weak-minded and inflexible people who need therapy (p. 382). Thus the utopian promise of colonial conquest, "*arbeit macht frei*"—work will set you free (which are the words over the gate of Auschwitz I). This "truth" we seek to not merely resist but to reframe and redefine as false. Indeed we have work to do, but it must take a different path.

Seeing the rising storm and retreating to the hills of northern Italy, Nietzsche (1887 Ger./1989 Eng.) ruminated, and there he coined an ugly term for an ugly thing, as he put it, to describe this prescription of surrender and self-sacrifice offered by those who would dominate the world—"misarchism" (p. 78). Misarchism is the surrender of agency in favor of conformity to the dominant ideology no matter its justice or nobility. The morality of this promises that under the influence of positive sounding "equilibrium," meaning psychological health achieved by acquiescing to a peacefully dead zero energy state where diverse and diverging creative powers of Others are extinguished, the Other will become one with the system. Nietzsche chafes, along with others of the time such as Thomas Huxley, arguing that under this condition:

> One places "adaptation" in the foreground, that is to say, an activity of the second rank, a mere reactivity; indeed, life itself has been defined as a more and more efficient inner adaptation to external conditions (Herbert Spencer). Thus the essence of life, its *will to power*, is ignored; one overlooks the essential priority of the spontaneous, aggressive, expansive, form-giving forces that give new interpretation and directions, although "adaptation" follows only after this; the dominant role of the highest functionaries within the organism itself in which the will to life appears active and form-giving is denied. One should recall what Huxley reproached Spencer with—his "administrative nihilism": but it is a question of rather more than mere "administration." (Nietzsche, 1887 Ger./1989 Eng., pp. 78-79)

Nietzsche argues that this utopian ideology ultimately leads to nihilism because it overtly promotes a meaning-killing process, which is the opposite of evolution. Life evolves by endlessly experimenting with new forms. It does not follow the efficiency of conforming to a single form that has proven successful. If the latter were so, then life would not have evolved past the spectacularly successful single-celled forms we find throughout the world's waters.

The point here is that too much will-to-power can also become self-destructive. The Nazis who followed not Nietzsche but his sister's distortion of his work proves this point. A rock star who is so powerful that she need not listen to any other interpretation or direction in life, can easily implode. Our species is at this point. We need intervention to allow Other wills to assert themselves. Otherwise, if we force compliance and conformity from all other cultures and species, we will find ourselves is a world full of redundant forms, which is nihilistic. If any single culture or form, even the most beautiful, becomes a monopoly, then it becomes meaningless. It would be like an art gallery full of many identical paintings or listening to one song over and over until it becomes ugly to the ear.

Modernity has become so powerful that it is spreading and pushing all other ways into extinction. This need not be the case. Moderns can stop themselves. Otherwise, life will find a way; it will endure and other forms will continually and spontaneously emerge like new genres of music. That, even the most fascistic ideology cannot stop. But in the face of a monolithic culture they will not be robust unless it allows them to grow. Initially globalization opened us up to each other. The world became immensely rich in forms. But globalization has now moved from exploration and discovery to imposing administrative conformity in the name of efficiency—communication competence assured through monolingual monoculture (Kramer, 2003a). A single positivistic system is growing.

For example, in the name of utility and efficiency many want to operationalize this belief and ethic as policy that would encourage everyone to speak English so that trade will be so much easier. If other languages disappear, our horizon will narrow dramatically. And each time a language, a culture, or a species disappears life becomes less meaningful. But philosophy, we are told, is inefficient. It is too critical. But how else can we imagine another reality, another way? Philosophy gave birth to utilitarian positivism and instrumental reason. The question we face is can these cultural forms give birth to something beyond themselves, or are they so arrogant and sterile as to see nothing possibly better than themselves?

This is the philosophical project. Just when we need it most, philosophy is dying. It is being pushed aside in the academy by "practical disciplines" that do not question but instead seek how to better conform to the status quo and excel at advancing the values and expectations of the dominant worldview. Conformists profit while those who question first principles are at best irrelevant and at worst trouble-makers to be eliminated. We see the latter approach being instituted by a surge of anti-intellectuals who are increasingly populating the legislatures of states and countries reacting to challenges that only critical thinking can resolve. This tendency is likely to continue as times get tougher. People want simple and easy solutions that demigods are quick to offer. But retrenching in traditionalism, in conservative beliefs, motives, and expectations, is not a solution. It is part of the problem. These behaviors and beliefs are what got us into this predicament. Now is *not* the time to adapt to the mess we are making. Now is the time to change directions.

Philosophy demands that we think before acting and being acted on, and thinking means critiquing first principles and deriving logical paths once first principles are established by means of rigorous interrogation. Instead of blindly defending our values, we must examine them. Positivism is not reality. Nor are its progeny, capitalism or modernity. Positivism is a philosophy. It is the secular religion of modernity, and like all religions, it is an invention of human beings and as such must not be excluded from interrogation but must be made available for cross-examination if we have the courage. We can identify who invented positivism, why, when, and how it has come to dominate our way of thinking. If we dare, we can make it available for critical examination based on its consequences.

THE SUICIDAL CONTRADICTION

So why have we fallen so deeply in love with positivism? Because we want to live forever in a frictionless world where all we desire comes to pass as if by miracles, be they miracles of science, which is a total contradiction, or by spiritualism, which is delusional. For every action, there is a reaction. We cannot escape our own actions. Therefore, we must critically examine our own behavior, motives, beliefs, and expectations—in a word, our modern culture.

Reprise and Clarify

In this book, we still hold out hope that writing and reading this text is not a waste of time. We would like to start this exploration by stating that we are not anti-technologists. We live in an age filled with technologies, with technological systems that span the globe. In fact, we argue that to be anti-technology is essentially to be anti-human. Any effort to modify the world, including subsequent efforts to limit the impact of such modifications, is an application of human-technologic. We are constantly surrounded by technology and utilize technology to *our* advantage every day. In fact, we argue that technology is an important form of meaning and sense-making for human beings (sense being a broader, less defined phenomenon of understanding than meaning).

Our overarching thesis in this book is that as humans seek to avoid mortality by developing and deploying ever more powerful and expansive technological "fixes," the more we are not just hurting our own habitat but the more suicidal we are behaving. This is the great absurdity, the great self-contradiction of the "advanced" industrially "developed" human condition.

This book should not be read as an argument to "go backward." There is no doubt that technology has and can provide society with greater meaning, purpose, justice, comfort, communication, and peace. As such we should seek its conception and implementation to those ends. This sounds good and reasonable. But such a platitude begs several questions. Notice that this apparently sane statement claims that we do and should use technology to our advantage every day. And in fact we do. But this claim quickly becomes complicated. The operant term for our argument is "our." We cannot continue to see technology as merely a human issue. Such a selfish, extremely fragmentary, and dissociated attitude is ironically suicidal. Just as the ancient story of Narcissus warned us, the more selfish we become, the more we risk destroying ourselves.

Such an attitude involves a narrow anthropic species bias that presumes we have the right to and should do whatever makes us happy, including geo-engineering the climate and oceans. The problem here is that happiness is a fleeting experience. Consequently, such a feeling raised to the level of moral canon leads to short-term thinking. Even if we grant this myopic perspective privilege, it increasingly looks like our selfishness may be suicidal because it makes two presumptions that need to be evaluated.

First, this notion of privilege presumes that we are special—not a part of the world system but above or outside of it, even given the right by divine decree to take dominion over everything else. This leads to the belief that nature needs us to manage it, to minister and administer it with our transcending "super-vision." But nature does not need our vision to make it whole or to work or to succeed. And this story is not all and only about humans. Second, the privileging of the anthropic perspective presumes that the nature of our needs, wants, and desires is uniform across cultures and times.

But notice these hedonic values such as happiness, comfort, and having a purpose, if reduced to a single universal set of beliefs, result in the emergence of what Kramer (2003a) calls a monoculture, which is specifically a Western cosmotopian vision—an anthropic bias but also a particular version of this bias. The emerging monoculture presents a hyper-valuation of an urban, industrial, technopolistic, capitalistic, and consumption-oriented worldview. Like all forms of egocentric fallacy, those who live by it take this worldview as natural, universal, and self-evident. Many believe in and live by such preconceived assumptions, that this worldview is absolutely necessary for the fulfillment of human potential and happiness itself. Many have argued that greed—greed for endless personal happiness—is the major human instinct. Instinct of course is fatalistic and mindless. We do not accept such a pessimistic opinion.

In this book, we begin a phenomenology of cosmotopian technopoly, a questioning back to first principles without presuppositions. This involves establishing technopoly's point of origin and its continued expansion. As we shall point out shortly, the unreflective, unbridled pursuit of cosmotopianism is literally killing the planet. That consequence is becoming increasingly clear. But why are we hell bent on this trajectory? Part of the answer is capitalistic wealth accumulation. The gadget market is obvious. It is part of the status race among individualists performing dominance displays by exhibiting their ability to acquire the latest gizmo. We have huge landfills full of discarded televisions, cellular telephones, computers, non-biodegradable plastic stuff, diapers, and so on. From designer houses, super cars, art collecting, and fashion, to designer drugs for hypertrophic muscle development and luxury elective cosmetic surgery, wealth and power exhibitionism—this is how we strut our stuff—our hypertrophic individualism is expressed in various forms of private property and personal rights (Kramer, 2013). Meism is killing the planet.

No doubt such hoarding and record-keeping in the form of accumulating wealth and power in various material forms is a human activity. We don't see other species gathering trophies. But even among humans, the practice of infinite hoarding cultivated among the masses is fairly recent and culture-specific. Dominance displays are culturized by taking the form of externalizing our lust for power in the form of external technology. The concretion of our drives has much to do with culturized dominance displays as integral to mating competition and reproduction of the species. But only one culture massified this drive in the form of material industry. When this same culture began to expand across the globe, forcing conflict and competition (colonialism on a global scale), it proved itself relatively successful. But then it was forcing others such as the Chinese, Native Americans, Asian Indians, and others to play by its rules (Kramer, 2003b). The modern West in most instances arrived unannounced and began to dominate Others. Now everyone is rushing to mimic this form of success. This success was in part based on instrumental rationality and technological prowess. The more essential explanation of the two, however, is instrumental rationality that comprehends and apprehends everyone and everything as a tool. This subtends technology itself.

Guns and steel, as Jared Diamond (1999, 2006) has argued, made a difference when conflict was initiated. But something more was involved—an attitude, a cultural perspective (Kramer, 1992, 1997, 2008, 2011, 2012, 2013;

Kramer & Ikeda, 2001). One civilizational structure had the ambition and hubris to begin global conquest, and it was successful even though guns and steel by themselves cannot explain its repeated triumphs against not "societies," as Diamond calls them, but, importantly, communities; how, for instance, a few desperate Spaniards with two small 1-shot cannons and a few primitive single-shot pistols that were as likely to fizzle as to fire could overthrow thousands of robust and fearless Aztec warriors armed with razor-sharp obsidian-edged mallets, stone hammer axes, spears, and other weapons. There is only one explanation for how the Spaniards prevailed over both the Inca and the Aztec: They managed to capture their adversaries' living god-kings. It was not just material technology that made the Spanish victorious (Kramer, 2008, 2011, 2012, 2013). It was a particular worldview that was quite modern and arrogant. The seduction of this worldview has spread across the globe, testing the carrying capacity of the Earth itself.

Another example of dominance display expressed through elaborate technologies and their ceremonial exhibition in parades (for instance) is the arms race rooted in in-group versus out-group competition and conflict. This invariably involves the rhetoric of defending "our way of life." In this case, the dominating paradigm that is spreading across the world features industrial might and free, unlimited consumption. If you have the money, you can have anything, including armies to acquire more. Much of the modern technologic world is a direct result of weaponized competition and colonial conquest.

But such explanations beg an even deeper question. Why technology and why this obsession to dominion? This book attempts to answer these two questions. The answer is not rooted in technology because it is but a means. Rather the answer lies in a specific worldview that has valorized material technology above all else as the way to immortality. There are many other worldviews, but they are being rapidly eliminated and abandoned by those who are rushing to modernize and Westernize (for modernization and Westernization are utterly entangled) (Kramer, 1997, 2011, 2012, 2013). Many millions of people, mostly younger ones around the globe, are experiencing and manifesting a modern Western phenomenon, the generation gap. They are actively abandoning the ways of their own cultures where they were raised within a semantic field they have come to see as deficient, under-developed, weak, irrelevant, immaterial, counterproductive, and, in some quarters, no less than evil. At most they are willing to keep some of their own indigenous ways out of sentimental emotion but fuse those with Western ideology and technological culture (Kramer, 1997, 2000b, 2003a, 2008, 2011, 2013).

The obsession with perfection, with perfect knowledge, the perfect physique, the perfect beauty, the ultimate weapon; in a word, idealism is limitless and ultimately suicidal. In the modern perspectival world that promotes ego hypertrophy, this means limitless liberty, an unbridled freedom to do whatever makes one happy. This is a deficient, hypertrophic mutation of an earlier efficient attitude that spawned basic civil liberties in the face of serfdom and slavery. Ideal freedom is limitless, and that makes it ultimately suicidal. We see absolute idealism in the history of religious conflict and the desire to purge the world of sin, pollution, evil—the wicked Other—anything or anyone who threatens my eternal salvation (Kramer, 2004a, 2012). The unproductive must be eliminated, and in fundamentally idealistic terms, we are after the means of producing/achieving immortality.

The emergence of monotheism involves the death of all gods but one. This is the historical source of positivism—hypertrophic perspectivism, which sees only from its own point of view and denies the existence of all Others. The world is verging toward a single paradigm with a single set of values, beliefs, expectations, motives and socioeconomic patterns of behavior—even a single aesthetic and psychology (Kramer, 2003a, 2003b; Kramer & Isa, 2003; Rainwater-McClure, Reed, & Kramer, 2003). While there may be a few variations about how to achieve the one goal, the single goal of immortality is quite widespread, and we posit that technology is one of those paths to promised immortality. The medical field is an obvious indicator. But even when technology *sui generis* is not seen as the one and only path to eternal life, it is often fused with various forms of idealistic ideology to fight for dominance (Kramer, 2000b, 2008; Kramer, Callahan, & Zuckerman, 2013). Competition in business, and in military conflicts, including ideological confrontations rooted in economic beliefs and religious doctrines are fought with the use of technologies.

We postulate along with Gebser (1949 Ger./1985 Eng.) that this will-power-drive, this obsession for ever more unto totality, is rooted in ego-hypertrophy—hypertrophic perspectivism, which is expressed in positivism, the idea that only one perspective constitutes the whole truth and nothing but, the good in itself, the beautiful, and the just. In May 2013, the convergence of a monoculture of human beauty comically emerged in a beauty contest in Asia. News outlets began to publish pictures of all the Miss Korea beauty contestants side by side to illustrate that thanks to a single sense of beauty and with the aid of cosmetic surgery, the contestants were nearly identical. Every other facial structure, including indigenous Korean skin type, and hair, is minimally irrelevant if not an obstacle to the truth of pure beauty or, even worse, the ugly—an abomination (Kramer & Isa, 2003; Rainwater-McClure, Reed, & Kramer, 2003).

This is but one rather banal yet consequential example of what it means to claim what Nietzsche (1887 Ger./1989 Eng.) called the "ridiculous immodesty" of "decreeing from our corner that perspectives are permitted only from this corner" (p. 336). This hypertrophic egocentrism, this self-centered set of interests, is expressed in where, when, and how people spend their resources and the technologies they build. This complex is worthy of critical contemplation and regard. As has been noted, we are increasingly technologizing our world, including our own genome and phenotypes, enhancing our own bodies through medical techniques in the pursuit of an ideal, which we have internalized and which drives us to addictive levels (Kramer, 2003a). At all levels of life, an emerging monoculture is upon us. Unfortunately, this particular culture requires vast exploitation of resources.

We are in a world that is increasingly converging on a single form of modernism, constituted of billions of individualists who are narcissistic and ultimately suicidal. Competition is overruling obligation, appreciation, and altruism. What emerges here is suicide, the ultimate absurdity. If we pursue our own interests without restraint, we may disrupt ecosystems so profoundly, for the Earth is a living, dynamic entity, that we ruin our own habitat. We're demolishing systems in the pursuit of happiness, which has been degraded to material consumption and domination over others.

For decades groups such as the Club of Rome have been warning us. Evidence is mounting. Human impact has reached global levels. In the 2003 book *The Emerging Monoculture*, Kramer argued that we are on the verge of a truly global collapse of both biological and cultural diversity and that the two, culture and nature, are integrally connected. While many biologists such as Michael Samways (1999) speak of "homogenocene," they restrict the homogenizing process to biodiversity, failing to recognize the truly human cultural causes of the process. What Kramer (1997, 2003a) points out is that as cultural diversity collapses toward a singular positivistic mentality first reaching hypertrophic levels with European global colonialism, the threat to all forms of diversity (biological and cultural) has spread across the globe.

The cultural basis of the problem highlights the role of human agency and responsibility. To loudly and publicly proclaim, as many political "conservatives" do, that problems such as climate change are not humanity's fault is utterly irresponsible. Human culture has become so powerful on the planet that the acculturation of everything has tipped toward a manufactured world. This fusion of binary opposites—culture and nature—is undeniable (Kramer, 1995). The initial distinction between "culture" and "nature" as binary opposites by one culture's linguistic practices may be a powerful indicator of a cultural bias that is now spreading. It may well have programmed our thinking to magnify the desire a specific group had and continues to believe in; namely, that we humans are special, unique, god-like creatures destined to rule over all the rest of "creation." Herein may rest the hermeneutic roots of the technological mindset, which grasps everything as a resource base for manipulation at will, including our own physical bodies (Kramer, 2004a). But the relationship of culture to nature is more entangled than merely a craftsman and a separate medium of tooling. It has been well understood for decades that the human brain is a cultural product. The growth and development of the human brain is absolutely dependent on stimulation. What may seem utterly separate from culture, a purely natural process, brain growth, is not. In fact, as Kramer (1992, 1993b, 1995) has noted, the concepts of culture and nature emerged simultaneously as a single binary opposition (Kramer, 1995, 1997, 2013; Kramer, Callahan, & Zuckerman, 2013). Culture is that which is not nature or natural. However, both are cultural concepts (Kramer, 1995, 1997). One does not make sense without the other. Not all cultures or languages have corresponding words for culture and nature (Kramer, 1997, 2013). The dualism is a socio-linguistic expression of cultural bias. But the technologies that have emerged from this mindset are demonstrably powerful and therefore addictive.

This separation, this path of making sense, is particularly indicative of a culture's attitude toward the world, one that is spreading rapidly in part because its conceptualization of nature as a soulless material base available for manipulation at will has enabled it to develop technologies on a scale far more grand than those of other cultures. This power has seduced and compelled other cultures to mimic and adopt a materialistic technologic. Thus, the world is racing to industrialize with profound environmental consequences. As is explicated in this book, the magic consciousness structure that does not think in dualistic terms and the mythic structure that emphasizes introspective contemplation are being rapidly replaced by the modern perspectival spatial way of thinking (Kramer, 1992, 1997, 2013).

The spatial three-dimensional perspectival style of thinking conceptualizes things in spatial terms such as internal and external, subject and object, mind and matter, and then emphasizes visual, external material criteria for valuation. Technology, in such a world, is a self-evident power that is an essential criterion for the measure of another spatial concept, linear progress. For a group or culture to deny technology is to accept being "under" developed, retro, or regressive—powerful value judgments in the modern "objective" world. To remain "close to nature" is, from the dominant modernist regard, to remain "primitive."

3

The Grand Paradox

Technology as Suicidal Death Denial

AN INITIAL CRITIQUE OF TECHNOLOGICAL POSITIVISM

During the nineteenth century, positivism was conceptualized by writers such as Claude Saint-Simon, Auguste Comte, John Stuart Mill, and Herbert Spencer as a popularization of German romantic Enlightenment thought, specifically Hegelian philosophical speculation. Positivism was the philosophical justification for launching industrialization. Industrial culture was fated to be by the historical force of evolution. This philosophy and its implementation was the culmination of a long gestation of an idea, of a revolution in thinking and mindset that emerged during the Renaissance and has been discussed in great detail elsewhere (Kramer 1992, 1997, 2013). "Positivism," the arch value judgment that would characterize modernity itself, was a willful effort to be positive rather than negative, to embrace this life rather than favor the after-life, which had been the mantra of medieval religion. Positivism was a faith that humans, not gods, could control their own destiny. It was the fundamental philosophical justification for individualistic agency and the expansion of material industrialization. Unfortunately, this philosophy has ossified into a sacred mythology that commands identity and the deep emotional commitment of millions who see it as "our way of life," worth defending to the death. It is, in short, difficult to challenge without emotional backlash.

Once spiritualism and asceticism had eased its grip on Europe, Europe turned its focus on enhancing creature comforts of the flesh, on material innovations that would change this world—material technology. Positivism and pragmatic capitalism combined to form the worldliest of all philosophies. Introspection and emphasis on things spiritual was rejected for demonstrable survival of the physically fittest. Truth became what mechanically works and/or sells. After a 1,500-year hiatus, material technology, along with secular arts and sciences, even fashion, and other material enhancements as the power source of worldly empires, was once again embraced. The Renaissance meant the rebirth of classical Greco-Roman attitudes toward materialism and the sensual body.

Europe went through a metaphysical reversal like the periodic reversal of the magnetic polarity of the planet. Europe has two faces: one material and the other spiritual. We find this duality expressed in Christology, the study of the nature of Christ as both mortal human and supernatural being. The physical body and spirit form a strong metaphysical duality, even presented as oppositional. Sometimes Europe has emphasized matter over mind/spirit, defining matter as real and nonmaterial things as unreal. At other times, Europe has convulsed and switched, seeing matter and the physical body as dirty, contingent, temporal, and variable and therefore as untrue, even profanely evil, while the soul or spirit is eternal, pure, and sacred. It has been carefully documented that such a massive shift in belief and values has occurred at least twice in Western history, a revolutionary reversal in what is considered most real, true, sacred, and important (Kramer, 2004a).

The two opposing metaphysical systems yield different kinds of societies and individuals. The material worldview yields empires based on material might, risk-taking, and spatial exploration and conquest. The spiritual worldview yields conformity and an aversion to risk-taking principally because the world is perceived as the domain of spiritual conflict where spatial-material objects are irrelevant and the will of the gods fate the future of all people. All cultures, not just European societies, tend to fluctuate between these two realities, rooted as they are in opposing metaphysical structures. In one, material nature is universal, the medium of physical law, dominant, real, and the realm of truth. In the other, the supernatural is permanent, the domain of eternal law, and the dominant, real, and true. Whenever one is culturally dominant, the other is denigrated as "primitive thinking." Each postulates a different structure of human development. Both presume transcendental law, which, if broken, will result in destruction. One can break the law of gravity and jump out of a 30-story window but not without dire consequences. Likewise, defying a god's commandments yields very negative results for the trespasser.

Modernity tends to emphasize material metaphysics and natural law, which translates into technological progress. Technological materialistic progress is lacking in societies that emphasize supernatural law. While spiritual discovery exists in societies that emphasize spiritualism and supernatural reality, such discovery tends to be personal and introspective. In contrast, material discovery dominates societies that emphasize spatial thinking, even spatialized time as a line and quantity, the physical sciences. Material discovery is based on sensational evidence, and such discoveries require public demonstration before they are taken as true. In the latter worldview, subjective experience is not regarded as knowledge. Yet ironically, individualism dominates in societies where material resources are emphasized and can be hoarded and therefore where inequality can be plainly exhibited for all to see. While there may be spiritual competition, it is not so easy to exhibit as material competition. This is also why, in societies that favor materialism over spiritualism, physical beauty is embraced, sensationalism or knowledge from the senses forms the basis of truth, and physical culture or sports are massively popular.

Both polar metaphysical belief structures seek to extend the life of the individual. One belief structure seeks to extend life even beyond the merely contingent physical body through spiritual practices—ceremonies, rituals, asceticism, prayer or requests for good health and long life, and regulated acts. The other seeks to extend the individual's existence through material-technological means. Technology, being materially based, has a greater impact on the material environment, especially as technologies become more and more complex and global in terms of resource extraction, refinement, manufacture, distribution, consumption, material waste, and so forth.

While the reader may protest that the most material societies are also spiritual, we observe the following. While many religious people attend spiritual activities, when they get sick, they often also go to hospital for physical treatment. They participate in both and may well pray while in the hospital. However, there are many more people who go to the hospital but do not participate in spiritual activities. That is, when push comes to shove, spiritual people will relent and seek out physical treatment rooted in science and material technology while it is rarer for modernists to abandon hospitals for faith healing. The same is true for means of production. Nearly all self-professed spiritual people work in material services and manufacturing, but not all who work in material services and manufacturing are spiritual. And when it comes to money, while many with money are not religious, nearly all religious people and institutions concern themselves with material wealth. In the modern world, while being spiritual is a choice, being physical and participating in material institutions such as finance is not. A modernist sees this as self-evident and universal to the human condition. But others on the planet do not see it that way and are quite capable and even satisfied to reject modern materialism in favor of spiritual goals.

Most find a way to justify both. We are assured by many leading theologians that neither Jesus nor Allah has a problem with owning Ferraris, yachts, and mansions, and the Chinese often portray Buddha as literally made of gold and sitting in the midst of gold coins and sycee, *yuánbao* or ingot, smiling with ecstatic exuberance with raised hands of jubilation. Heaven is often portrayed as a place of "pearly" gates and golden streets inhabited by sensual pleasures such as vestal virgins and a carefree existence. While we rarely if ever see spiritualism creep into scientific investigation (e.g., scientists usually do not use a cross as part of their laboratory equipment), we see the promise of wealth, physical health, and physical luxury often explicitly claimed as proof of blessing and also promoted in religious activities as, for instance, when people purchase spiritual or "hell money" with real money and also buy paper effigies of luxury cars and goods to burn in Taoist and Buddhist temples. While prayer for money is not uncommon, there have also been efforts to basically buy one's way to heaven by tithing to the church and indulgences.

Both materialism and spiritualism have their modes of seduction. Both promise long life and happiness. Material positivism, however, has a far greater impact on the environment. And where the modern material metaphysic dominates, prosperity theology dominates. People go to pray for "real" blessings, such as ironically *miraculous* cures for *physical* illnesses and good luck in business. Prosperity is not real until and unless it materializes.

The most recent sea change occurred during the Renaissance with the rebirth in optimistic humanism and a valuation of all things of this world. Here we find the origins of modern positivism and an explosion in scientific and technological development. The Roman world of engineering was born again. It is rooted in this profound shift from the spirit and soul to the physical world, physical body, and physical sciences (Kramer, 2004a). The Romans were engineers and worshiped individuals and physical beauty. This emphasis on things of this physical world was reversed with the rise of spiritualism as barbarians overran the Classical Greco-Roman world. The body became denigrated. It was seen as the carnal prison of the eternal soul and the site of spiritual pollution/sin. Then, over a millennium later with the rebirth of the classical attitude beginning around 1200 AD, the soul was shunted aside in favor of the physical world and human agency to change material conditions, improve them, and once again see progress within human ambition and human history. Celebrating individualism and an emphasis on physical evidence reemerged after more than a thousand years of self-flagellation, and denial of human sensuality, art, fashion, commerce, science, and technology. With the Renaissance, a new focus emerged emphasizing physical visual space—its exploration and mapping, the invention of eyeglasses and the telescope, new material realism and depth perspective in the arts, logic, quantification, double-entry accounting, critical inquiry into the nature of things, and medical science all blossomed. This material world moved to the forefront of Western European interest. Instead of seeing this temporal world as fallen and ruled by the devil, a new positive attitude took hold. This world became something worth investing in, exploring, colonizing, developing.

Industrial civilization is essentially positivistic. It has become a sacred faith in individual agency and boundless material progress. Trade, the coronations of imperial colonial masters, "World's Fairs," and Nobel Prizes, among countless other activities, have celebrated this secular religion. Industrialization and positivism are in fact one and the same civilizational structure. Taken to a more fundamental level theoretically, this civilizational structure presumes linear time and space and the search for a frictionless mode of communication and transportation. It also emphasizes dissociation, the objectification of all things enabled by the belief that material things are dead and the value of a disinterested observer (Kramer, 1997, 2013).

Introspection, ethics, and spiritual or immaterial and supernatural phenomena have been relegated to delusion, to a primitive earlier stage in human evolution. What is right is what physically and demonstrably works, wins, and sells. All other concerns are regarded as emotional nonsense and, in gendered language, effeminate if not hysterical. Far from denying the animal appetites, modernity encourages them. The seven deadly sins—pride, sloth, greed, wrath, lust, envy, and gluttony—are inverted into virtues in the modern world. Ambition encompasses greed, envy, and pride, while retiring leisure and luxury, the just fruits of one's labor, encompass old-fashioned gluttony, lust, and sloth. And to know, to prove a hypothesis true or false, to debate, to contend a claim with a thesis versus an anti-thesis, a prosecutor versus a defense attorney, these involve anger/wrath—a litigious world of contestation (to contest claims). The modern world is based on competition whereas traditional peoples and communities stress harmonious relations. In the modern world, we value being right over being nice but wrong. And we moderns despise ambiguity. We strive for definitive truth, clarity, and resolution—problem solution and demonstrable results. Notice that the words *clarity*, *definitive*, and *resolution* are equally applicable to a worldview that stresses eye-witnessing and spatial acuity. While the medieval introspective spiritualist was content to stay put and ignore poor eyesight and overall health while contemplating eternal truths, the modern urge is to explore the great outdoors of this world—to taste all of its pleasures and partake in its promise of better tomorrows.

Ironically, the obsession with material technologies and natural science would end up destroying the physical environment. This is rooted in the belief that matter is ultimately, really, divisible into dead building blocks available for manipulation at will. Reductionistic thinking is essential to the modern worldview. When all the animistic spirits evaporated, there was no reason to be fearful or hesitant about manipulating the world to suit ego interests. The arrogance and pride of empirical accomplishment, the progress of all things, especially in material science and technology, marks the modern world. Positivism proclaims a linear process of human development, placing itself as the *non plus ultra* in human development. Fragmentation and individuation increased in all things (such as quantification), resolved as separate entities—objects. Specialization and divisions of labor and modes of production (step-by-step methodical processes) became the norm. One consequence was the inability to see how things, even things we are not interested in, that fall outside our sphere of interest, are interconnected. The danger of ego-centrism is the fallacy that if I do not know or care about something, it does not "count" or "matter."

Claims of a post-positivist, "post-colonial" worldview sound, once again and ironically, progressive, but the fact is that this civilization continues to expand and colonize every inch of the globe and every mind, with some minor cultural variations and tiny pockets of resistance here and there, many pathetically (meaning emotionally) seeking refuge in deficient modes of "new age" spiritualism (Gebser, 1949 Ger./1985 Eng.; Kramer, 1988, 1992, 1997). The Tokyo business man may regard a *meishi* or business card a little differently than a U.S. business person, but both presume the card, the suit, the tie, the shined leather shoes, the brief case, the haircut, modern time-keeping, high-rise office buildings and elevators, cell phones, e-mail, a vast financial apparatus, double-entry spreadsheets, and so forth; all constituting what Kramer (2003b) has called the cosmopolis, the global Western style of industrial urban world. Today, trains, planes, trucks, and ocean-going freighters and oil tankers endlessly ply traderoutes protected by international law and massive naval and air powers. Vast highway systems, electric grids, global financial institutions, telecommunications, university/research systems, and other aspects of this civilization exist almost everywhere.

The very idea of evolution and human development has become tied to how much a person or group has been assimilated into this cosmopolitan world system. A place without television, refrigeration, and cell phones is regarded as horribly "backward" (a spatial metaphor)—positively primitive. Faith in this path of "development" is so strong that it is widely regarded as natural and even divinely inspired. Missionaries and their efforts have typically accompanied Western expansion right alongside military and entrepreneurial change agents. Individuals are seen as instruments of this ambition to progress—God's will to "spread" the gospel of faith and capitalism. Not only is there no apparent contradiction between supernatural and natural ambitions, but quite the contrary, Western expansion has been widely regarded as a divine right and providence—even as salvation vis-à-vis the "white man's burden." In short, to become civilized means to be baptized, to have air conditioning, and to discard spear chucking for satellite-guided missile systems.

The singularly real and true Jewish or Christian or Muslim god (itself a form of theological positivism that comes from the same basic theological origins) has even been re-conceptualized as an engineer and a planner, the great clock-maker administrator of the universal enterprise with a singular linear path heading toward a single teleological destination, an eschatological final solution, the mysterious purpose. To see the world as full, finite, alive, and finished—to have no purpose or presumption that one can improve on nature—is anathema to the enterprise of modernity. Even the one true truth, the one god must have a plan, a purpose, for this is the nature of the modern will-to-power. This cultural principle of monolithic religious teleology supports a single vision of positivistic techno-economic progress. In fact nothing proves whose god is best better than superior technology, especially in military conflict, but also in wealth accumulation as argued in the notion of blessing and prosperity theology.

The Christian faith was launched by Constantine based on this belief. It is similar to the early Jewish proof of being in accord with God's will as evinced through acquisition and military conquest. Islam too equates proof of God's approval with successful expansion and conquest. It is God's will that determines who wins. In fact, if not identical, then certainly mutually supportive religious teleology and positivistic progress promote each other with only minor disagreements. The last two Popes have on occasion issued negative evaluations of modern capitalism and environmental degradation in the name of modern progress. But most religious leaders, and in fact most Catholic leaders, preach that the Earth is humanity's playground to use as we wish and that global capitalism, which can thrive only on massive exploitation of resources including people, is the best bulwark against evil atheism. Since Karl Marx stated that all critical thinking must begin with a rigorous questioning of religious claims, any attempt at communal identification with other people and/or the rest of life on the planet as equal partners has been branded evil atheism. The Christ is the super-individual, the One and Only exclusive path to salvation. Like all positivism, it is intolerant. Two or more competing claims cannot both be correct. And per positivism, only humans are made in his image and have souls worth saving.

Pragmatic utility dictates that hedonic calculus is utterly natural and exclusively valid. Egocentrism is the only truth. This modern worldly philosophy insists that unless and until something can be transformed and exploited, it has no value because inherency has been replaced by the belief in arbitrary value and meaning (Kramer, 1988, 1992, 1997, 2013; Kramer & Kim, 2009). Things and animals that have no souls have no inherent value except as tools to be exploited for human comfort. This monopoly on value and meaning concentrated exclusively in human beings, especially humans of the variety of Middle-Eastern monotheistic faiths, is the opposite of "primitive" animistic worldviews, which see the universe as alive, finished, and full of other beings of equal or even greater value and worthy of respect.

This recognition of the Other was the downfall of animistic peoples when they encountered modern cosmopolists who had no intentions of sharing this world or tolerating different worldviews. For the Modern, inherency came to be seen as a subjective delusion while objective evaluation measured as the movement of mass over distance—work and winning—is real. Reality is realized only when force is applied to a thing or person to displace them. This is the essence of modern progress. Progress is realized only when things and people are manipulated—ministered and ad-ministered to. Progress requires change. To accept the world as it is, by definition, is contrary to progress.

According to the modern worldview, which continues to colonize the world, a thing or person has meaning, value, and purpose if and only when they are exchanged. Progress is a form of change. Will-to-power is manifest through transformation of things according to desired outcomes. To be happy with things as they are is contrary to progress. This is the crux of the hedonic calculus espoused by pragmatists. It can be captured in a phrase or two; you're only as good as your most recent achievement and "what have you done for me lately." There is no such thing as inherent value or meaning. Value and meaning only exist in the act of exchange. What is my car worth? Whatever I can get for it, period.

Exploitation always has a perspective, and therefore value is determined by personal interest—ego. Objectifying dissociation renders everything equally available for exploitation without remorse. In fact, to give a person a job and make him or her a productive member of modern society is to do him or her a favor. The same could be said for a forest that has no value until and unless it is harvested and transformed into a commodity. The lumberjack can say that he is doing the primeval forest a favor by cutting it down and bringing it into the meaningful and valuable commodity world.

In the modern world, without being exchanged, a thing or person's value, meaning, and/or purpose remains in a state of indetermination, without identity. In modernity, being is replaced by doing or being done to. Technology is not art. Technology is all about doing with a purpose. Progress is about making things "better," improving them.

Increasingly this techno-logical landscape is structured by automation, by automated data gathering and analysis on both a micro- and mega-scale, and even automated weapons systems. On June 6, 2013, Christof Heyns, UN special rapporteur on extrajudicial, summary, or arbitrary executions, told the UN Human Rights Council that there should be a worldwide moratorium on "lethal autonomous robotics," which are weapons systems that once activated lock on and kill targets without further human involvement. Heyns said that such systems are being developed and are proliferating and that the primary problem is that weapons systems will be able to make the decision to kill without human intervention. "Machines lack morality and mortality, and should not have life and death powers over humans" (Heyns quoted by Pilkington, 2013, p. 1). Just a week earlier, the U.S. Navy successfully tested the X-47B, a drone that can fly itself and take off from an aircraft carrier. Britain has developed a similar drone called the Taranis. South Korea has deployed autonomous sentry robots (SGR-1s) along the ironically named Demilitarized Zone, which can detect people entering the zone by use of heat and motion sensors and fire on intruders. According to weapons systems expert Steve Goose, in 2012, the United States had spent around $6 billion on research into autonomous weapons and unmanned systems (Goose quoted by Pilkington, 2013). At this writing, it is unclear whether a robotic weapons system has made the "decision" to kill autonomously, meaning without a human in the loop to "pull the trigger" or not. But the capability now exists and is being rapidly enhanced and deployed. Technology has dissociated humans from nature, and now it is dissociating humans from other humans. Distant killing is happening and without legal proceedings or warning, making such killings extrajudicial executions. This is the case even when a human remains in the loop. Drone pilots, for instance, are increasingly removed physically, legally, and psychologically from decisions to kill other humans.

The positivists saw their moral duty to be social engineers. Being positive in their own beliefs about what is best, they set out to construct a new civilization. The ideology was popularized by two non-academic writers, Claude Saint-Simon, and especially his secretary, and tireless apostle Auguste Comte. Saint-Simon was an aristocrat who believed that the entrepreneurial class of emerging industrialists should lead the world into a new positive order that would include a whole new economic structure, educational system, polity, and even spiritual mentality. Comte agreed.

However, they were inconsistent, even self-contradictory in their ideas. Their proclamations continue to play out in industrial civilization. On the one hand, industrialization held as its aim the betterment of the human condition. But its actual implementation generated massive exploitation and alienation, so much so that this widespread alienation inspired the formation of the social sciences, as every major early writer of the genre focused on the problem. Not only has mass industrialization brought about both material abundance and widespread destruction of traditional communities, a contradiction Marx thought would force it to mutate into another form of social structure, but industrialized social relations have reduced happiness while also degrading the environment in unprecedented ways. Since the beginning, the human species has not had the dissociated impact on itself and its environment that it has had in the last 200 years. Much of that change has not been for the good, which belies the very word *positive*.

Positivism was to be a social morality based on the "heart." But it also was and remains explicitly dedicated to making materialistic humanism the religion of modernity. Hence, the four-volume work published by Comte from 1851 to 1854, *Instituting the Religion of Humanity*. Prior to this work, Comte published his six-volume *Cours de philosophie positive* (1830–1842). The "Course," as this major work is often called, had a profound impact on the development of British/American positivism, especially the works of Jeremy Bentham and John Stuart Mill, such as the latter's *System of Logic* (1843/2014). The thrust of positivism was that Europe was endowed with a superior civilization and mode of thinking that offered humanity the one best path toward progress. In a perfect example of colonial narcissism, positivism proclaimed itself the *non plus ultra* of human development.

As noted, the basic principles can be found already more developed in George Hegel's idealism. The Saint-Simonians took Hegel and attempted to operationalize him. The basic principles include a deep faith in objectivity, in spatial linear progress, and the spatial conceptualization of human relations as system. These principles subtend the belief in the evolution of society through three stages toward a utopian world of rational efficiency. The means to real progress is through systematizing thought and action. Right thinking leads to right action. The chronic sense of urgency that is characteristic of modern positivistic society is captured by Comte's argument that time is constituted of only the past and the future. The present is essentially unreal to Comte. His extreme idealism and dissociation is obvious and heralds the apex of modern ideological civilization. Our current existence is of no value. Positivism thus often finds an adversary among existentialists.

Like Hegel's idealism, positivism presumes that there is one and only one correct view of reality and that there is one and only one best way to do anything. The best way is not only the most economical, thus building on the value of Occam's razor, but positivism also clearly explicates an ethic and a morality. The ethic developed by the Saint-Simonians and John Stuart Mill is one of a single version of justice. Anyone or anything that hinders the realization of the one best, most rational reality and way to do things is a kind of humanistic sinner against progress itself. Karl Marx, the other great neo-Hegelian of the nineteenth century, had a similar worldview, arguing for a singular, universal process of human evolution toward a utopian world and a strong insistence that false consciousness was possible because one true reality could be established.

In the twentieth century, we saw warfare escalate with horrendous advances in technology, and Europe split between two versions of positive utopia: the right Hegelian Nazi idealists and the left Hegelian Bolshevik idealists. For positivism, there can be only one truth, and it should be operationalized from a central control. Systems with cybernetic feedback control guarantee efficient, rational operation. Everything else is error and should be eliminated for the sake of efficient progress. What proves most true is self-evident. It is the tactics, strategies, and technologies that win (or sell).

European and American Social Darwinism is one variant of positivism. Like the mutual exclusivity of traditional religious doctrines, positivism may tolerate the other but only so long as they do not seriously hinder efficient progress toward the goal (some form of utopia). Positivistic colonialism thus sought to tolerate, assimilate, and finally eliminate all rival lifeworlds as being "under-developed." Like other religions, imperial nation and common market building, as the primary colonial ambitions, were and continue to be promoted as messianic means to the salvation of the subaltern. The message to the world is: the way "forward" is to cease to be your traditional irrational self, to unlearn and disintegrate your traditional culture so you can progressively develop into a modern Western version of the good person living the good life. Colonial ambition has always been to expand a single cultural system to global proportions. It is working albeit with pockets of resistance along the way. But the final barrier may be the carrying capacity of the Earth itself. Utopia seems to be leading to an extinction vortex.

We begin with just one fact out of a multitude of facts that could be used to support the argument in this book. The one fact: Since the Industrial Revolution, the vast oceans have become significantly more acidic—more than 30 percent more acidic (Orr et al., 2005). Water bodies and the atmosphere constantly exchange gases. The wind mixes atmospheric gases into the surface levels of bodies of water, and over centuries currents spread those gases throughout the depths. At the current rate, by the year 2100, the oceans will be 150 percent more acidic than they were in 1800 (Hönisch et al., 2012). Anthropogenic, or manmade, releases of carbon dioxide are being absorbed by the oceans. This, along with the rising temperature of the oceans due to global warming, is acidifying the world's water mass. The current rate of acidification of the oceans is "unprecedented over the past 300 million years" (Hönisch et al., 2012). Through geologic and biologic history, four major mass extinctions involved rising ocean acidity. According to a 2012 study led by Barbel Hönisch of Columbia University's Lamont-Doherty Earth Observatory and Andy Ridgwell and Daniela Schmidt of Bristol University of seabed sediments built up over hundreds of millions of years, the current rate of acidification is 10 times faster than any past event, which does not give ecosystems time to adapt (Hönisch et al., 2012). When the oceans absorb CO_2, it forms carbonic acid, which reduces the pH of seawater and the concentration of carbonate ions that are necessary for the calcium carbonate many organisms need to form exoskeletons. When the pH drops too much, organisms' shells begin to dissolve. These include, but are not limited to, shellfish, snails, urchins, corals, and foraminifera. Dozens of corals are now endangered. Foraminifera (autotrophs and heterotrophs) constitute the base of the marine food chain, and coral reefs are the nurseries for many fish species (along with mangrove swamps, which are also being eliminated at an astounding rate around the globe for sea coast development). As these organisms become extinct, so do many others that rely on them.

A 15-year study that analyzed more than 77,000 seawater samples from all over the globe found that the oceans are absorbing about one million tons of CO_2 every hour and that the rate is increasing because much of the CO_2 in the atmosphere has built up over the last 200 years of human industrial activity, primarily by burning coal and oil (Chester, 2000). And the amount we are spewing into the atmosphere from factories and automobiles continues to increase as billions more humans industrialize in developing economies such as China, India, Pakistan, Indonesia, Mexico, Brazil, and pretty much everywhere. The much lauded notion that the rest of the world is catching up to the most "advanced" and "developed" nations and flattening out—that everyone will soon achieve the level of human "development," economic "maturation," and consumption globally known as the "American dream"—is turning into a nightmare and not just ecologically. The idea that the environment has nothing to do with economics, health (as the globe warms, dangerous bacteria and fungi are increasing), politics, population, and other human institutions is false. The failure to recognize the integrative and systemic qualities of this process is a fundamental error. What goes around comes around. The real problem is the proverbial tipping point. Many scientists believe it is already too late to fix what we have broken, that we have passed several vital tipping points, including the amount of CO_2 that we have liberated from coal and oil. Elizabeth Kolbert (2011), writing for *National Geographic Magazine*, summarizes the tipping point:

> The acidification that has occurred so far is probably irreversible. Although in theory it's possible to add chemicals to the sea to counter the effects of the extra CO_2, as a practical matter, the volumes involved would be staggering; it would take at least two tons of lime, for example, to offset a single ton of carbon dioxide, and the world now emits more than 30 billion tons of CO_2 each year. Meanwhile, natural processes that could counter acidification—such as the weathering of rocks on land—operate far too slowly to make a difference on a human timescale. Even if CO_2 emissions were somehow to cease today, it would take tens of thousands of years for ocean chemistry to return to its preindustrial condition. (p. 1)

4

Media Campaigns That Teach Us the Truth That Technology is Love

Organic community including the sun, moon, and stars, the wind and rain, and all living organisms (not just among human beings) is slipping away right before our eyes, and we are the cause. We have dissociated ourselves from everything, including other people. Hannah Arendt (1963) taught us that evil is not spectacular but mundane and banal. It is, to extrapolate from Edmund Husserl (1913 Ger./1982 Eng., 1952 Ger./1989 Eng.), *Einstellung*—an attitude—the way we comprehend things, a bias, *the* bias that is essential to our conscious awareness, that presents itself as objective and unbiased, as sane, as natural, as harmless, as normal and beyond reproach. What sane person would argue with reality? In fact that is the very definition of insanity. But we all know that sometimes we delude and deceive ourselves, and we do so typically as a defense mechanism—to escape discomfort.

A reality where thousands of species and cultures are literally dying, our reality does not prevail because it defeats us. Rather we embody it. It becomes our perspective, our standpoint. It is the truth of our world even if we deny it. We even become defensive of it. It claims hegemony. This is a huge problem for when my reality is threatened, my way of life, I react by defending "it," which is my perspective, as if it were my own body under attack. And it is because I embody my beliefs. But we are now in a peculiar situation where our way of life, like overeating, is killing us. We are defending a suicidal perspective. It is absurd. And to a logician, being absurd (self-contradicting) is akin to what others call evil or insanity. Why would we do this? Ignorance. Faith in false gods and/or a false belief that I, personally, am special, a chosen one, not part of the system; that I can withdraw behind guarded gates and rise above the mayhem to Elysium. We are in love with the idea of being special and with the promise of escaping pollution, disease, and time itself—that great criminal that we must "arrest" (Kramer, 1992, 1997, 2003a, 2013; Kramer & Ikeda, 2002).

Attitude is intimately me. It does not triumph over me through genuine and grandiose superiority and sublime power, but instead it presentiates me, and it convinces me—I convince myself and seek out reassuring and reinforcing voices that echo my worldview. Attitude and belief structure take hold because we, you and I, do not care enough to resist or our greed makes us easy targets for the con game. We give over to it, and it possesses us, becoming who we are. The more well adjusted to the current world, the more satisfied we are supposed to be, the more "in sync" we are. But yet, as Friedrich Nietzsche (1895 Ger./1990 Eng.), in his own form of optimism, which Husserl agreed with, argued, we can transcend our own perspective and transvaluate our values (Husserl, 1913 Ger./1982 Eng.). We can achieve the philosophical attitude that questions ourselves. Each of us *wants* to believe that we are exceptional. To deny this is difficult. To deny our own "happy place" and turn critically against our own attitude, standpoint, *my* perspective; to do this requires that I at least temporarily set my own desires and identity aside. What are we doing? That takes great self-reflexive effort. It is the realization that I have been unconscious, deluded, naïve, wrong. Muslims call it *jihad*, meaning struggle, resistance to weakness and *status quo* as it resides within myself. It is to wage revolution against one's own unquestioned tendencies—perspective. The path to change requires that we bracket our untested biases, which are nearly invisible to us.

We all know what it means to try to change from within, to kick a habit, and we are all addicted to the current techno-economic structures and institutions that promise unending progress toward a utopia of effortless and limitless wealth in energy, things, services, and most of all life. We dedicate ourselves to achieving what this world offers as rewards. And goal of all goals, the ultimate reward of progress is life everlasting. Technology promises to defeat death itself. That is why, for modernists, to question technology is to question their religion, their death-denying delusion, to be a negativist rather than a happy positivist (Becker, 1973, 1997). But as Ernst Becker observed, we are willing to do horrible things in our campaigns to defeat evil. Since we, especially we narcissistic moderns, see our own mortality as pure evil, then any activity to enhance life, fun, and leisure, and to prolong life, is justified as self-evidently good. And anyone who challenges that right to pursue happiness is more than a mere naysayer; such a person is on the "other side," a minion of evil, an enemy of reason and of personal liberty and progress.

Major polluters such as Monsanto, British Petroleum, Dow Chemical, Formosa Plastics, DuPont, Mitsubishi Chemical, Bayer, Saudi Basic Industries Corporation, Sumitomo Chemical, Chevron Phillips, Dutch Shell, Lyondell Basell, and BASF constantly reinforce our status quo, the reality we share with them, the values, beliefs, motivations, and behaviors including reductionism. Reductionism is a form of rhetoric. It attempts to convince us that things are not as they seem. That the natural truth is that nothing is real except the smallest component parts of a thing. And so, according to reductionism, you are actually really just a pile of vibrating atoms, essentially the same as the chair on which you are sitting. That is supposed to be the natural truth. You are actually really just 7 cents worth of chemicals. Qualitative differences are denied existence. What is the difference between you and your chair? Essentially, there is no difference except, we would argue against the reductionists and their natural attitude, that you are alive. What does this have to do with anything? Well, thanks to the naturalism of reductionism, you cannot counter-argue against such claims without appearing insane or minimally against reality. It is a powerful rhetoric. But here is where we must resist the enchantment of language, including the story of reductionism.

For example, chemical companies do little product advertising at the retail level. That makes sense since few of us buy chemicals. But they spend large sums of money doing public relations and image advertising. A good example is Dupont's phrase, "Better living through chemistry." This slogan does not promote any particular product but rather, as Dupont's director of advertising, Charles Hackett, put it, this slogan is meant to change people's opinions about the role of business in society and chemicals in our environment (McCarthy, 2010). It teaches us that we cannot live without chemicals and that the chemical industry is making our lives better. The confusion created by this rhetoric is that there is nothing natural about the chemical industry. Yes, chemicals are essential to life. But life did quite well—indeed it is arguable that it did better—before Dupont came along.

Two things are at work here. First is the implicit claim that the most unnatural things are in fact natural. And second that reductionism is the only real truth. What is real is natural and what is natural, and most real, are the "actual" component parts that make up everything including us. So natural science and technology are natural. Cosmetic ads make such claims explicitly, arguing that if you buy a certain kind of mascara, for instance, you will achieve the "natural look" (Williamson, 1994).

So love is not really love or the fictional subjective state of affection. No. We are assured that "Love is chemistry" in a public relations ad campaign put out by BASF. In the television ad, we are told by a nice voice over perky music and sunny fun-filled video images of happy people that:

We believe that if love is a chemical reaction, then chemistry has a good chance to make the world a more harmonious place [a couple embracing, kissing grammy fish, a clip from an old cartoon of a heart on a spring, children running, smiling, and holding flash cards with the signs of the elements forming a human periodic table]. Chemistry creates the relationships among the elements [people dancing, salt and pepper shakers dancing]. It finds secret formulas to unite rather than separate things [a piece of raw fish crawls over and humps on top of some sushi rice] . . . Chemistry ultimately creates good relationships between people and whatever they need in their lives [people skydiving and playing soccer and then forming the BASF logo]. That's why we don't just make chemicals we create chemistry. BASF. *The* chemical company. (View the ad at http://www.ispot.tv/ad/77nz/basf-love-and-chemistry)

The promise here is to make the world better than it already is and to do so by using the natural science of chemistry. So nature can be improved on by acting unnaturally. Of course chemical manipulation is a cultural and economic activity that only humans, so far as we know, do. Now that BASF has presented us with its emotional rhetoric of corporation as hero, we can look at a factual record it neglected to mention. In 1921, a silo storing 4,500 tons of a mixture of ammonium sulfate and ammonium nitrate exploded at a BASF plant in Oppau (now Ludwigshafen, Germany), killing 500 to 600 people and injuring about 2,000 more. In 1948, a chemical tank wagon exploded in the same location, killing 207 people. And then there is the famous Sandoz chemical spill that turned the Rhine River red, causing massive mortality of wildlife downstream including a large portion of the European eel population.

On November 1, 1986, BASF's Ciba-Geigy chemical subsidiary holding containers failed during a fire in Schweizerhalle (near Basel), Switzerland, releasing tons of toxic agrochemicals into the Rhine River. "Within 10 days the pollution had travelled the length of the Rhine and into the North Sea. An estimated half a million fish were killed, and some species were wiped out entirely. There was a public outcry, resulting in the Rhine Action Programme of 1987" (BBC News, 1986). Then of course we have the Union Carbide disaster in Bhopal, India, on December 3, 1984, where a faulty tank containing methyl isocyanate leaked, killing about 20,000 and injuring more than half a million more people (not to mention the animals in the area). Yes, "love" can be reduced to a natural process involving chemical reactions in our bodies. But it does not logically follow, therefore, that what the chemical industry does is either natural or what we call love.

But the love does not stop there. Of the myriad of smaller accidents, we offer one more big one as evidence for our argument that humans are destroying life as we know it. On November 13, 2005, a chemical plant belonging to China National Petrochemical Corp. (Sinopec) exploded in

Jilin City, China. More than 10,000 residents were evacuated. The explosion severely polluted the Songhua River, with an estimated 100 tons of benzene and nitrobenzene entering the water. An 80-kilometer-long toxic slick drifted down the Amur River, where the recorded benzene level was at one point 108 times above national safety levels (MSN News, 2005). Many cities and villages that use the water were not adequately alerted to the danger. No valid audit of the environmental damage to the rivers has ever been published. About all we have are official Chinese accounts of the effects on the people in the region.

Downstream in the city of Harbin, the provincial capital (population over 10 million), panic buying of water ensued. Harbin, which takes its water supply from wells and the Songhua River, launched massive efforts to ship thousands of tons of water in from outside the area, and the city hastily drilled 95 additional deep-water wells to complement the existing 918 to supply the city (BBC News, 2005). Due to initial denials and then slow response to the disaster by the provincial government, even the official press responded with criticism (BBC News, 2005; *People's Daily News*, 2005).

Why do we tolerate this sort of behavior? Because we are convinced that these are just isolated events that the environment can magically absorb without lasting effect. And we are convinced that those who perpetrate such "accidents" have our best interests at heart, even making our lives better. Ben Bagdikian (2004) noted that at one time, Gulf+Western (now Viacom), which owned and operated subsidiaries in media (Paramount Pictures, Paramount TV Stations Group, USA Networks, NBCUniversal Cable, the Sci-Fi Channel/formerly TVX, Desilu Productions, Simon and Schuster, Prentice-Hall, Esquire Inc., Allyn & Bacon, Modern Curriculum Press), agriculture (The South Puerto Rico Sugar Company), finance (The Associates First Capital Corporation), chemical production (New Jersey Zinc), oil tankers, nuclear waste carriers, and so on, simultaneously attempted to acquire *Time Magazine* in a hostile takeover and block the merger of Time Inc. and Warner Communications. Around the same time in 1978, Gulf+Western took out the largest corporate advertisement in history (to that date), an institutional promotion that was 56 continuous pages long for $3.3 million. Bagdikian points out that no one would do this unless they (a) had marketing evidence that it works to change people's attitudes and beliefs about corporations in general and this particular one specifically, and (b) feel the need to change people's attitudes and beliefs to bolster a more positive image of themselves. Gulf+Western's major message was that oversight and regulation hurt us all.

Major polluters assure us that what we want, limitless personal freedom and happiness (whatever that may be) and gratification as fast as possible, we deserve, and that helping them to deliver that happiness to us is obviously rational. Give the children all the candy they could ever want. It is not hard to convince us that such drives and aspirations are not merely good but God-given rights supported, ironically, by natural law. Greed is good by nature. Nonetheless, they purchase massive lobbying efforts and advertising campaigns to continually reinforce this natural truth. They are essential to and the defenders of our way of life, our status quo, which is absurdly—perpetual progress—progress for its own sake. This is our modern myth. It is our status quo. We participate in it, and so we must take ownership of our condition.

The technology as utopia ideology may have hegemonic tendencies, but many conflicting observations enable us to challenge our own desires. A few such observations have been offered, and more are forthcoming. We must also question the motivation of those, including ourselves, who seek to reassure us that they are looking out for us, creating our jobs, and protecting our future, our way of life—telling us to confidently trust them. They tell us they want to earn our faith, but the fine print that flashes unreadable at the bottom of their video ads should give us some inkling that there is more to the story than they are willing to disclose. And yet they understand us. They are us. We crave such positive, comforting messages. We want others to take care of everything for us. But only we can really change ourselves. We must evolve.

5

The Human as Maker and Increasingly Self-Made

The Collapse of Dualism and the Dialectic of Technology

•

A dialectical relationship exists between technology and what it supposedly determines and what determines it (Gouldner, 1976/1982). Such a relationship is not unilateral, not deterministic. However, technological determinism remains a popular theoretical position (Kurzweil, 2005). Insofar as technological systems defuse through a society they become normative and ubiquitous. They also run along economic class lines. Early adopters of technologies such as the automobile, the electric refrigerator, the computer, smart phones, the airplane, and so forth, tend to be wealthy people who are elite not just in economic terms but in technological terms as well. Such inequality, along with access to the latest medical technologies, afford the technological elite better health care, more entertainment, and the status of being able to consume the latest in the temporal war of competitive capitalism's mantra of the "fastest, newest and best." In terms of technological muscle flexing, such as the space race and the arms race around the globe, technology is a direct expression of status, power, and prestige.

Technology is a manifestation of not only physical prowess and status but also authorized symbolic violence (Bourdieu, 1977 Fr./1991 Eng.). When only a few could access Duesenberg luxury automobiles during the Great Depression, driving them around underscored both economic and technological inequality, hurting many people's feelings. So Duesenberg went out of business in 1937 because driving one around made one the target of retaliatory violence, both physical as in rocks being hurled at the car and symbolic as in insults being cast toward the owner.

But the luxury auto example is not the whole story. Being left out of a technological complex, a system that constitutes part of culture, can lead to not just bodily harm but psychological and economic harm too. The impact of being left behind and left out of a wave of technological change can affect a group or the self-efficacy, self-esteem, and self-image of an individual. In the modern industrialized world, being poor very much has to do with access to technologies, and this is well understood. This is why private foundations, non-governmental and non-profit organizations, as well as governments are all trying to make sure poorer regions of the planet do not become permanent information ghettos, places where cellular communication technology and the Internet do not reach, thus isolating individuals and groups. This is vital for as Alvin Toffler (1991) noted decades ago, knowledge and ideas beget more knowledge and ideas, and so people who do not have access to knowledge and ideas not only lag behind others but, more important, continually fall farther and farther behind. So the potential for symbolic violence is significant and practically unlimited.

Technology, in short, is much more than material artifacts crafted for ulterior ends (as compared with art for its own sake).

When people speak of technological determinism, they rarely define what exactly it determines. The technologies we live with determine—or, more appropriately, affect—our hermeneutic horizon, our sense of what is real and possible, probable and desirable. The limits of some of our brute capacities are to a certain degree determined but not our imaginations or experiences. In a word, technology is part of the larger human experience, the "total ideology," as defined and differentiated from mere political ideology by Mannheim (1936 Ger./1985 Eng.).

The telescope and microscope are examples of technology that not only changed the boundaries of our spatial reality but also affected our ambitions as individuals and as a species. At the same time, technologies are cultural artifacts, expressions of our desires, wants, needs, and capabilities, and our will to expand and extend our world.

Every technology has hermeneutic horizons, limits beyond which we cannot see. This includes synthetic instrumental aids such as telescopes. For example, a telescope cannot be used to show us a person's blood pressure. A hermeneutic horizon is what we can perceive and conceive, what is realizable. This aspect of horizon is an enabling prejudice, but the horizon also has a limit, a blind prejudice as Hans-George Gadamer (1960 Ger./1975 Eng.) explains. Gadamer insists that one cannot escape one's place in history, culture, and language, one's perspective: in short, the sum total of one's horizons. Gadamer and his student, Jürgen Habermas (1968 Ger./1972 Eng.), debated the claim that perspective and, therefore, relativism are inescapable. Habermas chose to preserve the possibility of transcending one's personal perspective to achieve an objective truth and to preserve reason—an extension of Edmund Husserl's (1913 Ger./1982 Eng.) original project aimed at staving off the absurdity of the claim that relativism is truth. As students of both Gadamer and Habermas, we claim that neither is fully correct. Neither fully understood Friedrich Nietzsche's (1901 Ger./1967 Eng.) position on perspectivism as expressed in his many writings, specifically the *aporia*—that I am limited and know it. This knowledge combines with my will to overcome my limitations. We can escape our personal perspective. It happens frequently—for example, anytime we learn something new or when our beliefs are proven false and we must accommodate the fact that reality has changed, as when Einstein was forced to acknowledge that the universe is not a steady state but rather an ever-changing, expanding universe, and that, ironically, relativism was much more real than even he had imagined.

Gadamer rightly understood the fusion of horizons as a process of integrating other interpretations of reality via one's own prejudgments. But beyond this, sometimes our reality can be confronted by such profound difference that it cannot be easily integrated. In these situations, one horizon simply gives way to another. Such forced compliance, as Leon Festinger and James Carlsmith (1959) observed, can involve a great deal of confusion and pain. Cultures go extinct and identities are lost. Scholars are forced to abandon their hypotheses, theories, or versions of realities. New technologies can open new vistas that render old worldviews incorrect and obsolete.

The irony here is that hermeneutics is not in contention with science because science proves to have histories and to be continually revising its own worldview, its paradigmatic perspectives as Thomas Kuhn (1962) has explained. Science, as with other human modes of awareness, has horizons. This hermeneutic fact appears to be universal in human experience, as Martin Heidegger (1927 Ger./1962 Eng.) maintained. Change, as Taoists, Hindus, Heraklitus, and others have understood, is the one constant of the universe. In fact, the major difference between civilizations and their descendant cultures is based on differences in mytho-religious foundations. Some cultures insist on permanent and universal truths, whereas others are based on mytho-religious foundations that hold change is the only constant. Modern cultures that embrace revolutionary change reject mytho-religious traditions. No societies change as fast as modern industrialized and highly technologized ones.

Therefore, Gadamer (1960 Ger./1975 Eng.) is incorrect to insist that one cannot escape one's own horizon—that we build new horizons is obvious. But he is correct in arguing that one's horizon can be radically altered if one is open to other voices. This is a curious position—because at the same time Gadamer (1960 Ger./1975 Eng.) insists that one cannot escape oneself, he also insists that art can change us and can articulate a form of truth transcending our personal perspective.

Joseph Campbell (1988) addresses the power of art and ritual to throw us out of ourselves, out of our parochial mindset. Technology also has the power to do this. The experience of one's first airplane ride or scuba dive or trip to the top of a great skyscraper or watching the space shuttle take-off or sitting in the grand space of a massive arena can be life-changing experiences. Carl Sagan (1996) writes about a trip to the 1939 World's Fair and how it changed his life trajectory by instilling in him an excitement and ambition about science and technology that lasted his entire life:

> In 1939 my parents took me to the New York World's Fair. There, I was offered a vision of a perfect future made possible by science and high technology. . . . "See sound," one exhibit bewilderingly commanded. And sure enough, when the tuning fork was struck by the little hammer, a beautiful sine wave marched across the oscilloscope screen. "Hear light," another poster exhorted. And sure enough, when the flashlight shone on the photocell, I could hear something like the static on our Motorola radio set when the dial was between stations. Plainly the world held wonders of a kind I had never guessed. How could a tone become a picture and light become a noise? My parents were not scientists. They knew almost nothing about science. But in introducing me simultaneously to skepticism and to wonder, they taught me the two uneasily cohabitating modes of thought that are central to the scientific method. . . . As I look back, it seems clear to me that I learned the most essential things not from my school teachers, nor even from my university professors, but from my parents, who knew nothing at all about science, in that single far-off year of 1939. (pp. xiii, xv)

Technology and religion have one-dimensional magic power to transform an individual's worldview and also that individual's sense of self. Technocrats, technologists, and scientists are often hailed as heroes. At the tribal and super-tribal (national) levels, we pray that our technologists will create the great "secret weapon" that will defeat our enemies. Beyond the tribal level, we wait for science to save us all from cancer, to enable us to live under the sea, to save the planets' atmosphere, to save the world's fish stocks, to go into the jungles and oceans and return with new cures for disease, to go into the laboratory and return with unlimited, nonpolluting, cheap sources of energy. People see technology and science as saviors.

Nevertheless, Habermas is also incorrect. Although our sense of reality changes, we can never be certain whether at any moment we have achieved an objective truth or even that a singular truth exists. And even if we did for a time align with some absolute truth, as Gadamer argues, that would be our perspective only at that moment. The problem is that we cannot get behind ourselves or as Nietzsche (1887 Ger./1974 Eng.) puts it, "We cannot look around our own corner" (p. 336). Yet through communication with other alter egos, including the horizons of technologies, we can be exposed to new horizons and thus be changed by the experience. The wonderful thing about universal semantization, as Roland Barthes (1957 Fr./1972 Eng.) called the meaningfulness of awareness, is that a sunset or a canyon or even trash swirling in an eddy of wind in an alley, as shown in the film *American Beauty* (1999), can mean something to us and expand us beyond the perceptual limitations of our present selves.

The grand arrogance and error of positivism is to sit in one's perspective-based corner and believe that it is the only correct and possible interpretation, the one and only truth. Positivistic science is merely one interpretation among many. The usefulness and value of an interpretation depends on our needs, interests, wants, and ambitions at a given moment. A set of equations can describe a sunset but so too can a poem or painting. Which description is privileged is not so much a statement about the sunset as it is a statement about the person speaking. However, when descriptions *are* taken at face value, the error of naïve perspectivism is present, as Immanuel Kant (1781 Ger./1929 Eng.) recognized. So the privileged interpretation about science or poetry is mostly a statement about the one who does the valuation, the privileging. What people see in the stars may or may not tell me anything about stars in fact, but it tells me much about the person describing the stars. And this includes empirical descriptions along with mytho-religious or magic-idolic ones. The person who insists that only an empirical scientific version of reality is real and true is thus exposed as having a particular set of biases against other perspectives. These biases can in turn be explored to see just what it is that makes the person reject the poetic version of reality, for example. Often what is unearthed is a prejudice based not in science or empiricism but in a set of values concerning pragmatism—a set of desires and wants that value the power to change physical conditions. This is the cultural bias of science and technology. The science/technology cultural bias asserts that while other versions/explanations of reality may not be less beautiful, less exciting, or less easily practiced than the scientific/technological perspective, these other views lack the pragmatic power to alter conditions (i.e., the predict-and-control illusion and the illusion we should desire to or find it possible to predict and control), a power that is inherent in the cultural perspective of science/technology.

Science and technology are magics that work (literally). (Cheap) labor and (high) productivity are the primary foci of the industrial capitalistic world, and capitalists determine the value of technology and science. For example, if a popular tune, a popular style of painting, or a popular form of manufacturing makes money, it is deemed realistic, practical, and/or beneficial. Given the quantitative bias of money (i.e., making more money is equivocated with having more success), the technological solution is favored because it is popular and efficient—not in solving problems but in selling products. Many possible solutions to disease have been ignored by laboratories because the cures cannot be patented, and therefore they are categorized as inefficient and impractical, even impossible—not at curing diseases but as money makers. The barometer for medicine has changed from curing disease to making money.

For example, in 2007, researchers at the University of Alberta reported that dichloroacetate (DCA) causes the regression of several kinds of tumors. However, because DCA cannot be patented, there is no private investment available for clinical trials. DCA could be a cheaper and more effective alternative to those cancer treatments currently available. The research at the University of Alberta was funded publicly by the Canadian Institutes of Health Research, and the researchers there have called for more public funding to further test DCA (Michelakis, Webster, & Mackey, 2008).

As Socrates noted, what tends to be most invisible to people are their own prejudices. To know thyself is the challenge because such knowledge enables growth. Such knowledge is never complete, and thus the potential for growth is never ending. Which interpretation we favor depends on our current needs, wants, capacities, beliefs, ambitions, and values (and the ability to realize the ways that wants, capacities, beliefs, ambitions, and values are constructed).

Each new horizon is an interpretation. Each new technology provides opportunities for novel experiences. As Nietzsche recognized, there are an infinite number of perspectives. Human experience is in constant flux, an endless process that includes stresses and challenges (Whitehead, 1929).

The optical telescope gives us a taste of what is possible. It, like all technologies, carries within itself the seeds of its own obsolescence. Every technology has hermeneutic horizons, limits to its capacities, limits beyond which it is no longer useful or informative. But at the same time, technologies are cultural artifacts: expressions of our desires, wants, needs, and capabilities, our will to expand and extend our minds and our world. This perspectival nature of technology (it is perspectival in the sense that it facilitates the expansion and extension of the will, mind, and world) enables us to see in a particularly enhanced way.

We often become frustrated with our technologies and their limitations. We suspect that technology can do more. Why? Because our technologies continually do more and more. When the telescope first revealed moons orbiting Jupiter and mountains on the moon, we were astonished, and this revelation proved to us that we had been denied these views before, that there was yet still more to see. So when technology has demonstrated our limited perspectives and exposed our worldview as obsolete, we logically suspect that with even more powerful technology, an even greater view can be achieved. And the modern Westerner presumed a right that ever-greater views *should* be forthcoming—that we are entitled to ever-greater views.

Thus, the more successful a technology is, the more we desire its continued expansion. If a particular telescope reveals mountains on the moon, imagine what a bigger one could do, what vistas yet await our eyes and minds if only we can manufacture the means. The expectation therefore is that we can and should seek better telescopes. As with the telescope, so with all technologies; we expect to better our technologies and thereby eventually see/know everything through the application of our improved technological developments.

Our conception of the "greater view" extends to things not yet achieved, much as a pier enables one to walk out into a space above a body of water and also points out—to the space beyond the pier. We stand at the end of the pier pondering the waters beyond. Technologies signify that which, in theory, should be possible. The disappointment of limits drives us on. Modern individuals continually strive to expand their perspectives as much as possible. The limit of the visible (i.e., the invisible), as Merleau-Ponty (1964 Fr./1968 Eng.) understood, drives our efforts to see farther. We curse the darkness and strive to create fire; darkness gives light its value. The longing for progress (as defined herein) is based on the ruminations resulting from dissatisfaction with our current limitations.

Discovery is the source of satisfaction and joy for the modern. Novelty is rewarded above all else. Even a maniac such as Hitler stole rather than destroyed art and wanted to be an artist himself. The "new" promotes everything from the ideas of progress, development, and evolution to commodity advertising. We want new things, leaders with fresh ideas, and entrepreneurs who take risks in creating new and innovative products. Research and development are responsible for making our (hopefully) successful future. In the modern era, an entire people can stake its identity on achieving something never before achieved, such as landing men on the Moon and returning them safely to Earth. Furthermore, much of group identity relative to these achievements is derived from the fact that we expect to do them *before* anyone else, rather than potentially doing these things *with* other peoples/groups.

A concrete example of this dialectical process between the human horizon and the technical horizon can be seen in telescopic technology. Optical telescopes with ever-greater power were imagined until we abandoned optics for infrared telescopes, which were in turn subsequently abandoned in turn for (rather than *ultimately* to) radio telescopes. Likewise, the desire to see more is generated and maintained by the success of optical microscopes.

Heisenberg's (1958) uncertainty principle states that we can see only one aspect of an atom—either its position or velocity but not both at once because the act of observation changes both. Our thirst for greater vision, and our modern visiocentric obsession (Kramer, 1988, 1993a, 1993b, 1993c, 1994a, 1994b, 1994c), rather than phonocentrism as Derrida (1967 Fr./1976 Eng.) argues, drives us to move beyond optical microscopes to electron microscopes. The modern individual falls in love at first *sight*, well before ritual recitations of sacred, secular, or legal texts. Technologies inspire us to want more, and ambition drives efforts to create ever-greater technologies. We are simultaneously frustrated and inspired by technology.

One might argue that technology is consciously determined, an expression of our desire to escape our limited hermeneutic horizons. One might also argue that technology helps us escape those horizons even as it marks the limits of human experience. But neither argument is completely true; the dialectical process is not that simple. The continual synthesis of new technologies yields indeterminate consequences. Perceived needs and desires are the mothers of invention. As Nietzsche (1887 Ger./1974 Eng.) puts it, "Do you really believe that the sciences would ever have originated and grown if the way had not been prepared by magicians, alchemists, astrologers, and witches whose promises and pretensions first had to create a thirst, a hunger, a taste for hidden and forbidden powers?" (p. 240). To seek to identify the chicken or the egg as the origin of change is misguided. What we find instead is co-determination and randomness, and not only that, we also find an open horizon, kept open by the interplay of humans, their artifacts, and the (beautiful) unpredictability of life events. The paths and events cannot be predicted. Science can do many things, but it cannot control and predict where people will go and what will happen along the way.

We must consider the reflexive moment, the philosophical moment of assessment. We grumble about the proliferation of technical standards and our inability to keep up. We marvel at the rate of change we can see in a single lifetime. For instance, a native of the state of Oklahoma told one of us a story about his grandfather. His grandfather had worked on cattle drives along the Chisholm Trail as a youth; he retired as an electrician at a nuclear power facility. To further underscore the rate of sociocultural change modern technological societies experience, one need only remember that the Wright brothers conducted their first powered flight on December 17, 1903, a flight of about 120 feet. Fifty-eight years later, on April 12, 1961, Yuri Gagarin became the first human to go into space and the first to orbit Earth. Only ten years later, the Boeing 747-100, measuring 210 feet long with a wingspan of 195 feet, began carrying hundreds of passengers at once around the globe in comfort and at a high subsonic speed of 567 miles per hour (Mach .85 or 913 kilometers per hour) and a cruising altitude of about 37,000 feet (approximately 7 miles or 11.27 kilometers). The Boeing was 75 feet longer than the entire flight of the Wright machine.

Technology has the properties of dissemination and grafting. As with grafting a tree that subsequently flourishes in order to create a new breed of tree or fruit, technologies are also transferred, replicated, refined, and improved through dissemination of favorable traits. However, cultural fusion influences both dissemination and grafting, which occurs when a foreign technology comes into a cultural milieu, and a process of co-evolution results. Each object changes the others and is in turn changed by others. The foreign technology is received within the perspective of the host culture. As a technology disseminates, it is modified, invented, adopted, and rejected; often these technical forms signify important or significant moments within the reality of continual difference. Change is the constant. Histories proliferate—histories of food production and processing, of the train, refrigeration, the automobile, of surgical procedures, of printing, the computer, broadcasting, cinema, the airplane, and so forth. These histories inspire temples dedicated to remembrances of things past in the form of museums, including museums of science and technology. No societies in history have spawned so much change as modern technologically driven societies.

An example of the type of significant moment described above is Galileo's conception of the physical properties of all swinging bodies. His father had invented various pendulum devices for timing music. The young Galileo observed and tinkered with these devices and, with some degree of serendipity, developed an idea from his observations; an insight into a bigger picture, a more fundamental property of the universe. The truth of the relationship between periodicity and amplitude was always there in Galileo's father's devices, so what did Galileo contribute? Clearly the behavior of pendulums was not altered by Galileo's explanation, but Galileo's insights did impact the manufacture of pendulums and their use in things like clocks. The explanation of the behavior is not the same as the behavior. Science is not identical to what it explains. Science is a body of procedures and literature. To think otherwise is akin to confusing a menu with the food it describes. Did Galileo's father see in the devices what Galileo did? No. So no simple notion of determinism is adequate here. Insight and invention are intertwined and complex processes that can be encouraged but not entirely taught. There is no simple recipe for genius.

Science strives to explain what *is*. Clearly observation comes before explanation (theory). Subsequently, theory helps guide future ways of seeing. A dialectical process is at work between culture and nature, between theory and experiment, and between rumor and result. Each takes turns guiding the other.

The promise of miracles is as a prelude to a distant age. Religion and science fiction share an identity as the primers of the pump of desire that leads to material magic, magic that delivers change. But satisfaction is short-lived; the demand for ever-greater speed and power continues. The enemies are anonymity, boredom, and normalcy. What the modern seeks is infinite (and therefore unsustainable) speed and power, to be unique, special, and to be identified as the one with the most and best of everything. When life is normal, it becomes boring. Our lives, via our things, become inadequate and obsolete. Things once on the cutting edge become passé.

MODERN SUPERPOWER, MODERN INDIVIDUALISTIC
SUPERHERO

Humans identify with power—hence we have the emergence of the pre-Cyborg, humans who enhance and extend their powers with chemicals and synthetic materials (from contact lenses to insulin pumps, pacemakers, artificial hearts, and beyond). The power of seduction (and self-image) manifested by breast implants is another example. What is presumed is an entire field of meanings and a semiotic system that reduces the physical human body to signalic status. In the era of modern hypertrophic individualism, the body is less lived in than used as a tool to signify identity. The modern individual cuts, nips, tucks, paints, and otherwise manipulates the body. This is not new, of course—cosmetic and ritualistic scarification and body modification are ancient practices. What is new is the arbitrariness of the manipulations.

In tribal societies, tattoos, clothing styles, body extensions, and modifications are not arbitrary; rather, they are magically idolic, binding the individual to a group identity. Modern individuals, in contrast, express themselves through personal choices of tattoos, hairstyles, and other physical modifications. This personalization/manipulation extends to the personalization of technology. As the body becomes individuated, individual will, rather than collective custom, takes precedence. This individuation leads to the fragmented nature of the postmodern world and the emergence of the posthuman condition.

The modern individual's identity-formation process involves the reduction of the human being. At first the individual is separated from the collective and its imperatives. The modern individual presumes the right to control his or her own body regardless of the beliefs and wishes of the dominant group, including one's parents. The individuated human then subdivides, fragments, and is reduced to only two components variously articulated as a body and soul, matter and mind, exterior and interior, shell and spirit, and so forth. Then as reductionism continues toward complete minimalism and isolation, the body remains as nothing more than a discrete mass of physical tissue.

Phenomena without physical extension or weight, such as ideas, logic, ethics, beauty, obligation, and so on, are deemed nonbeings that vanish with the chimerical subject. Body modifications are subjective expressions of self, from self, to self. This is the emergent superhero who not only merely defies organic limitations but also owns the means of power and is literally identified with the means. The powers *define* the person. Furthermore, the process for accumulating and enhancing power is promoted with all vigor. The modern superhero is not like the heroes of traditional societies, such as the eponymous heroes of ancient Greece who sire entire peoples and as such are identified with them (if not identical with them) through the magic fluids of blood, milk, and semen. The traditional hero has human frailties. His or her blood flows through my/our/the tribe's veins.

The modern hero, by contrast, expresses technological-like capacities and is fundamentally Other. These Others have supernatural (i.e., superhuman) powers and belong to no known tribe or species (with the exception of alien species of superheros like Superman). The modern superhero is often the result of technological accident—like Mary Shelly's Frankenstein—a monstrosity, perhaps, but without the depth of reflection that forms the bulk of Shelly's story. Given the ethical and moral vacuum the modern superhero Cyborg inhabits, hero valuation comes down to an overly simplified good-versus-evil reality without the ambiguities of Shelly's characterization—ambiguities that lead the observant reader to conclude that the doctor, not his creation, is the true monster.

In the modern world, powers define the person. Superheros are brutish, empirical, and physical (not to mention beautiful and rich). Little depth of consequence is considered, and little understanding of purpose or what directs the power is demonstrated. The identity of the person is therefore not celebrated as one of us, not *our* tribal hero who embodies *our* perspectives and promotes *our* interests and values. The modern superhero's isolation is enhanced by the need to remain anonymous.

Furthermore, with the modern sense of obsolescence, the process for accumulating, maintaining, and enhancing power is promoted with all vigor and to the exclusion of anything like the greater good or goodness for the sake of goodness, altruism, and so on. A greater power can always be imagined. In modernity, the aging hero is discarded for the new, whereas in traditional societies the aging hero remains fundamental for eternity as the source of current value and power. If the mythic god/hero falls, so too do we—via magic idolic identification. Modernity, with its emphasis on perpetual motion, sees generations drift away from one another. Gaps appear as collective identity fragments. One generation's hero becomes the next generation's joke. Individuation shatters collective cohesion and the sense of coherent social reality. As the body is objectified, it too becomes obsolete. Aging becomes a serious problem for moderns.

The mind resists being equated with the blood and tissue we observe when we cut open someone's head. We do not look inside and see the person's thoughts, memories, and emotions. We see blood and tissue. Synergies (the fact that the whole is more than the sum of its parts) require a different understanding. It indicates that even superheros are motivated. Our technologies do not displace our humanness but express our desires, ambitions, and fears.

This synergistic condition intensifies in late modernity, moving beyond the will to power to become the will to will, the effort to maximize ambition and effort itself, to maximize the process of maximization, not merely to push the envelope but to push the pushing of the envelope. Those with no ambition are seen as failures. We aspire to have aspirations and to alter the boundaries of the possible. Hence, we have the late-modern sense of intensity (extreme internal focus/drive) as well as extensity (focus on altering the external world). The goal is to be as intense as possible—to refine and concentrate everything (most preciously the will itself) and to endlessly do so.

The will is not the only thing left of the ghost in the shell. Popular superheros are fictional. Morality, ethics, and beauty are still operant in the life of the superhero as well as the rest of us. Design, the tension between form and function, is as alive today as ever. However, in late modernity, the will tends to exist only insofar as it is manifested materially. Hence, we have the will to will. We are compelled to try harder to try. The hypertrophic modern individual suffers from an urgent desire to avoid mediocrity, seen as a form of obsolescence. For the modern individual, being average is not acceptable. But of course, as a group member, one cannot escape the relevance of the mean. The dissolution of the group and the rise of hypertrophic individualism is a fundamental characteristic of modernity. With it comes the opposite of average, the endless striving for outlier status, the siren call of utopianism.

The ambition of the late-modern individual is not belonging to any tribe, not to be celebrated as such, but to be independent, reducing the tribe to mere herd. This constitutes the other side of modernity, which is expressed even in the specialization of social sciences, for example, sociology versus psychology. On the one hand, we have the "egocentric individualist exaggerated to extremes and desirous of possessing everything . . . who, despite his limitations, is permitted everything" and, on the other hand, "extreme collectivism that promises the total fulfillment of man's being . . . the utter abnegation of the individual valued merely as an object in the human aggregate" (Gebser, 1949 Ger./1985 Eng., p. 3). The modern world presents crowding rather than community, and the modern crowd is full of isolated individuals, strangers each dreaming of being a superhero who escapes this world.

The ideology of utopia and the conceptualization and drive for perfection, by definition, beyond reach (as *ou topos* means "nowhere"), contributes to relentless pressure to improve endlessly. Satisfaction is thus unattainable. The modern era, for all its materialism, is the era of ideology, and ideology is most pronounced in the goal- and-progress-oriented notion of utopia. With utopia being nowhere (and, therefore, unattainable), progress becomes unending. Goals are never achieved. A new form of judgment arises; people are only deemed to be as good as their most recent/last performance.

Curiously, modern individuals are at least as idealistic as they are materialistic; the dialectic tension between these two values is the essence of the modern condition and its chronic state of dissatisfaction. The effort to achieve materially is driven by idealistic ambition. Because material productivity and performance are easily measured, the mythic idea that one will be evaluated against the ideal only once—at the appointed hour of judgment day—has been abandoned. Today, within the late-modern milieu, evaluation is a way of life. It proliferates and becomes perpetual—a product of technology and abundant information readily and constantly available. It is objective and objectifying. It pits one against one's former tribal kin, contributing to the modern ideology of Social Darwinism. But we are pitted not merely against each other but also against our own inventions (in the form of our technologies).

The ideal against which the human is measured is increasingly exemplified by our machines. Their tolerances for error are far lower than humans can achieve. Thus, we have a utopia presented not by another species but by something totally Other, the machine. It competes with us as if it possesses human ambitions. The Other of the machine is utterly different, absent, distant, and alien (yet our own creation). Technology has its own scale. Because it never sleeps, the adage that one is only as good as one's last performance, which still allows for the tolerance of gaps between performances, has intensified into continual monitoring. Mechanical, unit/linear quantification has become hypertrophic. Quality is reduced to quantification. And so we are under constant surveillance and assessment (measurement)—the two being combined in the notion of the unblinking gaze. This form of measurement is viewed as both valid and necessary; the results of this measurement dictate our consequent actions even when the natural world "says" something different.

The human is objectified because nothing is so external, so Other, so objective as utopia. From the perspective of utopian judgment, the human (and everything else) is inadequate. This is the problem of extension transference that Mumford (1934/1962/2010) and Hall (1983) discuss. Our extensions intensify in material magnitude and feed back on us, finding us unable to "measure up" to the scale and standards of the external apparatus and what it comes to signify through the process of "objective correlative" measurement (Eliot, 1932, p. 145).

This is the essence of alienation, including technological alienation. An example is the human value of punctuality manifested in the mechanical clock, which then reflects back on us, labeling us "late" and even "unreliable"—and the clock (and the people who subscribe to it) does so with complete objectivity, intolerance, and disinterest. The object—in this case, the mechanical clock—becomes the authority, the purest form of technocrat. Platonic formalism comes to lord over us mere humans who conceived of such utopian dreams. In the process, the virtual takes precedence over the actual, ideology drives life. Consistency and uniformity of the type found in the ideal of the number line comes to expose the inconsistency of mortal behavior and to drive it toward endless improvement, endless dissatisfaction.

This obsession with precision comes from the effort to discipline, to limit tolerances. It is found in religion, with its codified canons that lend themselves to hairsplitting commentary and debate, resulting in splintering sects. The notion of order identifies the various orders of the monastic life within religions such as the Franciscan Order, the Dominican Order, and so on. The invention of the mechanical clock, with its relentless quantification, turns time into pure monotony via standardization and endless uniformity. Tolerances are reduced as hands were added to its face to fragment moments from hours to minutes, to seconds, and eventually to fractions of seconds.

It is no accident that strict, even ascetic regulation of all thought and behavior originated with the establishment of monastic ordination. St. Benedict's rule, a set of regulations concerning the times of prayer and virtually all other bodily activities, was initiated by St. Benedict—the father of Christian monasticism—at Monte Cassino around 500 CE. Monks strove to develop ever more precise means of regulating themselves, of measuring and telling time until the invention of the mechanical clock deployed by an Order (in this case, the Dominicans) to regulate their ecclesiastical functions (as canonical hours). Perhaps not surprisingly, this is the same Order that led the Inquisition with total intolerance for any deviation (which they defined as heresy).

The mechanical clock is *the* icon of the modern world. It is dissociated from human life and subjectivity. It treats all, from pauper to king, in the same manner. It is the grand regulator. To be punctual changed from meaning rudeness in Middle English to being "a good thing." Being reliable—"just like clockwork"—has emerged as a central ethic of our era. To be inconsistent, late, or unreliable are negative measures of character in the modern world.

It was left to Hegel (1812, 1813, 1816 Ger./1969 Eng.), 500 years after the introduction of the mechanical clock with its universal scale, to codify a single logic with the central and penultimate status of divinity, a logic that in turn led to the Left and Right Hegelians (i.e., the United States and the USSR) ripping each other apart in the twentieth century with a fervor worthy of absolute conviction and racing each other to technologically driven oblivion in massive arsenals of nuclear weapons. Each formed economies thoroughly dedicated to the military-industrial complex. As John Maynard Keynes (1971/1989) observed, both sides built huge arsenals that were never used and had the same economic effect of creating jobs by hiring millions to dig holes and bury money. Both Western capitalist and Soviet communist economies became equally and thoroughly militarized and technologized. Our economies, dreams (of glory), and families became both militarized and technologized.

War is often an expression of conviction that, if not explicitly religious (as in crusades), is as intense as religious conviction. Thus, technological determinism can be deconstructed. War is not new. Nor are its impulses and origins to be found in technology. Rather, it may be war that determines (at least hastens and/or hastens funding for) technological growth. In any case, the human desire to have a purpose, to be given a mission (preferably sacred and absolute in status so that there is no doubt), is the essential expression of will to will. It is a purified form of will. It is will awaiting content, and sometimes that content is simply a desire for more willpower, more conviction, more emotional commitment, and/or stronger identities and deeper meanings.

For instance, the computers used by many data entry people in the corporate sector constantly monitor their human users. They are programmed to periodically flash messages on their screens stating that the data entry person is moving too slowly. The computers tirelessly, relentlessly, and accurately count the keystrokes per minute and monitor their human appendage, evaluating the human against an ideal. This "quality control" process continually threatens the human with the label of inadequacy and is based on a grand absurdity. Progress presumes a goal. Relaxation can come with the achievement of the goal. But there is no final goal in the hypertrophic modern condition. Progress is never attained. Perpetual progress makes no sense, however, because without a goal that can be attained, progress is meaningless. Only under such absurd conditions can technological determinism make sense.

Standards are rising while records fall. Eventually, with the right biomedical training and chemistry, the logical conclusion of continuous improvements will be a winner of the 100-meter dash in the Olympics who finishes the race at the same instant it starts (or even *before* it starts). This tendency is what Gebser (1949 Ger./1985 Eng.) has correctly identified as the tragic effort of the modern individual to control time in the same way he or she has struggled to domesticate space by means of fragmentation. But the exact opposite is the case. The urgency about urgency, the anxiety about time, comes to dominate humanity. Fragmentation does not defeat time. It intensifies its dramatic effect. Time (the present) is the essence of life. Therefore, to defeat time (the present) in the name of efficiency is to defeat life, its spontaneity and creative powers, the tolerance of leisure from which emerges the most profound sources of reflection. The modern anxiety about time is, in the end, a self-contradictory obsession because if life is exciting only when it is in the throes of urgency, then it is devalued because urgency, by definition, cannot become chronic, and insofar as it does, it destroys life and any pleasure associated with it.

Humans are creating standards and scales that lack tolerance. The obsession with material and temporal efficiencies reduces resilience and tolerance (and opportunities for novelty). When no resources are kept in abeyance (e.g., "just in time" resource management), there is no room for error or for thinking in the face of unexpected events. If, for instance, the state of California maintains potable water reserves for its residents that will last only three days, then when an earthquake or other event disrupts that supply, there is no flexibility in whatever plans exist to secure that which is vital to life for its residents, thereby creating a dangerous situation for all involved.

Fragmentation (in the forms of operationalization, objectification, de-individuation, and faulty generalizations) is the essence of measurement. When tolerance decreases, fragmentation increases. For instance, when you have the 10 fastest humans on Earth running 100 meters against each other for only one gold medal, one cannot measure only at seconds, half-seconds, or even at tenths or hundredth of seconds. Instead, fragmentation must increase to measure time in thousandths of seconds, which is below the threshold of unaided human perception, thereby rendering the difference impractical and, in practical terms, meaningless. Such is the obsession of the modern. Only one winner exists and must be identified, even when determining a single winner requires Cyborg-level measurement skills.

Thus, a unilateral notion of determinism is inadequate; technology is developed to serve pre-existent and emergent demands while in turn driving changes in human efforts and notions of what is possible and desirable. Another problem with the dualistic cause-and-effect approach is that the approach cannot explain reciprocity in the system. Humans and technological artifacts co-exist and exert mutual influence over one another. To understand technology and the species that creates it, one must use a systems approach.

Finally, it may be most important to move beyond the notion that an individual human can and should be reduced to the behavior he or she exhibits. As one admissions officer at an elite university has complained, there is no joy in most applicants. They present their accomplishments—all their doing—but there is no being. The technique of doing can lead, hypertrophically, to the loss of the human being, but this danger is not attributable to technology alone. The danger is in the childlike attitude about what is valuable. In the hypertrophic late-modern milieu, only measurable production counts. Being is ridiculed or worse—ignored, not perceived at all—certainly not perceived as valuable. This is the source of the problem. It is cultural. The attempt to escape into technical systems is a consequence, a symptom of the disease. Optimistically, it can be stated that these escapist views are only symptomatic views and can be changed (although they must first be noticed and seen as dangerous or undesirable).

It is metaphysical bias to ask whether the chicken or the egg comes first (or whether technology drives our needs and desires or whether it is the other way around). Does technology determine our consciousness structure? Does it determine our reality, including our social relations? Or do our needs and wants determine what technology is developed? To ask these questions presents a false dichotomy. The relationship is neither unilateral nor one of cause and effect. Rather it is cybernetic and symbiotic. Worldview and technology are co-evolutionary. Each determines the other.

6

Mediated Empiricism (Electro-Egocentric Fallacy)

The More You Watch the Dumber You Get

During the last 50 years, and despite the explosion in new media technologies, the number of media owners has collapsed from about 50 to fewer than 10 today in the United States (Bagdikian 2004; Lutz, 2012; McChesney, 2013). Deregulation has changed the mediascape of the world, including in the United States. This too is part of the collapse in cultural diversity on the planet. Even within the United States, regional distinctions are vanishing. Out of concern that common ownership of media may stifle diversity of voices and viewpoints (not to mention aesthetics), the Federal Communications Commission (FCC) has historically placed limits on the degree of common ownership of local radio stations, as well as on cross-ownership among radio stations, television stations, and newspapers serving the same local area. According to a study done by the FCC looking at media ownership patterns from 1960, 1980, and 2000, "the count of owners was generally, relatively stagnant. This is mainly due to tremendous consolidation, especially in the radio industry, since passage of the 1996 Telecom Act" (Roberts, Frenette, & Sterns, 2002, p. 3). Another study done by the FCC looking specifically at radio station ownership found:

> The 1996 Telecommunications Act loosened local radio station ownership restrictions, to different degrees across markets of different sizes, and it lifted all limits on radio station ownership at the national level. Subsequent FCC rule changes permitted common ownership of television and radio stations in the same market and also permitted a certain

degree of cross-ownership between radio stations and newspapers. These changes have resulted in a wave of radio station mergers as well as a number of cross-media acquisitions, shifting control over programming content to fewer hands. For example, the number of radio stations owned or operated by Clear Channel Communications increased from about 196 stations in 1997 to 1,183 stations in 2005. (Chipty, 2007, p. 2)

Diversity of viewpoints has converged into basically two warring camps orchestrated by a media oligopoly that has become global in scope (Hess & Kalb, 2003; Kamalipour & Snow, 2004). Meanwhile, across industries, electronic networking has decimated the middle class by eliminating many once high-skilled and good-paying jobs (Lanier, 2013). This is also the case in the field of journalism.

The editorial workforce for daily newspapers in 1971 was estimated to be 38,000. The American Society of Newspaper Editors put total newspaper newsroom employment in 2010 at 41,600. This means that roughly the same number of journalists are working at newspapers today as in 1970, even though the population of the US has increased by more than 50 percent. The population in 1970 was 203,302,031, while the population in 2010 was 308,745,538. (Federal Communications Commission, 2013, p. 366)

The pattern of media ownership that has been the result of efforts to eliminate regulation is one of gigantism and national and international absentee ownership and control. This has led to less local accountability and control — exactly what many conservatives who champion deregulation also claim to be fighting against. Increasingly, in lieu of locally produced news, the content of cross-media ownership and chain-owned newspapers, radio stations, and television stations is shared across the nation. In 2011, the FCC published a major report on the state of media and community needs. Taking into account all the new media platforms and technology that have become available, the results do not show an increase in quality news production and availability. Rather the results are the opposite: a decrease in quality local news. In the executive report, the agency concluded:

In part *because of the digital revolution* serious problems have arisen, as well. Most significant among them: in many communities, we now face a shortage of local, professional, accountability reporting. This is likely to lead to the kinds of problems that are, not surprisingly, associated with a lack of accountability — more government waste, more local corruption, less effective schools, and other serious community problems. The independent watchdog function that the Founding Fathers envisioned for journalism—going so far as to call it crucial to a healthy democracy—is in some cases at risk at the local level. As technology offered consumers new choices, it upended traditional news industry business models, resulting in massive job losses—including roughly 13,400 newspaper newsroom positions in just the past four years. This has created gaps in coverage that even the fast-growing digital world has yet to fill. An abundance of media outlets does *not* translate into an abundance of reporting. In many communities, there are now more outlets, but less local accountability reporting. (Waldman & The Working Group on Information Needs of Communities, 2011, p. 5; italics added)

The conclusion drawn in the FCC study is summed up in three sentences:

1) While digital technology has empowered people in many ways, the concurrent decline in local reporting has, in other cases, shifted power away from citizens to government and other powerful institutions, which can more often set the news agenda. 2) Far from being nearly-extinct dinosaurs, the traditional media players—TV stations and newspapers—have emerged as the largest providers of local news online. 3) The nonprofit media sector has become far more varied, and important, than ever before. It now includes state public affairs networks, wikis, local news websites, organizations producing investigative reporting, and journalism schools as well as low-power FM stations, traditional public radio and TV, educational shows on satellite TV, and public access channels. Most of the players neither receive, nor seek, government funds. (Waldman & The Working Group on Information Needs of Communities, 2011, p. 6)

As globalization intensifies, foreign news correspondents have been laid off by the major media corporations in the interest of greater profits and the ability to simply "rip and read" from a common news feed. Science and environmental reporting has also been slashed. The Internet lacks rigorous self-regulation and professionalism, and "net neutrality" is disappearing, as the major media conglomerates are moving to reconfigure their contents and delivery into complex and variable rate structures, making entire sectors available only for a premium.

The one consistent source of expert science and environmental programming, nonprofit Public Broadcasting, has been under constant assault and threat of total defunding by conservatives. It is clear that conservative leaders do not want a true competitive environment including competing motives (profit vs. not for profit). Not surprisingly, private alternatives that initially held some promise have capitulated to a purely profit-driven motivation. For instance, the Science Channel and the History Channel now regularly program content about ghosts, UFOs, predictions from

Nostradamus, and reality shows about antique hunting, the antics of "mountain men," tracking people through the woods, "pumpkin chuckin," survivor man, "Counting Cars" (a show about buying and restoring cars), ice road truckers, the escapades of a family of Las Vegas pawn shop operators, men making a living traveling around to pick through old junk for resale on "American Pickers," men making a living out of finding meteorites in fields, "Swamp People," and "Mudcats."

What do we get on the 24/7 channel Animal Planet? Content such as "Call of the Wildman," the network's most popular show featuring a marginally literate fellow, "Turtleman" (and his sidekick who offers dramatic comments about the precarious state of the Turtleman's safety), who grabs "nuisance animals" with his bare hands and yells "yel, yel, yel, yel." Turtleman, ironically, lives in a house with no television (or telephone), or so we are told. Other content on Animal Planet includes "Ice Gold," which features the personal conflicts of people who do gold prospecting; fake documentaries about the existence of mermaids; competition among taxidermists for the most bizarre creations they can come up with by combining parts from different species; people catching catfish by hand (noodlers) on "Catfishin Kings" and "Hillbilly Hanfishin"; two men grabbing alligators with their bare hands on "Gator Boys"; amateur hikers searching for Bigfoot on "Finding Bigfoot"; dramatized depictions of parasites in "Monsters Inside Me"; and men and women competing in a game show format while wearing bikinis and such, capturing fish in their mouths, with bows and arrows, netting them from cages while flying over the water on a cable, and whatever on "Top Hooker"; prison parolees caring for pit bulls; men indiscriminately killing snakes on "Rattlesnake Republic"; and so forth. While millions of us are enjoying feeling superior watching stereotypes of "hillbillies" and "rednecks," we are the ones getting dumber.

The irony is that the more you watch and the more you listen to increasingly centrally formatted, banal TV content and overtly biased reporting via repeater radio "stations," the less diversity you get and also the dumber you get (Bauerlein, 2009; Postman, 1984/2005; Steinberg, Kincheloe, & McLaren, 2006). This is what Bagdikian (2004) meant when he called the media oligopoly a "private ministry of information and culture" (p. 3). As the *Columbia Journalism Review* said after carefully studying a major metropolitan newspaper in a conservative state, something the *CJR* previously thought impossible, the more you read it the dumber you get: "*The Daily Oklahoman* has become a newspaper in reverse, sucking intelligence from its readers" (Fry, 2012).

At the same time, education funding is being reduced while Internet and video gaming addiction is compounding the problem (Carr, 2011; Jackson, 2008; Kozol, 2006; Macedo, 2006; Postman, 1996; Roberts, 2010; Weinberger, 2008; Wong, 1999). The corporate model being applied to education along with the "commercialization" of education is leading to bloated administrations and management salaries, larger class sizes, demoralized teachers, angry parents, and the transformation of students' identities into that of customers demanding satisfaction even when they refuse to put effort into the process. This is changing our culture and what is deemed important to teach and learn: difficult content and critical thinking skills versus how-to job skills (which are not always the same but often conflictive) (Molnar, 2005).

So what has the Turtleman taught us about turtles? What has he not told us millions who pay cable bills to watch him grab terrified animals for our entertainment? All the grand technology from computer video editing to our investments in flat screen TVs and satellite distribution has told us practically nothing. For instance, turtles are in big trouble (Kiester & Olson, 2011). In the race to extinction among all large groups of common animals, turtles hold the lead with between 47.6% and 57% (depending on one's methodology) of the 320 currently recognized turtle species identified as "threatened" with extinction (Hoffmann et al., 2010). According to Hoffmann et al. (2010), this exceeds global threat estimates for amphibians (41%), mammals (25%), bony fishes (15%), and birds (13%). The level of threat to turtles is matched only by our cousins, other primates, with nearly half (48%) threatened. If one includes "modern" turtles and tortoises that have occurred in the last 400 years, then half are threatened or already extinct (Kiester & Olson, 2011). "By any of these approaches, turtles are in dire straits" (Kiester & Olson, 2011, p. 198).

Thanks to China's currency becoming easier to convert in the 1990s, demand for turtles for food and medicine has "skyrocketed" (Klemens, 2000). The result, according to herpetologists Swingland and Klemens (1989), is that chelonians, as land turtle and tortoises as a group are known, have become "one of the vertebrate groups with the highest proportion of endangered species" (p. 5). According to Yoon (1999),

> Collectors have made such a clean sweep of turtles in countries like Vietnam and Laos that it can be impossible to find a single turtle even in ideal habitats in national parks and remote preserves. In the regions of Southeast Asia where turtles do persist, biologists say, they are fast disappearing to satisfy the huge, some say infinite, demand for turtles in China. Scientists have been reduced to looking for turtles in China's markets as an entire fauna is being bought, sold and eaten into oblivion. (p. 1)

This includes endangered species whose trade has already been made illegal by the Convention on International Trade in Endangered Species. What we are seeing is nothing less than a crash in turtle populations. As recently as the 1980s, turtles were common around cities like Hanoi. In 1996, Dr. Ross Kiester of UC Berkeley and the Federal Forest Service in Corvallis, Oregon, spent an entire month searching Vietnam's national parks and remote areas, but he and his research team found only two individual turtles in the field. The same utter decimation is true in Laos, Cambodia, and Thailand (Stuart & Platt, 2004).

> Studies of actual export numbers corroborate the anecdotal evidence for large-scale exportation of these turtles. According to reports from Traffic, a wildlife trade monitoring program, more than 240 tons of turtles, representing more than 200,000 individual turtles, were leaving Vietnam each year for sale in China in 1994. By 1996, two to four tons of turtles were being exported each day from Phnom Penh in Cambodia. As a result, the easiest place to find these turtles today is in China's markets. In July 1997, Dr. William McCord, a veterinarian from Hopewell Junction, N.Y., who does research on turtles, made a video-tape recording of an estimated 10,000 turtles for sale during a visit to a wildlife market in the southern Chinese city of Guangzhou. Nearly all the species were from outside China. (Yoon, 1999, p. 1)

So herpetologists have abandoned field research in favor of going to Chinese markets to discover turtles. McCord has discovered more than a dozen species unknown to science in Chinese markets (McCord & Iverson, 1991). The fact is that many species of turtles are being eaten into extinction before scientists ever see them (Engstrom, Shaffer, & McCord, 2002). Why? For narcissistic reasons. For a tasty dish, to impress one's dinner guests, and to live longer and have better sex. For instance, in China, the three-striped box turtle (*Cuora trifasciata*) from Vietnam is believed to cure cancer. The price of turtles makes them "a status symbol" (Platt quoted in Yoon, 1999, p. 1).

So what? How can we expect the Animal Channel, an American network, to know about the plight of turtles or the Turtleman to be in any meaningful way informative? Well, the fact is that Chinese demand for turtles has been impacting the Turtleman's turf. There is no legal protection for the capture and export of U.S. turtles unless they are listed on the Endangered Species Act list. According to Traffic's North American office, "By 1995, the United States was shipping out more than 84,000 map turtles, 23,000 snapping turtles and 38,000 softshell turtles each year—increases of fivefold to fortyfold since 1990" (Yoon, 1999). Since 1990, the unregulated harvest of wild North American turtles for export has continued to mushroom. Thanks to the technologically advanced logistical networks in the United States, shipping turtles to China is easier than shipping from Africa or Latin America. "Dallas-Fort Worth Airport is a major regional shipping point for turtles collected in the wild and harvested on turtle farms in Oklahoma and Louisiana" (Hylton, 2007). The United States has become an ever-larger source of wild turtles because, according to Peter Paul van Dijk, director of the tortoise and freshwater turtle biodiversity program at Virginia-based Conservation International (CI), "We have seen the Chinese trade vacuum out one region after another—Burma, Vietnam, Borneo, Java, then Sumatra . . . 75% of Asia's 90 species of tortoise and freshwater turtles now are threatened" (quoted by Hylton, 2007, p. 1). Numbers of wild turtles, especially large old specimens that are highly prized in China, have crashed. Most U.S. states have finally started to regulate the harvesting of wild turtles, but some profiteers still resist all regulation such as "Bayou Bob" Popplewell, owner of Brazos River Rattlesnake Ranch near Dallas and founder of U.S. Turtle and Aquatic Resource Technologies (USTART), which is a cooperative with hundreds of members who collect and sell turtles to Asia (Hylton, 2007).

In essence, vast and powerful technological infrastructures including massive jets have "globalized wildlife," according to Matt Wagner, Head of the Wildlife Diversity Program at the Texas Department of Parks and Wildlife (Wagner quoted by Hylton, 2007). Perhaps the Turtleman knew this all along and has been harvesting and selling wild turtles in the United States all his life. Perhaps that is how he got his start? In any case, turtles, that ancient species which always counted on its hard shell to be enough to ensure its survival, has more than met its match.

The narcissism of people who do not want to study or read about their own environment is suicidal (Stout, 2001; Sykes, 1996). Be it the "gentle loser" who spends copious amounts of time watching TV through a marijuana-induced haze or the uninformed yet highly opinionated follower of "wingnut" talk radio pundits who make her feel good by ranting away hour after hour repeating her own biases for her to hear, we are not willing to put in the hard work required to responsibly engage in current events (Abbot, 2010; Drew, Lyons & Svehla, 2010; Pozner, 2010; Zengotita, 2006). And this is not a problem limited to greedy conservatives. It includes underclass people who end up the recipients of bounteous government funding, but as incarcerated individuals instead of students in our universities (Malone, 2011).

The excuse of being "disenfranchised" can no longer be validated. To paraphrase Jean-Paul Sartre (1943 Fr./1984 Eng.), freedom is what we do with what has been done to us. Our past is not a prison. Pride in accomplishment means that we can see that we have surpassed our own origins. In short, some are born to more privilege than others, but we cannot surrender our freedom because of this fact. Nor is the issue simply failing administrative institutions, for the one variable that is repeatedly demonstrated to be the best predictor of success in school is "family educational culture" (Kramer, 1997, 2013; Pearlstein, 2011). Millions who grew up poor and uneducated during the Great Depression were smart enough to insist that their children work hard and study. The problem of apathy and selfishness also includes millions of liberal leaning or apolitical individuals who are apathetic and selfish. Some may be disenfranchised dropouts and others drifting along as marginally literate subsistence-level working class who spend much of their free time intoxicated (Bireda, 2011). The point is that it is us, we, the guy next door, the guy in the mirror. We are all in this together, and we are not managing things well.

And then there is the narcissism of those who believe that simply because they have been financially successful at ventures such as promoting anabolic steroid juiced fake wrestlers or selling fast food that they are therefore qualified to be a U.S. senator (or vice president or even president) with power over environmental policy (Hofstadter, 1996; Jacoby, 2009). The irrationality and banality of evil enabling so much destruction in the United States and abroad is demonstrable and incalculably disastrous. We need some adults in the room.

PART II

GIVING UP ON LIFE TO LIVE FOREVER
THE DEATH-DEFYING DELUSION
OF TECHNOTOPIA

This book focuses on the setting (conditions) of communication. Changes in communication technology usher in transformations of time and space consciousness; as a consequence, alterations in the communication process (semiosis) occur. Similar to many critical communication theorists, especially Habermas (1995), the primary consideration of this book is how the technicization of the lifeworld results in the colonization or mechanization of Others in our environment (both human and nonhuman entities) and how we perceive and communicate with them. In this sense, the present study lies in the realm of critical communication approaches.

Rather than the passé Marxist, structuralist, or post-structuralist perspectives, this investigation is based on a phenomenological perspective. It offers a critical assessment of the modern technological drive as it imposes transformations on the communication process in a unilinear and uniform way. The unilinear way of communication and semiosis results in a crisis of communication as merely a transmission of object-information. Therefore, as a critique of this dangerous tendency in the communication field, this study can be regarded as a necessary investigation for all forms of communication.

Hence, this study has three specific purposes. First, it seeks to provide a critique of Cartesian dualism (subjectivism or objectivism) as an inadequate, unsustainable foundation for continued life on Earth and for meaningful communication study. Second, it outlines the dangerous situation that exists within the modern technological milieu through examining the process of technicization of the *lebenswelt* (lifeworld). Third, it investigates changes in

the modes of communication (semiosis), which occur as a result of technological change.

Chapter 7 sets the stage for Part II. It argues that the transhumanist's
dream of a future where the human body, indeed all natural bodies are for-
feited for cyborg existence is a proposal to operationalize Hegel's version of
arch-positivism as Absolute idealism. Ray Kurzweil (2005, 2013), a major
spokesperson for the transhumanist movement, defines the notion of singularity to mean, in classic positivistic fashion, that there is one reality and one
logic, one best way to do everything. For Kurzweil, technology is not the
problem but the ultimate solution to the meaning of life. He argues that by
eliminating life as we know it we have solved all of life's problems. Why?
Because life is nothing but a hindrance to our self-realization, especially
death. If we are cyborgs, we cannot die because we are not alive. To eliminate the dialectical conflict between life and death, Kurzweil proposes that
we become cyborgs. Kurzweil unknowingly embraces Kierkegaard's critique of Hegel's Absolute virtual system that is uninhabitable by humans or,
we add, anything else. What Kierkegaard and many others see as an insane
"solution" to dialectical conflict, in this case between nature and culture as
the utopian ideology of technicization, is the willful rejection of our physical selves. Kurzweil sees this as the ultimate good because such a solution
would eliminate once and for all the limitations in life that hinder our desire
to realize our self-interest. The solution to problems in life is to eliminate
life. This is positivism taken to its logical and horrific conclusion—pure narcissism. And it is suicidal. According to Kurzweil, utopia and the way to
save ourselves is to eliminate our own bodily existence and become pure
information. Kurzweil's thesis might not be worthy of reflection, but in fact
many agree with him and have made him a mainstay in the literature concerning technology.

Chapter 8 outlines and explores the limitations of the traditional notion
of technology as a material dialectic between human and nature.

Chapter 9 describes the theoretical background for this study, including
exegeses of the work of Merleau-Ponty and Gebser. The goal of Chapter 9
is to offer solid philosophical argument in order to criticize, deconstruct,
evaluate, and analyze the Cartesian subject-biased tradition as a whole and,
more specifically, to criticize the mechanization of communication in the
modern technological milieu. This chapter lays the groundwork for criticizing the materialization or mechanization of the *lebenswelt* in Chapters 10
and 11.

Chapter 10 provides a review of the literature relevant to the critical
analysis. Critiques of Cartesian dualism are presented, including those of
Husserl, Merleau-Ponty, and Gebser.

Chapter 11 consists of various explanations of the nature and tendencies of modern technology. It then explores the relationships between the

basic mathematical theory of communication (widely accepted today) and technology.

Chapter 12 presents methodological reviews consisting of two theoretical approaches: Peirce's semiotics and Kramer's theory of dimensional accrual/dissociation. Charles S. Peirce's approach to semiotics offers a valuable means for explaining the changes in the semiosis of signs within the modern technological context. Peircean semiosis is a method that does not fall prey to the Cartesian subjective bias, and, therefore, it is used herein to demonstrate the absurdity of that bias and metaphysic. To complete the methodological approach, Kramer's theory of dimension accrual/dissociation and Gebser's framing of comparative consciousness structures are utilized within the context provided by Peircean semiotics.

Chapter 13 investigates the different aspects of technology based on a Gebserian interpretation and by applying Merleau-Ponty's notion of the lived body. This chapter unfolds the relationships among the objectivistic-biased paradigm and technological utopia, technology and perception, and embodiment and technology.

Chapter 14 explores the concepts of visiocentrism and overdetermination in relation to the implications of technologized communication.

Chapter 15 presents an attempt to locate the placement of humanity within a technologized society.

Chapter 16 is a final summarization and conclusion of our work, including an outline of its implications and some suggested directions for future research endeavors.

7

Hegel's Twisted Dream

Pure Disembodied Consciousness

In the introductory chapter, we outline some of the claims made by the positivists concerning technological development and offer some preliminary critiques of this value-laden view, for after all, from its inception with Claude Saint-Simon and August Comte, "positivism" is blatantly a value position just like negativism. One claims the happy state of absolute certainty and progress whereas the other claims absolute uncertainty and dystopian futures. We are neither. Rather we are aware of both polar positions, and we propose in this book to logically examine the implications of the massive technological complexes now unfolding.

The goals of this chapter are multiple. First, in order to fully appreciate the critique of technology offered in the upcoming chapters, it is necessary for the reader to have a basic understanding of the viewpoint being advanced by those who view technology from a utopian (purely ideological, positivistic) perspective. Second, this chapter offers a preliminary critique of the positivistic, utopian view of technology that both enhances and is enhanced by the in-depth critiques contained in the rest of this book. Finally, this chapter outlines some of the negative potential implications of the continued convergence, even equation of humans, society, and culture with technology that will serve as points for reflection as the reader proceeds through the text.

CYBORG EXISTENCE AND TOTAL DISSOCIATION

Much of the positivistic utopian view of technology is found in Ray Kurzweil's (2005) book, *The Singularity is Near: When Humans Transcend Biology.* In this book, Kurzweil provides an extensive "map" of a proposed positivist, technological, utopian society. Kurzweil (2005) refers to this utopian state as "the Singularity," which he defines as "a future period during which the pace of technological change will be so rapid, its impact so deep, that human life will be irreversibly transformed" (p. 7). Kurzweil follows up this preliminary definition by providing a description of the Singularity:

> The Singularity will allow us to transcend these limitations of our biological bodies and brains. We will gain power over our fates. Our mortality will be in our own hands. We will be able to live as long as we want. . . . We will fully understand human thinking and will vastly extend and expand its reach. By the end of this century, the nonbiological portion of our intelligence will be trillions of trillions of times more powerful than unaided human intelligence. . . . The Singularity will represent the culmination of the merger of our biological thinking and existence with our technology, resulting in a world that is still human but that transcends our biological roots. There will be no distinction, post-Singularity, between human and machine or between physical and virtual reality. If you wonder what will remain unequivocally human in such a world, it's simply this quality: ours is the species that inherently seeks to extend its physical and mental reach beyond current limitations. (2005, p. 9)

Nothing more ego-centrically and hypertrophically perspectival, nothing more primitively positivistic can be imagined than intolerant and exclusive "singularity." Imbedded within his arguments about the Singularity, and largely comprising them, is the concept of the Cyborg. Kurzweil (2005) defines the Cyborg as follows:

> The human body version 2.0 scenario represents the continuation of a long-standing trend in which we grow more intimate with our technology. Computers started out as large, remote machines in air-conditioned rooms tended by white-coated technicians. They moved onto our desks, then under our arms, and now into our pockets. Soon, we'll routinely put them inside our bodies and brains. By the 2030s we will become more nonbiological than biological . . . by the 2040s nonbiological intelligence will be billions of times more capable than our biological intelligence. (p. 309)

It is our argument that Kurzweil's utopian view of the Singularity/Cyborg is ultimately neither realistic nor desirable. Kurzweil's vision (and, by extension, the general positivistic view of technology) constitutes a dangerous trend even while suggesting that the trend is fatalistic (in the sense of being unavoidable). Clearly in his moralizing sales job, Kurzweil immediately falls victim to a grand contradiction. If the approaching singularity of cyborg utopia is inevitable, then it makes no sense to proclaim free will and "power over our fates." If that power can only be realized through technology, then we are predetermined. Legitimation for the existence of technology and technological growth is tautological—self-justifying. In this sense, it is simply a material manifestation of one-dimensional magic self-identity. Nothing more fatalistic and irrational can be imagined.

In short, Kurzweil argues that to be free, we *must* develop cybornetic technology, which will then set us free. Only if we become cyborgs will we be free. There is no other way. There is only one path of evolution, and it is pre-established and must be manufactured. This is merely more dependence on technology sold to us as the path to utopia. It is human will caught in the tightest hairpin twist of feedback and control applied to ourselves (Kramer, 1997). It is the total obsessive and compulsive drive for control of everything including the self. But when everything becomes predictable because it is manufactured, this redundancy will lead to a meaningless existence.

So what is the grand motive behind this insatiable drive to survive forever and without limits? The great scholar Ernst Becker (1973, 1997) has a suggestion. It is the desire to deny death. The more we dwell on the subject of death and dying, the more we frantically seek to escape and defeat it, and typically such frantic efforts take the form of violence; violence against others whose beliefs and immortality myths may threaten our own or, in this case, violence against nature—the insatiable effort to conquer what may well be the most natural of all biotic events, death. We are now turning against our own biological selves, defining them as inadequate and obsolete vis-à-vis our utopian goals. The goal is hypertrophic narcissism taken to an infinite level, where the self need never be burdened with slow thinking or doubt and never be threatened with being extinguished. But this is the ultimate dualistic opposition between nature and technology. Naturally, all things from animals and plants to stars and galaxies, indeed the entire universe, seem to have a linear life span, which includes intensification followed by a diminishing, interpreted by utopian positivists as "bad decline," and a final extinction. The positivistic and insane fear of the inevitable is tied to the human problem of time and the human ability to forecast and foresee one's own death. Kurzweil and many others discussed below, including several entire industries, are proposing a materialistic religion, a materialistic solution to nature perceived as a gigantic problem, for nothing is more natural than decline and death.

This fear of death is captured by the philosophically immature conclusion that if all that I as an individual or we as a species have accomplished will one day be lost and forgotten, then there is no point to anything. It is a materialistic philosophy that presumes product over process, static object over life, structure over systasis. The immature ego needs an audience, a viewing, and a permanent memorial. The goal is to live forever or be damned. Yet a more sophisticated philosophical tradition offers itself to us for contemplating our situation. For even if medical science can make me impervious to aging and disease, still, and even more so, the contemplation of my own demise remains because if I were destined to live a thousand years and fell off a bridge and was smashed beyond repair, the loss seems even more egregious and unpredicted than if I only expected to live 75 years anyway.

Presumed in much of this modernist thinking is a reduction of all things to accumulation and quantification, ideologies that are neither universally held nor without limitations especially when one wishes to contemplate the quality of life and things.

In short, the promise of immortality through technology is a false one. It is an expression of despair and anxiety and a desire for power and control. The greater the anxiety, the more we are motivated to try to build technologies that will avert pain and death in an escalating trend Kirby Farrell (2011) calls "survival greed." Modernity strives to extend life, including a modernist way of interpreting life and living, and eliminate suffering by conceiving of, manufacturing, and deploying technological systems. Technology is modernity's answer to the violent forced construction of the pyramids and the grand cathedrals. The Saturn V rocket is modernity's cathedral, an integral part of the great struggle between the "Eastern" Soviet system and the "Western" alliance. The demise of such systems is seen as apocalyptic. Once hooked, one cannot live without the cell phone, for instance. Once dead, my Facebook identity will live on, extending my self as a machine ghost. Technology is just the modernistic, materialistic way of attempting to achieve immortality of the ego, and Kurzweil's choice of the word *singularity* to describe the material fusion of self and the machine complex to achieve this goal perfectly captures the egocentrism this ambition manifestly articulates.

While Kurzweil may believe that technology will set us free from time and the fates, we argue that it actually forms dependencies on society-wide scales—what James Burke (2007) calls the "technology trap." It is also an expression of the age-old struggle for dominance. For example, the modern world would utterly collapse without massive electrical grids and networks of fossil fuel production and distribution right down to the light switch on your wall and the gas station on your corner. Technophilical zeal, such as expressed by Kurzweil's notion of freedom and the promise of technology, is absurd.

To maintain such techno-industrial complexes takes resources and energy, and many writers, including Michael Klare (2001, 2012) and Geoff Hiscock (2012), have observed the rise of perpetual violence of the most dangerous sort in the form of "serial resource wars." Erik Assadourian (2013) of the Worldwatch Institute simply asks, "Is sustainability still possible?" Irony of ironies, organized murder on massive scales is justified by our attempt to avert death and suffering by maintaining our technological complexes (Lifton, 1999). Increasingly, as we have turned agriculture into massive agrabusiness with heavy use of petro-chemicals and water, and we have damned up all the great rivers for hydroelectric power, the fight is over not just local but the global fresh water supply (Pearce, 2007, 2012; Prud'homme, 2011; Solomon, 2011). In short, technology harkens back to the first efforts in magical systems to escape from nature by harnessing it, to control things such as fertility, disease, weather, and ultimately death.

This issue is made possible by a linear teleological mode of thinking that demands an eternal final score; an unbreakable eternal record of accumulated accomplishment, typically canonized in the notion of a record-keeping, bureaucratic god such as Yahiah, or Thoth, Osiris, Anubis, and Seshat; and evaluative power that is reflected in the imperial powers that invented such gods. The bankbook is a perfect example. The record-keeping god measures the good and bad in all things, including behavior and thoughts, and records the deeds and judgment permanently on a balance sheet. Accomplishment, or the lack thereof, thus becomes our most fundamental aspect of being and identity. Individuals are reduced to nothing but their net worth and resumes. If my father left me no measurable, exchangeable, liquid assets, he left me nothing at all. The self is reduced to a tool of production of other, valuable, things.

The problem of this existential crisis is that it fails to see the value and meaning of being here now or of life-time (living) and being for its own sake. The failure to appreciate what we have leads to a berserk sort of obsession with technology and power, making life miserable because it is spent fearing vulnerability and death or, as mass consumption and mass advertising exploits, the fear of not being loved. The most egoistic cultures where people are most individualistic and most vulnerable to rejection from group membership are the ones most susceptible to this fear, and, as one could surmise, these cultures have spent the greatest resources to develop dissociating technological systems. For instance, combating social disintegration and loneliness is the mother of massive telecommunications systems to help us "keep in touch." So I utterly ignore the person sitting next to me while I text a message to someone not here and not now.

Kurzweil (2005) does not suggest that we have much choice in the move toward a Cyborg-based future society, an ideology with embedded values, motives, and expectations (especially the concept that bigger is better and the notion that any/all technology is progress). Just as a computer (an individual machine) is not the same thing as computerization (a society or system based on computers), so too the Cyborg per se is not the same as Cyborg-ization. The critique offered in this chapter illuminates disturbing and complex issues surrounding the intimate merging of human beings with technology, addressing issues that the technological positivists do not.

One of the theses posited by Kurzweil in the prior quotation highlights the importance of critiquing technological utopianism at this particular point in time. There is evidence that humanity is currently approaching what is commonly referred to as an "event horizon" (Kurzweil, 2005, p. 23) or a point of no return regarding the inertia of Cyborgization. Once this event horizon is crossed, it will likely be accompanied by unexpected consequences and unforeseeable circumstances, and it is certain to represent the coming of a new age from which there can be no easy return. Thus, our critique of technological positivism gains importance; the time to analyze the possibilities (both positive and negative) contained in the post-horizon future, if we wish to approach that horizon as a matter of choice (as opposed to accidentally "stumbling over" it), is before that threshold is crossed. We are, however, quickly approaching a point in time at which critical reflection concerning our convergence with technology may be a case of "too little, too late."

Kurzweil's Perspective Concerning the Cyborg

Kurzweil's view of the Cyborg posits that intimately combining human beings with computer-based technology is a desired future phenomenon that will make up for the shortcomings and frailties of, in our case, biology. It is interesting to note (as it is directly related to the critiques to follow in later chapters) that the term *Singularitarian* (coined by Kurzweil, 2005) is a combination of philosophy, observations on the progress of technology, and religious faith. Kurzweil (2005) states:

> A Singularitarian is someone who understands the Singularity and has reflected on its meaning for his or her life. . . . George Gilder has described my scientific and philosophical views as a substitute vision for those who have lost faith in the traditional object of religious belief. Gilder's statement is understandable, as there are at least apparent similarities between anticipation of the Singularity and anticipation of the transformations articulated by traditional religions. . . . Over time this modeling of technology took on a life of its own and led me to formulate a theory of technology evolution. (p. 370)

Kurzweil sees Cyborgization as salvific. Given Kurzweil's quasi-religious, scientific, and philosophical views concerning technology, it is hardly surprising that he sees the blending of human with computer as a positive development. Throughout his book, he speaks of three distinct areas of promises of the Singularity/Cyborg: promises for individuals, promises for humanity/society, and promises for the planet/universe. A brief explanation of these promises is offered here in order to provide background and structure for the critique presented in subsequent chapters.

Ten Promises of Cyborgism for Individuals

Kurzweil (2005) presents numerous promises for improvement that the Cyborg will bring to individual human beings during the Singularity. These promises are central to the positivistic thesis of a technologically created utopian future state. Here we will simply examine Kurzweil's top 10 promises, representing the most interesting and ambitious of the promises for individuals living in the Singularity.

The first two major promises that technological positivists argue will be brought to individuals as a result of the Cyborg are, first, the end of biological diseases and, second, an eventual ability to reverse, eliminate, and/or control the pace of aging (Kurzweil, 2005). Nanotechnologies currently under development will allow for the insertion of nanobots into the body in order to combat diseases (e.g., replacing the functions of our white blood cells in a more efficient immune system) and eventually serve as an age-reversal system. These promises lead directly into the third promise of the Cyborg—the ability to live indefinitely (Kurzweil, 2005). It is easy to assume that a claim of immortality is thus implied, as it is improbable that a perpetually young, disease-free being would choose to die.

Of course, a growing population of immortal beings would place quite a demand on the food supply; fortunately, the technological-positivist view promises to alleviate the problem of hunger as well. The fourth major promise is that the technological future will bring us the ability to internally create our own nutrients, eliminating our need to eat (Kurzweil, 2005). This will also be accomplished through the technology of nanobots, placed in the individual to monitor nutrition needs and create/deliver needed nutrients accordingly.

The fifth major promise of the Cyborg is the ability to program our blood to move itself (Kurzweil, 2005). Combined with the ability of the nanobots to create and supply oxygen for the blood, this will eliminate our need for a heart, lungs, and many other internal organs, thereby eliminating more of the frailties in our biological selves.

The sixth major promise of Cyborgism is greatly improved physical strength (Kurzweil, 2005). Through a combination of nanobot technology and the replacement of skeletal bones with alloys like graphite, individual physical strength and endurance will be greatly enhanced. This leads into the seventh major promise, the ability to change our physical appearance at will (Kurzweil, 2005). While initially this ability will be limited to virtual experiences (like the ability to change the appearance of characters being played in a contemporary video game), eventually we will be able to affect literal physical changes in our appearance by a simple act of will.

The Cyborg will also bring a new level of communication ability. The eighth major promise is the ability to receive direct audio communication inside our heads and be able to enter "fun-immersion virtual reality" (Kurzweil, 2005). This will include the ability to travel anywhere instantaneously in a virtual (but absolutely realistic) environment, become anyone in that environment (referring through implication to the seventh promise), and manipulate the environment as we choose (creating a virtual scene in which future technological capabilities will eventually allow changes to be enacted in literal reality). Additionally, we will be able to receive communication from others via direct input into our brains and listen to music and other audio without hearing it through our ears.

The ninth major promise is that we will be able to experience someone (or something) else's experience directly (Kurzweil, 2005) by "plugging in" to his/her/its consciousness. Finally, the tenth major promise of Cyborgism to individuals is that we will be able to download knowledge directly into our brains (Kurzweil, 2005) through direct access to the Internet—or a future virtual knowledge database very much like it.

Kurzweil's vision for the Cyborg future indeed holds promise for the individual, apparently at little or no cost to that individual. These promises to individuals made by the Cyborgism ideology are not the limits of Kurzweil' s techno-utopian vision. In the next section, attention will be given to the promises that Kurzweil argues Cyborgism will bring for humanity and society as a whole.

Ten Promises From the Cyborg to Benefit Humanity and Society, Two Cyborg Promises for the Future of the Planet and Universe

The technologically based utopian vision includes plethoric promises for society resulting from the crossing of the Cyborg event horizon. In this section, we limit the discussion to the most important ones for the purposes of the current critique. Six of the 10 promises that Kurzweil sees in the Cyborg for humanity have to do (ironically) with increased capabilities in warfare. The seventh promise is tied into the tenth promise of the Cyborg for individuals (direct and immediate [real-time] access to knowledge); the eighth and ninth promises involve socioeconomic factors. The tenth major promise is tied into the fourth promise for individuals previously discussed (the end of hunger and/or the need for agriculture). The two promises for the planet and ultimately the universe complete this presentation of the utopian view of the Cyborg ideology.

The first major military-related promise of the Cyborg is the promise of fewer casualties of war (Kurzweil, 2005), to be brought about by the deployment of robotic forces, increased communication efficiency to control battleground conditions and deployments, and increased intelligence-gathering capabilities. It is worth noting that this promise focuses on limiting negative outcomes from warfare rather than addressing the more favorable goal of eliminating the need for warfare, a focus we find to be indicative of the generally dismissive view of the "hard sciences" (i.e., biology, computer sciences, etc.) toward the "soft" sciences (i.e., social sciences). The second major promise is for combined human and robotic war forces (Kurzweil, 2005), a trend we are already seeing in current warfare to an increasing extent (i.e., the use of unmanned surveillance and attack aircraft utilized in recent actions against terrorist cells by U.S. military forces). The third promise from the Cyborg is faster troop deployment through reducing the weight of soldier's equipment, which will be altered by the incorporation of nanobot technology into weapons and uniforms (Kurzweil, 2005).

The fourth military promise is the use of robots for the actual conduct of warfare, eliminating the need for human or Cyborg troops on the battlefield (Kurzweil, 2005). The fifth promise lies in the ability to increase surveillance capability through the use of "'smart dust" (sensor systems the size of a pinhead) that can provide surveillance on battlegrounds and in enemy fortifications (Kurzweil, 2005). The fifth promise of the Cyborg is for increased use of nanoweapons, smart weapons, and virtual reality warfare (Kurzweil, 2005), which will allow for increased distance between individuals and the battlefield. Taken together, these promises indicate that increasingly warfare will be conducted robotically and from a greater distance, making war a virtual experience for the Cyborg soldier.

The seventh promise for society (and one that holds vast implications for both social and academic structures) is the end of centralized education systems (Kurzweil, 2005). With the ability to download information (the Cyborg substitution for acquiring knowledge) directly into the Cyborg brain, schools will be obsolete. There will be no perceived need for buildings, classrooms (even virtual ones), mentoring, or instructors; information will be available to all members of the Cyborg community via download.

The use of "knowledge" (in the case of the Cyborg, read "information") will also be greatly changed in this technological future, as there will no longer be a need for work—the eighth promise of Cyborgism (Kurzweil, 2005). With non-biological systems providing for basic individual needs (such as food), the Cyborg will be free to explore leisure endlessly (probably in virtual realities). This leads to the ninth promise from the Cyborg for society—endless play (Kurzweil, 2005). Life will become leisure, and leisure will be sought in virtual realities while technology takes care of the upkeep of the "real world." With the promise of full-immersion virtual reality that can be altered according to the whims of the individual, Cyborgs will be free to indulge in fantasies that are at least as real (in terms of the Cyborg's perception) as reality itself. Others encountered can be either of the Cyborgs' own creation or perhaps altered forms of other real or virtually real Cyborgs and/or things, which to the Cyborg represent a distinction without a true difference.

Finally, the Cyborg promises a new socioeconomic status: endless free resources, including food (Kurzweil, 2005). The only valuable commodity in the Singularity is information (which is also free), so the entire socioeconomic structure of society will be based on unlimited resources and wealth. There will be no need for monetary systems, as there will be nothing that cannot be freely created either virtually or in reality by the Cyborg (or its/his/her robotic assistants). There will be no such thing as rich or poor, except as is measured by the extent to which one is Cyborg.

Having solved the problems of humanity, the vision of the future posited by technological positivists next turns to the problems of the planet and universe. The first promise of crossing the Cyborg event horizon in this regard is the ability to alter reality (in this case, the physical environment) to our will (Kurzweil, 2005). Kurzweil provides the following description of "foglets" as evidence for this impending ability of the Cyborg:

> J. Storrs Hall has described nanobot designs he calls "foglets" that are able to link together to form a great variety of structures and that can quickly change their structural organization. They're called "foglets" because if there's a sufficient density of them in an area, they can control sound and light to form variable sounds and images. They are essentially creating virtual environments externally (that is, in the physical world) rather than internally (in the nervous system). Using them a person can modify his body or his environment. (p. 310)

The second promise is that the Cyborg will be able to make the planet, the solar system, and eventually the universe "intelligent" [read computational] and cause matter itself to "wake up" (Kurzweil, 2005, p. 21). Kurzweil goes to great lengths to explain that all matter has computational ability. In this particular aspect of the technologically utopian vision, the ultimate destiny and purpose of humanity is two-fold: First, we are here to create the technology that will allow us to become Cyborgs; second, we are to use our Cyborg selves to bring intelligence to the universe. According to Kurzweil (2005), that is why the universe exists and why we were placed here to begin with—so that we can help the universe "wake up."

This view of our purpose in the universe represents a form of Hegelianism with a physical twist. Instead of the Absolute placing humans, specifically Germans, in the world to think about Pure Logic (and therefore for the Absolute to think itself and achieve reflective self-actualization, thereby bringing an end to time itself) as proposed by Hegel (Hegel, 1812, 1813, 1816 Ger./1969 Eng.), in the techno-utopian view, Pure Logic has placed in us the ability to create technologies that eventually allow us to dissociate from our bodies and become Cyborgs, which in turn will serve to spread intelligent self-awareness and self-actualization to the physical "dead matter" of the universe.

Preliminary Critical Comments on Kurzweil's Vision

Having laid out the positivist vision of the future that is posited as resulting from the crossing of the Cyborg event horizon (as this vision is described by Kurzweil), it is helpful before launching into the theoretical critique to make a few critical comments about the overall framework from which Kurzweil is working. First, Kurzweil (2005) argues that an exponential growth of technology and an impending explosion of technology is going to occur imminently (an exponential growth of the already exponential growth of technology). These arguments are unessential to the critique, as the arguments we present are not arguments against the projections Kurzweil makes with regard to technological development but rather against the advantageous nature of these optimistic predictions.

Our criticisms are based on historical world events and historical experiences with powerful technological systems. In other words, we believe that rather than making claims concerning technological developments based on utopian ideas, we are much better served and more likely to arrive at accurate predictions with regard to the outcomes of technological developments through looking at the outcomes of technological developments in history; by taking this "looking back to look ahead" approach to technology, a different (and significantly less optimistic) view of the potential outcomes of technology is derived.

Second, the arguments of the techno-utopian positivists are value-laden. By this it is meant that they make value-based assumptions that uncritically accept a pro-technological perspective. These arguments are based on a belief in the positive potential of technological power, the even distribution of technology across all aspects of life, and the equitable dispersion of technology among all individuals. As such, these projections assume the values of connection, convergence, peacefulness, equity, quantification, and efficiency. To refute the inherent worth or practicality of these values is to significantly weaken, vitally wound, or potentially disprove the techno-utopian arguments.

Third, the positivistic view of the Cyborg event horizon presents a series of paradoxes. On the one hand, the Cyborg is promoted as a means for achieving harmony and representing the best of humanity; on the other hand, it is conceived for war. On the one hand, it is asserted that because the Cyborg will be a human creation and endeavor, it will be within our control and represent our values; on the other hand, it is demonstrated that the Cyborg will function beyond our capabilities and will have unique values separate from the values of humanity—capabilities that extend far beyond those of non-Cyborg humanity. The Cyborg is supposed to be a product of humanity (and therefore history), yet as previously noted, no attention is paid to the manner in which technology has been used in the past for the development and maintenance of power and control systems. A final paradox noted here is that the universe needs the Cyborg in order to "awaken." According to the techno-positivists, that is why humanity was placed on earth—to create the Cyborg. In short, the utopian view of technology and the vision of the Cyborg as a positive development is a vision of faith, ignoring inconvenient facts that can be derived from the application of lessons based in history and logic.

A BRIEF PRESENTATION OF KRAMER'S THEORY OF DIMENSIONAL ACCRUAL AND DISSOCIATION

The theory of dimensional accrual presented by Kramer puts forth four basic dimensions of expressivity in society (Kramer, 1997): "The first type is magic/idolic, the second type is mythic/symbolic, the third type is perspectival/signalic-codal, and the fourth type is an emergent integral style" (p. xiii). According to Kramer (1997), societies can only exist in one dimension at a time, occur in a set sequence, and are cumulative (i.e., previous dimensions are present in all subsequent dimensions). Each dimension accrued presents further disassociation/fragmentation among ideas and individuals (Kramer, 1997).

The magic/idolic dimension is defined by Kramer (drawing from the work of Gebser) as a consciousness of being as opposed to having; it is characterized by collectivism, literal meaning, animism (everything has a spiritual element), non-individuality, and rules maintained for balance (Kramer, 1997).

The mythic/idolic consciousness, Kramer's second dimension, is ambivalent, androgynous, and polar (Kramer, 1997). It is further characterized by the split between literal and figurative meanings, the presence of emotional tension, and the ideas of guilt and responsibility attributable to monotheism.

The third dimension is defined by arbitrary meanings, individualism, quantification, mechanics, causality, and zerotheism and is referred to as modernity by Kramer (1997). Finally, Kramer offers a preliminary description of the onset of the currently emerging fourth dimension, characterized by "radical relativity," transparency, ambiguity, and multidimensionality. In this dimension, "[w]hat a thing is depends on how one looks at it. Matter cannot be measured as such . . . [t]he famous Hartle-Hawking proposal[1] even deconstructed the impermeability of the event horizon of *singularity*" (Kramer, 1997, p. 123; italics added).

Using Kramer's Dimensional Accrual Theory to Critique the Utopian View of Technology

Using the concepts found in Kramer's (1997) theory, it is possible to offer a critical examination of the Cyborg horizon as presented by Kurzweil (2005). The promises of the Cyborg as presented earlier are the primary focus. It is demonstrated that the utopian vision of the techno-utopians is represented in each of Kramer's established dimensions. Each dimension is utilized as a critical frame to draw conclusions about the Cyborg event horizon. As mentioned, negative effects are largely ignored by Kurzweil (and, we argue, are ignored by the majority of those sharing a utopian view of technology). In the remainder of this chapter (in terms of the critical examination), we use the techno-utopian's vision of the future to provide a fuller interpretation of the fourth dimension, the integral style, than that originally posited in Kramer's previous work.

The Cyborg as a Third Dimensional/Perspectival Creation

Using Kramer's third dimension (the perspectival/signalic-codal dimension) as a launching point for the critique of the Cyborg event horizon makes sense; the Cyborg is a product of either the third or fourth dimension (depending on one's perspective, as will be explained). The technological positivists' preoccupation with quantification as *the* valid proof for conclusions drawn further demonstrates the third-dimensional nature of the Cyborg. Addressing Cyborgism from a fourth-dimensional perspective is currently almost impossible; it is only in recent years that Kramer's fourth dimension has truly begun to emerge, and therefore the qualities of that dimension are still being developed and discovered. The utopian vision of the Cyborg can

---

[1]See Hawking (1998) for a complete description. The Hawking-Hartle proposal suggests that the precursor to the Big Bang was a singularity in which time and space were conjoined and in which time did not exist (as it is a function of spacetime, which did not occur until the universe began to expand as a result of the Big Bang).

be critiqued as a third-dimensional entity along three lines of argument: hyper-individualism, anti-socialism, and mechanical perspectivalism.

Three arguments demonstrate the concept of the utopian Cyborg with regard to hyper-individualism. First, the vision of the Cyborg presented by Kurzweil facilitates individual isolation through the end of the need for communities for purposes of work, education, and agriculture. However, various sciences have shown that human beings are inherently social animals, and much has been written about the fact that technology has been increasingly isolating individuals from each other in terms of physical human contact (Postman, 1992; Vanderburg, 2005). Kurzweil's vision of the Cyborg as bringing an end (especially) to the need for work and education causes further dramatic isolation, eliminating two of three (the third being religious congregation) remaining social institutions in which human contact exists.

Second, the ability of the Cyborg to "morph" into alternate beings (along with the ability of the Cyborg to inhabit numerous virtual spaces) contributes to further fragmentation of the individual psyche, creating internal isolation among the various selves inhabiting alternate (real and virtual) realities. Stresses on the human psyche that currently exist demonstrate damaging effects and are seen in the roles taken on by many adults in contemporary society, including work-related, family-related, educational, and other social roles. The term *balancing* is often applied to management of these various roles within the individual. The Cyborg adds further fragmentation (and a reasonable expectation of intensified symptoms and effects along with it) through the adding of selves within the individual, and these can be expected to produce schizophrenic states of being, occurring when balancing the selves becomes impossible to maintain.

Related to the second argument is the third: the ability to alter oneself at will (either in actually real or virtual space). This ability can result in the loss of the notion of a "true self." Following Kramer's notion of arbitrary meanings,[2] for the Cyborg the "real" self is arbitrary, changeable, and dependent on perspective: Is my real self the original body I inhabit? Is it the altered body created from the original? Is it the virtual self created for virtual encounters?

The Cyborg may lose the ability to distinguish or keep track of these selves. More important, for the Cyborg these selves are quite possibly no more than "clothes" (or a costume) to be worn or discarded at will. When the self is seen as subject to change depending on perspective, the self is virtual and therefore meaningless in any practical or perhaps even real sense. The Cyborg takes individualism to a heightened (perhaps meaningless) level,

---

[2]This concept represents the process of disconnecting a thing from what it means, resulting in a perspective in which everything is seen as being absolutely arbitrary in nature and having no ultimate, absolute meaning or purpose (Kramer, 1997).

fragmenting socially and internally the concepts of both self and others. Hence, we have a new type of mass-schizophrenia: hyper-individualism.

In addition to these individual-level considerations, the Cyborg can also be demonstrated (as a third-dimensional creation) to be anti-social in nature. Three arguments support this contention: self-reliance, amorality, and virtualization of reality. First, the Cyborg envisioned by technological positivists is self-reliant, having no need for outside-of-self support. Nutrition is produced internally, desires are met virtually, physical weaknesses are addressed by internally installed technological systems, and information is downloadable—none of this requires contact with outsiders, of course. There is no need that the Cyborg cannot meet for itself; hence, no need for community exists. Community becomes an inconvenience that distracts from play and restricts the Cyborg from acting out its personal fantasies in virtual space. Contact is inefficient and otherwise risky, directly contradicting the modern industrial-technological value of efficiency. Accordingly, actual contact and social obligations are obviously undesired (so therefore eliminated) in a Cyborg world.

Related to this argument is the idea that a being that has no need for others has no moral (religious or secular) obligation to serve others or society. Morality (in myriad forms) serves a central purpose in human society as a means of promoting community and interconnectedness (Postman, 1992). If a being has no need to connect to others, then the needs of others (Cyborg, human, animal, plant, etc.) are both an inconvenience and potentially a sign of weakness. The only moral obligation of a Cyborg in a world without work or limits is the obligation to satisfy the selves (actual and virtual). There is no society, only virtual playgrounds to be manipulated in the singular pursuit of personal pleasures. There is no obligation higher than self—no need for or sense of community to drive common beliefs—so by default the interests of and obligations to the Cyborg's "selves" supersede all others. If the self is virtual, then it stands to reason that all others encountered in the Cyborg's world are also virtual—further, they must have been created by the self and for the self; hence, others exist only for the pleasure of self if they are allowed to exist at all. If the others encountered become an inconvenience to the self, then they have violated their purpose and can therefore be eliminated.

The Cyborg lives in a world without enduring negative consequences. Nature is not real (not a monolithic, absolute, or singular reality); rather, it is internally created and can be destroyed, manipulated, or re-created at will. It is not needed for anything that can't be easily created in the virtual realm without bugs, snakes, rain, natives, spiders, and so on (or, conversely, with large numbers of these things based on the desires of a particular self).

There is no reason for Cyborgs to band together for social causes because everything can be bent to the individual will at any time. Destruction is entertainment because it leads to ingenious re-creations. Nothing is precious because everything is reducible to a personal (and perhaps temporary) manifestation of self desire. Everything is replaceable, unnecessary, or unwanted. If "this place" cannot be inhabited, a "new place" can be created and retreated into. Everything is a toy, a replication, a simulation, including the self and others. There is no permanent or real community: If you don't like your neighbors or they cause you inconvenience, you simply move them (or remove them from your world altogether).

The Cyborg envisioned by technological positivists has no reason to respect others, no reason to initiate contact with others, and no reason to believe that others exist except as a manifestation of internal desire. In light of these facts, there can be little doubt that the Cyborg will not "play well" with others—the others don't even exist independent of the self, and there are no long-term negative repercussions for anti-social or destructive behavior. Others are inefficient and "messy"; the Cyborg has no need to deal with anything unpleasant—except perhaps as (somewhat twisted) entertainment. The instant something becomes non-entertaining, it can be changed; the Cyborg can do anything no matter how dangerous or reckless because it doesn't matter—if it is injured or threatened, it can simply alter (or reboot) the circumstance to eliminate the threat from its world.

The third major line of argumentation by which the Cyborg can be demonstrated to be a third-dimensional being involves the perspective concerning the universe. The third dimension—modernism (as described by Kramer)—is one in which individuals are fascinated with perceiving everything as quantifiable and mechanical. The Cyborg's relation to the universe can therefore be examined in three ways: the universe as dead matter to be exploited, the use of the language of technology as explanation for all things, and the quantification of the universe.

The techno-utopian vision of the Cyborg presents a third-dimensional perspective in the manner in which it treats matter itself. Techno-utopians view matter as fodder to be converted into computational power, to be exploited at will for optimal personal gain. This view creates a "dead" universe in which the quest for (and gaining of) power through Earth-scorching practices is a justifiable means (not that justification is required, of course) to the end of gaining all power and bending everything to the desired outcome of the power—seeker. Nothing (including the self) is too small or big, too real or virtual, too secular or sacred to be exploited to achieve a desired end in this view.

The only language that makes sense to a Cyborg is technological language because the Cyborg is a product of a technological dimension. Everything must be quantified, be made efficient, produce value, or be reconstructed so that it can accomplish these things. No other values make sense, no other language can be spoken. That which is already quantified is fragmented so that its components can be quantified further (analysis), and that which is efficient is re-created to be made more efficient (continuous improvement). That which cannot be understood in the language of quantification and efficiency is irrelevant and therefore must be made relevant or eliminated from consideration (if not eliminated from existence altogether).

Following the modern perspective that created it, to the Cyborg, the status quo can and must constantly be investigated and improved; the universe is a subject for Cyborg experimentation. When an experiment works, greater efficiency is achieved; when it fails, the Cyborg re-creates the scenario at will and runs the experiment again. In a world where nothing is real and everything must be understood mechanically, the desirable option is to break down everything that is encountered to see how the parts fit together (i.e., to perform a modern scientific analysis, a methodical and ritualized dissection as a form of faith practice). Analysis requires destruction for the purposes of attaining increased information and/or producing the desired result, re-constructing and using insights gained. For the Cyborg, no project is either too big or too small to be analyzed; the rituals of analysis and reconstruction/recombination are infinitely applicable to anything in the Cyborg world.

These three third-dimensional critiques of the Cyborg (as described by the techno-utopians) lead to interesting insights into the Cyborg that Kurzweil does not mention in his vision of the Singularity. A Cyborg with no need for social institutions or other beings is not likely to be a social entity. The Cyborg is probably schizophrenic. The Cyborg sees nothing as real; everything is arbitrary and self-created. The Cyborg views destruction and construction as co-equal parts of the discovery process. For the Cyborg, power is both means and end, and there is no limit to either. The Cyborg respects nothing, values nothing, and seeks nothing for its own sake (except entertainment). The Cyborg speaks only one language: the language of quantification and analysis; that which cannot be incorporated into the Cyborg language does not exist for the Cyborg. We therefore argue that utopia may not be all that it is assumed to be by techno-utopians; the third (perspectival) dimension may not be the right place to raise a Cyborg.

The Cyborg as a Second Dimensional/Mythological Being

The primary analytical tool (further building on the critiques supplied from the third-dimensional critics) from Kramer's second dimension (the mythic) that is applicable to the Cyborg is that of monotheism. A secondary analysis is also presented concerning the death of culture (through a paradoxical combination of the forces of homogeneity and fragmentation). Other aspects of the mythic dimension are either inapplicable to this analysis or limited in their potential for providing additional insights; emotional tension, guilt, and responsibility are irrelevant in Cyborg culture.

For the Cyborg (and for the technological positivist), traditional reli-gion and its ideals are replaced by the religion of Science. This is demonstrat-ed in four ways: Science as the source of all explanation, the mystification of Science, the minimization of other systems of belief, and the worship of Science. The first aspect ties into the third-dimensional critique of the Cyborg as a "mono-linguistic" being. We are using the term *mono-linguis-tic* here not in the sense of a literal language (i.e., English, Spanish, French, etc.) but rather in the sense of a meta-language related to perspective (i.e., the languages of religion, philosophy, etc.). Although it is entirely possible that a singular literal language could be developed or utilized by the Cyborg, our over-arching point here is that barriers in literal language usage are likely to be made irrelevant by the use of technology in the form of translators, per-haps physically embedded in the Cyborg body. In other words, when we refer to language, we are referring to the body of concepts and terminolo-gies, not their verbal or written format (rendered irrelevant or obsolete).

In a world in which the language of science is the only language spoken, everything is seen to exist as a function of science. This is reminiscent of the adage "to a man equipped only with a hammer, every problem is a nail." For the Cyborg, equipped only with the language of quantification and analysis, everything is science. That which cannot be explained by science does not "exist" in the Cyborg mind (or in the world, as it is a self-created reality) because no vocabulary exists to name it (Foucault, 1969 Fr./1972 Eng.; Gadamer, 1976 Ger./1981 Eng.; Innis, 1951).

As demonstrated in upcoming chapters, Science is a complex language; as specialization increases, so does jargon. Everything discovered or created by Science needs at least one name. As Science and its sub-languages grow in complexity, the lack of ability to universally frame these sub-languages leads to specialized methods of understanding (and/or the mystification of Science and the framework around which the sub-language is built). In this sense, Science becomes a mystic experience for the Cyborg. As the Cyborg becomes more complex and the individual Cyborg becomes more varied and specialized, the ability to understand the complexity of another individual Cyborg is limited, and so is its interest in developing needless, inefficient rela-tionships. Finally, the Cyborg is a mystic being to other Cyborgs—no one understands the way in which the others have been created or the tasks that other Cyborgs conduct. In this way, Science and its language become godlike "entities"; no holistic understanding is possible (despite access to all informa-tion). Despite the homogenous mono-language of science as the singular acceptable subject and form of discourse, paradoxically, fragmentation is per-petuated through the specialization and expansion of information and tasks.

There can be only one "god" (i.e., Supreme Truth) for the Cyborg soci-ety. Dissension between Cyborgs relative to truth and meaning is inefficient and, on that basis alone, eliminated. The adoption of the terminology of science as the official "language" of the Cyborg nation necessitates that all other means of understanding and enlightenment must be eliminated if relevance and meaning are not clearly established (through Science). This is not unlike the trends we see today in our human society. Already the language of Science is claiming dominance and disallowing other languages to be heard via the argument of irrelevance (or the insufficiency of experience as a legitimate form of explanation in the modern view). There is no place in the scientific classroom for competing theories or for initiating a challenge to accepted myths in the form of alternate grand narratives. This can be seen, for example, in the ongoing debate in U.S. science classrooms between the competing "scientific" explanation for the physical universe (the Big Bang) and the "non-scientific" (in the view of many members of the scientific community) alternative explanations (romantic poetry, etc.).

That which cannot be observed and measured is either considered irrelevant or systematically ignored because it does not "exist" in any practical sense. Those who insist on alternative meanings are labeled as backward, close-minded (ironically), or unenlightened. For the Cyborg, this will be taken to the extreme; Science is the creator, and the Cyborg shall have no other gods before it (or any other ways of explaining or proving anything).

Based on the prior arguments, it is easy to ascertain that the Cyborg will only recognize true worship as being the worship of Science. Philosophy did not produce the Cyborg, and philosophical ideas cannot be measured (or laid out on the altar for sacrificial dissection and analysis). Traditional religion is even further removed from Science than philosophy is—as a matter of the "heart" (which the Cyborg will dispose of in the name of efficiency and the risk of unpleasantness) rather than the "brain." Those languages used in traditional religions are dead to the Cyborg. Words like *soul, faith, hope, love,* and so on are empty words and replaced by *information, progress, efficiency, data, analysis,* and similar terms.

The secondary argument from the second dimension is the death of culture, which follows in many ways from the primary analysis conducted using this critical tool. Culture is, at least in part, a function of two things: community (i.e., a physically proxemic, cohesive, and cooperative group of people with a sense of a shared identity and interdependence) and common beliefs (i.e., shared ideas about religion, justice, behavioral norms, etc.). With the death of community and traditional religion as foundations, the death of culture is a logical conclusion for the Cyborg society. Perhaps the choice of the word *death* is inappropriate here; culture will become what religion will become—singular. The Cyborg will create a new monoculture centered around the language of the scientific-technological god by which it was created. There will be no American Cyborg, no Russian Cyborg, no Japanese Cyborg, no Mexican Cyborg cultures. There will be only *the* Cyborg culture. This can be thought of as a process of the *Wal-Martization of culture*: As the

Cyborg expands across humanity, Cyborg culture becomes the only way of being—the state of being anything, anytime, and anywhere. The Cyborg sweeps other cultural elements away, including languages, economies, nation-states, politics, religions, and so on (much like what happens to many competing and diverse businesses when a Wal-Mart moves into a locale; hence, the term *Wal-Martization*). Difference is inefficient and therefore intolerable, and there is no need for inefficient discussions accepted as meaningless.

The analysis of Kurzweil's Cyborg using Kramer's second dimension provides further insights into the Cyborg psyche not mentioned by Kurzweil. The Cyborg is singular: one language, one religion, one culture. Science is God. No other gods exist. The Cyborg is a scientific mystic, worshiping that which it knows but cannot understand (and ironically does not understand that it doesn't understand). Given the outcomes of specialization, any given Cyborg is potentially a god to other Cyborg individuals when encountered (depending on the context of the encounter). Individual differences and increasing complexities caused by the process of analytic fragmentation lead to mystification of the Other, contributing ultimately to a lack of ability to comprehend and/or understand both self and Other.

Cyborg as a First Dimensional/Magical Being

Three arguments are posited from the critique constructed utilizing this dimension of Kramer's theory. First, the Cyborg is examined as an association of fragmented individuals, then an analysis of the meaning of collectivism and the Cyborg is presented, and finally the implications for leadership in the Cyborg society are examined.

The Cyborg is clearly a being of the first dimension through animism, although in a different way than that envisioned by Kramer (1997) in looking at early cultures. Early cultures view everything as being endowed with a spirit; the "neo-animism" aspect of the Cyborg sees everything as having a computational ability (i.e., reality can be reduced to a series of computations and/or can be made to perform computational work). This is rather appropriate, as the Cyborg has replaced the spirit of humanity with the codes of the machine/computer—a process that is currently well underway and we can see in aspects of our current society (specifically in the workforce). In our specialized roles within organizations, we become more and more machine-like in terms of both daily functions and the way in which individuals are treated in many modern organizations.

Cyborg is an association, as opposed to a community (due in part to the lack of proximity, cohesiveness, shared identity, and perceived interdependence). Unfortunately, it is an association of fragmented, schizophrenic beings. Individual Cyborgs, as previously discussed, are both internally and externally fragmented through multiple real and virtual realities, yet the association of Cyborg individuals consists of networks of these intimately connected, cybernetic entities. Information is directly exchanged, individuals download and upload data to and from the same source, and all are connected in some fashion to all others in the association.

In individual entities, this could be expected to increase internal fragmentation, as the voice of the Other(s) is added internally to the voices of the selves and must also be maintained in some fashion as separate voices. For the association, it would be expected that dysfunction could be a major concern. If all voices are equal and all voices are accessible to the network, divergent opinions and perspectives on collective decisions could cause system paralysis or even meltdown. It may also be possible that the schizophrenia of any given individual Cyborg entity could be downloaded into the system, contributing to a schizophrenic network created within the information bases. Control of which individual's "self" has access to the collective network may be problematic; a virtual sociopathic manifestation of a Cyborg entity with access to the "real" network could also be problematic, especially if he/she/it were armed with a network-compatible virtual "smart dust virus" mentioned earlier. The possibilities for conflict and control problems are virtually endless, creating questions concerning the possibility of democratic practice in a Cyborg society.

The Cyborg association is a neo-collective culture. It can best be thought of as a hive in terms of the innate hierarchical order it requires in order to function. As with all first-dimensional societies, there must be a form of hierarchy and an order for collective decision making to occur. In the Cyborg association, this introduces issues of influence, power, and control of the hive. Whichever Cyborg (the "queen Cyborg") is in control of the hive (most likely through being in control of the over-arching meta-network) possesses the ability to directly influence the actions of the hive members through simple download capability. This is similar to systems of website censorship utilized by governments to prevent access to undesirable internet sites by their citizens (Dickie, 2008; Goldsmith & Wu, 2006; Postman, 1992). In the Cyborg hive, control can be asserted over individuals by directly inputting desired messages into the network. Perhaps even more sinister in its implications and operations, the hive leader could simply choose to alter an entity's program so as to lock it into virtual space, allowing for control of the real body of that entity without the entity's awareness that anything had occurred.

Control can be masked, freedom can be made virtual, slight-of-hand (red herrings) can be used to divert attention. Assuming a benevolent hive leader, none of this is problematic; however, if the Cyborg hive is infiltrated or should a malevolent leader emerge, control would be both absolute and invisible. As such, a malevolent control system would be likely to remain in control longer than under nearly any other circumstances, perhaps even infinitely given the practical immortality of Cyborg individuals (including those in control). Dissenters could be eliminated immediately, being shut down remotely. In short, resistance is futile in the Cyborg hive. Compliance is not a choice; there are no choices. Individuality is an illusion; the network (in the form of the queen Cyborg) controls all.

The Cyborg hive cannot be democratic. The idea of a democratic hive is an oxymoron. When all individuals are connected, the maintenance of balance is absolute. The queen Cyborg is in constant contact with the mood of the hive and its members. Dissent can be instantly detected and eliminated. No member of the hive can have access to information from outside the network; all are connected and monitored. All data are processed by members of the hive using the same methods, yielding the same results (the ultimate form of positivist/scientific efficiency). Differences are not allowed to emerge because they would disrupt the efficiency of the hive. There can be only one queen of the hive at any point in time (likely to be an infinite time frame). Political parties cannot exist; they would cause difference in the political system of the hive. Without difference, no politics exist; without politics, no democracy or form of non-authoritarian government can emerge through political discourse. At best, the hive is a benevolent socialist dictatorship; at worst (and we would argue much more likely), it is an authoritarian Fascist regime. Either way, it is absolute and unchallenged. This is the reality of life and power within the hive.

Once again, Kramer's theory provides insights of concern into the Cyborg that Kurzweil does not address. Connection has its dark side—access to the network carries with it the ability to monitor and control all content and distribution. Democracy is obsolete—the collective can only function with a single leader (likely to be the first Cyborg as it will have the first opportunity to both attain and subsequently maintain control of the system). Resistance is impossible, and the queen Cyborg knows all that occurs within, controls all members of, and makes all decisions for the hive. Based on these observations, it can be seen that the Cyborg society envisioned by techno-utopians is actually likely to be very non-utopian in practice, demanding from its members the surrender of autonomy, privacy, individuality, and choice. Utopia thus becomes the logical conclusion of an escapist hedonic calculus.

The lessons about the Cyborg that can be derived from using the three dimensions of Kramer's theory demonstrates that Kurzweil's utopian vision of the Cyborg is not realistic and that the likely actuality of the Cyborg society is not desirable. Potential outcomes for the Cyborg culture, including consideration of issues of power, control, freedom, and so on, demonstrate that blending ourselves with our technology could mean the end of our humanity and of society as a place in which individual voice matters and difference is valued or even allowed. Kurzweil sees the harmony of a *Star Trek* crew in his utopian Cyborg society; the reality is probably much more like the ultimate nemesis the Borg.[3] These issues cannot await the coming of the technology before we decide what to do with them; once the Cyborg arrives on the scene (regardless of whether it is benevolent or malevolent), resistance is futile; the course is irreversibly laid. But even the Borg had a collective purpose. An aggregate of dissociated cyborgs would share nothing. All interest would be utterly individuated.

EXPANDING ON KRAMER'S THEORY OF DIMENSIONAL ACCRUAL USING KURZWEIL'S CYBORG

As previously explained, Kramer suggests that a fourth dimension is currently emerging in society. Using Kurzweil's suggestions about the Cyborg culture, additional information about the fourth dimension can now be generated to expand Kramer's theory with regard to this fourth dimension. Kramer suggests that the fourth dimension will consist of elements from the previous three dimensions combined in new ways; as has been seen in the previous critiques utilizing each dimension's traits, evidence for this intermingling of aspects of the first three historical dimensions of cultural development is produced by the careful consideration of the Cyborg as presented by Kurzweil.

Three major assertions can be made from this examination/application about the emerging fourth dimension (assuming it is represented by the impending Cyborg society). First, the fourth dimension contains elements gathered primarily from the first and third dimensions of accrual. Therefore, the fourth dimension could be characterized as neo-magical/neo-perspectival in nature. Elements from the third and first dimensions are being combined in new ways through technology; what was once mutually exclusive is now being re-created as a hybrid. Some of these intertwined elements include individualism/collectivism, animism/zerotheism, literality/arbitrariness, and others such as myth/science and so on.

This intertwining creates paradoxes in the fourth dimension. There are no gods, yet technology and Science are deified. Hyper-individualism morphs with the collective monoculture. All differences are accentuated (fragmentation) and then ultimately eliminated (homogeneity). Individual choice and freedom exist as façades for mass manipulation. Unlimited individual power becomes relative individual powerlessness (with the exception

---

[3]First appearing in Gene Roddenberry's television series *Star Trek: The Next Generation*, the Borg is a race of beings who have integrated machine-technological systems with their biological minds and bodies. Their race is driven to conquer other races by a desire to assimilate both the peoples they encounter and their technologies.

of the queen Cyborg). Unlimited information creates limited (or the lack of) understanding. Endless play creates meaningless work. The ability to create requires the sacrifice of creativity (Hegel, 1812, 1813, 1816 Ger./1969 Eng.). The fourth dimension is ordered chaos facilitated by technology, and it is perhaps ultimately unsustainable. Regardless, sinister motives and/or behavior (i.e., the exercise of absolute control and the relentless, inconsiderate pursuit of power) are found beneath the thin veneer of benevolence (the appearance of democratic decision making, service to the larger good, etc.).

Late modernity also contains meaningful implications for power in society. Power becomes limitless, but power is concentrated in the grasp of a very few (or perhaps even one) individual(s). Those who wield power are increasingly reliant on technology to maintain that power; the cost of technological failure for the powerful and for the collective/hive becomes extreme. The combination of extreme technological and individual power with the virtualization of reality in the absence of a morally guided culture contributes to the possibility of inhuman corruption in the "real world" with no possibility of resistance or restraint (although, of course, most Cyborgs will potentially escape these implications through immersion in created virtual realities through either their own choice or banishment to them). Regarding the fourth dimension, the careful consideration of the full implications of Cyborg society tells us that we enter it at our own peril and perhaps to the detriment or destruction of what is truly valuable in our (still relatively) human condition.

To summarize this chapter, our ability to create and implement new technologies in short order is drastically outpacing our ability to carefully process and consider the implications of our creations. Caution should be exercised and individual goals tempered with consideration for the numerous effects, positive and negative, of new technologies. We are quickly reaching the point at which an ill-conceived introduction of technology could spell disaster; the ideologies of democracy, justice, and empowerment of the people (among others) could be instantly relegated to antiquity and irrelevance in society.

Once technology is introduced into society, it is difficult (if not impossible) for it to be revoked, even when it produces clearly negative effects (i.e., texting and talking while driving). Careful and thorough deliberations and putting policies in place *before* introduction of a new technology are the only means by which societies can protect themselves from destructive technologies, although none of these deliberations or policies is a guarantee of problem-free implementation of technology.

This means that knowledge must be shared and opinions must be heard from outside the community of the technological sciences (and the "hard" sciences in general). The social sciences have much to contribute that may have significant implications for the role of technology in human affairs.

Technology does not exist in a vacuum and is not innocent. Social structures can be drastically altered by technology. Technologies create social paradoxes, which can in turn lead to disruption of social processes.

For example, politics can only exist if difference is allowed to exist. Cyborg applications of technology pose the potential to destroy politics through destruction of difference. The Cyborg society is totalitarian; benevolence is irrelevant to technological power. The coming of the Cyborg signals the end of true democracy. Politics and power are subject to technological control if technology is not thoughtfully considered before implementation and closely monitored thereafter.

Finally, additional aspects of the Cyborg should be critiqued—some of which are addressed in upcoming chapters. Other aspects must wait for future research endeavors; these aspects include the economic impacts of the Cyborg and what would constitute Cyborg economies, the impacts on the culture of collectivism and interconnectedness, the impacts (biological, psychological) on the integration of human and computerized machine, the ethical implications and considerations resulting from the Cyborg, and impacts of the Cyborg on various social institutions.

It is clear that concentrated effort from a variety of disciplines will be needed to accomplish the work in time to beat the birth of the Cyborg. Without this work, we may find that technology infiltrates us before we have fully considered the potential impacts of its incorporation. If that occurs, the consequences may be devastating, perhaps even in more ways than the ones we consider here.

8

Defanging the "Paradox" of Mutually Exclusive Determinisms

ON THE WAY TO UNDERSTANDING
TECHNICIZED COMMUNICATION

Our technologies often shape us as much or more than we shape technologies. This communication is a relationship between us and our creations. It is a living organic and dynamic process that has synthetic properties suggesting a dialectical form of change and transformation. In many ways, this operationalization of ideas and the subsequent living with material creations that inspire new ideas followed by new material solutions is already fully explicated in Hegel's (1807 Ger./1977 Eng.) cosmology and reiterated by writers such as Lewis Mumford (1934/1963/2010) and Alvin Gouldner (1976/1982). Technology is concretized logic and reasoning in the service of an idea, a want, a need, a desire. We work our thoughts out through the tools of our hands operationalizing ideas. Every tool, no matter how complex and dissociated, begins with human handiwork, be it at a computer keyboard controlling a lathe or computer-aided design (CAD) system, fingers moving over a calculator to reckon the proper measurements to calibrate a telescope in orbit, or working flint with a reindeer antler.

To make the most sophisticated technologies begins with the logistical process of directing the procurement of basic resources from mining and drilling, in short digging with a preconceived purpose in the rock and dirt with a goal of refinement toward the fabrication of tools and machine parts

133

logically conceived for synergistic orientation to other parts forming complex machines and networked systems of machines. From the Paleolithic spearhead to the samurai sword to the Blue Gene/P supercomputer at Argonne National Laboratory (currently the fastest ever), all technology begins with manual dexterity guided by an idea and inspired by a purpose.

The modern Western world has projected this mechanistic modality onto the entire universe, and in this sense, as populations modernize, they are to some extent Westernizing, which involves not just what but also how we construct the made world. This is a regard, a way of seeing the universe and making sense of it, namely, as one gigantic machine with interlocking and interacting parts. Hence, many Westerners follow from this premise that there must therefore be a maker, a divine designer of the cosmic clockworks. This is just one way to see the universe.

In discussions about what is and what is not the meaning of technology, something is missing. What is missing is an explanation of the relationship between the fetish and those who possess and are possessed by it, be it the new shiny car, the new computer, the new telephone, or the latest data about a distant galaxy. The nature of this relationship is hermeneutical, meaning that as we learn, the experience of learning changes the way we learn. The nature of this process is co-evolutionary (Kramer, 2011; Kramer, Callahan, & Zuckerman, 2013) or co-integrative (Kramer, 2008, 2010, 2011, 2013). Neither the maker nor the made are determinant. We evolve as we bring resources into our purview and control, domesticate them, be they other organisms from wheat to wolves or inanimate stuff regarded as resource base such as iron, silicon, and cooper. And as we do so, our world is changed, and we continually adapt to this new world.

As a new cultural artifact is conceived and deployed, such as the automobile, it changes our horizon, our sense of what is real and what is possible. However, we do not simply adapt our desires to our technologies, thereby limiting ourselves to our present technologies. Rather, our desires are projected onto our new technological reality that then leads to new wants and needs such as drive-in fast food, drive-thru groceries, auto repair garages, parking garages, highways, and the like. Consciousness and its material expressions continually change, in part, because we want faster and faster food, groceries, auto repairs, and so on. Each new meaning and the possibilities it suggests enable a new perspective calling for new techno-material articulations. When these technologies are realized, they in turn change the meaning of our world, our capacities, ambitions, motivations, wants, beliefs, and behaviors. They change our culture and our consciousness structure (the system of horizons of beliefs, motives, values, capacities, and behaviors, including our own sense of self and social identities).

On one side of the co-evolutionary process, it is undeniable that we tend to become integrated with our tools (i.e., we project ourselves into them and hence find aspects of ourselves in our things). Technology becomes a veritable mirror of our selves. This is so not only because of such imitative technologies as the Internet, television, or virtual reality (VR), but also because of the semiotic registration of human beings. For example, as a further extension of our selves via technology, we are reflecting our bodies onto the concept of the genetic code, the genes that make us who we are. Power comes in the ability to change things at will. The modern technological mind desires total plasticity, the ability to rearrange things at will, from the building blocks of nature to the enculturation of children. Like the plastic promises of cosmetic surgery, the ambition of the Human Genome Project demonstrates that we are *literally*, not merely metaphorically, increasingly *tooled* by our tools (we are reduced to a genetic code), a phenomenon that underscores the value of Mumford's (1934) original insight into the issue of the mechanization of nature and the calculation of life itself.

Media and communication technology are not merely part of this tendency toward universal mechanization. Communication technology is the main driving force in the postindustrial world, and, in the sense that new communication technology is shrinking the globe by eroding (if not eliminating) spatial, temporal, and cultural boundaries, this technology is ultimately serving to erase space, time, and cultural diversity (Kramer, 1997, 2003a). Communication technology (or information technology)[1] not only intrigues those who work in the field of communication, it is also of interest to scholars in linguistics, philosophy, education, and other fields. Despite such multifarious attention, the question remains: What exactly is media technology and what is communication technology? With no definitive answer, communication technology is a floating signifier, open and full of meaning.

The deployment and development of what is called new communication technology (a.k.a. new media), specifically of electronic equipment for linking computers and telecommunications systems into networks, forms the foundation of postindustrial society. The computer is without doubt the single most important element in the field of new communication technology. It is the machine on which everything else—increased productivity and efficiency, telecommunication hookups, networking patterns, data storage/transfer, and the like—depends. Given the computer's central role in modern society, it is to be expected that a number of ways of talking about the

---

[1]In this study, the phrase "communication technology" fits better than "information technology" (IT) because in using the term information technology, people tend to regard technology as a mere technique not an enframing power. This tendency of tacit, yet somehow intentional non-discrimination between information and communication by technologists is one of the important points of this study. We can notice this tendency in the hyperbolic pro-technology slogans of many institutions and countries concerning information technology and the future.

computer and networking exist. Carey (1981) suggests the debate about technology and its assessment is dominated by two perspectives that demonstrate a fundamental difference in how people see the computer: viewing it as either a liberating or an oppressing force.

In the first perspective, computers are seen as being programmable with the capacity to handle certain uninteresting tasks in order to free our lives for more leisure time. People with this viewpoint generally regard technology as an instrument for self-realization, a device that serves to liberate us from mundane tasks. The computer enables smart automation, the doing of tasks without needing human attention. According to this perspective, technology enhances the quality of life for people in any number of fields, including health care, education, banking, and so forth. This perspective is an optimistic ideology of technical determinism, which states that technology liberates society from nature and the worker from labor. Champions of this perspective include McLuhan (1962, 1964), Pool (1983), Bell (1973), and Kurzweil (2000, 2005).

In contrast to this perspective is the view made famous by English textile workers who followed Ned Ludd. In the early nineteenth century, these workers (called Luddites) protested the introduction of automated machinery bought with the profits they had made for their owners, machinery that produced inexpensive textiles that undercut the livelihoods of skilled knitters and weavers. Many Luddites were put on mass trial in 1913 and executed for smashing textile machines (Binfeld, 2004).

The Luddites' view of technology condemned not the machine per se; rather it focused on how the choices about the deployment of technology affected existing social structures (the technicization of the workplace that took control of production out of human hands). Their adversaries created an anti-machine caricature of the Luddite position in order to make them look anti-progress, anti-science, anti-technology, and generally unintelligent. This caricature was unfair; these workers' skills were the basis for the design of the machines in the first place.

The Luddites correctly recognized that the ideology of capitalism was pitting profit motives for absentee owners against the very labor that produced the source of profits and that this ideology was detrimental to labor's need for work (Heidegger, 1952, 1954, 1962 Ger./1977 Eng.; Mumford, 1970; Postman, 1992). In the industrial world, labor became a market so that a major path to enhanced profit was to cut labor costs—by either finding people who would work for less or using efficiency-enhancing machines. An ideology based on automation and economical processes was born. Efficiency and the speed of capital accumulation (profits) came to threaten social structures necessary for the survival of workers. Workers became obsolete (in terms of their relevance to production capability) under the new ideology.

People holding this position argue that humankind must restrain the ideology of efficiency (the modern super-value), which generates a world-view in which technology takes on a self-propelled dynamic. Beyond this ideological dichotomy, those holding the neo-Luddite perspective can argue that the machine is fundamentally irrelevant because it has nothing to say about the important existential questions of the lifeworld. Gebser (1949 Ger./1985 Eng.) goes so far as to point out that while technology originally brought culture out of nature—allowing craftsmen to put their stamp on nature—mechanization has driven art and nature out of humanity as skilled craftsmen are replaced by the "rootlessness and homelessness of today's salaried employees and factory workers" (p. 306).

This is the more pessimistic form of technological determinism—the view that increasingly communication technology is a tool of oppression and a means of elevating an elite minority of "remote-controllers" (Dusek & Scharff, 2003; Loon, 2003; Williams, 2002; Winner, 1988).[2] In 2009, for example, flash drives made in Communist China had programming that enabled the Communist Party to access the contents of such drives at will, even remotely via the Internet (Goldsmith & Wu, 2006). The Internet has increasingly become a modern panopticon—a way to access (and spy on) people's private lives (Godwin, 2003; Goldsmith & Wu, 2006; Kramer, 1994b, 2004b; Zittrain, 2008).

Even early proponents of the Internet, including Howard Rheingold (1993), Roxanne Hiltz and Murray Turoff (1993), Lawrence Lessig (1999, 2008)—with his famous dictum borrowed from Joel Reidenberg (1998) that "code is law"—Nicolas Negroponte (1995), and Mike Godwin (2003) are beginning to recognize problems with the Internet such as privacy, libel, cognitive problems concerning addiction, the inability to discern and cate-gorize information (Weinberger, 2008), the continual threat to our ability to concentrate and focus, and problems of distraction and attention deficit (Jackson, 2008). Although many often attribute the origins of technology to generally positive societal forces, the fact remains that war and industry have primarily been the great motivators for technological innovation, often at the cost of human lives and social cohesion. The Luddites recognized a fun-damental shift in societal values—with material efficiency displacing inter-personal relationships and socioeconomic cohesion. Instead of all members of society "being in the same boat," with industrial-scale mass techniciza-tion, an elite few (industrial capitalists with access to the technological means of production) would increasingly come to dominate the masses (the majority of the workforce). Technology, they understood, is about who has

---

[2]Mumford's critique of the concentration of power, profit, and prestige of the pre-existent hegemony through control of communication technologies closely aligns with the perspectives of Carey (1989), Schiller (1989), and Mosco (1989). And the concept of "control" is prevalent in Innis (1951).

it, resulting in the concentration of power into fewer and fewer hands (with control becoming centralized, absentee, and increasingly narrow in interest). Control of technology is power—especially in highly technologized societies. The new power—knowledge—is concentrated in a class of experts (Lyotard, 1979 Fr./1984 Eng.). This includes expertise in all sorts of instrumentation, ranging from complex and mystifying financial instruments such as hedge funds and actuarial calculi, to medical technology, to public and private surveillance data gathering and processing, and the power that results from the technicization of communication itself—arguably the most important ability of the human species.

For the Luddites, the answer to the question of whether technology affects social relations was self-evident. Concentration of power is a fundamental and profound shift in social relations. Some might argue (to the contrary) that in a preindustrial, pre-technical time and culture of dynastic rulers, all power was concentrated in a single head-of-state. However, due to great inefficiencies in communication and travel, most people never saw their rulers or felt their power to any great extent because everyday life was loosely organized. Given the limitations of the time and space, pre-industrial, pre-technical governments could not exercise the degree of control possible today. One of the hallmarks of modernity is increased fragmentation of community into mass aggregation that subsequently lends itself to standardization and greater precision—facilitating profound increases in top-down command and (in the desire to be good, successful, and efficient) large amounts of self-control in the form of conformity. Organizational feedback and control is a modern way of structuring and controlling the everyday lifeworld.

The cellular network, for instance, exemplifies this reorganization of everyday life via communication technology. The industrial world is broken down into singular "cells" that are kept in constant communication with a close network of others. The cellular phone (via geo-positioning satellites) is enabling authority to be exercised (be it parental, law enforcement, or corporate oversight) in the form of constant tracking of individuals. The cellular phone is also enabling work to become a constant process—deconstructing the line between home and work, labor and leisure, work time and free time. Mobile wireless devices (smart phones) and laptop computers are bringing the office literally into the beds of workers—affecting sleep patterns and intimate interpersonal relationships. Gadgets marketed for our convenience are in fact pushing us to longer and longer hours of work (and killing us by the thousands on our highways) in the employer-serving illusion that multitasking is both possible and desirable.

Today powerful communication technologies may pose not only a threat to privacy but also (ironically) the freedom to communicate. For instance, many argue that the Internet is diffusing power and democratizing communication (Godwin, 2003). But the service providers that own and manage the Internet have turned the Internet into the ultimate panopticon so that all communication (including private correspondence) is recorded and tracked. No mail is private now, and giant Internet providers such as Yahoo and Google have provided algorithms to dictatorial governments so that those governments can monitor, track, and block millions of attempts to communicate (Goldsmith & Wu, 2006; Postman, 1992; Vanderburg, 2005). As people become more dependent on cell phones and computer-mediated, satellite-assisted (i.e., online) communication, the more they are vulnerable to surveillance. No traditional dynastic ruler had such powerful means to monitor and control their subjects before these technologies became widely available.

The right to assemble in a virtual community or chat room is enabled by technology; however, the technology that enables virtual assembly also enables the tracking of all communication. Reliance on the Internet has enabled many governments in addition to China—including Russia, Egypt, Iran, Vietnam, and others—to constantly monitor, track, censor, and arrest cyber-dissidents (Goldsmith & Wu, 2006; Postman, 1992; Vanderburg, 2005). Thus, we have enabled the capacity of governments to shut down the system altogether, eliminate views and perspectives that governments do not wish to exist, and create and perpetuate any propaganda it may wish to disseminate.

For example, in early 2008, Guo Quan, a professor and leader of a pro-democracy party in China, was fired from his university position and threatened with jail. In 2009, Professor Quan attempted to sue both Yahoo and Google for blocking his name on their search engines in China and for violating his human right to communicate (Dickie, 2008).

Many dissidents including Hú Ji have worked to gain release from prison for Internet activists and dissidents such as Liu Di, who was imprisoned for satirizing the government of the People's Republic of China. These dissidents have found that global Internet providers are seducing young people to join their services, becoming increasingly dependent on it for their view of reality, and then setting the agenda for what they can know. Walter Ong (1982) called this effect of technology on the structures of thought a fundamental altercation of identity at the noetic level. With the invention of the Internet has come the invention of a new type of space, time, and even new criminals (hackers and now cyber-dissidents).

Those who control the means of communication (and it is worth mentioning that this control is increasingly enacted in real time) have a powerful tool for controlling the means of production of reality, of controlling people's minds because communication, culture, and consciousness are so closely related as to be fundamental to the human condition (Hall, 1966, 1983).

But such assembly (e.g., the Egypt rebellion/Arab Spring) is so dependent on technology that it is highly vulnerable. Due to the concentration of Internet functionality, entire nations can lose their communication capability with the flip of a switch, sabotage, an accident, or by a breach in the channel caused by a natural phenomenon. In addition, increased centralization of communication makes the structure vulnerable to natural events that can disrupt massive numbers of communiqués.

A perfect example was the damage to the Fiber-Optic Link Around the Globe (FALCON) Europe-Asia telecommunications submarine cable operated by India's Reliance Communication Ventures Corporation. FALCON connects several countries with high-speed fiber optics, including Japan, the United Kingdom, India, and several Middle Eastern nations. On January 23, 2008, FALCON was damaged, cutting off Internet service between the Indian subcontinent and the Middle East. One week later, the SEA-ME-WE 4 and FLAG cables were damaged in the Mediterranean near Alexandria, Egypt—disrupting Internet communications among India, Saudi Arabia, Kuwait, Bahrain, Bangladesh, Pakistan, and several other countries. Then only four days later, on February 3, 2008, the DOHA-HALOUL cable connecting Qatar to the United Arab Emirates was damaged, causing disruptions in the already crippled Middle Eastern communication network. From January 23, 2008, to mid-February, damage to just four cables caused billions of users to lose Internet access. In short, the Internet is not nearly as dispersed, redundant, or private as written correspondence. While each handwritten letter was a self-contained channel, billions of Internet messages are funneled through a single cable constituting major parts of the backbone of the Internet network infrastructure.

The malfunction of a technology that one has come to depend on is one thing. However, many scholars, including Mumford (1934/2010), Heidegger (1952, 1954, 1962 Ger./1977 Eng.), Murphy, Mickunas, and Pilotta (1986), Mickunas and Pilotta (1997), and Carey (1975), argue (and we agree) that the problematic points of the modern technological milieu are not the mal-*function* of technological applications but rather the *nature* of modern technology and the viewpoint that technologists, scientists, and communication theorists share (Carey, 1975; Heidegger, 1952, 1954, 1962 Ger./1977 Eng.; Mickunas & Pilotta, 1997; Mumford, 1934; Murphy, Mickunas, & Pilotta, 1986). Some modern computer enthusiasts may be willing to share their data with anyone (i.e., freeware); what they are not willing to give up readily is the entire technocratic worldview that determines what qualifies as valuable fact. It is not the data per se that technocrats wish to monopolize; rather, they wish to cling to the approved, certified, authorized, and safe modes of thought that define what it means to be reasonable—because, as Heidegger (1952, 1954, 1962 Ger./1977 Eng.) noted, technology is not some mere collection of artifacts but, in fact, a "way of seeing or a mode of revealing" (p. 3) or a kind of being.

We argue that technology can be better understood in the sense of a language-analogue rather than a thing-analogue. When we consider technology as a way of being in the world (rather than as a thing or a tool), the nature of technology becomes more clearly understood as a part of the human life-world. Cultivating this view means a larger number of communication features become available for consideration.

Regarding technology as a mere tool allows it to be considered apart from those who use it and the use they make of it, as illustrated in the frequently invoked cliché, "Guns don't kill people, people kill people." Ellul (1954 Fr./1964 Eng.) warns there is danger in this kind of reasoning because it leads to the "attractive notion which would apparently resolve all technical problems: that it is not the technique that is wrong, but the use men make of it" (p. 96). Ellul (1954 Fr./1964 Eng.) continues, "Consequently, if the use is changed, there will no longer be any objection to the technique" (p. 96). However, the problem is that the *use of technique* (utilization of technology) is ontologically inseparable from the technique (technology) itself; hence, the terms technology and technique can be used interchangeably. The being of technology is its use. Once we reintroduce *phronesis* or judgment (what positivists claim to be a terribly subjective pollutant), then *techne*, which is pure doing, regains its theoretical dimension. When we take back control of technology by means of judgment, we not only bring technology back into human scale and control, but also technology becomes available for moral and ethical interrogation.

When we view technology as a structuring force in the lifeworld (more similar to a language game than a separate and disinterested machine), Foucault's (1969 Fr./1972 Eng.) claim that language speaks us and not the other way around becomes exceedingly important. Reflecting on the horrors of the first highly technicized war (World War I), Winston Churchill and Edmund Husserl (among others) realized what Albert Einstein finally recognized after World War II—namely, that our technological abilities were outrunning our humanity. Objectified technics were over-determining our capacity to control our own aggressive tendencies.

Mumford (1934/1963/2010) recognized the process whereby our inventions (such as the mechanical clock) can come to control us through the process of dissociation. Following his lead, Hall (1983) named this process "extension transference," whereby an activity or product resulting from an "externalizing-extension-process is confused with the basic or underlying process that has been extended" (p. 229). Thus, for example, writing is confused with language itself. According to Hall (1983), extension transference occurs when an extension of an aspect of our selves (be it tooth, nail, or fist) takes the place of the process that has been extended. Thus, plump old men rarely throw punches or engage in hand-to-hand combat anymore. Instead they extend their fists by giving the command to launch missiles.

Hall (1983) claims that extension transference "not only can, but usually does eventually take the place of the process which has been extended" (p. 131). We come to treat the artificial extension as more real than the organic process it extends. Objectification of organic processes makes them seem more real. Thus, Kramer (1997) argues:

> We have taken our own subjective sense of time and moved it outside ourselves and standardized it. Then we begin to treat mechanical clock time as the only reality and it turns on us and begins to standardize and synchronize us. We become stressed by technologies we invented. Our identities even become defined by their measure so that a person who is often late according to the clock comes to be negatively seen as unreliable, undependable, a bad person. Thus judgment itself, that most subjective of phenomena, is not eliminated by externalization and objectification of values in technologies and technical process, but instead inflated absolutely. It becomes positivistically defined as the only one and true criteria for judgment, the only one and true reality, an absolutely intolerant fetish. (p. 107)

Do we structure technology or does technology structure us? Does it shape the limits of our actualization—our imaginations, thoughts, desires, and our lifeworld? When one thinks of the reliance on the automobile in the United States, for instance, the grammar of transportation language immediately appears to be constricting. In many parts of the United States, if you cannot drive, you practically cannot live. If a single transportation technology can have such a major impact on how we build and live in our everyday worlds, then certainly other powerful and vast technological complexes such as communication networks are profoundly changing how we live our lives and how we communicate (which is fundamental, the essence of human social being). With new communication technologies, identities, statuses, and expectations change. For instance, with e-mail, people expect prompt responses, much more prompt than in the days of manually carried correspondence (hence, the term snail mail). If a response is not prompt, then the receiver side of the dyad may be seen as lazy, rude, disinterested, disorganized, incapable, or (perhaps worse) inefficient. Technicization is a shift in our way of being and interpreting it as not merely a discrete object that can be contained (despite being reified and personified).

Some critics (e.g., Roszak, 1969; Toffler, 1970) reject Heidegger (1952, 1954, 1962 Ger./1977 Eng.) and Ellul (1954 Fr./1964 Eng.) for their "extremely pessimistic" conclusions. Cautionary though they may be, few of these critics have successfully penetrated public awareness. Instead of helping to shape and inform the public's consciousness of what technology is and where the threat lies, optimistic approaches have (in many cases) captured the public's awareness, creating unrefined notions of technology and the groundless optimism that whatever the problem is, humans can solve it. Toffler's (1970) *Future Shock* is one such example.

Despite the tendency of futurologists to promise a wonderful techno-logical future, we tend to side with the "pessimistic technophobes" (as they are labeled by the technological positivists) such as Ellul (1954 Fr./1964 Eng.) and Heidegger (1952, 1954, 1962 Ger./1977 Eng.), in the sense that we fully appreciate the depth and latitude of the warnings regarding the serious-ness of the modern technological milieu. Rather than following the futurists' proposed path to more leisure and happier endings, technology has been uti-lized almost exclusively as a means for enhancing the productivity and prof-itability of business (and government). For example, in pre-17th-century Catholic countries, there were about 100 holidays a year (Mumford, 1934/1963/2010); comparatively, in 2007, only 50 percent of working Americans took a summer vacation, and of those who did, 46 percent planned to continue working while vacationing (Kirn, 2007). While the Blackberry® allows us to leave the office physically, it ironically makes it much harder for us to escape it mentally. Thus, we have what has been coined "absent presence" (Gergen, 1994) while on vacation.

Heidegger (1952, 1954, 1962 Ger./1977 Eng.) claims that treating every-thing as a form of standing reserve makes possible endless disaggregation, redistribution, and re-aggregation of material and people for its own sake. In this respect, information, especially digital information, is endlessly trans-formable. Flexibility (or the ability of the master to manipulate the slave) is the issue. Whose agendas are served by these technologies? When every-thing becomes classified as a standing reserve or an endless resource, people and things will no longer be understood as having essences or identities. Enduring qualities and characteristics are no longer stable, but rather they are transient; multiple identities can be created and maintained in various Internet profiles, for example. In this sense, Heidegger's (1952, 1954, 1962 Ger./1977 Eng.) view then suggests that the modern technological world is reduced to systematic concerns; as Kramer (1997) states, "the whole world is identified as a system of operations and functions" (p. 85). As a conse-quence, communication becomes rationalized and reduced to being a sequential exchange, strictly informative or instructive. This rationalized reduction of communication was also recognized by Foucault (1969 Fr./1972 Eng.). According to the positivistic ideology, there is one best way to communicate, one best interpretation exemplified by the dictator of the dictionary and other authorities. Experts who set the standards—and the followers who conform to the standard most strictly—are admired (and more likely to be "successful"). The standards are definitive and definite. Human nature is seen as flawed, biased, and less capable than machines, whereas machines are seen as superior (not only in speed and scope) and also virtuous (i.e., unbiased, fair, impartial, etc.).

Everything, reality *sui generis*, is reduced to the same thing, an aggrega-tion of uniform building blocks of "bits" (bytes) that are interchangeable at will. This metaphysical faith then enables the rise of purely arbitrary conventions to the status of objective truth (and preferred ways of being) and is similar to the drive to contribute to a body of knowledge even if it is a proverbial house of cards. Which conventional scale will prevail is a power issue (and is clearly not the same thing as a quality issue). Whose will prevail and how that is determined is increasingly a function of technological prowess, including behavioral technologies brought to bear on a massive scale through mass mediation and marketing (including the "branding" of public, domestic, and global policies). Qualitative differences are eliminated in favor of endless redundancy. Redundancy is convincing even when basic facts are wrong. Of course, it often doesn't matter if the facts are wrong; often people don't seek facts but rather mimic the messages of people they like and/or trust. Content becomes increasingly irrelevant. In fact semantics and meaning are ignored. A good marketing campaign guided by rigorous behavioral technologies brought to bear on a massive scale can produce sales of just about anything—given enough money, time, and media saturation. Reality itself thus becomes increasingly the property of those who have the technological and economic resources to exert their will.

This reductionist attitude is essential for (and manifested by) technological comportment, which supercharges our capacity to conceptually atomize, systematize, standardize, streamline, and install processes as *the* way of doing or being. Hence, quantity supersedes (or even supplants) quality. Political discourse is reduced to bumper-sticker efficiency as time becomes (perceptually) increasingly—and ironically—scarce in our modern utopia of labor- and time-saving devices. During the National Football League's Super Bowl game in 2008, advertising spots shrank from the traditional 30-second time slot down to a single second. Quality is reduced to quantity, which is to say quality disappears altogether or remains a metaphysical delusion— haunting quantitative reality, an epiphenomenon, an illusion. With the rise of efficiency to the throne of Ultimate Value and Virtue, time indeed becomes money (and in the case of capitalistic societies, power). Speed is of the essence in the modern technicized world. Technology becomes integrated with the very idea of utopia (i.e., utopia becomes an expression of pure will to power rather than the predicted collective harmony and escape from worldly cares).

Gebser (1949 Ger./1985 Eng.) and Mumford (1934/1963/2010) both point out that technology has supplied the final metaphor of the rational cosmos: nature as gigantic machine performing with the precision of a clock (and with attendant personifications; i.e., father time, mother earth, mother nature, etc.). Similarly, Ellul (1954 Fr./1964 Eng.) and Foucault (1975 Fr./1977 Eng.) argue that the human body, as a part of nature, came to be looked on as a mechanical thing, an automaton or robot (e.g., it is often compared to an automobile engine in biology classes involving discussions of digestion). This view was personified in Rene Descartes's (once considered odd) affection for a robotic mannequin that accompanied him in his travels. Technology does not merely enhance efficiency; it also is viewed as a companion (and even a savior). When television is removed from prisons, riots erupt; this does not happen if a particular show is removed but in reaction to the technology being removed. People "watch" television as a companion more than to watch a particular program (Postman, 1984/2005). Consequently, when "nothing is on," they do not turn away from the apparatus but rather continually search for the least objectionable program available (Postman, 1984/2005). The link between television violence and aggressive behavior in children is stronger than the link between smoking and lung cancer (Strasburger, Jordan, & Donnerstein, 2010). People now spend more time watching video images than sleeping or working (Roberts & Foehr, 2008). Surfing the Internet continues to encroach into work time and space, just as work encroaches on home life and leisure time via technology (and perhaps as a form of passive resistance to these encroachments on home/leisure time). Viewing in the televisual world has been linked to many fundamental changes in human beings and their modes of being, including obesity and its attendant problems, such as the early onset of type 2 diabetes in children (Hannon, Rao, & Arslanian, 2005).

According to Kramer (1997), "efficiency in the pursuit of a system's interests threatens to transform humans into [C]yborgs" (p. 136). In the same vein, Heim (1993) posits that "the danger of technology lies in the transformation of the human being, by which human actions and aspirations are fundamentally distorted" (p. 61). With the use of computer technologies, a radical change of our everyday communication patterns, thought, and work occurs. It becomes possible, theoretically, to visually monitor the operations of the entire system. There is finally an omnipotent presence (in the form of the all-seeing computer) to oversee and monitor the clockwork-like operation of organizations. Soon, though, information overload occurs, and given the extermination of quality and judgment as nonsense (or at a minimum some empty exercise we don't have time for), rationality is threatened (devalued, at a minimum). Now that a communicative system exists that collects and accesses the entire communicative field, everything (including human beings) is reduced or resignified as a resource base—something to be used to benefit us without regard for the health and/or well-being of that resource. While it could be argued that this phenomenon is not new (i.e., managers have been exploiting workers before the technologizing of the workplace), it can be stated with certainty that technology has provided a powerful tool via which worker exploitation and reduction to mere resource has been taken to new heights. Exploitation becomes the meaning of reason itself. Just because one can access all kinds of information does not mean that one should access or utilize it (just because the dress fits doesn't mean one should wear it), but exploiting this power becomes the ultimate seduction of the Internet.

This move is grounded in (or built on) the modern ego. According to this distortion, reason (or what is rational) becomes that which is "good for me" (i.e., good for me = rational). And there is only one solution—the one that satisfies my needs. Once a solution that suits me is developed, it becomes *the solution* (in the absolutists' positivistic sense). Value is either utterly eliminated or reduced to exploitation (viewed by its utility within the system). That which cannot be exploited (e.g., diamonds or oil too deep in the earth to be transformed into commodities) is worthless (Kramer, 2004b). Thus, the world becomes a form of translation (i.e., removed from the original meaning or purpose—Baudrillard's simulacra/hyperreality), the nexus of which is the human ego and its individual, subjective interests. Consequently, an absurd condition arises by which reason is reduced to subjective want. The world fragments into competing interests and ultimately is destroyed, as shown in the massive extinction of other life forms on the planet as a direct result of the uncontrolled human pursuit of personal happiness (which has come to mean progress as measured by consumption). Individuals argue (out of self-interest) that the facts are debatable and that the consequences are open to interpretation, even in the face of irrefutable evidence that entire ecosystems are vanishing. People have made an epistemological shift: Politicians are now allowed to tell us what science is, means, and so on. Ultimately, we can't really blame anyone but ourselves for allowing this (mindless) shift in sensibility. We have allowed ourselves to become so ignorant about earth, water, air, science, and so on that we are reliant on experts and their technologies, and accordingly we are at their mercy. Without a transcending force, there is nothing to temper human will, power, and drive to buy, buy, buy (which, according to many humans, is actually good): Greed is good because it gets things done.

Such shifts require a tremendous prejudice in the form of dehumanization, most starkly manifested in various forms of slavery and other atrocities. It is argued herein that this tendency toward the mechanization of nature and lifeworld is a legacy of the Cartesian subject-biased prejudice.[3]

---

[3]The Cartesian subject-biased view is the same as the Cartesian object-biased view. Both terms indicate the subject-object dualism that has influenced almost all modern rationalism. Although there are many differences in specific topics and aims of various areas of postmodern and deconstructive critique, what they share is this bias: Although they differ in specific topics and approaches, many postmodern and deconstructive critiques share the Cartesian bias of rationalism. In the current study, the concept "present-obsessed way of thinking" indicates the same bias manifested through different aspects (Culler, 1982; Kramer, 1988, 1997; Seung, 1982). Heidegger (1952, 1954, 1962 Ger./1977 Eng.) insists that the last stage of this bias is evinced when everything is regarded as standing reserve/resource; he calls it the end of thinking—calculation. Chapter 12 details these concepts.

Basic Issues and Themes

The position that conceives of technology as a set of instruments used to transform things can be regarded as having Cartesian and subjectivist biases. From this biased standpoint, it is supposed that an individual can use a thing as an instrument to affect a desired result in the outer world. This presumes an unsophisticated and inadequate notion of will that fails to comprehend the availability of alternatives and the reversibility (not simple dialectical interaction) of the language-world as being spoken (and as speaking, heard, and/or interpreted). A critical investigation of the Cartesian subject-biased viewpoint will be outlined in Chapter 11 and further elaborated in Chapters 12 and 13. These chapters establish that the clear-cut differentiation between subject and object is absurd. Rather an ecological paradigm is used because it better explains the human-technology relationship. Technology is viewed as both text and context at once. Humanism—the human condition—is altered by the text and context in our contemporary, highly technicized world.

In his work *The Crisis of European Sciences and Transcendental Phenomenology*, Husserl (1954 Ger./1970 Eng.) displays a strongly critical attitude toward modern science and technology. He describes a great divide between physicalistic objectivism and transcendental subjectivism. In assessing the reconstruction of modern mathematics via the technical use of formulae in the sciences, Husserl (1954 Ger./1970 Eng.) concludes that the process he calls technicization (*technisierung*) is the central cause of the division and consequent crisis of modernity. Herein, the word "technicization" is used to mean *technisierung* rather than David Carr's (1970) English translation, "technization," which appears in Edmund Husserl's (1954 Ger./1970 Eng.) *Crisis of European Sciences and Transcendental Phenomenology*.[4]

Technicization connotes the narrowing of experience through abstraction from other meanings. The consequence is an oversimplified focus on (e.g., in science) the method instead of deep sense-making or an emphasis on following empty rules rather than working toward fuller understandings. This pathological form of technicization turns reality into a resource for possible pragmatic worlds. According to Husserl (1954 Ger./1970 Eng.), the process of technicization achieves an increase in efficiency at the cost of meaning (a lot of know *how* but not much know *why*).

Influenced by Husserl, Merleau-Ponty (1945 Fr./1962 Eng., 1947, 1955, 1964 Fr./1964 Eng.) suggests the notion of the "embodiment" of technolo-

---

[4]"Technization" is the translation used by David Carr (1970) in the English version of Husserl's (1954 Ger./1970 Eng.) *The Crisis of European Sciences and Transcendental Phenomenology*. But actually "technicization" is more appropriate as the word "technic" is used by Lewis Mumford (1934/1963/2010) to connote a process and way of life.

gy. But "embodiment" for Merleau-Ponty does not presume the Cartesian mind-body dichotomy. Rather, he conceives the material relationship between humans and the world as a symbiotic and mediated relation instead of a divided, instrumental one. Technicization is a relationship, not a thing in itself. Thus (as we have noted repeatedly), computerization is not the same as a physical computer (Berdayes & Murphy, 2000). Humans are the only agents who can experience and reflect this relationship. Humans cannot reflect the relations from outside, from a god's view, for example; rather we must do it from within the relations themselves, with a navigational and embodied view — a perspective, a reality.

The more the lifeworld is technical, the more our perception of the world is technical (Postman, 1992; Vanderberg, 2005). We come to perceive technology through a technical perspective, and as this perspective gains currency, all things (including Self and Other) come to be seen as technical objects available for technical function. At the extreme, this can lead to the dehumanization of humanity. All becomes base resource, subject — that which subjects itself to a higher, transcending reason or purpose in the name of efficiency. For instance, the sacrifice of thousands of soldiers can be seen as a "necessary" and "acceptable" sacrifice given a larger or "higher" strategic purpose (and, of course. the view is very different when your son or daughter comes home in a box or with missing limbs or mental capacity, even if the box does have a flag on top). A spatial metaphysic emerges here — expressed as a hierarchy of tactical movement in pursuit of a higher strategic goal. A logic of perspectival pragmatism of expediency (with the transcending goal as its pivot) becomes reason and logic itself. Reason thus becomes an expression of the modern hypertrophic ego, utterly subjective, goal oriented, and valuated as perspectival positivism. The cause transcends all and life is reduced to a (stated, i.e., public) purpose outside itself. The meaning of a thing, process, or person is reduced to use-value and is measured against progress toward goal attainment. Materialism is the metaphysical basis of this technological ontology. Thus, despite its rationalist reputation as the ultimate purveyor of unbiased, pristine fact, technology is hardly free of values and ethics.

According to Merleau-Ponty (1945 Fr./1962 Eng.), the human body is a center that always finds the "maximum or optimal grip" (p. 302; see also Merleau-Ponty, 1947, 1955, 1964 Fr./1964 Eng.) in its relations with technology in particular and with the existential world in general. In a different description of this fundamentally embodied (i.e., symbiotic) relationship, Ihde (1990) argues that, "technics (technology) is a symbiosis of artifact and user within a human action" (p. 73).

In his book *Technology and the Lifeworld*, Ihde (1990) focuses on human-technology relations and the cultural embeddedness of technologies. Following a relativistic ontology, he draws a distinction between the "direct

bodily and perceptual experiences of others and the immediate environment" and "technologically mediated experiences" (p. 15). Based on the
notion of embodiment, he suggests that we look for different degrees of
mediation in our technologically textured world. Ihde (1990) argues,

> There is . . . a deeper desire which can arise from the experience of
> embodiment relations. It is the doubled desire that, on one side, is a wish
> for *total transparency*, total embodiment, for the technology to truly
> "become me." . . . The other side is the desire to have the power, the
> transformation that the technology makes available. Only by using the
> technology is my bodily power enhanced and magnified by speed,
> through distance, or by any of these other ways in which technologies
> change my capacities. These capacities are always different from my
> naked capacities. . . . The desire is, at best, contradictory. I want the
> transformation that the technology allows, but I want it in such a way
> that I am basically unaware of its presence. I want it in such a way that
> it becomes me. Such a desire secretly rejects what technologies are and
> overlooks the transformational effects which are necessarily tied to
> human-technology relations. This illusory desire belongs equally to
> pro- and anti-technology interpretations of technology. (p. 75)

This description of the connection between human beings and technology
clearly articulates one of the arguments of this study: the existence of *technological embodiment* or *embodied vision*.

To understand the meaning of communication technology, it is crucial
to understand the notion of embodiment based on the critique of subject-
biased perspectives. In addition, it should be obvious that there are no
grounds for supposing that the technological revolution takes place in one
moment at a specific time. Instead, this transformation occurs throughout
long periods of time, at various paces, and to differing degrees. Further, we
should also take into account the following consideration: The influence of
the use of media on the structures of the mind should not be interpreted as
traveling along a unidirectional path or in a single plane.

Are we doomed to be merely a ready-to-use resource? Does communication end as thinking has arrived at the final stage: calculation? Not necessarily. The development of modern, state-of-the-art communication technology relieves physical (not communicative) effort. The aim of this study is
to investigate ways of grasping the meaning of communication technology
in the context of this modern technological milieu. In this investigation,
Gebser's (1949 Ger./1985 Eng.) insights serve as an exceptional guide.

Gebser (1949 Ger./1985 Eng.) does not side with the prophets of doom,
nor does he believe that our civilization's progress is inevitable as many
futurologists assert. For Gebser (1949 Ger./1985 Eng.), technology is a projection of the rational consciousness that needs to be understood and

retracted from a position that transcends the inherent limitations of rational consciousness. Gebser (1949 Ger./1985 Eng.) argues that this retraction need not entail an annulment of technology: That would only amount to a denial of the constitutive structures of consciousness and the dissolution of existing forms and effects of civilization. Rather, Gebser (1949 Ger./1985 Eng.) argues for a perspective that recognizes a balance based on the actualization of an intensified consciousness: aperspectivity. Aperspectivity allows rationality to be integrated into a diaphanous *awaring* of all the modes of human consciousness, creating an integral, coherent whole. This study suggests that aperspectivity can be utilized to grasp the meaning of communication technology as it offers a means to appreciate the technology of systematization as well as pre- and un-perspectival forms of truth/reality (e.g., taste and smell, although difficult to share "objectively," are shared rather effortlessly, nonetheless).

Rationale of the Study

According to country, climate, and population, the definition of "one best way" will undoubtedly vary, thereby creating the illusion of substantial differences. Nevertheless, Ellul (1954 Fr./1964 Eng.) argues, "all those differences will have been calculated by some technician with the same automatistic logic" (pp. 130-131). Under these modern technological cultural conditions that regard any difference as deviance, deviation implies more than mere difference. The central difficulty is that technology's current mode of rational-scientific legitimation encourages a style of intercultural delivery and implementation that is insensitive to cultural exigencies and, thus, subverts existing social meanings and practices (Kramer, 2003a; Pilotta & Widman, 1986).

Through the mediation of now omnipresent information, communication, and image technologies, the notion of "country" is no longer meaningful because the "global village" is not a village, but rather an urban complex of global diversity, including all the ethnic neighborhoods contained within the city (Kramer, 2003a). As Kramer (1997) suggests, "the call for monoculturalism is a consequence of this fundamentalistic reductionism. The empirical reality of multiculturalism is not conducive to the values of utility, efficiency, and profitability, which are held supreme by modern pragmatism" (p. 120; also see Kramer, 2003a). Within this context, recognizing the tendency to "streamline" multiculturalism for the sake of efficiency, this study will explore and criticize the modern paradigm from which problematic understandings of communication and communication technology stem. Examples of technology streamlining cultures can be demonstrated through consideration of the various characters found in languages that are rapidly being eliminated in the hardware/software of computer-mediated communication (and in the users too), such as the two dots above certain vowels in Swedish or the tilde over the n in Spanish.

Rooted in this exploration, the second aim of this study is to investigate the notion of embodiment through comparison between the modern notion of vision (visiocentrism) and Merleau-Ponty's (1945 Fr./1962 Eng., 1947, 1955, 1964 Fr./1964 Eng.) embodied vision. This comparison illustrates the absurdity of the Cartesian viewpoint and provides a different way of seeing the relationship between humans and technology. In addition, this study explores the semiotic transformation occurring in the technological milieu and explains the meaning of that transformation: semiosis and communication as mere calculations, coexistent with communication and semiosis as forms (processes) of aperspectivity. Finally, the implication of the explorations mentioned above are discussed in terms of the critical situation of intercultural communication and the meaning of alterity (Otherness) (e.g., the encounters with alterity in the modern technological milieu).

The contentions in our study are supported through the use of examples. Zimmerman (1990) offers a sagacious recognition of the technological situation that he calls a paradox:

> Instead of trying to "solve" the problem of modern technology by furious actions and schemes produced by rational ego, then, Heidegger counseled that people learn that there is no exit from the "problem." We are cast into the technological world. Insight into the fact that there is no exit from it may, in and of itself, help to free us from the compulsion which characterizes all attempts to become "masters" of technology—for technology cannot be mastered. Instead, it is the destiny of the West. We can be "released" from its grip only to the extent that we recognize that we are in its grip: this is the paradox. (p. 220)

Hence, our understanding of our technological dilemma is constrained by our situatedness within the context of technology. Therefore, the first step on the path to freedom is to realize the paradox of freedom in the modern technological milieu. Acceptance of the paradox does not guarantee that one will be free; however, it does remove the concealing shroud, thereby creating an opening—a crack in the veneer of our constrained perceived reality—just as realizing the structural limits of language allows us to think with greater awareness and clarity.

Central to this study is the exploration of how we are to live with and in our technological society without becoming just another component in the machinery. However, theorizing about communication will never be more than an exploration, in the sense that exploration does not entail end. The purpose of this work, therefore, is not to provide a solution but rather to question the meaning of communication and its technology in this technological milieu. As Heidegger (1952, 1954, 1962 Ger./1977 Eng.) suggests, questioning builds a way.

9

Theoretical Background

This study draws primarily, although not exclusively, from the works of Maurice Merleau-Ponty and Jean Gebser as proponents of the phenomenological tradition. Not only are they the dominant figures in this tradition, but they are also the two figures most concerned with critiquing the Cartesian objectivistic paradigm of reason.[1] Each of these writers provides a different way of understanding, grounded ultimately in the differences between consciousness structures (that shape human experiences) and the lived experience of the human world.

MERLEAU-PONTY

Merleau-Ponty's Phenomenology: The Body

The starting point for Merleau-Ponty's (1945 Fr./1962 Eng.) analysis is Husserl's (1913 Ger./1982 Eng.) phenomenology. Husserl suggested that the

[1]Building on the work of René Descartes, particularly *Meditations on First Philosophy* (1641 Lat./1647 Fr./1901 Eng.), in which he discarded all knowledge of which he was not absolutely certain and then attempted to rebuild knowledge from that which was indubitable, the objectivist paradigm demands that knowledge must exist on universal truths that exist prior to and apart from thought, observation, or direct experience.

Kantian world *an sich* (thing itself) should be perceptually enclosed in parentheses, as a means of shifting the focus to the ways in which the world takes shape and is organized by the self. For Merleau-Ponty (1945 Fr./1962 Eng.), reality is most engrossing when it appears to people as a phenomenon (Low, 2000; Madison, 1981). Merleau-Ponty (1947, 1955, 1964 Fr./1964 Eng., 1960 Fr./1964 Eng.) does not consider human perception to be analytical; in other words, our perception does not progress in stages such that one first observes something and then unites discrete elements on the level of thought, intelligence, belief, or emotion. Instead, humans interpret elements as entities (i.e., holistically). Every perception is therefore automatically significant. Different perceptions constantly open new horizons for people in the world of experience, and through these horizons, our relation to the world takes shape (Merleau-Ponty, 1947, 1955, 1964 Fr./1964 Eng., 1960 Fr./1964 Eng.). This is veritional diaphaneity (Gebser, 1949 Ger./1985 Eng.; Kramer, 1997a).

In describing the experience of perception, Merleau-Ponty (1945 Fr./1962 Eng.) seeks to divorce himself from what he terms *pensee objective* (objective thought). From the perspective of objective thought, an observed space is a system of mathematical coordinates in which objects are clearly defined (Merleau-Ponty, 1945 Fr./1962 Eng.). In contrast, Merleau-Ponty (1945 Fr./1962 Eng.) asserts that "visual observation is perhaps better described as a landscape on a foggy day; the objects we observe are always blurry to some extent" (p. 12). Perception points toward a world characterized by always being already there, as well as having the quality of overdetermination, whereby things in the world have their own eloquence, as objects are not dependent on being perceived. In Merleau-Ponty's (1945 Fr./1962 Eng.) view, objects cannot be fully grasped as mere objects waiting to be perceived.

From his speculation about perception, Merleau-Ponty (1945 Fr./1962 Eng.) arrives at conclusions contradictory to those of Cartesian philosophy: "Givens" are neither simple nor unconstituted wholes. For phenomenology, intuitions are constituted not given. Only already constituted intuitions are given within an already sedimented context. The subject of perception is not a Cartesian consciousness; rather it is the body as being in the world or existence (Langer, 1989; Madison, 1981; Matthews, 1999).

Merleau-Ponty's Critique of Cartesian Bias

Merleau-Ponty (1947, 1955, 1964 Fr./1964 Eng.) criticizes objectifying thought (he alternately calls it "scientific thinking" or "operational thinking") because it reduces everything to a shallow state of being. Objectifying thought considers the object-in-general and claims to view things "as they really are." As a consequence, the notion of things as related to a universe of being disappears, leaving us with mere objects of an independent shallow nature that exist only to be manipulated (Kramer, 2000a, 2004b). The loss of a sense of ontological depth also turns human beings into human material (i.e., resources waiting to be used). Objectifying thought, then, creates an existential crisis. In his warning against such thinking, Merleau-Ponty (1947, 1955, 1964 Fr./1964 Eng.) states,

> Thinking "operationally" has become a sort of absolute artificialism . . . where human creations are derived from a natural information process, itself conceived on the model of human machines. If this kind of thinking were to extend its reign to man [*sic*] and history; if, pretending to ignore what we know of them through our own situations, it were to set out to construct man [*sic*] and history on the basis of a few abstract indices (as a decadent psychoanalysis and a decadent culturalism have done in the United States)—then . . . [hu]man[kind] really becomes the *manipulandum*. (p. 160)

The most critical implication of the reduction of people and things to shallow being is that they are meaningful only insofar as they can be manipulated based on mechanical, calculative law. Thus, the "'objective human' turns self into an instrument, a 'self-polishing mirror' of Reality—as if this is an end itself, indeed the salvation of man [*sic*] from himself [*sic*], achieving the *caput mortuum* [worthless remains] of all virtue" (Kramer, 1997, p. 94).

In further clarifying the Cartesian bias, two phenomenological critiques are helpful. First, for phenomenology, there can be no such thing as a worldless, independent subject. Doubt may be cast on how to interpret the world; that is, the question remains open as to whether the world is grounded in material, mental, or some other metaphysical tradition or combination of these. However, there is no doubt that there is a world that is present, constantly to be experienced. Second, there is no subject without a world, nor is there any immediately self-transparent subject. The subject in the phenomenological world is deprived of its singular immediacy and presumed self-evidence. In other words, the subject can know itself only by means of the world (the subject meaningfully exists only in its context).[2]

Heidegger's (1927 Ger./1962 Eng.) concept *dasein* illustrates the preceding two phenomenological critiques. *Dasein* is not to be known directly, but rather indirectly, by means of its world. That is, as the world of *dasein*

---

[2]In an interview with Richard Kearney (1984), Derrida clarified his views on subjectivity, expressing a similar attitude: "I have never said that the subject should be dispensed with. Only that it should be deconstructed. To deconstruct the subject does not deny its existence. There are subjects, 'operations' or 'effects' of subjectivity. This is an incontrovertible fact. To acknowledge this does not mean, however, that the subject is what it says it is. The subject is not some meta-linguistic substance or identity, some pure cogito of self-presence; it is always inscribed in language. My work does not, therefore, destroy the subject; it simply tries to resituate it" (p. 125).

changes, so does *dasein*. The subject knows itself in terms of its world, its Other (Kramer, 1988, 1997). Despite the claims of objective thought, the subject cannot be reduced to a worldless shallow being, to an object for manipulation. With subject as being in the world, more is meant than is intended in each expression. Thus, a hermeneutic process is needed to explicate the unsaid (such as features of the context).

Obsessed with presence, objectifying thinking posits that meaning exists in self-presence, and hence, that to speak is to put a ready-made signification under each thought. Alternatively, Merleau-Ponty's (1945 Ger./1962 Eng., 1964 Fr./1968 Eng.) notion of being as horizon suggests that what generates meaning for a sign is not the sign itself but rather an invisible differentiation between that sign and others. Merleau-Ponty's situated subject (regardless of whether it is seen as the practical actor on the world or as the expressive subject) is already involved in a historically finite system of instrumental and expressive conditions and capacities. For example, as Heidegger (1927 Ger./1962 Eng.) illustrates, in using a tool, the body acts on the world with extended capacity. In so doing, the body is modified and defined by the tool (see also Dreyfus, 1995; Zimmerman, 1990).

The Primacy of Perception

In the preface to *Phenomenology of Perception*, Merleau-Ponty (1945 Fr./1962 Eng.) explicitly situates his work within the context of phenomenological philosophy, issued earlier from Husserl (1913 Ger./1982 Eng.). Merleau-Ponty, particularly in his early writings (e.g., 1945 Fr./1962 Eng., 1947, 1955, 1964 Fr./1964 Eng.), radicalizes the perceptualism of Husserl and so insists that "the perceived world is the always presupposed foundation of all rationality, all value, all existence" (Merleau-Ponty, 1947, 1955, 1964 Fr./1964 Eng., p. 13; also see preface of Merleau-Ponty, 1945 Fr./1962 Eng.). Merleau-Ponty sees his own development of phenomenology as a nuanced divergence from certain aspects of Husserlianism.[3]

Three distinguishing points of Merleau-Ponty's (1945 Fr./1962 Eng., 1947, 1955, 1964 Fr./1964 Eng., 1964 Fr./1968 Eng.) critiques on Cartesian ideal subjectivism are evident (Langer, 1989; Low, 2000; Madison, 1981). First, the primacy of the perceptual world is the base from which one must begin and the primitive field that must be thoroughly explored. It must be understood that perception here means the perception of phenomenology (that of lived body, lifeworld, time consciousness, etc.) and not that of

---

[3]In this respect, "the most important lesson which the reduction teaches us is the impossibility of a complete reduction" (Merleau-Ponty, 1945 Fr./1962 Eng., p. xiv). This is not a negative comment about Husserl's work, but rather it is the affirmation of what Merleau-Ponty understands an existential phenomenology to be (Merleau-Ponty, 1945 Fr./1962 Eng.; also see Madison, 1981).

Cartesian or modern, neo-Cartesian physicalism. Second, the examination of this primitive field yields certain essential ambiguities about humans and our relations to our world that are better revealed by focusing on the genesis of meaning than by attaining a description of stable essences (i.e., traits). Third, the Cartesian generic emphasis results in the development of an existential philosophy rather than a transcendental idealist one (Merleau-Ponty, 1945 Fr./1962 Eng., 1947, 1955, 1964 Fr./1964 Eng., 1964 Fr./1968 Eng.).

The Body and Optimal (Maximum) Grip

According to Merleau-Ponty (1947, 1955, 1964 Fr./1964 Eng.), in reality an observed space is not a set of coordinates but rather a situation that takes shape in experience. The positions of observed bodies are not points of equal value in a system of coordinates. The observed space is divided into areas of different value, such as right and left, up and down, far and near. Thus, objective reality is an inadequate abstraction to Merleau-Ponty (1947, 1955, 1964 Fr./1964 Eng.). Rather, the perceptual experience of embodied subject must have primacy.

Merleau-Ponty's (1945 Fr./1962 Eng.) argument that perception has primacy expresses an understanding of the centrality of the body. The way the body responds directly to the world inspires Merleau-Ponty (1945 Fr./1962 Eng.) to introduce the concept of "maximum grip" (p. 302). Dreyfus (2001) succinctly describes Merleau-Ponty's point: "[W]hen we are looking at something, we tend, without thinking about it, to find the best distance for taking in both the thing as a whole and its different parts. When grasping something, we tend to grasp it in such a way as to get the best grip on it" (p. 56; also see Madison, 1981). Merleau-Ponty (1945 Fr./1962 Eng.) explains,

> My body is geared onto the world when my perception presents me with a spectacle as varied and as clearly articulated as possible, and when my motor intentions, as they unfold, receive the responses they expect from the world. This maximum sharpness of perception and action points clearly to a perceptual ground, a basis of my life, a general setting in which my body can co-exist with the world. (p. 250)

This notion of lived body is meant to both contrast with the objectified sense of body used in the sciences and refer to a primary, non-reduced sense of living being as embodied being (Madison, 1981). The embodied or incarnate subject is the perceiving counterpart to the perceived world. Thus, the lived body is the perceiving subject in a perceptual world, and the concrete finitude of the body corresponds to the perceived presence of the world (Madison, 1981).

There is no useful or meaningful perception without embodiment. In addition, embodiment is culturally, ideologically, and invisibly situated and saturated; the lifeworld appears between the subject and the world within the focus of perception. So the lived body (which is an embodied subject immersed in a world pregnant with significance) becomes the basic theme of the existential version of the primary perceptual situation. In this sense, relational ontology is held to transcend the dualism of Cartesianism and provides the perspective of multiculturalism. Multiculturalism becomes plausible when Cartesian thinking is set aside and replaced with the view of embodied experience as central. Cartesianism holds that all subjects are basically the same and reason in the same way—meaning that objective morals (The Way) and The Truth (rather than truths) are the goals. But, understanding that each body is different and that subjectivity is an embodied experience makes the tolerance of multiple perspectives possible (Madison, 1981).

Horizon and Silence

The notion of being as horizon brings to light a different explanation of the nature of meaning: Meaning is a matter of differentiation (Merleau-Ponty, 1945 Fr./1962 Eng.). If objective thought is incorrect (and assuming that an opposition between subject and object is not what makes visibility possible in the world), then visibility appears as an object-horizon structure in which something is seen as well as seen with or against (in the midst of) something else. One perceives objects by reference to differentiation, although one does not perceive differentiation (i.e., the process by which we perceive is invisible). Hence, differentiation is the invisible ground of all perception, the unperceived phenomenon on which one's seeing rests (Seigel, 1991).

In addition to perception being multidimensional, it also becomes ambiguous and/or polymorphic in Merleau-Ponty's (1947, 1955, 1964 Fr./1964 Eng.) extension of the Husserlian view. Merleau-Ponty (1947, 1955, 1964 Fr./1964 Eng.) states, "It is remarkable that the uninstructed have no awareness of perspective and that it took a long time and much reflection for humans to become aware of the perspectival deformation of objects" (pp. 74-75). This opening to the macro-perceptual state is, in one sense, made more explicit in Merleau-Ponty's later work (1964 Fr./1968 Eng.), yet in another sense, this perception becomes enigmatic in relation to cultural factors (Low, 2000). In *The Visible and the Invisible*, Merleau-Ponty (1964 Fr./1968 Eng.) illustrates:

> I say that Renaissance perspective is a cultural fact, that perception itself is polymorphic and that if it became Euclidean, this is because it allows itself to be oriented by the system. . . . What I maintain is that there is

an informing of perception by culture which enables us to say that culture is perceived. (p. 212)

Here we have macro-perception. The spatiality of being in the world
clearly describes the bodily existence of perception. However, spatiality
takes its shape in a much broader macro-perceptual context. Perception is
strongly related to culture. Perception is an intangible but primal artifact.
According to Merleau-Ponty (1947, 1955, 1964 Fr./1964 Eng., 1964 Fr./1968
Eng.), the field of implicit silence (or the macro-perceptual context) is
always broader than the focus of explicit speech or perception.

In the metaphor of field and focus, the field is the totality of presence
that may be differentiated according to the question addressed to this totality of presence. Thus, if our question is visual, the field is the whole of the
visual field before us. Focus is the region within the field we attend to in any
given moment. If the example is visual, the focal center may be a certain
object that stands out against the background of the visual field. When we
extend this notion, the field is the phenomenological world, and the focus is
the phenomenologically explicit attention within the world (Low, 2000;
Madison, 1981; Merleau-Ponty, 1947, 1955, 1964 Fr./1964 Eng., 1964
Fr./1968 Eng.).

In the metaphor of silence and speech, silence — as Merleau-Ponty (1945
Fr./1962 Eng.) holds — is the field of pregnant, latent expressiveness *always
already present* for the living subject. Speech is the focal center, the explicit
foreground of meaning that floats and varies. However, speech always
stands out against the background of silence. Therefore, the clarity of explicit meaning is a relative clarity (i.e., relative to the implicitness of the background). Merleau-Ponty (1945 Fr./1962 Eng.) states, "The clearness of language stands out from an obscure background, and if we carry our research
far enough we shall eventually find that language is equally uncommunica-
tive of anything other than itself, that its meaning is inseparable from it" (p.
188). In Merleau-Ponty's (1945 Fr./1962 Eng., 1964 Fr./1968 Eng.) sense,
meaning appears in the non-present (i.e., historical — the past and/or the
future) movement of differentiation that is rendered present through the
body in a particular temporal duration. In other words, meaning emerges as
the invisible movement of differentiations is rendered in the present moment
and with a subject or subject(s). But this present is, as Husserl (1905-1910
Ger./1964 Eng., 1913 Ger./1982 Eng.) points out, an ambiguous phenomenon, a "standing-streaming" (1913 Ger./1982 Eng., p. 197), which occurs as
differentiations are combined in temporal duration. According to Merleau-
Ponty (1945 Fr./1962 Eng.), what makes an object visible and meaningful is
not the object itself; it is an invisible (a continual, seamless, and subconscious
evaluation of the) difference between the object and others. The difference
embodied in what the object is *not* is called "silence" (Merleau-Ponty, 1945

Fr./1960 Eng.). Silence is, therefore, the realm in which meaning originates (Merleau-Ponty, 1945 Fr./1962 Eng.; also see Merleau-Ponty, 1964 Fr./1968 Eng.).

Phenomenologically, the relational distance between focus and horizon is the intentional distance that must include both the perceived referent object as well as the act of perceiving the object. The perspectival lived body is presumed, although not in the same way as in Cartesian-Newtonian frames. One cannot separate the perceived from the act of perception, although this is a necessary presumption for all framing, including the Cartesian-Newtonian variety. Phenomenological measurement is reflexive and utilizes means that determine the (apparent) distance within the correlation of the perceived and the perceiving. As Ihde (1998) indicates, what must be avoided in claims is the false belief that a perspective is equal to an ideal observation or godlike omniscient sight. Because the phenomenological space-time method is reflexive, it does not forget its own embodied situatedness. Therefore, hypertrophic subjectivism—the ego-centric fallacy writ large that one culture has instituted as the Cartesian-Newtonian external perspective—is avoided.

Hence, in perception there are only appropriate or inappropriate contexts and a diversity of fields. Appropriateness is determined by the internal logic of a perceptual system and does not necessarily pertain to other systems. Our power to perceive is intertwined with linguistic and cultural features that are distinctly human—all too human. It is inadequate to claim that perception is a lower or more primitive action than linguistic action. Quite the contrary—perceptual-bodily activity is both the basis for and implicated in all intelligent behavior (Merleau-Ponty, 1947, 1955, 1964 Fr./1964 Eng.).

This point demonstrates why the present study of technology begins with the ideas of Merleau-Ponty and Gebser. The impulse to create mathematics, science, and technology cannot be fully explained by mathematics, science, or technology themselves because this impulse is not mathematical, scientific, technological, or logical. Science is not a scientific invention. Insofar as mathematics and technology are self-generative, they are pure magic. When a mathematician expresses validity by saying that an operational definition is valid when it measures what it claims to measure, such a tautological claim resists reflection. It is a significant instance of the definitive power of making, of pure magic. Similarly, it is no accident that we still concern ourselves with the proper spelling of language. Naming emerges from silence as pure motivation that refers only to itself; it is absolutely arbitrary. Attempts to stop floating meaning, to fixate language, are born of politics, theology, and ideology. Western law in all its forms (from natural law to judicial law to sacred law) involves attempts to establish permanent foundations and maintain a canon, position, wealth, and (in most cases) the status quo (Pospisil, 1978). This process is done by recording laws in material media that exhibit durability to entrench in the lifeworld (Mumford, 1934/1963). Thus far, however, no medium has proven to be permanent.

Such efforts at enlightenment, at knowing (which is nothing more than becoming familiar with something), constitute an attempt to defeat the darkness and silence that contextualize all texts. Knowledge (i.e., the known) is definable only by the boundary that separates it from the unknown—that is, the unknown is known as that which defies domestication and familiarity. We can see the invisible; the absence meets the eye, the field for the focus, the silence for the speech (Merleau-Ponty, 1947, 1955, 1964 Fr./1964 Eng.).

To summarize, Merleau-Ponty's phenomenological approach coheres on three major points. First, Merleau-Ponty rejects notions of pure data, sensory or conceptual. Instead he accepts an essential ambiguity of the perceptual object—an incompleteness, an openness to multiple possibilities; for Merleau-Ponty, those ambiguities are true in actual lived experience. Second, Merleau-Ponty rejects both an objective (mechanical) body and a transparent intelligence (mind) as relevant interpretations of experience. He accepts the embodied subject whose every action is subject to an initial movement from the unformed to the formed, whose gesture precedes any later attained clarity of intellection. Third, Merleau-Ponty rejects an objectively given world in which reality is merely to be discovered (constructed) by the (only) correct method of formal, abstracted geometric structuring. On the contrary, he insists the world is pregnant with significance, and meaning is emergent through an interrogation of the movement of differentiation on, around, and through the body.

Merleau-Ponty (1945 Fr./1962 Eng., 1947, 1955, 1964 Fr./1964 Eng.) argues that the lifeworld appears between the subject and the world within the focus of perception. Thus, the lived body, the embodied subject immersed in a world pregnant with significance, becomes the primary perceptual situation. This unitary and relational ontology transcends the dualism of Cartesian thinking. The essence of the Cartesian dilemma is that the subject and the object have no means by which to communicate. Descartes (1641 Lat./1647 Fr./1901 Eng.) failed to recognize what Hume (1739/1973) saw—the fundamental import of differentiation. Following Husserl's (1954 Ger./1970 Eng., 1913 Ger./1982 Eng.) insights concerning perception, Merleau-Ponty (1945 Fr./1962 Eng., 1947, 1955, 1964 Fr./1964 Eng.) grasps the significance of relational differentiations for communication. The medium is invisible, but the invisible is a necessary condition for the visible, the unknowable is necessary for knowing.

JEAN GEBSER

Consciousness for Gebser (1949 Ger./1985 Eng.) is primarily an expression *of* something. In any expression, specific structures of consciousness are visible in their differing modes, such as language, art, and so forth. Therefore, consciousness is intrinsically tied to the experienced world. This correlative nature may be expressed as consciousness-world, in which world as experienced (i.e., lived reality) is manifested through or by an event, object, expression, context, or horizon (1949 Ger./1985 Eng.).

Every expression is a product of a particular structure of consciousness. Gebser's (1949 Ger./1985 Eng.) project, then, is to gather expressions/phenomena of a culture and discover what kind of consciousness would make such expressions. Particular expressions/phenomena share a common field of implications into which other expressions/phenomena fit; by becoming aware of this commonality, a structure in consciousness is rendered apparent. Gebser's usage of consciousness embraces concepts such as the Cartesian ego's consciousness, biological consciousness, and more, including the term *unconscious*, which is assumed, silent, tacit, unseen, and unfelt, but nonetheless operates, and can be made transparent or visible.

Gebser (1949 Ger./1985 Eng.) identifies five consciousness structures as constitutive sense-worlds. They are delineated by their essential qualities: the zero-dimensional archaic, the one-dimensional magic, the two-dimensional mythic, the three-dimensional mental, and the four-dimensional integral structures. While more structures or substructures may exist, any discussion of them would be metaphysical speculation because evidence for such structures is not robust. The evidence amassed by researchers such as Gebser (1949 Ger./1985 Eng.), Mickunas (1998), Kramer (1992, 1993b, 1997), and others thus far consistently evinces the five structures.

Consciousness dimensions did not/do not evolve along a linear path by slow degrees across time. They do not unfold in a gradual framework as postulated by classical Darwinian evolutionary theory. Rather, the change in consciousness structures occurs in quantum-like, discontinuous leaps. Already in the late 1940s—well before Stephen Gould's (2006) work on the evolution of consciousness—Gebser (1949 Ger./1985 Eng.) concluded that consciousness mutates in an unpredictable manner to a new intensity or dimension that does not negate previous structures. In the same way that Merleau-Ponty's (1945 Fr./1962 Eng.) field informs focus or silence shapes speech, in Gebser's (1949 Ger./1985 Eng.) consciousness structure, the dominant mode of awaring (i.e., forming perceptions) is informed by those latent modes that are ever-present. The importance of Gebser's idea lies in the fact that all expressions of consciousness are intimately tied to space and time, although not in a linear progression (for space itself is not a spatial phenomenon per se; e.g., it makes no sense to ask how long space is). Expressions, beliefs, attitudes, behaviors, and the like are manifest interpretations of the world and being in it through the space-time "lens" of the current consciousness structure. For the past 100 years or so, the dominant consciousness structure of humanity has been mutating from the mental structure to the integral. The first manifestation of this new aperspectival, integral reality is the inclusion of time perception as a fourth dimension (Gebser, 1949 Ger./1985 Eng.).

Gebser's Notion of Perspective

According to Gebser (1949 Ger./1985 Eng.), this emergent aperspectival awareness reveals itself in modern physics no less than in fine arts and poetry. He first conceived of the idea of the aperspectival as a description of observed expressions not limited to art but applicable across manifestations of (especially Western) civilization, including science. According to Gebser (1949 Ger./1985 Eng.), among the three formations of perspective—unperspectival, perspectival, and aperspectival—there exists the same meaning-relationship as (for instance) among the illogical, logical, and alogical or the immoral, moral, and amoral. We should not take "aperspective" as contrasting with or as a negation of "perspective." The opposite of perspective is non-perspective. Instead, the aperspectival is liberation from the exclusive constraints of unperspectival mythic and perspectival mental rational worlds. This is why Kramer (1992, 1997) argues that Gebser was one of the first great postmodern thinkers because Gebser recognized—as Nietzsche (1901 Ger./1967 Eng.) had before him—the fundamental danger of modern fascism, including the exploitation of illogical myth as embraced by Heidegger (1952, 1954, 1962 Ger./1977 Eng.), thus revealing the latter's failure to understand the deficiencies of reductionism, whether materialistic or linguistic.

Gebser articulated a profound understanding of the aperspectival nature of emergent postmodernity while Derrida was six years old (Kramer, 1992). Gebser's (1949 Ger./1985 Eng.) scholarly rigor is immediately evident in his care with words and concepts. With the aperspectival, Gebser uses the Greek prefix "a-" (aperspectival) to break the presumed exclusive validity of mental-rational (perspectival) and mythic (unperspectival) structures, *not* to negate them or reiterate the modernist project by synthetically ordering all consciousness structures within a single unit. Gebser (1949 Ger./1985 Eng.) states, "Our designation, then, does not attempt to unite the inherently coexistent unperspectival and perspectival structures, nor does it attempt to reconcile or synthesize structures which, in their deficient modes, have become irreconcilable" (p. 2). According to Gebser, the aperspectival indicates a form of being and awaring that transcends the dualism of mental affirmation and negation. Here, the prefix "a-" has a liberating character, as mentioned. Gebser's designation does not attempt to unite the unperspectival with the perspectival; he views them as co-existent. Nor does his insight about the emergent integral represent an experiment in synthesis that can at best promise only momentary validity before fragmenting. Finally, Gebser's view is a reconciliation of what has become irreconcilable by becoming self-destructive. Rather, the integral aperspectival is diaphanous, a transparent consciousness structure that enables our awaring of the mental perspectival and the mythic unperspectival, as well as the magic pre-perspectival structures (Gebser, 1949 Ger./1985 Eng.).

Pictures of the pre-perspectival magic period were painted during pre-dawn consciousness, when objects are shadowless and flat, when darkness absorbs space so that only its immaterial component remains to be expressed. By virtue of perspective, depth and space are made visible and brought out into the daylight of waking consciousness. As a result, the human self attains visibility of self as separate from other things. The comprehension of the human as subject is conditioned by a comprehension of world as object, thus situating the modern perspectival human as an object among objects (Gebser, 1949 Ger./1985 Eng.).

To see or think perspectivally means to see and think with spatial fixation. Today, human beings are suffering from the deficient dominance of the perspectival mental consciousness (Gebser, 1949 Ger./1985 Eng.). The gradual emergence of perspective, which became a principal concern of Renaissance humanity, had the effect of expanding the world while narrowing it through spatialization. Ellul (1954 Fr./1964 Eng., 1977 Fr./1980 Eng.), Heidegger (1977), and Mumford (1934/1963/2010, 1967) have all expressed concerns about the consequences of this spatialization, concerns about overpowered and overpowering perspectivism, and the kind of self-empowerment that leads to self-entrapment. The human being is merely part of the world. But hypertrophic perspectivism unconsciously (unreflexively) postulates its finite perspective as not only the dominant position, but the exclusive one from which all knowing is possible. The partial thus becomes the absolute. Many faux postmodernists are just as trapped, just as obsessed with such perspectivism as are the modernists they decry. While modernists refuse to allow or acknowledge any other less "positive" episteme, the deconstructionists stress perspectivism to the point of solipsism. They fail to see any way out of one's own egocentric existence. Both modernists and deconstructionists ignore the dynamic integrating process of communication that liberates one from ego-centrism, opening up and challenging the self-centered perspectival universe with what both Levinas (1987) and Merleau-Ponty (1968 Fr./1970 Eng.) term *alterity* (Otherness).

The ego-driven dominance of the perspectival is threatened by alterity. If a person is powerful, then this power is manifested as control, including the control of what information is considered to be real (or, at the least, relevant). Ironically, often the more powerful a person is, the less contrary talk, opinion, and unpleasant information he or she tolerates. Hence, a powerful person may be defined as having control over what information will be tolerated and thus introduced to that ego. Elimination of the alterity of serendipity and genuine Otherness may cultivate a sense of security, of self-sameness, but it also breeds an increasingly narrow purview of who and what exists, and what is possible. Thus, the more powerful a person is, the more isolated he or she tends to be (Kramer, 1991). An intensely powerful ego tends to control incoming information and the valuations of information so that growth is inhibited and the status quo is maintained. If this power enforces resistance to alterity such that those around the powerful person dare not contradict what the powerful person says or does, then the powerful person becomes surrounded by "sheeple" whose primary function is to assist the powerful to insulate themselves from different opinions. Even having neutral perspectives is inappropriate—sheeple must actively reinforce the voices of the powerful, including his or her personal prejudices (Kramer, 1991).

It is important to underscore here that alterity is not a moment in interaction. Rather, as Nietzsche (1887 Ger./1974 Eng.) recognized when reflecting on the "genius of the species," it is the structure of reality, thought, and awareness. Alterity is essential to humanity as a communicative species. Humans who claim to be divine or all-powerful exhibit a lack of humanity—an inability to grow, to learn, to hear alternate voices. The human being is fundamentally a thinking, communicating animal. In communicative terms, alterity presumes the chiasm—the boundary difference from which informative variance emerges rather than redundant sameness. The invisibility that marks the nature of implication characterizes the chiasm. Neo-Nietzscheans such as Derrida have not grasped the radicality of either Nietzsche or Husserl, and thereby they have failed to benefit from the insight of their benefactors. Nietzsche (1887 Ger./1974 Eng.) states that thinking, consciousness, language, and knowing are never trapped within a self-contained perspective. Rather, they are communicative phenomena that emerge within self-structuring—the conversation within the difference—that makes exchange and conversation possible. Likewise, Husserl (1905-1910 Ger./1964 Eng.) decenters the metaphysics of thingism, arguing that reality is relational. Even under the extreme conditions of interrogation, the interrogator does not control the outcome of an encounter; interrogation is inherently a foray into the unknown. Interlocutors belong to a conversation, not the other way around.

For the perspectivist, the part is the whole. This worldview is the world's view. For this reason, it is important to consider those incisive events that Gebser (1949 Ger./1985 Eng.) calls mutations in the consciousness of humankind. Mutation is the most profound violation of sameness. Mutative differentiation has global (i.e., holistic) consequences. The possibility of mutation is latent within each of us in the form of the different structures of consciousness. These mutational possibilities both constitute and are constituted by our own being, as they are manifested in our sense of being (and expressions, communication acts, etc.). Mutation proceeds as a reintegration, a restructuration of all relationships, of consciousness. Gebser describes four mutations of consciousness that have occurred in the history of humanity. These mutations are not merely changes of perspective, nor are they simple paradigm shifts. Rather, they are fundamentally different ways of experiencing reality or, more accurately and less dualistically, different ways of being. These four mutations reflect five separate eras that are not distinct and isolated from one another, but rather appear intermingled so that all previous consciousness structures are found in subsequent ones and all subsequent structures lie latent within the previous ones (Kramer, 1992).

Each of these five structures is associated with some degree of dimensionality. The first structure is associated with archaic zero-dimensionality that exhibits no distinction between Self and Other. The second, magic consciousness structure, is one-dimensional in accordance with the point-like identification of Self *with* Other, while the mythic consciousness (the third structure) emphasizes polarity as reflected in its two-dimensionality. The fourth structure is the three-dimensional mental perspective involving objectification of Self and Other, situating them in dualistic opposition. Finally, there is the emergent integral (the fifth structure), in which latent structures compound, allowing the eventual exhibition of the fourth dimension. To say "third" or "fourth" in this situation implies the existence of the previous structures (plus the archaic zero-dimensional structure). Each structure is experienced at any privileged time (i.e., a particular moment) as implicating the others and involves any combination of the previously occurring structures, for privileging latently incorporates that which is denied (Gebser, 1949 Ger./1985 Eng.). Thus, the fourth dimension, associated with the integral consciousness structure, allows the latent awaring of zero-, one-, two-, and/or three-dimensional consciousness by privileging the perception and the perspective associated with a given structure in a given moment, time and space, or context.

This aperspectival awareness frees the integral consciousness structure to incorporate the other consciousness structures. No longer limited by perspectivism or unperspectivism, and no longer confined to the dark of preperspectivism, the integral aperspectivism nonetheless does not invalidate the other structures—quite the opposite. Through the integral consciousness, all ways of being are manifest and transparent in human experience; we perceive and express in any mode of the five structures (or combinations of the structures) of consciousness (Gebser, 1949 Ger./1985 Eng.).

FIVE STRUCTURES OF CONSCIOUSNESS

In Gebser's (1949 Ger./1985 Eng.) explanation of the five consciousness structures, the conception of mutation is of central significance. Essentially something new can only be discovered if one becomes aware of the old. For Gebser, the adage that there is nothing new under the sun is only conditionally true. Everything has indeed already been, although in another manner, in another light, under a different value system, in some other realization, in another manifestation. Gebser's work has a strong historical-evolutionary component; however, this must be understood within the appropriate context. The different structures of consciousness do *not* represent a progressive shedding of structures into the past in order to evolve into higher states of consciousness. Rather, as he consistently argues, the various structures are co-constituents, all essential features of our current, predominantly modern world/consciousness. That is to say, we are part archaic, magic, mythic, and integral as we are mental-rational (Gebser, 1949 Ger./1985 Eng.).

Currently, the archaic, magic, and mythic are most generally integrated according to the premises of the mental structure, manifested as deficient rationality in the modern (objectivist, positivist) view. Thus, the other structures are somewhat distorted, latent, and sometimes invisible as they are understood in mental-rational ways. Yet they are operant in our daily lives—we hold irrational beliefs, follow irrational hunches, and irrationally identify with things. This is an important insight that has great practical relevance. Gebser (1949 Ger./1985 Eng.) does not regard the rational consciousness as the culmination of the evolution of human consciousness. On the contrary, he claims that much of modernity, including its characteristic obsession with value-freedom that liberates *techne* from *phronesis* (prudence), has repeatedly proven catastrophic. This is because when mental consciousness becomes deficient,[4] rationality becomes confused with intolerant logic, moving from a qualitative reasoning to a quantitative rationalizing. Thinking is reduced, truncated to being a mere tool for (nearly exclusively financial) ambition. Still, this deficiency in mental consciousness is nevertheless the harbinger of the collapse of perspectival dominance in the

---

[4]For Gebser, each form of consciousness has both an efficient and a deficient form. The efficient, or emergent, form measures itself in relation to the other modes of consciousness and enhances life. The deficient form only relates to the world in its own terms and thereby destroys life by cutting humanity off from other vital parts of itself. For example, Parmenides saw thinking and being as one in the same, and thus his reason was on an equal plane with the rest of his being. For Descartes, his being is a result of his thinking. In the deficient form, the rest of being becomes subject to (and thus is neglected by) the dominant mode of awaring (the current/local/social way of being).

face of the current mutation to the aperspectival, which diaphanously integrates the five structures of consciousness (Gebser 1949 Ger./1985 Eng.).

The Archaic Structure of Consciousness

Within the archaic structure, consciousness lacks differentiation. Things are not discrete. The process of individuation within the field of awareness is not apparent. Hence, this structure is not consciousness in any sense that we understand today (Gebser, 1949 Ger./1985 Eng.). Instead, it can be linked to a state of deep sleep; as the Chinese philosopher Chuang Tzu (1961) says, "The pure man of old slept without dreams" (p. 72). If we bracket Chuang Tzu's notion of "purity," what is apparent is a way of being in the world without the spatial "in." The archaic is the structure present while the soul sleeps. It is the dreamless and the timeless, in which there is a complete lack of separation or distinction between the individual and the whole, for archaic consciousness is prior to such fragmentation (Gebser 1949 Ger./1985 Eng.).

The word "archaic" derives from the Greek root *arche*, meaning "beginning" (in the sense of origin rather than indicating a specific moment in time). Origin, according to its nature, is ever-present, a quality not contained in the word "beginning." Using archaic origin as ever-present, Gebser (1949 Ger./1985 Eng.) asserts:

> It is our task to presentiate the past in ourselves, not to lose the present to the transient power of the past. This we can achieve by recognizing the balancing power of the latent "'future" with its character of the present, which is to say, its potentiality for consciousness. (p. 43)

We do not want to lose the present to the power of historical determinism and do not want to proclaim the past eliminated by present progress. Understanding origin as ever-present rejuvenates the past without letting it dominate.

Very little direct, tangible evidence is available with regard to the archaic consciousness structure. For Gebser (1949 Ger./1985 Eng.), consciousness is "neither knowledge nor conscience but must be understood for the time being in the broadest sense as wakeful presence" (p. 42). This state of presence or being present does not overpower or delimit the past (past-orientation) or any future-oriented finality, as the notions of past, future, and finality imply change toward an end without considering mutations. The archaic or original structure is not something in the past; rather, it is an ever-present condition necessary for all "subsequent," more complex structures. Although we may not be aware of the archaic or other structures of consciousness, they nonetheless tacitly operate (Gebser, 1949 Ger./1985 Eng.). Just as previous layers of epochal worlds are necessary to support the "top soil," and just as if one digs down, these buried layers are found to be ever-present although not obvious, so too one finds such accrual in genetics and the meta-perspectival world. This accrual process involves not only genetic accrual but also the awareness of genetic accrual and other instances of seeing, thinking, and speaking about perspectives. Such an interpretation is a basic condition of human existence (Gadamer, 1960 Ger./1975 Eng.; Heidegger, 1927 Ger./1962 Eng.; Kramer, 1997; Nietzsche, 1887 Ger./1974 Eng.). Linear modern history writing implies that the past is nothing more than a chaotic pile of remnant artifacts and texts that any historian may compile.

In contrast, hermeneutics (i.e., interpretations) demonstrates the past as a dynamic, synergistic, and ever-present process (or component of the present). It also demonstrates what Derrida (1977 Fr./1988 Eng.) (for his notion of presence as central to all Western metaphysics is more fundamental) means by logocentrism. Hermeneutics reveals the arrogance in the writing of linear histories and what they say about the present—the sense of entitlement at stating and defending (and entrenching as reality) what are nothing more than hypothetical scenarios about the past. The term "history" betrays this arrogance of transcendence, for traditional historians arrange a privileged version of the past that is actually little more than a bricolage. The what, why, and how of any current historian's effort to forge a story with continuity from such disparate bits are expressions of the (a priori) living idea of what a historian is and does—the notion of who does history and how it is passed down. Both a historian's compulsion to "come up with" something and what he or she comes up with are historically conditioned, which is to say history writing is contingent. This is why and how the endeavor can remain a viable challenge to generation after generation of historians. They are free of final conclusions even as they attempt to forge a story that is factual and positively conclusive. Hence, history writing ebbs and flows as different interpretations vie for prominence (Derrida, 1977 Fr./1988 Eng.).

So it is that we say of previous structures (including the archaic are everpresent), although their manifestations may be overlooked or misunderstood, their influence is no less profound. Consciousness structures do not reduce to a story of linear progress that produces the current state, whatever and whenever that may be. This is not to say that all perspective is eliminated—that would be impossible. The point here is that human history does not progress through a series of mutually excluding stages. The simplistic, positivistic notion of progress (as a linear, unidirectional progression) is an expression of a particular time and place; by recognizing it as a particular perspective, we are freed from its prejudice. The past—including origin—remains vital, even in the sense that without it there could be no new (Gebser, 1949 Ger./1985 Eng.). Past and future implicate each other.

For its lack of technology, archaic consciousness has proven profoundly successful for human beings. Technical manipulation presupposes spatial
distantiation (distancing) of an embodied will from the rest of the world as
a resource base, a characteristic of the mental structure, not the archaic. This
distantiation is so successful that it thrives and endures, even enabling the
emergence of "higher order" spatial-logical forms of consciousness with
competitive/conflictive attitudes. Although origin is a necessary condition
for such forms, there is no consciousness of tension between Self and Other
in the archaic. In this world (in which there is no differentiation to even
make the notion of unperspectival possible), the human is sheltered and
enclosed in the world of the "we" — a world without outer objective space
or internal isolation (Gebser 1949 Ger./1985 Eng.).

The Magic Structure of Consciousness

The mutation from the archaic to the magic structure is the emergence
of humanity from a zero-dimensional archaic structure of nonidentity into
a one-dimensional structure of unity. The ideal symbol for one-dimension-
ality — the point — is illuminating as a reference for and a characteristic of
magical humanity. The point expresses the spaceless and timeless condition
in which the magic human lives. Magic consciousness is not yet "awake" to
time and space as either extremely abstract constants or existential coordinates; consequently, it does not "manage" the world as object manipulating
other objects. Magic consciousness has neither a rational structure nor a psychic one; it is a fundamentally *vital* structure that permeates the world of
things, of time(lessness) and space(lessness), only to be experienced, not to
be contemplated or symbolized (Gebser, 1949 Ger./1985 Eng.).
   In the magic world, there is no individualized ego as such, only the ego
of the group or clan: The "I" is not a factor, the "we" is dominant. In this
egoless state, responsibility is lodged in the world as a whole, a world in
which the part is the whole and the whole is the part. The magical human
experiences nascent detachment or fragmentation from and of identity with
the whole, thus becoming "conscious." Magic humanity is marked by an
explosion of conscious reflection, of a new kind of understanding involving
an emergent distinction between self and nature. Consciousness in this
structure is characterized by the magic human's fundamental reflection as
the individual begins to dissociate and therefore becomes able to associate
with nature. Magic structure is a state of becoming aware, and thereby the
necessity emerges for the magic human not only to *be* in the world but also
to *possess* it. Magic power, the essence of the artifact, marks the beginning of
culture as that which is not nature, including the supernatural (Gebser, 1949
Ger./1985 Eng.).

The magic consciousness structure is characterized by its point-like unitary world and point-like egolessness. The point indicates the first "centering" in human consciousness that will later lead to the realization of self. Magic is a break from "harmony" (i.e., from absolute identity with the whole). The individual begins to suffer anxiety due to this dissociation, and the nascent ego begins to stir as manifest confrontation and exertion of will. A rudimentary sense of self emerges, and the need to bridge gaps—to communicate and create networks—gives rise to a consciousness on the way to language and thinking. Purely emotive (primal) calls solidify into standard words; words as vehicles of power emerge, as does incantation as a precursor to prayer (Gebser, 1949 Ger./1985 Eng.).

But this emergent, communicating sense of self is not the three-dimensional, fully distantiated (separated from the surrounding world) sense of self that is endemic to the mental consciousness structure. The magic human only begins to consciously coordinate in various relationships, such as hunting, whereby the not yet existent "I" (ego) is a point within a collective intent of other "mes." I go this way so the prey animal (i.e., not me) will be flushed that way toward the other mes (tribe members) who will kill it. This point-related unity is grounded in a vital nexus that pervades everything, not a rational causal nexus restricted to humankind. Magic people recognize the whole as part and vice versa. In the magic world, blood, milk, and semen— the vital fluids—are sources of power and identity; to drink the blood of an animal or man is essentially the same thing in the vital nexus. Through this interweaving with nature, magic consciousness *experiences* reality as extended self, as agency through external objects, deeds, or events separated from each other as points in an overall unity but bound by the common vitality of things. Therefore, the magic structure is the most vital and honestly emotional of all structures (Gebser, 1949 Ger./1985 Eng.).

Magic consciousness involves an unintentional association in which things that may seem merely similar to the modern perspective are mutually sympathetic to the magic world (i.e., bound by their shared vitality or felt connection). The part cannot and does not *stand for* the whole—it *is* the whole. Each point may, with full validity and effectiveness, take the place of or take on the value of any other point. Such exchange in the magical sphere is not deception; it is a genuinely valid expression of what is "equal." In this equal validity of the whole and the part, there appear two further essential features of the magical world, consisting of the perceived equality of place and equality of value. Equating one thing with the whole has as its consequence what we could call analogical or associative thinking (which is less a form of thinking than an accidental association supported by the analog). Herein lies the root of the magical human's feeling that things that seem similar are mutually sympathetic. The magical human connects them by virtue of the vital nexus as sharing the same spiritual essence. This reaction to the world gives the magic consciousness power (through incantation) and makes the magical human a creator (Gebser, 1949 Ger./1985 Eng.).

Gebser (1949 Ger./1985 Eng.) indicates that from these magic roots arise our machines, our technology, and all our attempts to rule nature and others. Regarding the present study, it is crucial to understand that magic (which is etymologically related to "make," "machine," "mechanism," "might," and similar terms) is the essential means of fulfilling needs. Magic is an effort to control external forces. Thus, casting spells and conducting rituals are ways in which basic vital connections are exploited. The power of the national anthem at a sporting event during a time of national turmoil is an apt example. It is important to note that, "All magic, even today, occurs in the natural-vital, egoless, spaceless and timeless sphere. This requires, as far as present-day [humans are] concerned, a sacrifice of consciousness; it occurs in a state of trance, or when consciousness dissolves as a result of mass reactions, slogans, or 'isms'" (Gebser, 1949 Ger./1985 Eng., p. 49). Magic exhibits completely honest (some might say barbaric, brutally honest, primitive, or even rude) want and need that, when coupled with modern technology, can be catastrophic.

The Mythic Structure of Consciousness

The magical consciousness structure is characterized by the emergent will and becoming aware of nature as Other. Similarly, the mythic consciousness structure is characterized by an emergent awareness of the soul, of the essence of being human. Such a shift signifies the cusp of mythic dimensional increase and the passing of the radical insight of human (as something other than nature) into a normative presumption. If we look on the mythic from the point of view of a growth in consciousness, surprising and illuminating results become evident. This structure is typified by imagination and is therefore distinct from the magic structure, characterized by emotion. In the magic structure, there is a felt unity, a nascent awareness of externality in emotional forms and activities. The mythic structure, in contrast, has an imaginative awareness different from what is imagined. The emergence of image is manifested in the symbolic character of myth and is responsive to the soul, to heaven, to the cosmos, and similar constructions (Gebser, 1949 Ger./1985 Eng.).

The mythic structure is the expression of two-dimensional polarity. Thus, for example, mythic consciousness is attuned to such polarities as light-dark, life-death, heaven-earth, and masculine-feminine, and it reflects these in symbolic imagery. The archaic structure leads (through loss of zero-dimensional wholeness) to one-dimensional unity in the magic structure, foreshadowing an increased awareness that dawns in humans through a process of nascent individuation. The magic structure brings about extrication from nature through struggle against it, making humanity aware of an external world. Yet for archaic and magic humans, dreams, premonitions, and feelings are not private but diffused throughout world-awareness (the lifeworld). In contrast, for the mythic human, the external world begins to coalesce against the internal world, polarizing the dream and waking worlds as co-present opposites (these two poles will not become mutually, dualistically exclusive until the mental rational mutation, explained later). Via co-constitutive genesis, interior and exterior emerge together. Although at first their sense is ambiguous, through this polarity, the mythic structure exhibits an awareness of soul, that is, of an interior world vis-à-vis an exteriority (Gebser, 1949 Ger./1985 Eng.; Kramer, 1993b).

Gebser (1949 Ger./1985 Eng.) submits that whereas magic is point-like, mythic is circular, that mythic human becomes aware of patterns with the cycle emerging as the most dramatic and prominent pattern of the lifeworld. The circle symbolizes the awareness of repetition (i.e., the consciousness of the polar relationship of cycles). In linear temporal terms, the rhythm of nature becomes time-laden. This is the decisive step that magic human took upon emerging from the womb of the group consciousness into the more dissociated story of myth, from unexpected (often terrifying) nature to organized narrative drama (Gebser, 1949 Ger./1985 Eng.).

The symbolic consciousness that characterizes the mythic structure fluctuates between magic timelessness and natural time-bound sense. It is still remote from space-awareness, although already close to time-awareness. Magic is utterly timeless and spaceless; the more a myth is remote from magic awareness, the more time-bound it is (and the more aware of latent spatiality). Myth expresses nascent temporal and spatial awareness manifested as a narrowing or localization, a fragmentation of primordial unity. In this sense, myth is a crisis for the magic human because with myth the cosmos begins to polarize into exterior/interior and good/evil along with consequent reward/punishment. Guilt and shame become not only possible but inevitable as honest emotional need and desire become evaluated, explained, and articulated within storied context (Gebser, 1949 Ger./1985 Eng.).

Mythic human gains a greater awareness, a recognition of self as distinct from Other. In the mythic structure, the "I" of self-contained human ego is not yet fully developed. However, it has developed to the extent that it recognizes and demands a separation from nature, from unity with its environment. This can be regarded as evidence of an increasing crystallization of the ego. This trajectory on the way to selfhood may seem a logical progression to Hegelians and an inevitable one to Spencerians. However, Gebser (1949 Ger./1985 Eng.) does not postulate an overarching plan or logic to emergent dimensionality and its correlate, increased dissociation. The shift to mythic polarity that demarcates the soul/self is not a consequence of a linear process. No final goal is presumed and, therefore, progress is not inferred (Gebser, 1949 Ger./1985 Eng.).

In connection with the current investigation, it is important to recognize that the embryonic consciousness of time lies in the mythic structure as a natural phenomenon in the world. In the mental structure, mythic consciousness of cyclicity becomes abstracted and mechanically fixed as clocktime. Despite this mental-rational mutation, mythic temporal consciousness remains vividly alive and effective in many aspects of human comportment (the lifeworld) (Gebser, 1949 Ger./1985 Eng.).

The Mental Structure of Consciousness

In reaction to the deficiencies of mythic consciousness (e.g., the ambiguity of myth's circular oceanic thinking and the contradictory and directionless plethora of stories of creation and gods and goddesses), classical philosophers such as Socrates, Plato, Aristotle, and Pythagoras stepped out of the mythic circle to confront its convoluted world of ambiguities with the lucid, abstract logic of directed mental consciousness. The effort was to clarify, to think linearly and without contradiction. While mythical thinking (insofar as one may designate it as thinking at all) is an imaginative symbolic projection within the confines of polar cycles (i.e., circles), mental thinking is directional and starkly dualistic as the analyzing mind reaches out into the open space of three-dimensional objects that can be manipulated. Thinking is no longer polarized in the mental structure; the world is no longer complementary pairs. Instead the world is composed of oppositional dualities. Hence, mental consciousness involves a world perceived as fundamentally different from the self—as alien, objective, and external. Abstraction becomes a key word to describe mental activity, and we find humans using their minds to overcome and master the world around them (Gebser, 1949 Ger./1985 Eng.).

The transformation from the civilizational dominance of mythic consciousness to the dominance of mental consciousness was an occurrence so extraordinary it shook the world. Just as the mythic's move to polarize the human-nature unity into an interior soul that was rewarded/punished by an exterior cosmos presented a crisis for magic humans, the mental reality of a disinterested and uncaring universe that destroyed previous valuations presented a crisis for mythic humans. The mythic incorporated humanity into the embrace of the world-soul, wherein humanity lives in polar harmony with nature, cosmos, and time. The modern perspectival human, with a newfound independent ego, leaves the temporality of this protective plane for an empty and dead world, stepping out of the mythic two-dimensional circle into the mental three-dimensional space that the individual will attempt to conquer in thought and deed (Gebser, 1949 Ger./1985 Eng.).

The modern individual is detached from overarching obligations or injunctions. The deification of the independent thinking ego almost universally replaces the plethora of gods; dogma, in both allegory and creed, replaces the symbols of previous times (although of course that which is replaced remains latent in the subconscious). Similarly, contentious ideology displaces sacred story. Linear method displaces the mysteries as humans exhibit an ever-increasing desire to penetrate and, of course, master nature. In the mental structure, the independent world of spheres of influence, power politics, and willpower drive emerges with no restraint from gods, spirits, the collective, or any other mythic authority (Gebser, 1949 Ger./1985 Eng.).

This inauguration of the mental consciousness as a dominant civilizational structure coincides with the "discovery of causality"—that is, the faith in one's ability to trace any phenomenon directly back to a single initiative (i.e., its origins). The straight lines of mental consciousness cut across and through the convoluted and the curved that are reduced to distractions and digressions. Shortcuts as in Occam's razor[5] become valued. Minimalism in clothing, architecture, logic, grammar, music, and so forth marks the modern style. Honorifics and etiquettes, reflecting the authorities and relationships of the mythic world, come to be seen as superfluous as the elaborate and time-consuming ritual obligations of collectivistic culture are minimized in favor of personal freedom of pursuit (Gebser, 1949 Ger./1985 Eng.).

Deriving its power from the individual self, mental consciousness establishes self-world duality. The modern ego is dissociated (alienated) from the objects of the world, which it must conquer, manipulate, and accumulate. For the mentally conscious human, even one's own body becomes an alien object to be managed. For example, the modern is more concerned about his or her physique than his or her soul (deemed nonexistent anyway), working out to shape the body into a pleasing object. The world becomes something for the self to pioneer, something to struggle with and domesticate, to map and subjugate; the world becomes a built world. Thus, three-dimensional, quantitative aspects of the world (i.e., matter and space) are all-important for mental consciousness (Gebser, 1949 Ger./1985 Eng.).

The materialism and duality of the mental structure leave it vulnerable to the rational tyranny of objectivist measurement. Philosophers of the modern era have employed the term "rational" to describe human thinking, yet rational does not encompass all that mental consciousness includes. In fact, Gebser considers rationality the deficient aspect of the mental consciousness structure because of its reduction of the lifeworld to function. Galileo, for example, demonstrates the exaltation of the quantitative when

---

[5]Occam's razor is a philosophical principle taken from the works of William Ockham and holds that plurality should never be posited without necessity. In other words, all else being equal, the simplest explanation is usually the correct one. The term Occam's razor was first coined by Sir William Rowan Hamilton in 1852 at the height of pragmatism in British philosophy.

he attempts to measure everything that is measurable and to make everything measurable that has not been made so before—a project that gave rise to the idea of science as the dominant "religion" of today (Gebser, 1949 Ger./1985 Eng.).

Given its worship of science and functionalism, it is not surprising that mental-rational consciousness prevails in most industrialized societies. This prevalence as well as the structure's inherent duality leads to unavoidable clashes between the mental-rational and the mythic and magic versions of reality. Consider how differently technology and the power to make things happen are structured in the three dimensions. The act of making (i.e., creating) for the magic human is a consequence of the vital nexus—a sacred act of unity. It is less so for the mythic human, yet concerns about harmony between maker and made, and about good and evil as cosmic forces, pervade technology. But for the mental-rational human, making is dissociated from the sacred and cosmic. Making is the individual manipulating the disconnected objects of the detached dualistic world, and technology is neither good nor bad (in the moral sense). Instead it is either pragmatic or not (hence redefining good and bad). With the desirability of creation truncated to what is pragmatic, to what "works," efficient functionality comes to the fore as the primary standard of value (Gebser, 1949 Ger./1985 Eng.).

Hence, technology in the mental-rational world is meaningful only in relation to egocentric interests: It is not possible to speak of good or evil technology but only of its practicality, its rationality/efficiency vis-à-vis the accomplishment of personal benefit. Humans and their interests take center stage in all affairs. What is good is good (not in cosmic terms but) in pragmatic egocentric terms as convenience also emerges as a gauge of technological worth. The expression "biggest bang for the buck" articulates values of both efficiency and convenience projected from an egocentric perspective. Perspectival goals involve what works, and what works is what is self-evidently true (Gebser, 1949 Ger./1985 Eng.). As Nietzsche (1901 Ger./1967 Eng.) points out, technology in the modern world moves beyond good and evil to become amoral-indifferent and value-free. Humans become work machines without regard for personal fulfillment or the righteousness of "right occupation" (as a Buddhist might say). Consequently, workers are dehumanized and evaluated strictly on disinterested measures of efficiency defined in terms of physical work, productivity, and various performance evaluations (Gebser, 1949 Ger./1985 Eng.).

Efficiency and convenience stress the chronic sense of urgency of the modern perspectival world. A temporal anxiety characterizes mental-rational consciousness (e.g., fear of aging, fear of looking fat, fear of being slow, and fear of being late in a punctual environment). The modern version of time is expressed in primarily spatial terms—that is, as a product of the mechanical clock. Time for the mental-rational human is technologized.

Efficiency links spatial motion to time in terms of miles per hour, light years, keystrokes per minute, IQ, time and motion studies, and so forth. In this way, human labor is reduced to work defined as mass multiplied by distance (W = md), which is to say the transfer of energy to an external object causing displacement. Some equate work with the speed of displacement by defining work as equal to distance divided by time (W = d/t). In either case, work, technology, and other aspects of life are reduced to physical measurement (Kramer, 1997).

Exalted as a standard of functionalist value, time thus joins space in the mental-rational world as the other primary measurement, which stresses movement, building, and empirical production over reflection. We can't allow silence in our conversations (as modeled by ever-present media that become a near-circadian rhythm) because pausing to think is an intolerable lapse in noise. With time reduced to three-dimensional abstraction, it can be divided (not to mention killed, saved, wasted, stolen) and is the great divider and measurer. Time is conceptualized (spatialized) as a line, as an arrow that points from the past to the future by way of the present (Feuerstein, 1987; Kramer, 1997, 2004b; Kramer & Ikeda, 2002). History becomes a single thread weaving its way to the present with logical necessity. The mental-rational structure equates this linear sense of temporal progress with the triumph of egocentric objectivism by stipulating perspectivism as the ultimate truth and the end of philosophy as metaphysical speculation through modern scientific certitude. This, however, is an epoch at its end.

During the 1930s and 1940s, before the word "postmodern" was coined, Gebser began cataloging observations that support the claim that we are currently undergoing a mutation that is marked by a predominant concern with and perception of time as the fourth dimension of integral human consciousness. Gebser (1949 Ger./1985 Eng.) observes:

> Whereas the preoccupation of the Early Renaissance was with the concretion of space, our epoch is concerned with the concretion of *time*. And our fundamental point of departure, the attempt to concretize time and thus realize and become conscious of the fourth dimension, furnishes a means whereby we may gain *an all-encompassing perception and knowledge of our epoch*. (p. 16)

Yet many late-moderns—those who are attempting to retain modern values and ways of being (Kramer, 1997)—are "tragically" (in Gebser's description) trying to spatialize time. They can only grasp time as a measurement, enabling the clock to be deified, to become a fetish. As a result, time becomes fixed and the clock a fixture. To be freed from the tyranny of the clock, the process of time-concretizing must "lead beyond" a mere synthesis of time and space, for if we synthesize, we lapse into mental duality despite all our efforts expended in pursuit of aperspectival temporality of the integral whole (Kramer, 1997).

The Integral Structure of Consciousness

The integral structure of consciousness achieves the concretization of time by realizing (conceiving) time's existence as a four-dimensional world constituent and embracing aperspectival awareness. In so doing, integral consciousness makes the other four structures (archaic, magic, mythic, and mental) transparent, thus enabling the human mind to transcend limitations of three-dimensional mental spatialization and perceive all forms of consciousness as valid experience (Gebser, 1949 Ger./1985 Eng.). Rather than the inadequate current conceptualization of time (which limits and fragments time by spatializing it), the integral structure manifests the "irruption of qualitative time into our consciousness" (Feuerstein, 1987, p. 130), thereby creating a comprehensive understanding of time. This understanding is what empowers the integral individual to realize the archaic, magic, mythic, and mental as manifest (co-constitutive) realities.

The integration of consciousness structures that occurs in the integral structure is not simply a synthesis, a union of seemingly disparate opposites; it is the latent, partial incorporation of structures in the rendering of the whole that neither necessitates nor eliminates synthesis. The ideas of arationality (rather than the rationality of the current deficient mental structure), aperspectivity (rather than spatially determined perspectivity), and diaphaneity (the transparent recognition of the whole, not just parts) are significant characteristics of the integral structure. Reflected in these characteristics is the worldview that the tensions and relations among things are more important at times than the things themselves. Hence, integral consciousness focuses on how a relationship develops as (not over) time rather than on the fact that a relationship synthesizing two or more parts exists (Gebser, 1949 Ger./1985 Eng.).

The concretization process fundamental to integral consciousness thus involves more than recognizing things, events, values, and the like as integral manifestations. An individual who wishes to integrate must not merely have concretized material and mental phenomena but must also have the ability to concretize one's own consciousness structure. That means that not only do the different structures become transparent and conscious in that person, but the person also becomes aware of the effects of the structures on his or her own life and destiny. Furthermore, it means that by virtue of this insight, the person acquires mastery over the deficient elements working within the individual and attains the degree of maturation and equilibrium that is a precondition of every concretization. Only those components that have thus become equilibrated (i.e., matured and mastered concretions) are the "stones" that build the integral structure (Gebser, 1949 Ger./1985 Eng.).

One difficulty that may seem insurmountable to achieving integrality is the fact that no idea of the aperspectival can be formed. The integral world transcends our current ideas. Even the bare mention of the mutation from the mental to the integral consciousness structure can contribute to misunderstanding when our currently normative modes of expression are inadequate to make the integral fully intelligible. The aperspectival designation means "a process of liberation from the exclusive validity of perspectival and un-perspectival, as well as pre-perspectival limitations. . . . Aperspectival is a definition which differentiates a perception of reality that is neither perspectivally restricted to only one sector nor merely unperspectivally evocative of a vague sense of reality" (Gebser, 1949 Ger./1985 Eng., pp. 2-3). Those who object to the aperspectival world as incomprehensible and indemonstrable flounder because of the limitations of their own ideas of the world, fettered to perspectival comprehension and visual perception. The mental-rational world at one time similarly transcended the capabilities of mythic human to experience it; nevertheless, it became a reality. Gebser (1949 Ger./1985 Eng.) claims that even though the mental-rational structure clings to its societal dominance, the mutation of human consciousness to the integral is becoming ever more apparent. He thereby devoted his life to describing the emergent manifestations of the aperspectival lifeworld.

The level of difficulty in describing the integral structure depends a great deal on our experiences—not just on the fact that we have them, but also on how intense they are and what we take away from them. Intensity is key in this mode of consciousness; it comprises more than simply the emotional relationship to experience or the deepening of emotion itself (which is a magical response rather than an integral one). Rather, the intensity of integrality is the intensity of the whole, of the combined and reconstituted consciousness structures. It is the potency of time as fourth dimension and as world constituent, manifested through *systasis* and *synairesis* (Gebser, 1949 Ger./1985 Eng.).

SYSTASIS AND SYNAIRESIS

The mode of perceiving that makes possible the comprehension, or more exactly the appearance of temporal elements, is that of *systasis*. *Systasis* is an active and aperspectival worldview. As Kramer (1997) states:

> *Systasis* is not causally determined. *Systasis* is neither a modern mental-rational concept, nor a mythical image, nor a magic presumption that all things are interchangeably identical. *Systasis* is not integral, but integrating. (p. 142)

It is important that *synairesis* not be considered the outcome of building a *systatic* system in the current three-dimensional understanding of the term. As a mode of four-dimensional awaring, *systasis* (*systase*) does not mean "system"—that distinction belongs to three-dimensional consciousness. System deals with parts rather than the whole, with the product rather than the process. Yet *systasis* and system are not antithetical either. Gebser (1949 Ger./1985 Eng.) notes:

> *Systasis'* acategorical element is the integrating dimension by which the three-dimensional spatial world, which is always a world of parts, is integrated into a whole in such a way that it can be stated. This already implies that it [*systasis*] is not an ordering schema paralleling that of system. We must especially avoid the error of considering *systasis*—which is both process and effect—as that which is [a]ffected, for if we do we reduce it to a causal system. We must be aware that *systasis* has an effective character within every system. *Systasis* is not a mental concept, nor is it a mythical image (say) in the sense of Heraclitus' *panta rei* ("all things are in flux"), nor is it a magic postulation of the interconnection of everything to and with everything else. And finally, it is not integral, but integrating. (p. 310)

If we take into account *systatic* concepts (e.g., time concretization, aperspectivity), the mere methodology of systems is intensified to *synairetic diaphany* that makes the categorizing of system transparent. Up until now (particularly within the scientific community), the firm, even forcible, separation of subject from object has been required. If this categoric dichotomizing is transcended through *synairetic diaphany*, we can arrive at a more comprehensive, deeper (or richer) understanding of the world around us and of ourselves. As Gebser asserts, the intensification/diaphany of *synairesis* allows *systatic* integrating of system as a useful mental construct without entrapment in the three-dimensional scheme of thought, exemplified in its extreme and deficient configuration as Cartesian dualism in the forms of objectivistically or subjectivistically biased paradigms, polarized and detached from the lifeworld.

Although it is important to avoid Cartesian mental-rational bias when attempting to discuss integral characteristics such as *systasis* and *synairesis*, it is difficult to do so. For instance, Feuerstein (1987) is correct to say that, "*Systasis*, in contrast to systematization, deals with the proper 'arrangement' of intensities (rather than quantified 'extensities')" (p. 194). But then he falls back into dualism when he defines *synairesis* as "an integral understanding, or perception, of reality" (Feuerstein, p. 194). In the integral, the integrity of the whole is presentiated (including the observer), so that the dualistic meaning of a "perception of reality" (reality as object observed by perceiving subject) is avoided (Gebser, 1949 Ger./1985 Eng.).

Because Gebser (1949 Ger./1985 Eng.) is presuming the Husserlian move to bracket modern metaphysics, he does not differentiate between objective reality and subjective perception of it. Comparing system with *synairesis*, Gebser (1949 Ger./1985 Eng.) explains:

> *Synairesis* comes from *synaireo*, meaning "to synthesize, collect," notably in the sense of "everything being seized or grasped on all sides, particularly by the mind or spirit." Whereas synthesis is a logical-causal conclusion, a mental (trinitary) unification of thesis and antithesis (and falls apart because it becomes itself a thesis as a result of the dividing, perspectival perception), *synairesis* is an integral act of completion "encompassing all sides" and perceiving aperspectivally. (p. 312)

While the idea of space and time freedom is critical to Gebser's entire approach, freedom from them does not mean to be unaware of their various adumbrations through magic one-dimensionalism, mythic two-dimensionalism, and perspectival three-dimensionalism. Rather than discarding these forms of time and space consciousness, integrality involves the awaring of the modalities and their interactions, giving rise to an unlimited (holistic) understanding. By realizing consciousness latency and transparency, what has passed is not dropped and forgotten, although this is the temptation of the mental-rational structure of consciousness. Instead the integral systatically incorporates latent structures into our consciousness as transparent, effective elements (Gebser, 1949 Ger./1985 Eng.).

SUMMARY

Merleau-Ponty and Gebser create a framework that allows us to step away from the Cartesian paradigm — the view of individuals as fairly uniform subjects who analytically experience an objective world — and instead embrace an embodied subjectivism in which alterity is a critical component of the subject's identity and experience. Recognizing the critical relationship between the focus and the field as it relates to consciousness allows us to take an ahistorical perspective as Gebser does. If we approach the current technological milieu with the Cartesian paradigm, the dominant mode of understanding time and space would preclude us from acknowledging the reality of the latent modes of consciousness, and hence we would be unaware of how they inform the current dominant mode. By pursuing an aperspectival understanding of technological communication, we can lay the foundation for an efficient incorporation of integral understanding.

10

Comparative Assessment of Theories of Technology

This chapter focuses on the Cartesian object-biased paradigm that provides the foundation for technological utopianism. Critical assessment of this paradigm comes mainly from the works of Husserl and Merleau-Ponty. The interconnected nature of the objectivistic bias and the characteristic of the modern technological milieu, which together form technological utopianism and its unavoidable consequences, is critically reviewed in terms of modern notions of "progress" and Gebser's view of the role of mutation in the life-world.

CRITICAL ASSESSMENTS OF THE "OBJECT-BIASED" PARADIGM

Husserl's Critique of Modern Science

To develop a more appropriate understanding of the modern technological milieu, it is useful to start from the crisis of European sciences—a crisis that Husserl (1954 Ger./1970 Eng.) finds evident in the failure of reductionistic and mechanistic programs in psychology. More precisely, he illuminates the failure of such programs to reach an understanding of human experience and the meaning of human behavior. Grasping the chemistry of love and understanding love as an integral part of the human experience do not occur in the same dimensions. The correlation of one phenomenon (brain chemistry) with another (the direct experience of love) is not the same as understanding either of the two. Nor are the paths to or dimensions of understanding the brain and experience identical. If a skull is opened, we see chemicals and tissue, but we will not "see" love. Husserl (1954 Ger./1970 Eng.) has nothing against the study of brain chemistry; he acknowledges its value for altering mental states. He merely points out that understanding the correlation between chemistry and direct experience is in fact a correlation between two different phenomena. To point to a formula and proclaim that it is "love" is similar to confusing the menu with the food. The neurosurgeon may have direct access to a brain but not to thoughts and emotions.

Husserl (1954 Ger./1970 Eng.) remarks that, "the stage of development of ratio represented by the rationalism of the Age of Enlightenment was a mistake, though certainly an understandable one" (p. 290). It seems that the crisis of the modern European sciences is rooted in the misguided theory of rationality that lies at their base. Husserl (1954 Ger./1970 Eng.) leads us to understand the constituting role of conscious subjectivity in the shaping of the human situation. By pointing to the limitations of the prevailing conception of rationality, Husserl (1954 Ger./1970 Eng.) intends to point the way toward a more appropriate conception: The always pre-given lifeworld *becomes* a world through the function of our conscious processes.

In *The Crisis of European Sciences and Transcendental Phenomenology,* Husserl (1954 Ger./1970 Eng.) tells us that we must strive "to bring latent reason to the understanding of its own possibilities," for there is no other way to put "universal" philosophy "on the strenuous road to realization" (p. 15). Husserl rejects the narrow scope of modern rationality as an inappropriate characterization of reason. According to Husserl, the roots of the present crisis can be traced to the Galilean mathematical rendering of nature as an objective, measurable, predictable, and controllable universe.

In Husserlian (1954 Ger./1970 Eng.) terms, Cartesian-Galilean objectivism is biased in presuming that the lifeworld is a realm of mere subjective appearances and needs to be measured "for a well-fitting *garb of ideas,* that of so-called objectively scientific truths" (p. 51; italics added). According to the objectivist view, without measurement and "objective" analysis, experience is raw nonsense. Thus, a tremendous dualism divides the modern European world. The sciences do not see themselves as emerging from or as part of the lifeworld but rather apart from and superior to it. The lifeworld is viewed by science as a world of untruths; the lifeworld of social agents is viewed as fiction, anecdotal evidence (i.e., nongeneralizable, and therefore useless). The process of measurement is the only way to salvage any value from it. Any culture or person who does not follow the scientific method exclusively has nothing meaningful to say—such a person is utterly suspect. Thus, most of humanity and its opinions are rendered worthless unless ordained useful, valid, representative, objective, significant, and generalizable by independent (i.e., objective) scientific authority. And this authority alone is legitimate because it alone observes objective (without bias) reality. According to Husserl (1954 Ger./1970 Eng.):

> It is through the garb of ideas that we take for *true being* what is actually a *method*—a method which is designed for the purpose of progressively improving, *in infinitum*, through "scientific" predictions, those rough predictions which are the only ones originally possible within the sphere of what is actually experienced and experienceable in the life-world. It is because of the disguise of ideas that the true meaning of the method, the formulae, and the "theories," remained unintelligible and, in the naïve formation of the method, was *never* understood. (pp. 51-52)

Method is the privileged means of *dressing up*, of ordaining the subjective lifeworld and presenting its "'objectively actual and true' nature" (Husserl, 1954 Ger./1970 Eng., p. 51). Thus, what is deemed true nature is actually a product of culture, of the highly socialized, learned culture of science (i.e., the scientific method[s]). A consequence of this methodical bias or preferred way of grasping the world is that we are tempted to interpret the world as if it exists apart from a worldview. This attitude remains central to the overall Western arrogance vis-à-vis other people and cultural contributions (as uneducated, unrefined ideas or "mere opinion") and the willingness, even the eagerness, to push other worlds aside as useless, with the possible exception that they may be used as a trinket (i.e., to entertain, soothe, serve, etc.). These other worlds are negated, when they are noticed at all.

According to Husserl (1954 Ger./1970 Eng.), the interpretation that the world exists apart from a worldview constitutes the naïveté of the objectivistic paradigm as it takes the so-called "objective" world "for the universe of all that is, without noticing that no objective science can do justice to the very subjectivity which accomplishes science" (p. 295). As Husserl (1954 Ger./1970 Eng.) reminds us, "What characterizes objectivism is that it moves upon the ground of the world which is pregiven, taken for granted through experience, seeks the 'objective truth' of this world, seeks what, in this world, is unconditionally valid for every rational being, what it [this world] is in itself" (p. 68).

To Husserl (1954 Ger./1970 Eng.), the central naïveté of modern science is the unquestioned presupposition of a world existing "in itself" and knowable as it is, in itself, apart from the lifeworld, wrought with the biases of human subjectivity (biases that science has supposedly exempted itself from). A second naïveté is the belief that science is not only rational but that it circumscribes all that could possibly be called rational. It is a naïve faith (and misguided desire) that we can have an observation, scientific or otherwise, without a perspectival observer. It is a claim that perception can be h without an embodied perceiver. As Kramer (1997) has noted, this scientific faith is extended to humanity as an object of investigation (but excluding the scientist him or herself) with the presumption that even though human beings may exhibit cultural variance, a true science of humanity is possible. It is possible, according to the doctrine of positivism, because cultural and historical variance (and therefore behaviors and other cultural and historical artifacts) can and should be ignored in science (indeed cultural and historical studies are routinely denigrated as fictions). The lifeworld must be ignored in the name of objectivity and in favor of the presumption that humans manifest inherent and invariant sets of motives, responses, and character traits. These invariant external facts can, should, and (if they are to be useful) must be categorically reduced to redundant, measurable, and therefore predictable affective and cognitive functions (i.e., operationalizations). Social science must presume that an invariant human nature exists that can be known and that guides—a priori—all true scientific investigations. Social science positivists must presume that human nature is independent of and more important than cultural variance, and that it is not only biologic but also psychologic, sociologic, and economic. Given such a perspective, culture and history are merely confounding variables to be ignored. Indeed, all human activities, with the glaring exception of science itself, are reduced to irrational behaviors programmed by universal instinct. Thus, many social scientists pride themselves (and teach their students to be proud, as their professors taught them) on being utterly ignorant of cultural and historical aspects of the human condition (i.e., the lifeworld). As this bias expands, psychology, sociology, communication, and other fields are increasingly (and virtuously) disinterested and therefore ignorant of their stated subject. The positivist's focus is on measuring an unrecognizable, operationalized sliver of a behavioral event sliced from its contextual surroundings, its history, its meaning (i.e., isolating a static event from myriad components of a complex active process), and/or creating data via self-reported thoughts about disremembered behaviors and, from the perspective of the objective subject (college students fulfilling this category are overrepresented to say the least), often insignificant events.

The rise of social physics during the Age of Reason is advancing, reducing the fields that have staked out human behavior as their area of explo- ʾtion to physiology, and at the same time defining cultural and historical ʾies as invalid and unreliable precisely because of their presumed lack of ʾizability (they are generalizable, of course, or we wouldn't recognize ʾbservations of actual, contingent lifeworld conditions are useful if if they can be collapsed via the formulae of averages (measures of ʾdency). Thus, the actual variance of experience is deemed a fiction ʾcts The Truth of Trends. What is sought as natural turns out to be of mathematical operation, an operation and ambition that is unique to the post-Enlightened modern European humanity. And this is the virtual line (straight or curved) that remains after the peaks and valleys are averaged out (i.e., negated and disregarded, controlled out of existence).

As Husserl (1954 Ger./1970 Eng.) reminds us, the supporting role of the pre-given cultural horizon goes unspoken and invisible; what the objectivistic scientist fails to recognize is the fact that his or her cultural horizon "is always presupposed as the ground, as the field of work upon which alone his [sic] questions, his [sic] methods of thought, make sense" (p. 295). Thus, the pre-given, invisible cultural horizon is "forgotten" in scientific accomplishment. "[T]he working subject . . . is forgotten" (p. 295). This forgetfulness, this ignorance in itself, lacks rationality. With no analytic knowledge gaining purpose, this ignorance instead serves a rhetorical purpose (i.e., to inoculate science from the charge of relativism).

It is little wonder that the modern tradition embraced the naïveté, the illusion of objectivism, with the belief that their thinking was somehow not motivated—unaffected by a worldview or an ambition. But as it turns out, the scientific attitude proves to be one of the (if not the) most ambitious and ethnocentric on the planet, rejecting all alternatives unless and until alternative ways of seeing are proven valid by science itself (and its ruling gods) in whatever fashion, and whenever it may see fit. Objectivists who eschew history as bunk are self-blinding—conveniently or otherwise unaware of the embodied contingencies that constitute and feed their own growing bodies of knowledge. Under such resistance to history, they become self-deluded, assuming, often naively (and by willfully ignoring the history of science itself and their own cultural subjectivity in pursuit of a utopian omniscient identity), that they are addressing "things themselves," eliminating bias via scientific methods of inquiry. Although methods yield precision, what is precisely measured remains a slice of reality randomly selected for measurement, described as "privileged" by some. An instrument attends to only a tiny fraction of the world as already known and available, relegating all the rest to the realm of invisible disinterest. Basically put, one does not know what one does not know. Dialectical ingenuity remains the best way to decenter the Self, thus exposing it to genuine alternative views. But increasingly, rhetorical studies are being driven from the academy by social scientists exploiting the current cultural (or epistemological) fashion and extracurricular power. The definitions used in operationalization of research concepts generally disregard the rhetorical and lifeworld aspects that (necessarily) exist in positivistic studies (whereas the opposite is not true). Things like the literature review, the definition of terms, and conclusions are rhetorical; when writing the results of his or her research, the scientist extends the operationalizations into the lifeworld (in order to have something in any way relevant to conclude).

Consistent focus, which yields precision, is manifest human interest, not objective disinterest. Focusing means to narrow the field or horizon of investigation in accordance with a priori interests. Focusing is a necessary condition for precise types of knowledge and thereby co-creates ignorance; ignorance (i.e., that which is ignored) includes all aspects of the lifeworld that are excluded from the narrowed scope of attention–the so-called statistical outliers. These data are selectively discarded by a researcher because they are too deviant, too aberrant given the mean. Furthermore, the rule about what is real (i.e., significant statistically) and not real is a mathematical decision, one made a priori according to the rules rather than a human judgment. Precise knowledge (as defined by objectivists) and ignorance are co-constituting phenomena. When a method creates knowledge, it inherently creates ignorance at the same instant.

Furthermore, as Kramer (1997) argues, the scientific method is not a naturally occurring phenomenon. It was not found lying in a forest by Francis Bacon. It is a product of subjective invention. Science is a human achievement. It is a historical, cultural artifact, an active process of communal effort. Historically and cross-culturally, as it has ascended to the mantle of legitimate engine of knowledge; other forms of knowing such as direct personal experience (the anecdote) and spiritual revelation have descended, having been rendered illegitimate and/or irrelevant.

Another aspect of reality to consider is that science changes through time. Therefore, it is contingent on, in fact less universal in incidence than, the anecdote. The anecdote is common knowledge (i.e., it exists *as* a generalization—my story is relate-able to by Others), but on the basis of what positivists call a *lack* of generalizability, all common knowledge is suspect by the much less common scientific rendering. Scientific comportment is a far less common mode of being in the world. Over time the meaning of science, its facts, its targets of observation (units of analysis), and its ways of observing have changed. Eventually many rules, methods, facts, and instruments end up in the Smithsonian and other museums of science and invention scattered throughout the lifeworld. This happens because science is a human accomplishment. It is, as Dilthey, Husserl, and Kerényi observed (with Kuhn [1962] in their wake), a historical and political process, and, as such, science is *inextricably* a product of and exists within the lifeworld.

The concept of a fixed thing-in-itself, independent of observation, is pure metaphysical speculation. So far as is known, only an embodied consciousness can acknowledge the existence of a thing. Even with artificial intelligence, a computer manifests the perspective of its programmers. Naturalism proves to be one of the greatest founding myths of modernity. It is a self-sustaining myth in that it inoculates itself from reflection by deploying a rhetoric that claims that only insane people argue with natural fact (i.e., scientific reality).

According to Gurwitsch (1974), with the achievement of Euclidean geometry as a demonstrative sort of reasoning, the Greeks suddenly found themselves in possession of a true exemplar of *episteme*. Further, for the learned people of Renaissance Europe, geometry became the guiding "model and standard" of true scientific accomplishment. Concerning geometry, Husserl (1954 Ger./1970 Eng.) indicates that the cultural roots of geometry were cut off, and the pure but abstract idealization of geometry was given a life of its own. Moreover, geometry was raised to the level of a true object of knowledge. This tendency contributes to the conception of universal science: a conception of the world as being "in itself a rational systematic unity . . . in which each and every singular detail must be rationally *determined*" (p. 65; italics added). The rationale behind this attitude, Husserl (1954 Ger./1970 Eng.) argues, is that our scientific standpoint will treat us to a panorama of more than just objectively determinable reality (which is not possible anyway). Like Nietzsche (1887 Ger./1974 Eng., 1901 Ger./1967 Eng.) before him, Husserl (1954 Ger./1970 Eng.) comes to recognize that positive science promises to deliver happiness and (as Herbert Spencer espoused) a definition of good as the useful, the practical, "as the valuable in itself"; to deliver humanity from its "shame," which is its very subjective often "useless" quality of life (Husserl, 1954 Ger./1970 Eng., p. 27). Husserl (1954 Ger./1970 Eng.) notes that the salvific, hypervaluated so-called "value free" posture of modern science actually harbors an attitude, an approach that promises to make possible knowledge of "what is true in itself about values and goods" (p. 66).

Husserl (1954 Ger./1970 Eng.) wants us to recognize the nature of the transformation that took place between the Greek conception of geometrical idealization as grounded in the lifeworld activities of Greek craftsmen and the modern concept of geometrical demonstration as a self-enclosed, rigidly deductive process of rational methodology. According to Gurwitsch (1966), in Galileo's time, geometry had already undergone this transformation of sense. Gurwitsch rightly points out:

> [Galileo] inherits geometry as an established science which, on account of its absolute and universal validity, he considers as the prototype model and standard of knowledge. . . . Consequently, geometry must be applied to experience in order to discover reality as it is in itself, in contradistinction to varying appearances and phenomena. (1966, p. 408)

What Gurwitsch indicates is that the nature within which the Greek craftsman experienced the vision of idealized perfection was neither the exact universe of Galilean or Newtonian mechanics. As Gurwitsch (1966) illustrates, the experience of the Greek craftsman's sense of nature was within the cultural horizon of ancient Greece and also, we add, within his or her own embodied (anecdotal) experience of working at a craft. It was nature as *experienced*—a realm that required a concept (i.e., physics), which was inseparably interconnected with other concepts such as *arche*, *psyche*, *nous*, and *telos*.

However, in the Galilean and Newtonian universe, the concept of nature is occupied by the objectivistic worldview. Gurwitsch (1966) asserts that, "Under the import of the growing prestige of the developing physics, a prestige stemming from its success, both theoretical and practical, that tissue of ideas . . . has come to be considered, by scientists and laymen alike, as reality, as 'nature as it truly and objectively is,' to the total disregard of the life-world (p. 411).

Thus, *nature as it really is* stands in contrast with lived experience, and yet it is an accomplishment, the achievement of rendering a mathematical manifold. In other words, the objectivistic worldview—otherwise called the Galilean and/or Newtonian objectively true nature (i.e., The Truth)—is merely a construction of ideas or ideal constructions. It is personal experiences "dressed up" in methodical garb, accessorized with highly valued detached-from-the-lifeworld data and fashionable interpretations.

Husserl (1954 Ger./1970 Eng.) finds the key to overcoming objectivism in the skeptical position arrived at by both Berkeley (1710/2008) and especially Hume (1739/1973). To Husserl (1954 Ger./1970 Eng.), the significance of Hume's (1739/1973) position lies not in the conclusions themselves. Rather, he finds Hume's (1739/1973) insight into the weaknesses of the objectivist paradigm of reason. In other words, Husserl (1954 Ger./1970 Eng.) finds in Hume's conclusions a bankrupting naïve objectivism. According to Wolff (1966), Hume (1739/1973) begins by assuming that, "All empirical concepts could be explained in terms of some combination of the [sensory] contents of perception," but "very quickly comes to see that knowledge and belief result from what the mind does with its contents rather than simply from the nature of those contents" (p. 103).

This demonstrates that Hume's empiricism turns away from objectivism because Hume (1739/1973) discovers that there are no sense impressions from which we could ever have derived beliefs that take the form of empirical generalizations. Likewise, Hume argues that there is no impression from which to derive the idea of necessary connection. In other words, the mind forms a "habit of association," which is not a sense impression but which connects them (Hume, 1739/1973, pp. 12-15; see also Wolff, 1966, p. 107). Therefore, if we believe in causality, the force of our persuasion cannot have come from experience. Rather, it must have arisen on the basis of a mental process detached from the lifeworld and one's own mind and view, and operating on the givens of previous sensory experiences that are also removed from the lifeworld.

As Hume (1739/1973) indicated, our everyday beliefs about the "real" world and its content are grounded not simply in impressions but rather (and more importantly) in non-empirical factors that serve to determine the experiential nature of the world and objects in it. Hume (1739/1973) calls these non-empirical factors *principles of association*. Behind the operation of these principles, Hume says, is not reason but custom (i.e., habit). We grow accustomed to forming expectations in advance of experience. They are proper ways of experiencing and relating to stimuli. Without these (what become normal and) sensible ways of being, we would experience neither a flow of events nor the world within which this flow occurs. Therefore, the scientific project of building an edifice of objective knowledge cannot be rationally or empirically justified; the best we can hope for is a set of convictions and beliefs that serve us either effectively or ineffectively. These convictions and beliefs become ideology, that is, they become a form of social sediment serving as the predispositions that organize our experience into global and invisible structures (i.e., ideology and bias).

According to Husserl (1954 Ger./1970 Eng.), Hume (1739/1973) failed to recognize that the subjectivity that engenders the world is also the living subject whose experiences take place *in* the world. Husserl (1954 Ger./1970 Eng.) states, "[T]hat 'world-constituting subjectivity' might itself be 'incorporated' as an object-content within the horizons of validity set up by its own constituting activities" (p. 182). This means that even though Hume (1739/1973) succeeded in overcoming the objectivistic bias, he still failed to recognize the co-constitutive process between the subject and the world. This is what Kant (1781 Ger./1929 Eng.) keenly recognizes.

Kant (1781 Ger./1929 Eng.) accounts not for the *fact* of scientific truths about nature but rather for the *conditions* that underlie the possibility of a given fact. Kant's position is that Descartes and Hume (1739/1973) made fatal mistakes when they embraced the objectivistic assumptions about the nature of world and experience. By assuming that the world that would correlate with objective knowledge is transcendent to human experience and conscious life, they were led to reject the possibility of an indubitable connection between the subject of experience and the objects in such a transcendent world.

Husserl (1954 Ger./1970 Eng.) argues that the scientific attempt to pin down a correct sense of reality (i.e., absolute reality) represents an effort that takes place within the horizons of the world we take for granted, as existing in advance of all practical and theoretical cognition. Carr (1977) indicates the implication of Husserl's point:

> The scientist sees himself [*sic*] as overcoming the relativity of our "merely subjective" pictures of the world by finding the objective world, the world as it really is. Husserl shows that the scientist can just as easily be seen, by a shift in perspective, as a man [*sic*] who himself [*sic*] has a particular sort of picture of the world, and that as such both he [*sic*] and his

[*sic*] picture belong within the "real" world, which Husserl calls the life-world. (p. 207)

Husserl (1954 Ger./1970 Eng.) describes the way that *being* is present to us in experiences. His final claim is that the key to understanding the presence of things in experience lies in the intentional nature of our conscious access to things. Studying the intentional nature of conscious experience is done by the phenomenological method. Following Husserl, Merleau-Ponty (1945 Fr./1962 Eng.) explores the co-constituting process that engenders the subject and the world. The focal point, the necessary condition for and locus of this co-constitutive process, is the "lived body."

Merleau-Ponty's Notion of Perception and His Critique of Objectivism

Merleau-Ponty is suspicious of the "received" view,[1] observing that the received views on perception have been unproductive when applied to case studies in psychopathology. Merleau-Ponty (1945 Fr./1962 Eng.) makes fully explicit the point that perception is neither passive reception of data (as in the case of Hume) nor a product of meaning amplification (as Kant or Husserl might argue).

On the basis of his reflections on case studies of psychically damaged patients, Merleau-Ponty (1945 Fr./1962 Eng.) concludes that there is a dimension of bodily experience that is neither cognitive nor physiological—a dimension that is our living insertion within the common sensible world.[2] Perception is the ground of reflexive thought, insofar as Merleau-Ponty claims that our predicative level of conscious awareness is somehow "awake" and continually sustained by the body's living insertion.

However, instead of renouncing the significance of reflexive thought, Merleau-Ponty (1947, 1955, 1964 Fr./1964 Eng.) attempts to capture the significance of reflection. Merleau-Ponty (1945 Fr./1962 Eng.) asserts, "Without reflection, life would probably dissipate itself in ignorance of itself or in chaos: but this does not mean that reflection should be carried away with itself or presented to be ignorant of its origins" (p. 19). In other words,

---

[1]Terms such as "logical positivism," "logical empiricism," "deductive-nomological," and "causal law system" are used to articulate what some call the "received view" (Polkinghorne, 1983, p. 90). Following the received view, all rational explanations, including explanations of the life of the human spirit and consciousness, must ultimately lead back to physical, quantifiable processes. Bernstein (1983) explains this "received view" in detail, including various implications.

[2]Concerning Merleau-Ponty's (1945 Fr./1962 Eng.) analysis of deficient modes of perceptual activity, the case of the "phantom limb" is discussed on pp. 76-89, "Schneider" is discussed on pp. 98-147, and the "girl who learns not to speak" on pp. 160-166

the evident-ness (evidence) of a thing's presence is not something, which is built up by intellectual synthesis.

Furthermore, Merleau-Ponty (1945 Fr./1962 Eng.) elaborates on the phenomenological insight into the fundamental nature of episteme:

> All my knowledge of the world, even my scientific knowledge, is gained from my own particular point of view, or from some experience of the world without which the symbols of science would be meaningless. The whole universe of science is built upon the world as directly experienced, and if we want to subject science itself to rigorous scrutiny and arrive at a precise assessment of its meaning and scope, we must begin by reawakening the basic experience of the world of which science is the second-order expression. Science has not and never will have, by its nature, the same significance qua form of being as the world which we perceive, for the simple reason that it is a rationale or explanation of that world. (p. viii)

Hence, as already mentioned in Chapter 9, Merleau-Ponty's position is (in many respects) a refinement more than a rejection of the Husserlian position. Husserl (1954 Ger./1970 Eng.) sees the lifeworld as arising from the constituting activity of transcendental subjectivity. However, both Heidegger and Merleau-Ponty choose to view the world as a field of access that first opens itself for interrogation in the instant of our coming to birth as existential beings.

From Merleau-Ponty's (1945 Fr./1962 Eng., 1964 Fr./1968 Eng.) viewpoint, consciousness is not experience through the body; rather, it comes to life in the body, as a dimension of the body's interrogative posture (a product of thinking rather than of experience). Thus, Husserl (1954 Ger./1970 Eng.) places the principal focus on "consciousness (although, as embodied)," whereas Merleau-Ponty (1964 Fr./1968 Eng.) chooses to begin with "the body (together with consciousness)" (pp. 190-191). Stated differently, to Husserl (1954 Ger./1970 Eng.), the conscious subject organizes the body's capacity for movement, giving intentional direction to the movement of the body. It would seem that consciousness subtends the function of the body, whereas Merleau-Ponty argues the body clearly subtends conscious life (Madison, 1981). In short, Merleau-Ponty is interested in how the body gives rise to conscious life (Ihde, 1998).

Merleau-Ponty (1945 Fr./1962 Eng.) suggests that the efforts of phenomenology are concentrated on "re-achieving a direct and primitive contact with the world" (p. vii). Merleau-Ponty (1964 Fr./1968 Eng.) describes the nature of this "direct and primitive contact" as originary, writing:

> With the first vision, the first contact, the first pleasure, there is initiation, that is, not the positing of a content, but the opening of a dimension that can never again be closed, the establishment of a level in terms of which every other experience will henceforth be situated. (p. 151)

The goal of phenomenology is to describe the world as it is lived by the experiencing subject. Therefore, Merleau-Ponty (1964 Fr./1968 Eng.) is immediately drawn into an investigation of the nature of our perceptual access to the world. This access allows people to be oriented to the horizons of involvement within which people must position themselves both spatially and temporally.

Merleau-Ponty (1964 Fr./1968 Eng.) discovers that horizons are not given through the act of mind or consciousness but instead through a bodily interrogation that serves as the anchor for our perceptual orientation. Merleau-Ponty (1964 Fr./1968 Eng.) insists:

> We do not have a consciousness constitutive of the things, as idealism believes, nor a preordination of the things to the consciousness, as realism believes . . . we have with our body, our senses, our look, our power to understand speech and to speak, *measurants* for Being, dimensions to which we can refer it, but not a relation of adequation or of immanence. The perception of the world and of history is the practice of this measure. . . . If we are ourselves in question in the very unfolding of our life . . . it is because we ourselves are one sole continued question, a perpetual enterprise of taking our bearings on the constellations of the world, and of taking the bearings of things on our dimensions. (p. 103)

The role of the body sustains "the underlying movement through which we have installed ourselves in the world" (p. 104). Merleau-Ponty's (1947, 1955, 1964 Fr./1964 Eng.) concept of the body is not the conventional notion of the body as "*an object in the world*, under the purview of a separated subject" (p. 5). Rather, the body is "on the side of the subject; it is our *point of view on the world*, the place where the spirit takes on a certain physical and historical situation" (Merleau-Ponty, 1947, 1955, 1964 Fr./1964 Eng., p. 5). In other words, Merleau-Ponty's body is *embodied world* or *institutionalized body*. This point is discussed in detail in Chapters 9 and 13.

In the realm of objective space, all points, including the objective position of my objective body, lie in objective relation to one another. On this objectivistic account, it would be nearly impossible to understand the relationship that builds between the body and the world (e.g., a blind person, a cane, and things in the world).[3] As Merleau-Ponty (1945 Fr./1962 Eng.)

---

[3]Similarly, Nietzsche (1901 Ger./1967 Eng.) insists on the provisional character of the *logos* of the moment: "Against positivism, which halts at phenomena—'There are

explains, "The blind [person's] stick has ceased to be an object for [that individual], and is no longer perceived for itself; its point has become an area of sensitivity, extending the scope and active radius of touch, and providing a parallel to sight. . . . To get used to a hat, a car or a stick is to be transplanted into them, or conversely, to incorporate them into the bulk of our own body" (p. 143).

According to Merleau-Ponty's discernment, the body into which we incorporate things of this sort is not the objective (i.e., physical) body, but instead it is the *lived* body—one that is intentionally related to the world.

Summarizing the view of body in relation to mind and consciousness, Merleau-Ponty (1947, 1955, 1964 Fr./1964 Eng.) suggests:

> The perceiving mind is an incarnated mind. I have tried, first of all, to re-establish the roots of the mind in its body and in its world, going against doctrines that treat perception as a simple result of the action of external things on our body as well as against those which insist on the autonomy of consciousness. These philosophies commonly forget—in favor of a pure exteriority or of a pure interiority—the insertion of the mind in corporality, the ambiguous relation which we entertain with our body and, correlatively, with perceived things. (pp. 3-4)

For Merleau-Ponty, the body is not originally given in my experiences through a phenomenal description or prescription. Rather, the body is the very anchor of intentional activity. Stated differently, the body is intentionally related to the world. Merleau-Ponty (1945 Fr./1962 Eng.) states, "We merely want to push back the boundaries of what makes sense for us, and

only facts'—I would say: No, *fact is precisely what there is not, only interpretations*" (p. 267; italics added). Derrida (1967 Fr./1976 Eng.) criticizes objectivistic approaches based on the differentiation that proliferates without limit. According to Derrida, knowledge unfolds as a dialectical movement of thought whose mutation over time cannot be reduced to a fundamental structuring opposition. Therefore, to Derrida, "reality" is an endless slippage of meaning that conforms to no predictable itinerary. For Derrida, the mind attempts to evade the unpleasant reality of *différance* by interpreting the psychological experience of speech as confirmation of the self's presence to itself. This privileging of speech as a token of timeless, unmediated meaning entails a corresponding devaluation of the written word that is denied any specific attributes as a medium of communication. Writing is merely an instrument for the representation of speech. That is, in order to entertain the fantasy of enduring truth, the mind must obscure the revelation that writing affords of thought as a historical process. Derrida suggests that the longing for the centered universe of meanings represents a willful forgetting of the reality of *différance*. Modern humans habitually overlook the productive character of knowing in order to reside within a world of reassuring certainties. Language itself, due to its abstract nature, continually obscures the specific character of the present.

rest the narrow zone of thematic significance within that of non-thematic significance which embraces it" (p. 275).

Therefore, "the feeling that one feels, the seeing that one sees, is not a thought of seeing or of feeling, but vision, feeling, mute experience of a mute meaning" (Merleau-Ponty, 1964 Fr./1968 Eng., p. 249). Merleau-Ponty concludes, acknowledging the foundational role of the living body in perception, "[I]t is the body and it alone . . . that can bring us to the things themselves," and in such a way that we "coexist with them in the same world" (p. 136).

My flesh literally encroaches on the world, and so too does the flesh of the world encroach on my flesh. The flesh that is my living body reaches out, and in so doing, is taken in the world, thereby opening a dimension or level in which subsequent experience will be situated (Merleau-Ponty, 1964 Fr./1968 Eng.). As a refinement of Husserl's (1954 Ger./1970 Eng.) critique on the objectivistic bias, Merleau-Ponty makes clear in his notion of perception that the flesh-body is the anchor in the co-constituting process between conscious subject and the world. Moreover, Merleau-Ponty provides us with a rigorously developed way of understanding the relationship between body and technology. Chapters 13 and 15 explore this point, embracing the insights of Gebser and Peirce.

Gebser's Critique of Dualism as Objectivistic Bias

Whereas Merleau-Ponty demonstrates the absurdity of objectivistic bias from his analyses of embodiment, Gebser (1949 Ger./1985 Eng.) provides a broader context for the matter. For rationalists, everything non-rational is abjectly irrational. As Gebser (1949 Ger./1985 Eng.) indicates, the pre-rational has not only had validity in the past but remains active today; along with other structures, it is part of our constitutional makeup (constituted reality). Beyond that, Gebser speaks of the *impossibility* of losing the archaic structure; it is the mode of (ever-present) origin manifested by our pre-reflective world.

It is nearly impossible to adequately represent here any of the structures of consciousness. The magic structure is difficult to represent because it can be distinguished only by experiencing it. The mythical structure is also difficult to represent and is distinguished by its capacity for being experienced. The mental-rational structure is thinkable and demonstrable, neither of which is the same as experience. Finally, the integral structure is distinguished only to the extent that it is perceptible. Gebser's (1949 Ger./1985 Eng.) use of "perceptible" is close to Merleau-Ponty's notion of perception. It may be called embodied vision, in the sense that Gebser (1949 Ger./1985 Eng.) claims that perceptible is not related to the condition of objectified space or time, but instead to the matter, "I can—," which is embodied potential. According to Gebser (1949 Ger./1985 Eng.), "At one time . . . the human body was the instrument of sight or thought across distances—tele-vision and telesthesia—or the perceptor of the faint radiation of the aura, while today [humans create] instruments for such purposes" (p. 131). It means that as consciousness mutates from magic and mythic to the mental-rational structure, so does the potential of "I can—," which constitutes the context or radius of embodiment.

For Gebser (1949 Ger./1985 Eng.), perception is not merely observing, which preeminently typifies the mental/rational structure. Rather, perception is a potential that conjures all forms of appearances and expressions. Each perspective yields insights, blindness, understanding, and misunderstanding. Consequently, perception is capable of apprehending the *diaphane* (transparent luminosity), which cannot be realized by merely seeing, hearing, or feeling. However, it should be emphasized that perceiving is not a transcendental super-sensuous act. Concepts such as intuition would be inaccurate to describe what Gebser (1949 Ger./1985 Eng.) means by perception. However, through multiple perspectives, through experience, we learn that every point of view has strengths and weaknesses; every point of view limits as it concurrently reveals. Access to this knowledge is diaphanous. Knowledge in this sense is a seeing-through or comprehension of the meaning of perspective itself. Once we understand perspective, we are no longer unconsciously trapped by it. As Laing argues (1969), "Unless we can 'see through' the rules, we can only see through them" (p. 28). We have achieved a new insight that impacts our own self-assessment. Thus, Gebser (1949 Ger./1985 Eng.) says that when consciousness intensifies, there is a realization that time affords difference and difference defeats the ignorant arrogance that entraps someone living a perspective which they believe encompasses all there is to know and that could be knowable. Exploration takes time; it is a temporal endeavor, and exploration presumes that one does not already know everything. Science recognizes the need for reliability, but it refuses to explore or accept knowledge generated by methods other than its own. Thus, the great insights that gave birth to science are regarded as being of dubious value by scientists themselves. But Nietzsche and his followers point out that science is not a scientific invention. Darwin may be relegated to the dustbin as a mere naturalist and not a true biologist (given his unreliable methods), but he was in the process of discovering and pioneering those methods.

Scientific reliability is likely given a culture that enforces tight and exclusive controls on means of replication and ways of seeing and doing. If I run the exact same survey with a similar audience or duplicate your experiment, it is likely that I will arrive at similar conclusions. This has its strength but also its weakness. Much knowledge arrives serendipitously; it was stumbled on outside the structures of methodical replication (Kuhn, 1962).

Einstein couldn't conceive his problems in conceptual terms. He had visions of an entire event that he would then attempt to translate into terms that could be communicated to the scientific community (Deloria, 1999). This is the case with science itself.

What we are pointing to here is a level of creativity far more profound than science. A level of creativity that is emergent from the lifeworld. The conservative nature of science (i.e., positivism) restricts the possibility that there may be a better way of generating knowledge than itself. It is marked by the arrogance of hyper-perspectivism (the tallest ivory tower). It may be, as Kramer (1997a) has argued, that science is a spoiled and sterile child of creative medieval parents who conceived of and gave birth to the Renaissance, to something that reached beyond their own ability to imagine. Can science allow itself to conceive of something better than itself, something more integral, a way of seeing that is superior to itself? For many positivists, positivism is the *non plus ultra* of human development. It manifests the end of the evolutionary line and is deified accordingly. Finally, reason has come to rule. But what sort of reason is this?

Such perspectival arrogance was already put under suspicion by Nietzsche as soon as it began to bellow. Gadamer (1960 Ger./1975 Eng.) forcefully asks, in the age of science does art have nothing meaningful to say? Does art not contain and communicate insight and truth? Gebser (1949 Ger./1985 Eng.) answers in the affirmative. Is it not reasonable to recognize the value of art and religion for humanity? Gadamer (1976 Ger./1981 Eng.) asks what has become of reason in the age of pure mathematization and quantification, modalities that Gebser (1949 Ger./1985 Eng.) calls "deficient rationality." The logical positivists and logical empiricists of the famed Vienna Circle, including Carnap (1928 Ger./2003 Eng.; 1934 Ger./2011 Eng.), Popper (1934 Ger./2002 Eng.), and Quine (1960/2013) argued, if a thing cannot be reduced to symbolic logic and/or quanta (to a measurement), it cannot be permitted existence. Operationalization comes to dominate as a particular yet universal mode of being. This is what Landgrebe (1981) called "metaphysics gone virulent," a totalizing and intolerant metaphysical bias (*mathesis universalis*). Numerical representation is carried to the point that the universe is claimed to be a giant algorithm, a sort of computer program.

According to science, art (poetry, music, novels, plays, painting, etc.) is merely a diversion designed and restricted to providing emotional entertainment. If such amateurish hobbies (and other pointless, non-productive activities) dare to create a less than flattering portrait of science (such as its handmaiden status and lack of reflective power when harnessed for mass war), they are labeled hysterical.

For Gebser (1949 Ger./1985 Eng.), perception is a holistic happening, an integration of the Self (*"Sich"*). One can neither hear nor show nor see the *diaphane*. Rather, through perception the world is heard, displayed, and seen and becomes the living presence of wholeness through the institutionalized (embodied) body. Gebser (1949 Ger./1985 Eng.) insists, "Descartes [the father of modern objectivistic bias], with his premise of *cogito*, transposes the action or movement confirming or substantiating the existence of the ego essentially from the psychic-vital realm into the psychic-mental; and this is merely a kind of hypergradation that does not eliminate the *ego*" (p. 97).

The either-or of dualism comes into prominence as an unbridgeable alternative and threatens to place everything in doubt. We are presented with a choice: Either we must have progress as advocated and promised by the exoterics (i.e., technicians and technocrats)—more quantification and progression away from origins—or we must undergo a return to origins as preached by the esoterics (i.e., the occultists). In either case—forcing the wheel forward or turning it back—we are confronted with illusion.

Following Gebser (1949 Ger./1985 Eng.), the term "duality" signifies one of the major consequences of the perspectival structure. The dualism that marks modernity is considerably stronger than the polarities of earlier centuries. By comparison, contemporary dualism is uncompromisingly fixed and unequal. This is so because perspective fixes the observer as well as the observed and then assigns to one side all existential validation. It fixes the subject or human, on the one hand, and the world, on the other. As a consequence, the modern person is compelled to emphasize Self ever more strongly due to the isolating fixity of perspectivism. This contributes to two things: an ever-more intolerant egocentrism and, as a result, a hostile confrontation between subject and object. This confrontation takes the form of conquest and dominion over the world of things. Human drama is even defined (in arts and sciences) as humans against nature, humans against other humans, and even (in total egohypertrophy) humans against themselves. An emphasis on having (possessing) displaces being. Experience is something to *have*, to be purchased and documented, rather than lived (experience *for* rather than experience *of*).

According to Gebser (1949 Ger./1985 Eng.), "The world, in turn, reinforces this confrontation by taking on an ever-increasing spatial volume or extent (as in the discovery of America) which the growing strength of the ego attempts to conquer" (p. 94). Furthermore, Gebser contends, "This dualistic opposition of contraries, whose positive aspect is the concretion of [humans] as well as of space, includes, at the same time, the negative component recognizable in fixity and sectorization" (p. 95). Such fixity contributes to isolation. This fixity provides the foundation for the modern technological milieu and is the conclusion of a process that is traceable to a negative possibility in the beginnings of the mental structure.

Gebser (1949 Ger./1985 Eng.) argues that the roots of the negative possibility of the modern technological milieu can be traced to the inadequacy of the synthesis of duality, an inadequacy manifested in abstraction and quantification, for synthesis immediately becomes the nexus of conflict as it is converted to a provisional thesis and threatened with opposition—the anti-thesis. Time, history, and life are conceived as moving only under the stress of inconsistent yet relentless attack. Life comes to be perceived from a defensive position—a perspective that is always threatened with losing something (or everything). Life is understood as a battleground between good and evil, subject and environment. It is up or out, conform or die. Thus, temporal anxiety indicates the insecurity that modern humans feel for contingencies in knowledge and history. Modernity is infused with a sense that it must keep advancing, moving, often frenetically—direction unknown; movement for movement's sake. It is assumed that bigger is always better. A lack of measurable growth or change does not indicate satisfaction but rather stagnation. All aspects of life are continually monitored, measured for change. Mythic conscience is operationalized in modernity. Quality of life and frame of mind are displaced by sheer quantity of units of change, as quantities have meaning only relative to each other, which is to say they have no inherent value or meaning, whereas qualities do not require relative comparison to make sense. I can feel happy or sad without comparison to how you feel, and such feelings are self-evident. But I can be tall only relative to you. Thus, the modern obsession with quantification has unwittingly plunged humanity into nihilistic relativism even as it seeks to fix value as quanta. Gebser (1949 Ger./1985 Eng.) insists:

> As long as the moderating quality of the mental consciousness was still effective, abstraction and quantification were only latently capable of negative effects. But when moderation was displaced by the immoderation of the *ratio*, a change most clearly evident in Descartes, abstraction began to transform itself into its extreme form of manifestation (best defined by the concept of isolation), while the identical process led from quantification to amassment and agglomeration. (p. 95)

Perhaps the most clear expression of this amassing quantification, which functions to isolate and reduce individuals to units (called subjects, participants, workers, FTEs, etc.) and strip them of qualitative value, is to be found in the application of statistical methods to human beings beginning with the founders of eugenics, including Francis Edgeworth, Francis Galton, Karl Pearson, and George Yule (see Kramer, 2003a, for a detailed discussion). Humans are thus stripped of inherent dignity and are considered (and used) as beasts of burden to be bred in the interest of wealth creation. Those who create wealth most efficiently are to be bred while the poor should be discouraged from breeding (if not sterilized)—all for the greater good of the collective global interest.

To summarize, the conception of humans as subjects to be submitted to a transcending logic emerges concurrently with the emergence of a world or an environment that is a disinterested object. As the world is emptied of inherent value, value must be added by means of human action. The world, emptied of any sacred dimension, becomes available for indiscriminate plundering by ego-interests. Humans are not just in the world, but rather are here to possess it. After objectivistic duality is established, the world no longer manifests a spiritual dimension. As pure object, it becomes appropriated by and for human possession and consumption. This shift is, as Gebser (1949 Ger./1985 Eng.) notes, "a gain as well as a loss" (p. 12). As care for the Other is eliminated as an obsolete emotion and an obstacle to progress, humanity no longer perceives itself to be a part of the object-world, as an inhabitant within and of the world (magic, or as a caring custodian of the creation [myth]), but instead as an outside owner, a manipulative yet legitimized exploiter (mental-rational perspectivism). For the perspectival, life is reduced to a ratio of cost to benefit.

The Subject and Object are polarized as opposing entities, as fundamentally divergent ontic fields. This attitude is the necessary condition for the technological world to emerge. Modern humanity is thus alienated from the object world. Existence is interpreted as a constant struggle with the object-environment to make things work. As Harvard economist Juliet Schor (1993), Jeremy Rifkin (1989) of the Foundation on Economic Trends and a Fellow of the Wharton School's Executive Management Program, professor Benjamin Hunnicutt (1996) of the University of Iowa, John Sweeney and Karen Nussbaum (Sweeney & Nussbaum, 1989), former Director of the Women's Bureau of the U.S. Labor Department, and others have noted, people in the most "advanced" industrial societies spend longer periods of their lives devoted to training for work and work more hours per day (to the point of chronic fatigue caused by a perpetual sleep deficit) than any previous generation or less industrialized society. As Hunnicutt and Hunnicutt (1996) noted, in the most technologically advanced countries, leisure has changed from the active pursuit of personal hobbies and interests (avocations) to collapsing before the television after having the best hours spent on production outside the personal realm of the home or personal interest. The distance between Subject and Object enables one to take possession and manipulate with careless impunity, but this plundering destroys identity with the environment and with what one produces. This possessive culture is reversible, too, so that the person is taken by the system, and production and consumption (and its techniques) come to dominate everything imaginable.

Gebser's (1949 Ger./1985 Eng.) idea has important implications for the exclusively objectivistic view of the world. First, the acting person is viewed as an isolated subject. Second, individuality is understood to be co-constituted by mass collectivity; community gives way to aggregates of disinterested individuals. Third, the external universe is grasped as a field of unsympathetic objects. The physical and/or lifeworld is now understood to both be in conflict with and resistant to human will. In an utterly indifferent universe, morality and ethics are ultimately regarded as nonsense. Life becomes an endless struggle to subjugate and rationally order the object-world. Integral awareness, however, does not manifest the rigidity of Cartesian objectivism. The four consciousness dimensions of the world (that were formerly thought to be mutually exclusive) are, in the integral world, recognized as interpenetrating each other.

THE OBJECTIVISTIC BIAS AND
TECHNOLOGICAL CONSCIOUSNESS

As discussed in Chapter 10, Husserl (1954 Ger./1970 Eng.), Merleau-Ponty (1945 Fr./1962 Eng., 1964 Fr./1968 Eng.), and Gebser (1949 Ger./1985 Eng.) claim that something about human experience and the human world cannot be adequately dealt with (i.e., understood) by the methods and practices of the quantifying objectivistic standpoint. If this is true, then we have more reason to take seriously contemporary criticisms of our increasingly technological way of being, such as those offered by Heidegger (1952, 1954, 1962 Ger./1977 Eng.), Ellul (1954 Fr./1964 Eng.), and Mumford (1934/ 1963/ 2010).

It is not enough to point out the anomalies of our technological milieu. Rather, we must show why the anomalies in question are more than simple research protocol problems. The phenomenological investigations of Merleau-Ponty (1947, 1955, 1964 Fr./1964 Eng.) and Gebser (1949 Ger./ 1985 Eng.) are attentive to the non-quantifiable dimensions of human experience. We must be willing to recognize the fundamental contingency inherent in all human thinking if we wish to generate an accurate explanation of technology. As the development of humanity is increasingly determined by values grounded in a technological viewpoint, which is grounded in the misguided notion of exclusively quantitative reason advocated by the Cartesian rationalists, it becomes pertinent to appreciate the relevance of the ideas of Merleau-Ponty and Gebser for philosophical considerations of technology in particular and social science in general.

The promise of phenomenology lies in the resolve of its followers to resurrect the world of everyday experience—to make evident the role of the lifeworld as the fundamental reality from which all conceptions and constructions of other domains start, and to which these domains essentially refer (Gurwitsch, 1966; see also Schutz, 1953/1997, for an understanding of the essential nature of the lifeworld in relation to social science in particular). The birth of the scientific method came about from a blending of rational and empirical procedures, a blending that figured most prominently in the work and thought of Galileo. Galileo was hardly the first to blend demonstration with empirical observation, but the results of his efforts had the greatest impact on subsequent generations of scientists. For this reason, it is not uncommon to see references to the "Galilean worldview" in discussions of the birth and impact of the new scientific attitude (Gurwitsch, 1974).

The Galilean worldview transformed the modern Western view of nature and restricted the definition of the essence of human rationality. The Galilean view operates on the assumption that this view captures the true sense of rational explanation and also provides the true sense of "reason" as the guide to the rational development of humanity. In the process, the methods of the "natural" (physical) sciences are embraced by the human (social) sciences (in what Freud might have referred to as "method envy" on the part of the social sciences), to the point that it is taken for granted that all rational explanations must ultimately depend on the physical, spatially quantified products of positivism. Even explanations of the life of the human spirit and consciousness count (i.e., are considered valid) only if they are articulated as quanta. Other modes of expression, regardless of their content, are evaluated (ironically) to be invalid. Results reported in non-quantitative ways are frequently devalued, ridiculed, or ignored—dismissed as garbage in, garbage out, junk science (or, more commonly, as not even being scientific at all).

By the early decades of the twentieth century, the new idea of rational calculation had entered the domain of the workplace. The idea was to train workers and design technological interfaces in ways that would promote an optimal relationship between worker and environment—optimal in terms of quantity of production, not quality for those doing the producing (Braverman, 1974). The goal of engineered efficiency became the dominant theme of reflection and the intense preoccupation of managers and producers. The dream of efficiency leads eventually, as described by Feinberg (1977) and other futurologists, to the utopia of a rationally determined future, with well-appropriated and ample resources to care for the wealthy, and with only enough resources for the rest to survive in order to serve the wealthy (keeping the ratio between resources expended and labor hours gained favorable to the wealthy). The great chain of causation is instituted as the future shall be caused by the fixed, indifferent, incorruptible ratios—the bottom line, the top price, the cut-off point, the acceptable range. Thus, all future states are to be made rationally, but they are also absurdly posited as logically inevitable (fatalistic).

Stemming from this idea of radical calculation is the culminating form of objectivism (which enables itself to avoid responsibility for any and all future states): the world is defined as precisely the subjective-relative dimensions of human beings. This realm of uncertainty rooted in subjective caprice was evaluated as not only full of fallacy but also as the very cause of fallacy. Thus, it had to be methodically removed from consideration (by the smoke and mirrors of the so-called "exact" sciences) in order to pave the way to their "objective" reality. Thus, naturalistic psychology (including behaviorism) began from a picture of reality that had been developed on the basis of careful abstractions. The cognitive science movement that dominates psychology today (and that serves as the foundation for much research in the field of communication studies) is guided by the same sort of attitude and metaphysical presumptions. To the extent that scholars who adhere to this movement fail to recognize the crucial difference between *data* and *sign*, their studies (and, by extension, the disciplines they operate in) suffer from being cut off from lived experience.

Perhaps the most extreme case is the mathematical theory of communication that is purely quantitative and, as such, neglects the phenomenon most important in any communication act—what the message means. For example, communication frequency and communication channels utilized are easily and infinitely quantifiable, but the numbers generated from studying the quantified data do not adequately address human communication (and most other social) phenomena (i.e., they cannot tell us the *value* of the communications studied or the *meanings* generated in them). These positivistic approaches treat communication as a static event rather than the active process it undeniably is. The technological achievement nourished from abstraction comes to birth in a world that is neglected yet full of human intention and purpose—a world more complex and ambiguous than anything considered (i.e., allowed) by positivism. Convenience and power are interests that contribute substantially to this neglect of value and meaning (through fantastic over-simplification). However, humans live in a world of signs and symbols that are not univocal. Unlike electrons, we continually evaluate conditions and potential and make decisions based on our unique conclusions. The lifeworld (ironically, including certain experiences interpreted as data) is a realm of meaning. What Skinner (1999) never explained is how a reward can also be a punishment, how the difference is established by a person, or how a thing can change from a reward to a punishment with a change of mind, each a substantial point to be sure.

Positivistic science, with methods so carefully (and ironically) eliminating all bias (except the bias for true objectivity), has been popularized as the exemplar of linear causal science in the academy; even in the human sciences (and especially in psychology)—entrenched as the one and only god. Behavioral scientists aspire to reach the levels of achievement realized by the physical sciences (Bernstein, 1983). In the process, the human sciences have taken on the metaphysics, methods, and goals of the natural sciences and have embraced the worldview that foolishly dichotomizes mental life and physical life.

If we develop an objective-scientific method aimed at extracting the meaning of this world from its presence to us, it becomes difficult to see the meaning. Under such a bias, we focus on the thing, not the pre-experiential structures that make the appearance of the thing possible (again, treating the active process as a static event). Husserl (1954 Ger./1970 Eng.) indicates that:

> This idea of objectivity dominates the whole universitas of the positive sciences in the modern period, and in the general usage it dominates the meaning of the word "science.". . . [But] the contrast between the subjectivity of the life-world and the "objective," the "true" world, lies in the fact that the latter is a theoretical-logical substruction, the substruction of something that is in principle not perceivable, in principle not experienceable in its own proper being, whereas the subjective, in the life-world, is distinguished in all respects precisely by its being actually experienceable. (p. 127)

If people remain unaware of the nature of perceptional process, it is easy to see that people will simply take for granted the "obvious" existence of a wholly independent world within which people think and operate as subjective beings. From this naïve conception of the relationship between human beings and their world, it is easy to uncritically assume the posture of objectivism, and from the new posture, then, to work for an objective determination of the true nature of our understandings (our obviously flawed conclusions).

The ideal of a technological utopia or a rationally determined future of humanity comes from this positivism-as-truth orientation. At the base of this ideology is the belief that human beings can eventually gain enough conceptual leverage over their situation to be in a position to control the consequences of their actions. People can, then, choose the actions that will benefit their situation and abstain from any actions that are inhibitive or harmful. However, as discussed in Chapters 9 and 10, and as Gebser and Merleau-Ponty emphasize, the rationalizing viewpoint (positivism) is absurd.

In short, objectivistic and rationalistic assumptions yield a view of human circumstance as something that can be rationally determined in accordance with the reductive, calculative, abstractive methods of exacting mathematics. However, we cannot hope to understand the nature of technological phenomena from a standpoint that seeks to isolate the physical from the mental, the user from the device. Rather, we must seek to understand the intentional and complex nature of our relationship to technology, for in the end, this relationship generates the prescriptions through which we experience technology and en-world ourselves within an increasingly encroaching technological milieu. Before exploring critical approaches, it is necessary to clarify what technological utopia is—an extreme yet exemplary configuration of the objectivistic bias.

TECHNOLOGICAL UTOPIA

The promise of technological utopia presumes the objectivist paradigm (or, more simply, objectivism). This aspect is particularly evident in Feinberg's (1977) work:

> More and more of what happens in the world is subject to human intervention and control, so that more than ever before, *we have the power to determine the future, rather than to predict it.* Given this rapidly developing power which is the result of what we have learned about the world and ourselves, *we should be more concerned with choosing what future we want for the world* than with divining what providence or blind chance has in store for us. We should recognize that to an ever increasing extent, *the future is what we make*, and endeavor to make it what we want it to be. (p. 8; italics added)

Feinberg (1977) argues that it is especially crucial for people to recognize that the future is ours to determine, especially in light of the increasingly refined and powerful potential for drastic change in humans and their societies, a potential that comes from advances in the "engineering" technologies (especially nanotechnologies and biotechnologies).

Furthermore, Feinberg (1977) continues, "computer technology . . . has raised the possibility of creating artificial intelligence comparable to human intelligence" (p. 11), and "[T]here is reason to believe that we can accomplish almost anything we wish" (p. 14). Feinburg further insists, "[I]t seems reasonable to suppose that we will eventually be able to understand the scientific laws relevant to any aspect of nature and [humanity] that interests us" (p. 130). This fearless optimism follows from Feinberg's conception of the nature of complex systems:

> The problem is not that there is something more to the system than science can reveal, or that some mysterious laws act in complex systems that are not found in simple ones, but rather that we are not in a position yet to deduce what the known laws of science imply when the components of a complex system act upon one another. (p. 98)

In this view, human beings will continue to need and use computers, and that means, among other things, learning how to compute the laws of interaction that hold among human beings. Even though people have not learned how to compute laws of this sort yet, if one follows this optimistic viewpoint, there is no basis for the claim that such a feat is impossible. Feinberg's three basic optimistic claims are indispensable for clarifying, supporting, and perpetuating the objectivistic technophile position. Feinberg (1977) argues first:

> We could imagine an especially effective computer which had been programmed with the known laws governing the interaction of components of some system . . . and which by numerical solution of these equations would be able to make predictions about the behavior of the system in a variety of circumstances. . . . Such predictions might well be made without the programmer or the computer having an intuitive understanding of the behavior of the system. (p. 100)

Accordingly, what is left for human beings is to simply ask the "right" questions.

Second, Feinberg (1977) claims:

> There is nothing intrinsic to complex systems that differentiates them from simple systems. It is rather a weakness of the human intellect in dealing with complexity which makes it appear to us that there are intrinsic differences. Therefore, we must look for the improvement of our way of thought, rather than the obtaining of some special insight into the nature of complexity, as the direction that post-modern science will follow in bringing more of the world into human understanding. (p. 106)

Continuing from the first two claims, Feinberg (1977) argues his third point:

> If we are going to continue to intervene on a major scale in the environment, or eventually in our own biological processes, we must develop better intellectual tools for the prediction of long-term effects. This task is made more difficult by the many interacting factors that exist in the environment, and in human society. But the challenge of dealing with such problems should attract the most gifted among us, and I fully believe that they will successfully respond to it. When that is done, we may have a true ecology or science of the environment, as well as a true sociology, or science of society. . . . We can then rationally decide how to achieve the world that we want. (pp. 130-131)

Feinberg (1977) argues that humanity's limitations can be removed through the proper development of scientific reflection, computational approaches to the study of complex systems, and accurate long-range forecasting techniques. What should be remembered is that Feinberg begins with the assumption that humanity's chief aim is to become "as independent as possible from environmental fluctuations" (p. 112).

Finally, Feinberg (1977) states:

> From the point of view of basic science, no aspect of the natural environment is really essential to human life. For example, we could make our food by chemical synthesis, extract our minerals from sea water . . . etc. Indeed, in many cases we are doing just these things on a small scale, and nothing in the laws of nature forbids us from doing them on a large scale. (p. 113)

Feinberg (1977) concludes, "It seems much more likely that it is possible to design artificial environments that are more conducive to human well-being than the one in which we evolved" (p. 117). Accordingly, the fundamental question is not, "What must we do to maintain the balance and harmony of our natural milieu?" Instead, we should be asking ourselves, "What sort of environment do we want?" (p. 117). Through his argument, Feinberg (1977) would have us quantify the essence of our human existence and input those data into a computational matrix devoid of all ambiguity and contingency. In the lifeworld, however, Feinberg's view is substantially distorted; it is a fantastic wish—the utopian dream of total technological control. But ambiguity is the essence of communication and semiosis. Without ambiguity there is no communication. Perfect clarity constitutes the end of semiosis. Nothing is left but calculation.

Feinberg's (1977) vision of a rationally determined future, along with the ideal of a technological utopia, is as misguided and indefensible as is the objectivist conception of scientific rationality. Not surprisingly, both are grounded in the same illusion about our capacity "to see more clearly" than the structure of human experience will allow.

The problem is not that people have yet to fully realize their capacity to see with the mind's eye, as Descartes (1641 Lat./1647 Fr./1901 Eng.) was fond of imagining. Rather, the problem is that we must first see with the eye of the body. Therefore, people must reason from the perspective of the living body—the embodied life, the context that affects all social encounters—and from within the commonsensible world. We must understand initially that we are an integral part of the system, and it of us. In other words, we cannot hope to conceive the proper relationship between reason and technology without first taking into account the implications of the different consciousness structures involved in the relationship and the nature of intentionality, the point at which Gebser (1949 Ger./1985 Eng.) starts his investigation.

Mutation, Not Progress

With regard to the technological worldview, it should be said that the description offered here is not presented as a new conception of the world. As Gebser (1949 Ger./1985 Eng.) indicates, a new image would be no more than the creation of a myth, as all imagery has a predominantly mythical nature; that is, it does not have linear logic. A new image would be another new mysticism, another irrationality. Furthermore, "a new *conception* of the world would be nothing else than yet another standard rationalistic construction of the present, for conceptualization has an essentially rational and abstract nature" (Gebser, 1949 Ger./1985 Eng., p. 7; italics added).

According to Gebser (1949 Ger./1985 Eng.), all making (creating), whether in the form of casting a spell or the reasoned technical construction of a machine, is an externalization of inner powers or conditions; as such, it is merely the visible, outward form of these powers/conditions. Every tool, every instrument, and every machine is only a practical application that manifests a perspectival-directed usefulness. This desire to make/use tools is not guided by transcendental laws; instead, the laws are of one's own body rediscovered externally. Therefore, the (desire for) technical achievement and discovery is pre-given.

Gebser (1949 Ger./1985 Eng.) argues that every invention is primarily a rediscovery and an imitative construction of the organic and physiological pre-given symmetries or laws inherent in the structure of the human body (including mental structures) that becomes conscious by being externally projected into a tool. This is also true of the natural capacities at the disposal of the magic human, such as fantastic feats of endurance and sympathy with other animals. The magic human lives, moves, and is absorbed in a spaceless-timeless world of which the individual is a part, not thinking in terms of extension or projection (of power). For the magic human, a spell is not cast across empty space but iterated and immediately effective. In this respect, such acts are not miracles but normal occurrences for magic humanity.

But this is not true of radio and television. The mental-rational, modern human forfeits the capacity for such miracles and has replaced such powers with a projected objectification or externalization in the material form of television and radio. However, as Gebser (1949 Ger./1985 Eng.) acknowledges, we might also say that we would not have such instruments if we did not have within ourselves the genuine capability to create and achieve and to use the tools we have made. This consideration also points to the limits of technology: "[T]echnology is definitely unable to bestow on human the omnipotence that [they] imagine [themselves] to have. On the contrary, technology necessarily leads to an 'omn-impotence' to the extent that the process of physical projection is not realized" (Gebser, 1949 Ger./1985 Eng., p. 132). However, Gebser insists, we have the possibility of resolving the problem of technology, a problem that cannot be solved merely by more technological advancement.

The rearrangement of certain capacities within humanity—from the qualitative, natural instrumentality of early human into the externalized instrumentality of the machine—entails more than quantification. Early archaic and magic humans, for instance, with their vital or magic powers, were not able to "think" in the modern sense. Yet it would be a misunderstanding to regard the practice of magic as a deficiency (as modern people frequently do); for such an evaluation is equivalent to questioning the sense or meaningfulness of life. In the modern mental-rational worldview, magic does not work. And yet many cling to myriad faiths and find a deep sense of security in them. Nevertheless, in the modern world, two threats are apparent. First (as with the rise of Nazism), there is the possibility of a resurgence of magic consciousness, occurring in a lifeworld with the technologies of perspectival humanity—technologies that magic humans cannot produce. Second, the spatializing and materializing of the world threatens to atomize everything from community to knowledge—from operationalization to the absurdly relativistic situation criticized by Husserl (1900 Ger./2001 Eng.) as "regional ontologies" (p. 37). There is no difficulty in determining that this atomization has already taken on tangible and palpable forms.

As Gebser (1949 Ger./1985 Eng.) specifies, it is incorrect to regard the machine as being the initiator of all present-day horrors (or to suggest that humans aren't complicit in being controlled). The emergence of modern conceptions of time, followed by the invention of the machine, lies outside humanity's mental or rational manipulation; retaining their autonomy in the modern technological milieu. That is, they remained free of humanity's waking conscious control. Consequently, "[T]he motoricity of the machine arbitrarily began to dominate and compel [humanity] into its dependency" (Gebser, 1949 Ger./1985 Eng., p. 301). Feinberg's (1977) claim clearly shows that there are those who in their technological overconfidence fail to recognize the seriousness of our situation. Thus, they insistently reiterate that human beings have "advanced majestically" with their "progress" (Feinberg, 1977, p. 545). For those with an optimistic view of technology, progress is measured by how far humans have come in atomization and in technological prowess, ultimately operationalized as economic gain (i.e., how much money is made from the production of technology or as a result of technological developments). No other sense of progress is thinkable by them.

We have become accustomed to conceptualizing the evolution of humankind as a temporal procession, but we should keep in mind that this is merely an attempt to structure the past for the purpose of making a survey of history. The interpretation and application of concepts including "evolving creation" and "progress" are often misleading—they are matters of faith presented as fact (with rather high penalties for what we might call scientific blasphemy, such as rejecting the idea of a confidence interval or inferential statistics in general). However comfortable, we must regard the idea of a progressive, continuous development as inadequate to understand our situation. To formulate this in biological rather than physical terms, we might say that such a process is mutable—that is, it operates *in the manner of mutation*—spontaneous and independent of ambitious controlled instrumentality, and it develops by leaps. It is illusory to think the lifeworld is or can be predictable or controlled in the ways positivists conjure.

Regarding the notion of "mutation," Gebser (1949 Ger./1985 Eng.) writes:

> The manifestation of this mutational process should not be construed as a mere succession of events, a progress or historicized course. It is, rather, a manifestation of inherent predispositions of consciousness, now incremental, now reductive, that determine [hu]man's specific grasp of reality through and beyond the epochs and civilizations. Once more, it should be emphasized that we must remain suspicious of progress and its resultant misuse of technology (to the degree that we are dependent on it and not the reverse), as well as of the doctrines of evolutionary superiority and voluntarism. The voluntarism which is clearly evident since Vico has transferred the capacity of signification from an origin presumed to be "behind" all being, into human reason and will. (p. 41)

Understanding Gebser's notion of mutation is crucial for understanding the meaning and nature of the technological milieu. Thinking in terms of mutation instead of linear progress enables one to perceive the process that is ongoing yet invisible.

What appears to be continuous and to have an inherent causal-logical continuity is nothing but a series of (un- or minimally related) transitions (as Kuhn, 1962, would argue, too). People endow what is happening with a logical, causal, determinate, often final character. The concept of *mutation* better depicts the discontinuity that marks the differences among consciousness structures (i.e., worlds or realities). Moreover, use of this term enables people to keep their distance from such concepts as progress, evolution, and unfolding.

Every mutation in consciousness is marked by a sudden eruption of possibilities and properties that are incorporated into a new structure. These sudden occurrences are attributed to the idea that certain processes take place apparently outside spatio-temporal comprehension and conceivability, so that people are not able to place the causal nexus in time and space. In other words, mutation has an emergent character.

Attempts to describe such mutations of consciousness often exploit concepts such as progress, evolution, and unfolding. However, such concepts at best only reiterate dialectical and psychological or biological frames. Within mutations of consciousness, a process of rearrangement takes place beyond the reach of mere space-time-bound events. As previously stated, emergent processes manifest themselves in discontinuous leaps and bounds; these processes have made possible the assimilation of the sense-making operation of the origin throughout human consciousness. Origin iterates itself in consciousness through mutations in awareness, which is what Gebser (1949 Ger./1985 Eng.) calls the *integrational process*.

Defenders of the idea of progress, such as Feinberg (1977) and de Sola Pool (1990), assert that our age (or era) and civilization are synonymous with a superior development, but this view has clearly been put into question by their very achievement. The results and their applications demonstrate why people must guard against self-esteem, especially presumptuous overestimations such as the arrogance of the biological postulate that development is inherently something higher and better—the view that has engraved itself deeply as a primary aspect of the modern mentality and must be monitored carefully. For example, Comte (1975), whose ideas formulate one core of beliefs that constitute the received view in social science, postulates progress as purposive and goal-directed. Such an ideology reveals his perspectivistic fixation and objectivist, positivist bias. The concept of development associated with continuity allows no room for the possibility of mutation that is discontinuous and non-directional.

As discussed in Chapter 9, Gebser (1949 Ger./1985 Eng.) offers a working hypothesis. The four or five different structures that he designates as archaic, magic, mythic, rational, and integral do not present a continuous progression with typical developmental characteristics. These structures do not exist in the past tense; each is "ever-present" in every one of us today, is more or less latent (or relevant) at a given time, and is sometimes accelerated in its development.

Origin is ever-present (Gebser, 1949 Ger./1985 Eng.). It is not a beginning; beginnings are linked with time. So far as the choice of the word "structure" is concerned, structures are distinct from "levels," "planes," or "states." Such terms imply something spatial and hence foster the mode of looking at things in perspective. Structures, for Gebser, are not mere spatial textures but may indeed be textures of a space-time or even non-space-time character. The results of these mutations are latent within us in the form of various consciousness structures and continue to be effective.

11

The Nature of Technology and Communication

This chapter provides three concrete diagnoses concerning the nature of the modern technological milieu, including the works of Ellul, Heidegger, and Mumford. Before introducing these critical assessments, Borgmann's (1984) argument that deals with three different approaches to technology is presented. His argument clarifies the viewpoints of Ellul (1954 Fr./1964 Eng., 1977 Fr./1980 Eng.), Heidegger (1952, 1954, 1962 Ger./1977 Eng.), and Mumford (1934/1963, 1967), discussing the views they share and how the three differ from other futurologists including Feinberg (1977) and de Sola Pool (1990). This chapter demonstrates that many communication theories are under the influence of Cartesian-biased objectivism and the obsession of modern technological futurological utopian optimism.

DANGERS OF THE MODERN TECHNOLOGICAL MILIEU

Three Views of Technology

Borgmann (1984) argues that views of technology fall into one of three approaches: instrumental, pluralist, or substantive. Instrumentalists view technology as simply a means to an end or a value-neutral tool in the service of human values and goals. Instrumentalists argue that political activity directs technology. Thus, instrumentalists represent a broad range of views and debates about technology ranging politically from far left to far right. The liberal democratic view that pervades Western democracies, as well as socialist and Marxists views and those of Marcuse, perpetuate the simplistic instrumental view that technology is a means to an end.

According to Heidegger (1952, 1954, 1962 Ger./1977 Eng.), the instrumental view was outdated by the degree of technical proliferation and the subsequent qualitative changes that have resulted in social, psychological, and intellectual processes. The instrumentalists refuse to relinquish the idea that someone, some group, some governing body, or humanity in general is in control of technology. The instrumental view fails to differentiate technology in our modern culture from technology in traditional cultures where means were "always and inextricably woven into a context of ends" (Heidegger, 1952, 1954, 1962 Ger./1977 Eng., p. 6). Therefore, Heidegger claims that the instrumental view is "correct" but yet not "true" because it "still does not show us technology's essence" (p. 6).

Second are the pluralistic approaches that receive the least attention in Borgmann's analysis because those advocating these approaches suffer from an inability to see the proverbial collective technological forest for the individual technological trees. As Borgmann (1984) puts it, the pluralists see "no clear problem of technology at all, merely an interplay of numerous and various tendencies" (p. 15). They focus on individual systems and technologies, the details of their evolutions, specific interactions between one technology and another, and particular counterexamples to both the instrumentalist and substantive approaches. By attempting to master the abundant minutiae of any given technology and human interaction with it, pluralists get lost (or tossed around) in a sea of information, without any vision of an underlying pattern or essence of the whole. For example, in a given developmental stage of a certain technology, pluralists might adhere to one theory whereas in another interaction or evolutionary stage, they might uphold an opposing or different one.

In contrast to the pluralist approach, Borgmann (1984) describes the most ambitious (and least popular) substantive approach to technology, for which Ellul (1954 Fr./1964 Eng., 1977 Fr./1980 Eng.) is the chief representative and in which Heidegger (1952, 1954, 1962 Ger./1977 Eng.) is also included. According to Borgmann (1984), the substantive view is characterized by the affirmation of technology as an autonomous force, "a force in its own right" that "shapes today's societies and values from the ground up and has no serious rivals" (p. 9).

The substantive view is typically anti-technological, Borgmann (1984) says, because autonomous technology is portrayed as a malicious force.[1]

---

[1]At this point, Borgmann reveals a controversial understanding of Ellul's view on technology. As Lovekin (1977, 1991) illustrates, technique (the technical phenomenon) is a form of intentionality. Without any sense of the technical intention involved in the technical phenomenon, Borgmann has missed the most crucial dimension of

Borgmann claims that "efficiency" is an incomplete notion, incapable of being the sole goal of technique, as Ellul (1954 Fr./1964 Eng.) describes it, because it requires, in Borgmann's (1984) words, "antecedently fixed goals on behalf of which values are minimized or maximized" (p. 9). This statement alone exemplifies a gross misunderstanding of Ellul's (1954 Fr./1964 Eng.) idea of technique that operates with "absolute efficiency" (p. xxv) not efficiency as Borgmann describes it (Lovekin, 1991).

Producing "Absolute Efficiency"

Ellul (1954 Fr./1964 Eng.) describes "absolute efficiency" as that which is determined by the quantitative calculations of technicians in order to illustrate the self-regulating character of modern technology that rejects any antecedently fixed values. Defining efficiency in the traditional sense, Borgmann (1984) fails to recognize the modern self-justifying function of the appeal to efficiency in the technical phenomenon Ellul describes (Lovekin, 1991; also see Lovekin, 1980).

An illustration of this modern self-justifying appeal to efficiency can be seen in the following example. When someone insists that wilderness and nature be treated with more respect because respect for nature represents the most efficient use of these resources in the long-term view, their reasoning should be regarded as that of "absolute efficiency." The desired result of the argument is that we should try to manage natural resources with more care and respect. However, this is not equivalent to treating wilderness better in its own right, nor is this view a deviation from the instrumental paradigm. It is not another paradigm, but rather it is fine-tuning the paradigm.

Zimmerman (1990) argues, "[T]he limitless domination of modern technology in every corner of this planet is only the late consequence of a very old technical interpretation of the world, which interpretation is usually called metaphysics" (p. 166). Following this idea, technology is conceived as the final stage, the fulfillment, the end of the Western tradition that began with Plato and Aristotle. Therefore, technology is the lamentable conclusion of thinking (metaphysics) that has given way to its final form, calculation (Zimmerman, 1975; also see Zimmerman, 1990).

Zimmerman (1975) insists that the origin of the instrumental paradigm can be traced to the ideas of Greek philosophers. He summarizes Heidegger's critique of the Greek philosophical metaphysics as follows:

Ellul's concept. Sometimes this kind of misunderstanding (Feenberg, 1991; Mitcham & Mackey, 1971) leads to describing Ellul's and Heidegger's views as fatalistic despite the objection of Ellul and his defenders.

The metaphysical schemes of Plato and Aristotle, Heidegger argued, were based on the view that the structure of all things is akin to the structure of products or artifacts. Aristotle's metaphysics, for example, is "productionist" insofar as he conceived of all things, including animals, as "formed matter." The most obvious example of such "formed matter" is the work produced by an artisan who gives form to material. Plato and Aristotle seemingly projected onto all entities the structure of artifacts. (p. 157)

Based on Heidegger's (1952, 1954, 1962 Ger./1977 Eng.) critique, Zimmerman (1975) states, "[I]f people in the technological era are treated instrumentally, this is because the Greeks defined humans in terms of categories which originally applied to artifacts such as equipment" (p. 159). Gebser's (1949 Ger./1985 Eng.) description of the burgeoning stage of mental consciousness and Heidegger's (1952, 1954, 1962 Ger./1977 Eng.) insight that technological instrumentality traces back to Greek philosophers are not coincidental in their similarity of description. The similarity between the emergence of mental consciousness and technological instrumentality illustrates the process of dimensional accrual/dissociation. Kramer (1997) argues that as human culture strives to become more and more objective (or productionist-like in the Heideggerian sense), a process of dimensional accrual/dissociation occurs (also see Kramer, 2004b).

Marxist revisionists, including members of the Frankfurt school such as Marcuse (1964), Habermas (1968, 1971 Ger./1973 Eng.), and Borgmann (1984), do not grasp (or choose not to address) the seriousness of the modern technological milieu.[2] These theorists affirm the deterministic character of technique and technological enframing, but because they can describe and talk about technological determinism, they appear to believe that determinism can be avoided or overcome. For instance, in his concluding chapter, Marcuse (1964) describes a revolutionary change that would overcome the dangers of technology and return dimension and depth to humanity. But he appears to deny the recognized character of technology. These theorists describe the danger of technology and then, because the dangers have been identified and brought to consciousness, offer an ambiguous revolution leading to freedom that overcomes those dangers. Ellul (1954 Fr./1964 Eng.) illustrates that freedom is harder to achieve than revolutionaries think.

---

[2]Habermas (1968, 1971 Ger./1973 Eng.), for example, criticizes the colonization (or mechanization) of the lifeworld. But it is hard to find any argument made by him directly concerning technology or the nature of technology (Dreyfus, 1995).

ELLUL'S EXPLORATION ON TECHNOLOGICAL SYSTEM AND SOCIETY: TECHNOLOGICAL IMPERATIVE

According to Ellul (1954 Fr./1964 Eng.), the everyday world may become so thoroughly dependent on technology that our capacity for choosing and judging may well be completely framed by technological criteria relevant to the safety and prosperity of the technological system. In that event, our lives would be determined and modified by technological factors deeply rooted in the objectivist paradigm (and objectivists will also hold the keys to the buildings where these systems are housed/worshiped and will make all the rules and select punishment for breaking them, etc.). The system becomes a cybernetic loop, a tautology in which the only acceptable reason for altering the system is to maintain (or further enhance) the system (repairing it as opposed to reconstructing or dismantling it).

The technological milieu (and attendant dissociation) has saturated the lifeworld so that we no longer understand nature as something separate from technology. We cannot see the natural world without the lens of technology. If technology is to be comprehended as a system, then one must overcome the temptation to consider one's relationship to technology as one of dealing with isolated objects. Instead, we should recognize that our involvement with technology engages us in a network in which the interrelations among parts are not of the same type as those among the parts of an engine.

The view based on the objectivist paradigm of reason suggests that technology is a set of objects crafted by and at the immediate disposal of humans. Those holding a view such as this assume that the human being is free to recognize the need for changes without questioning the possibility that the systematic nature of the environment within which humankind functions is dynamic, a source of change. Ellul (1954 Fr./1964 Eng.) indicates that humans are free to choose, but the freedom is limited to a range of pre-structured choices circumscribed by the limits of their technology. While (arguably) individuals may choose to avoid technology (i.e., becoming hermits, going "off the grid," moving to a Luddite colony, etc.), for society as a whole, what exists are kinds or zones of choice, not absolute choice.

The vaunted freedom of interaction is always already structured by pre-given parameters. Freedom to choose is reduced to (an ever-shrinking set of) parameters. Technology and commodity structuration is evinced in the corporate motto that industry gives us choice, but that choice can be exercised only if we buy (an act that is presumed). Thus, I have beyond-ample choices—hundreds of types of ice cream or shampoo or socks—but only in the act of purchasing.

Ellul (1977 Fr./1980 Eng.) concludes that humankind is not in command of technology but is instead thinking and operating (living) in *response* to technology:

The human being who acts and thinks today is not situated as an independent subject with respect to a technological object. [The individual] is inside the technological system . . . modified by the technological factor. The human being who uses technology today is by that very fact the human being who serves it. And conversely, *only the human being who serves technology is truly able to use it.* (p. 325; italics added)

Action and thinking are thus structured by the technological milieu. Technology manifests the limits of the possible for daily life. As the lifeworld becomes increasingly mechanized, the possible range of motion and thought conform (adapt). For example, small cameras allow us to monitor (virtually— meaning both "nearly all" and in the VR sense) anything: our homes, pets, children, teen drivers, elderly parents, strangers in hotels (feloniously), and so on, so we move and think differently as a result of this monitoring capability.

Furthermore, Ellul (1977 Fr./1980 Eng.) reveals the misunderstanding of the naïve, objectivistic perspective on mechanization and the technological milieu in general. Ellul (1977 Fr./1980 Eng.) says the problem with the objectivistic perspective is:

It leads to regarding technology as put together out of disparate bits and pieces, with random and uncertain relations between them. Yet the opposite is true. Each technological element is associated with all the others in a preferential way. When mechanization is introduced into offices, it represents a kind of spearhead launched in that direction by the technological system. (p. 81)

This seems particularly true in the case of computerized operations. With the transfer from manual labor-based systems to computerized ones (or even to newer, updated forms of pre-existing computerized systems), invariably new job definitions and new problems develop, requiring expertise that serves to integrate the user into new work environments. For example, moving from a traditional paper-based filing system to a computerized one causes these developments, as does moving from a DOS-based computer filing system to one that is Windows-based, and so on.

The increased capacity of computerized systems and the greatly reduced "turn-around" time between work requests and work completion produce a new horizon of expectation (e.g., the near extinction of secretaries and typing pools—all replaced by the CPU) that is often frustrated by unforeseen difficulties or breakdowns in the computerized system. People can perform tasks in an hour that used to take a week; at the same time, people expect the tasks to be completed faster and faster (speed as progress), so that a 24-hour slowdown in operational capacity often strains relationships of those involved in the transaction.

The point here is not that computers should be unplugged and used as doorstops. The point is that a computer transforms the user of the computer, the world in which it is used, the nature of the tasks to be performed, and the horizons of expectation; it introduces a new equilibrium to the lifeworld. This altered environment has new parameters for the relations among elements. The computer becomes the nucleus and fulcrum of all relations, creating an environment that has the capability of sustaining its own evolutionary rhythm. The lives and activities of those involved in the computerized world ultimately become geared to the new pace and rhythm, frequently conforming seamlessly, often silently, to the demands of system. People are succumbing to the "technological imperative" for the same reason that they have embraced the objectivist paradigm of reason (Ellul, 1977 Fr./1980 Eng.). Of course, this tendency closely relates to the obsession with progress (discussed in greater detail in Chapters 14 and 15).

As the demands of the technological system increase, there is a corresponding further solidification, institutionalization, and normalization of technology as the central factor in our lives. This does not mean that technology has a mind of its own, nor does it entail that technology functions independently of human desires and needs. Instead, Ellul's (1954 Fr./1964 Eng., 1977 Fr./1980 Eng.) position can be interpreted to mean that the technological system has become an integral feature of the lifeworld, and through this process, the system has generated a subtle transformation in the horizon. Ellul (1954 Fr./1964 Eng.) more clearly illustrates the danger, in particular, of the modern technological milieu, emphasizing the technological imperative as the determining characteristic. Ellul (1954 Fr./1964 Eng.) writes:

> In the past, different civilizations took different "paths"; today all people follow the same road and the same impulse. This does not mean that they have all reached the same point, but they are situated at different points along the same trajectory. The United States represents the type that France will represent in thirty years, and China in possibly eighty. . . . Technique is the same in all latitudes and hence acts to make different civilizations uniform. (p. 117)

For Ellul, if technology has become the dominant or determining factor in our lives, it is because we have made the conscious investment and commitment necessary to deliver ourselves to the technological imperative. The obsessions of avoiding error and achieving exact calculations are examples of our desires and needs both created and delivered by technology. Already mentioned in Gebser's (1949 Ger./1985 Eng.) critique of dualism, these obsessions are consequences of dualism, of fixity and sectorization (specialization). This is so because fixity and specialization contribute to isolation and calculation. If people desire to remove human error, then they must ultimately convert their understanding of the world into a medium that can be processed by computers.

Ellul (1954 Fr./1964 Eng., 1977 Fr./1980 Eng.) envisions three milieus in human history—the natural, the social, and the technological. Humanity has not left the natural milieu behind on entering the social milieu. Rather, according to Ellul (1954 Fr./1964 Eng., 1977 Fr./1980 Eng.), the natural milieu is mediated by the social milieu. The natural milieu co-exists with the social milieu even as it has been both preserved and negated (Lovekin, 1990, 1991).

Technique now mediates social relations. In the same dialectical manner through which society emerged as the negation and preservation of the natural milieu, the technological milieu sublimates and mediates human relations to both society and nature. If we want to understand our world, Ellul (1954 Fr./1964 Eng.) claims, we can no longer consider it in terms of traditional social forces, nor can we consider technology as simply one social force (or object) among myriad others.

Following Ellul's (1954 Fr./1964 Eng., 1977 Fr./1980 Eng.) thinking, all social forces are negated, preserved only insofar as they are mediated by technology. To see this, it is necessary to look at the dynamic forces and currents within technology. Technology is today that which permits humans to live, providing what they need while presenting humanity with its greatest threat—dehumanization through systematization to the technological milieu.

From this comprehensive picture, Ellul (1954 Fr./1964 Eng.) argues that technology is not one isolated factor among others that predominantly influences modern society. In fact, Ellul objects to the term *technology* because it suggests it is only one factor among many others, as in the usages space technology, medical technology, communications technology, and so on. Technology brings to mind images of machines and specialized procedures. Ellul (1954 Fr./1964 Eng.) insists on the term *technique* to describe the phenomenon that shapes our technological milieu:

> The term technique, as I use it, does not mean machines, technology, or this or that procedure for attaining an end. In our technological society, technique is the totality of methods rationally arrived at and having absolute efficiency (for a given stage of development) in every field of human activity. (p. xxv)

Thus, Ellul (1954 Fr./1964 Eng.) differentiates technical operation from the technical phenomenon because, "every operation [is] carried out in accordance with a certain method in order to attain a particular end" (p. 19). The technical phenomenon is that qualitative difference distinguishing modern technique from that of the past. Ellul insists:

The twofold intervention of reason and consciousness in the technical world, which produces the technical phenomenon, can be described as the quest of the one best means in every field. And this "one best means" is, in fact, the technical means. It is the aggregate of these means that produces technical civilization. The technical phenomenon is the main preoccupation of our time; in every field [people] seek to find the most efficient method. But our investigations have reached a limit. It is no longer the best relative means which counts, as compared to other means also in use. The choice is less and less a subjective one among several means which are potentially applicable. It is really a question of finding the best means in the absolute sense on the basis of numerical calculation. (p. 21)

The drive toward efficiency is a rational drive, but it becomes irrational when it supplants all other drives. The technological phenomenon is as much a form of consciousness and human desire as it is a sociological phenomenon. Given this singular goal and attitude, similar techniques could easily develop independently of each other. Prior to the emergence of this technologically driven form of consciousness, there was not yet comparison or competition that could lead to formulation of "The one best way in the world!" (Ellul, 1954 Fr./1964 Eng., p. 30).

Following Lovekin (1977, 1991), the universal pervasiveness of technique has two aspects for Ellul (1954 Fr./1964 Eng.). First, simple geographical maps of countries where technique has already prevailed and is presently invading other regions indicate that the field on which technique plays out its development is the entire globe. The dominion of technique negates geography, which presumes difference, replacing it with "universalism."

Second, Ellul (1954 Fr./1964 Eng.) describes a qualitative universalism. The global expansion of technique minimizes the uniqueness of countries and cultures to the degree that they have become technical. Ellul (1954 Fr./1964 Eng.) says:

Technical civilization means that our civilization is constructed *by* technique (makes a part of civilization only what belongs to technique), *for* technique (in that everything in this civilization must serve a technical end), and *is* exclusively technique (in that it excludes whatever is not technique or reduces it to technical form). . . . Herein lies the inversion we are witnessing. Without exception in the course of history, *technique belonged to a civilization* and was merely a single element among a host of nontechnical activities. Today *technique has taken over the whole of civilization.* (p. 128; italics original)

As Ellul (1954 Fr./1964 Eng.) indicates, while the United States may be (in today's world, we would indicate "may have been") 20 years ahead of

France technically and China may be 50 years behind the United States, all three of these countries are on the same trajectory. Thus, we are witness to a cyber-march toward global uniformity.

Heidegger's *Question Concerning Technology*

It seems beyond question from his book, *The Question Concerning Technology and Other Essays*, that Heidegger (1952, 1954, 1962 Ger./1977 Eng.) is the anti-technological philosopher *par excellence*; his negative account of technology is a critically antagonistic and nostalgic assault against it. Ihde (1998) criticizes the Heideggerian position, writing, "[T]he preference for embodiment relations over other human-technology relations is what could be called a nostalgic element in the romantic thesis" (p. 109). However, Heidegger's position is hardly unique to Heidegger. It is also to be found in Marx (1962/2000). Insofar as his alienation theory is bound to any nostalgic element relating to the worker's relationship to his or her product prior to machine tools in a factory context, the same bias may be found in any number of analyses.[3]

Although Heidegger is frequently regarded as antagonistic to modern technology, Heidegger's (1952, 1954, 1962 Ger./1977 Eng.) project describes a free relationship to technology, in which the freedom of the relationship between humans and technology is determined by human response to the essence of technology. In the present study, we share the interpretation that

---

[3]For example, the mechanical reproduction of art works allows the achievements of the great masters to be available to everyone, but the aura surrounding the work disappears entirely. Walter Benjamin (1969) made this point in his famous essay, "Das Kunstwerk im Zeitalter seiner technischen Reproduzierbarkeit" (translated by Zohn as "The Work of Art in the Age of Mechanical Reproduction," but which may be more accurately rendered as "the work of art in the age of its technological reproducibility"). This essay appears in the 1960 collection *Illuminations: Essays and Reflections*, edited by Hannah Arendt (Benjamin, Arendt, & Zohn, 1955 Ger./1969 Eng.). In it Benjamin argues that even the most perfect reproduction of a work of art utterly lacks authenticity because it lacks the presence of the original. That is, it lacks the original's singular "presence in time and space, its unique existence at the place where it happens to be" (p. 120). Benjamin (1969) calls the authenticity or uniqueness of artwork "aura," explaining, "The concept of aura which was proposed . . . with reference to historical events may usefully be illustrated with reference to the aura of natural ones. We define the aura of the latter as the unique phenomenon of a distance, however close it may be. If, while resting on a summer afternoon, you follow with your eyes a mountain range on the horizon or a branch which casts its shadow over you, you experience the aura of those mountains, of that branch" (pp. 222–223). Heidegger (1952, 1954, 1962 Ger./1977 Eng.) described aura as the capacity of a work of art to organize a world as the clearing in which human life can transpire and through which the earth can manifest itself (see also Zimmerman, 1990).

it is inadequate to accuse Heidegger of being simply antagonistic toward modern technology. Heidegger (1952, 1954, 1962 Ger./1977 Eng.) speaks in the name of liberation—of the proper understanding (or way of seeing) but not of mastery.

Technology is not equivalent to the essence of technology (Heidegger argues) because the essence of technology is nothing technological. One does not become free by dedicating oneself to conforming to the operative needs of a specific technology, by becoming an expert technician. Nor is one free by mystifying technology as being beyond one's comprehension. The free or open relationship of human to technology is not a matter of technical facility or experience with technology; ideas often invoked by those arguing for or against Heidegger's analysis of the technological essence of modernity (Lovekin, 1991; Zimmerman, 1990). We are excluded from establishing or maintaining a relationship to the essence of technology when we conceive technology as technological tools or specific techniques.

To be free of technology, we must understand it *essentially*, not as technical contingency. We must learn about the aspects of technology that do not become obsolete—its essential way of being in the world; its impact on our lives and on our identities; its human, moral, and ethical implications; and practical extensions as willpower and drive.

Therefore, Heidegger (1927 Ger./1962 Eng.) makes clear the point by claiming that technology is a mode of *revealing*. Zimmerman (1990) accurately describes Heidegger's focal point:

> Philosophers have traditionally presumed that entities are really first present-at-hand and can become tools under certain circumstances. However Heidegger insisted that this reverses the true situation. The fundamental way in which entities "are" for us is as ready-to-hand. Only by an act of abstraction can *Dasein* remove itself from its involvement with the activities of everyday life and adopt instead the attitude of a passive spectator or observer, for whom what was once a useful device now becomes a mere "object" with certain properties analyzable by specific scientific procedures, and so on. (p. 139)

Where Heidegger (1952, 1954, 1962 Ger./1977 Eng.) is wrong is in presuming that his analysis has essential universal application. Differing consciousness structures present different meanings and types of material configuration (i.e., technology). By studying technology, much can be learned about the people who create and use it, their beliefs about space and time, the sacredness of habitation, fundamental metaphysical and epistemological presumptions, how people orient to their own desires and ambitions, and myriad other lessons. Heidegger (1952, 1954, 1962 Ger./1977 Eng.) is right, however, about the dominant Western configuration of nature as a resource for human consumption. What is uniquely Western about this view lies mostly in its connection to systematic mechanization (i.e., mathematization of nature and the systematic emptying of nature of qualitative dimension rendering it mere object, a resource devoid of sacredness, care, or identity).

Ge-stell (Enframing)

Heidegger (1952, 1954, 1962 Ger./1977 Eng.) describes the essence of technology as *Gestell* (Enframing). Translating *Gestell* as "enframing" may lead one to mistakenly think that technology for Heidegger is mainly a structure or sociological framework. *Gestell* does not, however, designate a thing or structure, but rather an activity, a process, or a way of being in the world. As a mode of being in the world, enframing also entails the manner in which entities are revealed to us. In this sense, Heidegger's (1952, 1954, 1962 Ger./1977 Eng.) approach to the issue of technology has the potential to accommodate different ways of revelation, different civilizations, cultures, and consciousness structures. According to Heidegger (1952, 1954, 1962 Ger./1977 Eng.), the essence of technology describes both the manner in which we relate ourselves to the world and the manner in which everything in the world is revealed and appears to us (see also Glazebrook, 2000, especially pp. 240-246).

The claim that technology is a mode of *revealing* and not only a human *doing* implies that technology is not solely a human activity, nor is it only a means within human activity. This is Heidegger's (1952, 1954, 1962 Ger./1977 Eng.) strategy for eliminating the multitude of instrumental and anthropological definitions of technology that assert, in one way or another, that humanity is actively in control of technology. Such definitions insist on humanity's freedom and, at the same time, delude human beings. For Heidegger (1952, 1954, 1962 Ger./1977 Eng.), this very aspect (i.e., affirming human freedom with profound delusion) is the true essence of technology.

Heidegger wrongly assumes, however, that people before him have failed to critically assess their relationship to the material world and the technologies they generate. For many people(s), technologies are gifts of the gods. For others, they are alive with vital force. Technologies—from writing to agriculture— have often been carefully assessed from the perspective of suspicion as a form of critical reflection. In the *Phaedrus*, Plato's concern about writing is that it can promote weak mindedness; to the Taoists, writing is seen as delusional in that it must miss whatever point it attempts to restrict and articulate. In short, Heidegger's (1952, 1954, 1962 Ger./1977 Eng.) insights have value, but we must remember that what he says is most relevant to the way he and the industrialized culture around him conceived of technology. Not all are deluded, nor are we deluded in the same ways. Delusion is a form of enabling insight, as it circumscribes the luminescence giving it form. It is a form of darkness that constitutes the edge of focus. It is part of what enables perspective (and therefore knowledge), although we may find that perspective undesirable.

Technology, the process of enframing, requires that nature be ordered and available in a specific way, which Heidegger (1952, 1954, 1962 Ger./1977 Eng.) calls "standing-reserve" (pp. 21-22)—the process through which science reveals nature (and Others) to us.

Not all cultures conceive of technology as presenting that on which it works (i.e., nature) as mere standing-reserve. The standing-reserve presentation is only one way to enframe. The availability of a tree to a Western lumberjack working for a modern corporation is a different presentation of a tree from how a tree exists (is presented) within the field of interests and powers of a traditional native of Amazonia. Indeed these two attitudes are so different that the word *available* is no longer appropriate to describe the Amazonian relationship. To the native Amazonian, many trees are considered sacred, not available for indiscriminate cutting. Such trees are saved, worshiped, protected, and venerated with garlands. As Kramer (1992) points out, those who do not have a concept of culture also do not have a notion of its opposite, nature. Magic human is not dualistic. Magic human does not enframe the universe as standing-reserve, in place to serve individual interests. Individual interests placed before broader human interests, including the natural world, are detrimental to all, including the individuals. Conversely, post-modern humans don't act to preserve long-term survival of self, of our corporations or governments, and so on, but rather the survival of the technological system to which all of these entities and individuals are rapidly becoming slaves.

Having said this, aspects of Heidegger's (1952, 1954, 1962 Ger./1977 Eng.) work might be salvaged for use here by arguing that magic people do not have technology. But this would be wrong, as the magic impulse to control and create is the essence of technology; not all technique and technology are strictly materially manifested. Many aspects of magic (incantations, rituals, etc.) are, in fact, a form of spiritual technology—technique designed to control spiritual forces as a means of creating (or maintaining) favorable conditions in the lifeworld. Once magic is recognized as a technique, we can reasonably start with Heidegger's (1952, 1954, 1962 Ger./1977 Eng.) notion of enframing and expand it to include different modes of enframing; his mistake is in seeing only one modality of consciousness structure. Keeping this limitation in mind, we can think through Heidegger's insights.

The delusion involved in the modern instrumental and anthropological definitions of technology is that they are *technological* definitions of technology (i.e., they manifest the materialistic objectivist bias discussed earlier). These definitions presuppose the availability of the world as a separate and material standing-reserve as Heidegger (1952, 1954, 1962 Ger./1977 Eng.)

described. Such definitions of technology are one factor among many involved in the conspiracy to conceal the essence of technology and humanity. Dehumanization occurs when other humans are objectified (and when corporations become individuals legally), included in the enframement of standing reserve. Examples include slaves and workers, soldiers, and anyone who has less money than we do. Paltry pay does not defeat the dehumanizing form of enframing, but rather manifests it (and institutionalizes it) in such a way that enframing generates acceptance of itself. For example, the logic of industrial production cannot persist without consumption, so we consume. However, we can only consume to the level that we are paid (or to the extent that we can attain credit). Therefore, our worth (in the overall industrial system—by extension ultimately in ourselves) is directly reflected in the price of the goods or services we can afford to consume or possess—hence, our pride in the things we can buy (as symbols of our status/value). We accommodate, maintain, and make robust the technology system as we conform and become less robust as individuals. The individual's internal and external sense of worth is no longer attained through what that individual *provides* to the family, tribe, or society; value is a function of what the individual can *consume from* society (i.e., large houses, expensive cars and clothes, lavish/exotic foods, etc.). The ideology of consumerism thereby becomes a technique of perpetuating the current technological complex. The standing-reserve aspect is evident when one dies or fails—many are waiting to step into place/function, becoming a ready resource, that is, standing-in-reserve.

Modern science sets up nature as a calculable standing-reserve existing for humanity's use. Hence, we have the aptly labeled practice of "scientific management." Heidegger claims that modern science is actually in the service of technology and not vice versa. In the modern world, science serves and is dependent on technology despite the chronological priority of science (Ihde, 1998; Kramer, 1997; Lovekin, 1991; Zimmerman, 1990). For example, medical science depends on technological developments such as magnetic resonance imaging (MRI) and sonogram; and in earth and space science, satellite and digital transmission technologies are indispensable (Ihde, 1998). Ellul (1954 Fr./1964 Eng.) also proposed an almost identical thesis concerning the relation of technology to science. Ellul (1954 Fr./1964 Eng.) argues that the common belief "that technique is an application of science (science being pure speculation)" (pp. 10–11) is misguided. Technology is not only a point of contact between scientific theories and the material world. Ellul's (1954 Fr./1964 Eng.) point is that the theoretical distinction between pure science and applied science is, in practice, untenable—all science in the modern world is applied.

To Heidegger (1952, 1954, 1962 Ger./1977 Eng.), the supreme danger of enframing (i.e., the danger of technology) consists of triple-tiered concealments. The first-order danger (most commonly discussed) is the appropriation of nature as object in the world, a standing-reserve or resource. Next is the second-order danger, the final appropriation of the appropriator, *Dasein*, as a standing-reserve. Human beings are "human resources," now revealed in the same category as everything else in the world, just another object. Heidegger adds a third-order delusional by-product of the first two dangers, namely, that human beings get the impression that they are entitled to the earth and all it holds because all standing-reserve (i.e., everything) exists because of and through their own making, as a resource for their own use.

For Heidegger (1952, 1954, 1962 Ger./1977 Eng.), then, the supreme danger of enframing is the delusion of human as lord that hides the illusion that human and nature are standing-reserve, which conceals the misconceptions that technology is a means to an end set by human activity. The delusion, illusion, and misconception prevent the revealing of technology as more than human doing (Lovekin, 1991).

Poesis as Revealing

Heidegger (1952, 1954, 1962 Ger./1977 Eng.) suggests that *poesis* is a key process in revealing. It is the way of revealing found in "the arts of the mind and the fine arts" (p. 13). Heidegger (1952, 1954, 1962 Ger./1977 Eng.) refers to *poesis* as a mode of revealing. He calls it "mediated thinking," which is to be affirmed over rampant "calculative thinking" (p. 52). In other words, people are in danger of losing their power to think meditatively. Heidegger's term "destining" applies primarily to the manner in which the world is revealed and/or the manner in which humans think about the world. Even though there is a subtle difference between *synairesis* and *poesies*, both concepts share the necessity of meditative thinking. In addition, both enable technization of the lifeworld to be revealed as a serious change. In this sense, the single most important danger and the last possible danger of technology is humanity's inability to respond to it in their thinking (i.e., to be meditative toward technology).

To summarize his main points, Heidegger (1952, 1954, 1962 Ger./1977 Eng.) suggests that it is crucial to look beyond technology's all too familiar shape as strictly an instrumental object, as a mere tool. He argues instead that technology is an elusive phenomenon. Without this appreciation of technology as more than a tool, one cannot come to terms with the possibility of its historical appearance. For Heidegger (1952, 1954, 1962 Ger./1977 Eng.), the question concerning the role of modern technology is already answered when technology is taken to be—essentially—instruments for our use. However, the question begs for an answer when we don't take the tech-as-tool position. The view of technology as machine (and nothing more) is actually an ambiguity; the possibility of instrumental familiarity is not simply a choice that we can make or unmake whenever we wish. Rather, the possibility involves the emergence of a historical and perceptual decision that is the essence of technology itself.

As technology becomes increasingly viewed as "natural" in our lives, as it becomes more familiar, people feel themselves to be more empowered by it. Yet this view of technology as natural-in-life, as something that people can take or leave, obscures the fact that modern technology is substantially more than an outside force acting on modern perception within the perspectival rational consciousness structure.

Mumford: Myths of the Technological Complex

Mumford (1967) argues that *abundance* is the promise of technology. Moreover, abundance is assumed to determine the quality of life. The quality of life should, then, be operationalized, objectified, and defined by or as abundance. Therefore, the question of life–value is not qualitative. It is not about what the good life is; instead, it is reduced to quantitative measure. The good life becomes an abundance of dualisms, the *goods of* life.

Mumford (1967) observes that Darwin superimposed the ideology of Malthus and Adam Smith onto the biosphere and ignored the diversity of life, including mutual aid and kinship. Competition displaced cooperation as the fundamental principle of life. It is important to remember that neither Gebser (1949 Ger./1985 Eng.), nor Innis (1951), nor Geddes (1915), nor Mumford (1967) embraced the fatality of Social Darwinism. Mumford (1967, 1970) blames many of the ills of the modern technological milieu on a quantitatively based ideology he calls the *myth of the machine*. The machine, as the entire technological complex (what might be called the meta-machine), is pervasive in its influence and extensive (although mostly invisible) in its structure and process.

The part of Mumford's argument that is relevant here is his comparison of quantitative mechanism and qualitative organism. As Mumford (1934/1963) explains:

> The method of the physical sciences rested fundamentally upon a few simple principles. First: the elimination of qualities, and the reduction of the complex to the simple by paying attention only to those aspects of events which could be weighed, measured, or counted, and to the particular kind of space-time sequence that could be controlled and repeated—or, as in astronomy, whose repetition could be predicted. Second: concentration upon the outer world, and the elimination or neutralization of the observer as respects the data with which [the observer] works. Third: isolation, limitation of the field, specialization of interest and subdivision of labor. In short, what the physical sciences call the world is not the total object of common human experience: it is just those aspects of this experience that lend themselves to accurate factual observation and to generalized statements. (p. 47)

As described by Mumford (1934/1963/2010), the scientific approach was framed in measurement and instrumentation, operationalization, simplification, and delusion. This indicates the relationship between mechanization and objectivism as a contingent and biased paradigm. Mumford (1934/1963/2010) illustrates this relationship:

> The tools and utensils used during the greater part of [human] history were, in the main, extensions of [the person's] own organism: they did not have—what is more important they did not seem to have—an independent existence. But though they were an intimate part of the worker, they reacted upon . . . capacities, sharpening [one's] eye, refining . . . skill, teaching [one] to respect the nature of the material with which [one] was dealing. The tool brought [humans] into closer harmony with [the] environment, not merely because it enabled [individuals] to reshape it, but because it made [them] recognize the limits of [their] capacities. (p. 47)

Following Mumford (1934/1963/2010), we regard power as the chief manifestation of divinity or, if not that, the main agent of human development. Much like the *technological imperative* in Ellul (1954 Fr./1964 Eng.) and *ge-stell* in Heidegger (1952, 1954, 1962 Ger./1977 Eng.), Mumford (1934/1963/2010) similarly describes *absolute power* as the driving force of the modern technological milieu. According to Mumford, absolute power, such as absolute weapons, belongs to the same magico-religious scheme as ritual human sacrifice. Such power destroys the symbiotic cooperation of human beings with nature. This is so because too much or too little is equally fatal to organic existence.

Mumford (1934/1963/2010) adopted Geddes's (1915) transformation of the terms *Paleolithic* and *Neolithic* into the terms *paleotechnic* and *neotechnic* to describe types of culture, technology, and ideologies. Mumford (1934/1963/2010) insists, "[O]ne can divide the development of the machine and the machine civilization into three successive but over-lapping and interpenetrating phases: eotechnic, paleotechnic, and neotechnic" (p. 109). Geddes (1915) coined the neologisms *paleotechnic* and *neotechnic*.[4] These terms describe not only epochs in the development of technology but also cultures and types of actors in the roles that supported the ideologies of those epochs and cultures.

---

[4] Each of these phases roughly represents a period of human history and is characterized even more significantly because they form a technological complex. Each phase has its specific means of utilizing and generating energy (Mumford, 1934/1963/2010, pp. 109-110). Speaking in terms of power and characteristic materials, the paleotechnic is built on the products of mining, of coal and iron, while neotechnic culture is based on metallurgical processing, on alloys, the lighter metals produced with elec-

Following Mumford (1934/1963/2010), the machine is not a product of an industrial revolution; rather, it has existed in some form since the time of the divine kings of Egypt. Although Mumford identifies the first mechanical clock in a monastery during the tenth century as the crucial machine, the machine is prefigured in the ritual procession of quarried stone to build the pyramids. Not wheels, nor tools, but standardized, interchangeable human parts (objects standing-in-reserve) comprised the proto-machine. Mumford (1934/1963/2010) asserts:

> Civilization brought about a double transformation of [humanity]. On the one hand it developed in the pharaoh or ruler, the autonomous personality; and on the other, by the subdivision of labor and the specialization of work, it produced the submissive, if not servile, *Teilmensch*, or divided man, who has lost his [*sic*] primitive wholeness without yet gaining the new attribute of his [*sic*] ruler: autonomy. (p. 47)

What matters to Mumford is not the specific machine, instrument, or skill but rather the transformation of life and thinking in the technological milieu. Mumford (1970) insists that the gates of the technocratic prison will open automatically, despite their rusty ancient hinges, "as soon as we choose to walk out" (p. 435).

For Mumford (1934/1963/2010), Gebser (1949 Ger./1985 Eng.), Ellul (1977 Fr./1980 Eng.), and Heidegger (1952, 1954, 1962 Ger./1977 Eng.), to re-conquer the machine and subdue it to human purpose, one must first understand and assimilate it. According to Mumford (1934/1963/2010),

> From the beginning, indeed, the most durable conquest of the machine lay not in the instruments themselves, which quickly become outmoded, nor in the goods produced, which quickly were consumed, but in the *modes of* life made possible *via the machine* and in the machine. (p. 323; italics added)

What remains as the permanent contribution of the machine, carried over from one generation to another, is the technique of cooperative thought and action it has fostered rather than specific machines and their functions. From this standpoint, Mumford (1970) states, "[T]o understand fully what

---

tricity. The neotechnic complex is based on electricity, including electronic communication technologies. The use of lighter metals and the electric grid that fostered clean industry and communication networking is characteristic of the neotechnic epoch. The neotechnic megalopolis arises in the wake of technological advances based in the sciences that bring forth the technologies of electricity and instantaneous communication.

happened earlier, one must read backward from the present to the past" (p. 312). Therefore, Mumford's theme is not that of technological determinism; rather, it is the antithesis of it.

Morris (1969) provides an alternate explanation, arguing that the machine does not enable cooperation among people (and between humanity and nature) but instead manifests a competitive attitude via the exaggeration of certain selected capacities, prominently including the ability to consume (e.g., the status struggle manifested as conspicuous consumption). According to Morris, the natural (and preferred) state of humanity is cooperation, which requires abstract thinking and language. In a world of predators, ancient human teeth, jaw, claws, and other tools of killing were woefully inadequate; the human ability to coordinate both hunts and childrearing, and to share food and information, proved the keys to survival. The machine comes along only after surplus is available (and surplus is a function of social behavior). Selfishness and a refusal to share and cooperate are luxuries. Machine extension empowers the operator beyond natural abilities. One might speculate this view is the origin of Marx's bourgeois, the owner of the means of production—voluntarily segregated from the rest of the working community—affording owners disproportional power and surplus value (through exploitation of both community resources and the community of workers). Machines enhance our ability to exploit with exponential efficiency.

However, for Mumford (1934/1963/2010), the machine is ambivalent because it is both "an instrument of liberation and one of repression" (p. 283). The machine complicates the organism and the organism elaborates the machine. The machine manufactures complexity; the organism, by ingestion and digestion, breaks down complexity. Mumford (1934/1963/2010) claims that in the beginning, "[T]he machine was an attempt to substitute quantity for value in the calculus of life" (p. 282). In this vein, Mumford (1934/1963/2010, 1970) insists that social science is an extension of the machine ideology as it manifests reinforced (and blind) faith in the scientific method of reducing—not only inorganic matter, but also culture, human beings, and society to the ontological status of mechanism. Accordingly, as discussed in Chapters 10 and 11, we commonly assert that qualities of life that could not be measured as quantity were ignored in an effort to simplify and order life as a mechanized process. Social philosophy does not become social science; precious little social science has been done. Instead, in the name of progress (making a soft science harder), social philosophy became social engineering. In the desire of sociologists to be legitimate scientists, social scientists did this to themselves and continue to do it. Positivism is not merely descriptive of what *is*; it is also a vow, a promise, to improve society by (initially at least) improving the human race by application of scientific (i.e., objectivist or positivist) principles of experimentation via standardized technique. What counts as improvement is posited without debate—because debate involves polluting science, delaying progress with subjective nonsense such as personal opinion, anecdote, interpretation, and philosophizing. The positivists always already know what is best for all; anyone with questions should get out of the way of progress—just try to keep up.

The accelerating tendencies of the mechanizing processes are obvious (Kurzweil, 2005; Mumford, 1934/1963/2010). The apparatuses of life have become highly complex so that today the processes of production, distribution, and consumption have become so specialized and subdivided that the individual is muddled and has lost confidence in his or her own unaided capacities. Training and continual retraining is the new lifestyle. For example, ageism has emerged. The older a person becomes, the slower and more obsolete his or her abilities are (or are perceived to be). The elderly are not seen as wise, for their experiences are outmoded, meaningless for the young (in the view of the young)—their wisdom no longer relevant. Instead, the elderly, as with their equally unproductive preschool comrades, are warehoused in daycare facilities and nursing homes—one facility for awaiting death, the other used to prepare for a life of ever-accelerating work. People are increasingly subject to commands they do not understand. They must submit to what Lyotard (1979 Fr./1984 Eng.) calls "expert knowledge" systems that are beyond any one person's ability to craft or comprehend. Humans are at the mercy of forces over which they exercise no control, moving to a destination they have not chosen (autistic economics).

Regarding the explosive development of state-of-the-art communication technology, Mumford (1934/1963/2010) observes, "[T]he possibilities of good and evil here are immense." However, at the present moment, as with so many other technologies, "[T]he dangers of the radio and the talking picture seem greater than benefits" (p. 241). Further, Mumford (1970) asserts that our situation is becoming ever more dangerous, ever more mechanized, arguing:

> Those already conditioned from infancy by school training and television tutelage to regard megatechnics as the highest point in [humans'] "conquest of nature," will accept this totalitarian control of their own development not as a horrid sacrifice but as a highly desirable fulfillment, looking forward to being constantly attached to the Big Brain, as they are now attached to radio stations by portable transistor sets even while walking the streets. By accepting these means they expect that every human problem will be solved for them, and the only human sin will be that of failing to obey instructions. *Their "real" life will be confined within the frame of a television screen.* (p. 331; italics added)

What Mumford describes here is a preparatory stage for full-blown cyberlife, a life increasingly absorbed by interacting with/through a (television or computer) screen (Turkle, 1995). Whereas television did not track the viewing habits of the audience, the Internet has become panoptic as companies have emerged that do nothing but track people's movements on the Internet, including what sites they visit, when they visit them, how often, and for how long. Electronic mail can easily be perused and, importantly, without our knowledge; we are subject to near-constant surveillance in our public excursions and in our purchasing habits, telephone, and web surfing. Describing computer screens as *monitors* turns out to be increasingly more appropriate. Monitoring is now two-way, not one-way (as in traditional over-the-air broadcast arrangement). Even cable systems enable the television to communicate to a central authority, allowing the automatic and continual tracking of viewing habits (and, in the case of technologies like TiVo, the selection of programs for the viewer to watch). The IP address, which is the address each computer has on the World Wide Web (not one's personal e-mail address), enables even wireless communication to be tracked. Anonymity on the World Wide Web is a myth. The global network of communication technologies, especially through complex and interconnected communication technologies such as the Internet, smart phones, Personal Data Assistants [PDAs], tablet and laptop computers, as well as remote and often secret surveillance cameras, function to impress on people the myth of the absolute power of the machine and of those who suppose they control its workings.

However, Mumford (1970) states, "The ironic effect of quantification is that many of the most desirable gifts of modern technics disappear when distributed en masse, or when—as with television—they are used too constantly and too automatically" (p. 337). There is no satisfactory answer to this phenomenon on the basis of technics alone. In other words, it would be a gross mistake to seek technological solutions wholly within the field of technics.

To summarize, what is essential about technology is not that one can look through it and see the world, but rather that the world is created anew in and through it. As Mumford (1934/1963/2010, 1970), Ellul (1954 Fr./1964 Eng.), Gebser (1949 Ger./1985 Eng.), and Heidegger (1952, 1954, 1962 Ger./1977 Eng.) commonly contend, technology is not machines or some style of using machines that can be repeated again and again; rather, technology is an inherent tendency of perception; it is the technical transformation of everyday perception and the way in which this transformation is taken for granted. Seen from Gebser's (1949 Ger./1985 Eng.) notion of *plus-mutation*, what separates ancient and medieval technology from the form that we intimately and ceaselessly experience today involves the accomplishment of a certain perceptual and technical fusion, what Carey and Quirk (1992) call "sublimation."[5]

---

[5]Carey and Quirk (1992) have provided an interesting and heuristic definition for electronic interpretation. In investigating the "electronic sublime" (p. 113) of our time, these authors have shown it to be a thematic and chronological continuation of

For example, in their investigation of the "mythos of the electronic revolution," Carey and Quirk (1992) refer to specifically new technical innovations: "As agents . . . at hand to bring everything into harmonious cooperation . . . triumphing over space and time . . . to subdue prejudice and to unite every part of our land in rapid and friendly communication" (p. 120). Carey and Quirk (1992) are not referring to McLuhan's global village but rather to steam, the miracle-working natural power of the nineteenth century, and the railroad on which the communications network was built.

COMMUNICATION THEORY AND TECHNOLOGY

As Williams (1983) points out, the word *communication* contains an unresolved double valence. Reacting to shifting sociocultural contexts and changes in both the means and modes of transferring information, communication has developed an unstable semantic field—at once both one-way transmission and mutual sharing. This semantic bivalence or instability of

---

the mechanical sublime of the nineteenth century. In terms of conceptual content, both forms of sublimes can be considered part of the larger meta-category of the technological sublime. According to Carey (1992), the mechanical sublime was born in the 1800s of a contemporary culture stamped by new mechanical technology, especially the techno-romantic and Utopian expectations concerning the steam engine, steam power, and the railway. During the last third of the century, however, belief in the mechanical sublime began to decline significantly, and its place was taken by the electronic sublime, based on electricity and systems of electric technology. Later in the twentieth century, the television, computer, and electronics industries mutated the sublime thoughts and expectations previously directed toward the telegraph and telephone. We have moved into the age of the "electronic sublime" (Carey, 1992, p. 113). The electronic sublime includes the central idea or faith in electronics and electronic systems advancing with nearly teleological if not messianic power. It also includes an emphasis on the continuous state of change. Revolutionary innovations are seen as following each other in a progressive, highly prescribed series of developments. It is important to note that in shifting from the mechanical to the electronic sublime, the verbal metaphors for speaking of technological change often remain the same, although the subject they portray has become altogether different. As steam and railroads were in the nineteenth century, so multimedia, hypertext, the Internet, information highways, and other electronic inventions in our own time are the embodiment of the technological (and specifically the electronic) sublime. This mentality and way of thinking can be seen clearly in contemporary technological discourse. A strong future orientation and optimistic, even enchanted ways of talking about the possibilities of technology are identifying features of the discourse of the electronic sublime. As history repeatedly demonstrates, the idea that technical and technological changes automatically lead to positive developments in society, to cultural evolution, is regularly presented in the visions of our time.

the word *communication* puts communication theorists in an interesting situation: Unwittingly we have become bifocal scholars, setting out to investigate two incompatible phenomena. As Nelson (1985) rightly suggests, models and theories of communication are "designed to give us the illusion of controlling, or at least, structuring this uncertainty" (p. 3).

The technological annihilation of space is articulated in information theory and cognitive science, and before that by Cartesian epistemology.[6] According to information theory, communication is the exchange of information, be the channels wide or narrow, long or short (Borgmann, 1984; Shannon & Weaver, 1949). As Finlay (1990) demonstrates with the aid of discursive analysis, contemporary explanations and practices of new communication technology conform to the age-old procedures of classical representational theories based on objectivism despite claims that the new approaches are revolutionary.

One of the dominant paradigms in communication theory stems from the influence of the mathematical theory of electrical communications that employs a model describing communication as the transmission of information between a sender and a receiver, through a channel that links them in some way (Shannon & Weaver, 1949). The central object of this model is, then, the message that contains the information: Information is encoded into message by A, transmitted, and then decoded by B. Such an operation is made possible by the fact that both A and B share knowledge of the same message code.

According to the mathematical theory of communication (or the media effects tradition in general) that relies on what Kramer (1997a, 2004a) calls "received orthodoxy" (p. 89), the fidelity of a message is measured by how much agreement there is between the sender and the receiver. Following Kramer (1997a, 2004a), this configuration of communication contributes to the problem of social engineering—what Ellul (1963 Fr./1972 Eng., 1977 Fr./1980 Eng.), Gebser (1949 Ger./1985 Eng.), and Heidegger (1952, 1954, 1962 Ger./1977 Eng.) discussed. This is so, according to Kramer (2004a), because:

---

[6]The technological annihilation of space, in the sense that all different modes of the consciousness of space have collapsed into one abstract, mathematical geometric space that has supported the Cartesian epistemology and Galilean style sciences, is discussed in detail in Chapter 14. In this chapter, the relationship between technology and the different manifolds of time and space is explored. Briefly, the importance of the technological annihilation of space and time lies in the fact that the annihilation of various time and space consciousness structures (by making them unilinear and unidimensional based on modern technology) leads to the annihilation of semiosis and communication.

> [T]he correspondence sense of "good" communication is concerned
> with compliance gaining and control, and not just of the message but of
> its interpretation, for these two discrete atomic entities, the sender and
> the receiver must somehow understand each other if they are to coordi-
> nate behaviors. *This is really communication as utility or technology.* (p.
> 57; italics original)

Echoing Ellul's (1954 Fr./1964 Eng.) argument, Kramer (1997a, 2004a)
insists that agreement between the sender and the receiver, in the received
view, "does not mean that the two people agree about the truth-value of the
message but only that they understand the meaning of the claim first and
foremost as *the same*, in the *same way*" (p. 53; italics original).

The mathematical theory of communication, initially intended to
explain how machines communicate with each other, deals only with technical features of communication; it has been adopted by many in the field
and has had a major influence on the development of communication theory—especially those theories deriving from psychology and linguistics. The
process of communication has been, therefore, conceived as a psychological
process of two subjects, alternately functioning as sender and receiver, correctly utilizing a linguistic system (that is to say, using a grammar that we
assume to be known by both subjects) to produce propositions that demonstrate their own mental activity.

From the standpoint of mathematical communication theory, dealing
with communication means only considering grammatically correct linguistic propositions. What does not fit into this restricted category is banished
into one of the two peripheral categories available (both of which are also
borrowed from the mathematical theory): redundancy and noise. A fairly
substantial portion of the interactive process, including much of the non-
verbal communication (and a good part of the verbal communication as
well), is shunted into one or the other of these categories. Consequently,
communication is reduced to a basic structure that is logical and verifiable
(i.e., mechanistic).

A key to the mathematic understanding of communication is the connection (a strict relation of symmetry) between *thinking* and *the proposition*,
in which the mind is conceived of as a tank of objective contents transformed provisionally by a code making it possible to transport them
through a channel. Needless to say, communication theory cannot escape
the essential characteristic of the modern technological milieu or rational
consciousness. This model is a rationalistic (and drastic) reduction of the
communicative process, a concept based on psychological, Cartesian subject-biased aspects of communication, abstracted from context and thus mis-
representing the process as a whole.

It is almost shocking how simplistic this model is and how widespread it has become. Perhaps, given the confused state of communication studies among quantitative writers—almost exclusively in the United States, and proliferating especially after Joseph McCarthy's red scare drove critical reflection (thinking) out of the academy for the better part of four decades—such an oversimplified model is embraced. It is perhaps curious that a writer like James Gibson (1950) is valorized for teaching scholars like Edward T. Hall and Marshall McLuhan a "whole new way to see and think" (i.e., to simply become aware that the medium is a, if not the, message).[7] Such a need for elementary instruction evinces their utter failure to understand the most basic aspects of phenomenological psychology and the corresponding body of literature. It is surprising (to say the least) that a vast audience of communication teachers would find Hall and McLuhan edifying in their second-generation claim that how you say something (along with what you say) is salient within the act of communicating. One reason that this book has been written is as an effort to bring greater sophistication to the effort to understand and theorize communication.

Hall (1966) views the communication process as external to the subjects involved, based rather on the factor of experience as an anthropological and intercultural meeting point. Birdwhistell (1973) insists that it is a mistake to reduce communication to a simple passage of verbal information between two monads, effectively conceptualizing both communication and humans as mechanistic and atomic fragments. Birdwhistell argues that a human being is not a black box with one orifice for emitting a chunk of stuff called communication and another for receiving it. At the same time, communication is not simply the sum of the bits of information that passes between two people in a given period of time.

As will be discussed in Chapter 15, the official policy of many nations that guides their technological futures (and futurologists' promises about the virtues of information technology) robustly promotes the fundamental ideas of traditional communication models and perspectives (e.g., the mathematical theory of communication). It will be argued in the following chapters that such planning indicates a widely held satisfaction with an illusion that we can gain mastery over communication by means of communication.

---

[7]To use the exclusionary intent of the definite article "the" as in "the medium is *the* message," rather than "the medium is *a* message" (as Mumford originally stated it before McLuhan borrowed the insight without understanding it), is to repeat the error of dualistic metaphysics only on the formal side. To reduce the message to its medium is to fail to recognize the importance (relevance) of content. This amounts to simply switching one bias for another, one stupidity for another. The important point to note here is that form and content cannot be separated in any meaningful way. The effort to do so reveals at least as much about the separator as the phenomenon being dissected.

From this standpoint, as Chang (1996) asserts, "[T]o derail communication from its teleological track, to exteriorize the microevent of communication to its macrostructure of determination" (p. 186) may be an alternative to the objective-biased paradigm.

SUMMARY

The development, study, and use of communication technology have been dominated by the objectivistic-biased paradigm. As Husserl (1954 Ger./1970 Eng., 1913 Ger./1982 Eng.) argues, a Galilean pursuit of a mathematically rendered objective view of communication does not constitute a full understanding of the process of communication. The current scientific approach to communication produces method not knowledge. This quantitative pursuit only represents the physical life and dismisses the mental life as a fiction. Such an approach is dangerous for studying the technological milieu because focusing on a sender-receiver relationship only measures the utility of the communication and cannot account for how the medium changes the sender, receiver, and content of the message. This approach is naïve, treating technology as merely a tool that we can use without being affected by it. The objective/positive approach that dominates scholarship and policymaking must be replaced in order to make visible the cultural horizon. The more we attempt to render our conception of communication in mechanistic terminology, the more communication will come to resemble the machine.

12

Methodological Approach

INTRODUCTION

Three philosophical approaches are used to guide the study of meaning and transformation of communication in the modern technological world. The main method of inquiry derives from the semiotics of Charles Sanders Peirce (1931, 1958). To augment the Peircean model of the semiotic process, the investigation draws on the theories of Kramer (1992, 1997), Gebser (1949 Ger./1985 Eng.), and Husserl (1954 Ger./1970 Eng.). Peirce's (1931, 1958) 10 types of signs derived from his concepts of firstness, secondness, and thirdness; Gebser's (1949 Ger./1985 Eng.) ideas about consciousness structures and the process of plus-mutation; and Kramer's (1992, 1997) frame of dimensional accrual/dissociation each offers pertinent conceptualizations of communication in the technological milieu. The simultaneous use of these three theoretical approaches may seem unnecessarily complicated. However, when used in combination, these theories help reveal different aspects of the same phenomena, each theory and explanation expanding the others in explaining the communication process.

The three theories are similar in three important ways. First, they demonstrate the vagueness of Cartesian subject-object dualism. Second, they represent the nature of communication or sign action—semiosis—as a process. Third, they present useful conceptual frames for analyses that are more comprehensive than traditional communication approaches.

Integrating these three approaches affords a new means of exploring the topic of communication as semiosis within the technological world and provides optimal leverage for engaging the dynamics and possibilities confronting us within our technological milieu.

This chapter begins with an overview of semiosis as a communicative process, touching briefly on the work of Peirce (1931, 1958) and contrasting this view of semiosis with the objectivistic semiotics of structuralism. This is followed by a segment on bracketing objectivistic bias. Next, Kramer's (1992, 1997) theory of dimensional accrual/dissociation is presented, followed by an in-depth discussion of Peirce's semiotics.

THE NATURE OF COMMUNICATION AND SIGN-ACTION (SEMIOSIS)

Process and Transformation

Recent research indicates that the cognition of language may be much less arbitrary and much more grounded in the body's sensory perception than previously theorized (Iyer, 2002; Moriarty, 1996; Shettleworth, 2009). Kramer (2004a) states language works by dissociative generalization, that is, by means of perceptually sampling the world and reducing it to a "surface-and sign-world" (p. 69). This dissociation can become extreme abstraction, as Nietzsche (1887 Ger./1974 Eng.) warns, fetishizing language by withdrawing into a virtual sign-world.

Signs do not simply "represent" a thing, as Cartesian referential theory and the mathematical, mechanistic theories of communication assume; signs emphatically relate to more than a thing. Although the conceptualization of "communication as exchange, or downloading, is called into question already in the fifth century B.C." (Kramer, 2004a, p. 56), the modern dominion of the objectivist science paradigm encourages the idea of signs as abstract designations with preset meanings. According to traditional social science, communication consists of two atomic fragments (i.e., a sender and a receiver) that are connected by a channel along which a message is conveyed (Shannon & Weaver, 1949). This view of communication assumes that messages are encoded with abstract signs bearing information, and that these signs decode (precisely) the same information. Any change in meaning from sender to receiver is due to "interference" in sign transmission or reception; the signs are held to be absolute in meaning, with precise one-to-one reference to the signified object. Yet if the metaphysical bias of objectivism is bracketed, then neither "pure" information nor meaning exists—both emerge full of contingency and complexity from the embodied human in the lifeworld. In this sense, signs are more like verbs than like nouns—they are temporal interactivities, not spatialized passive objects. Therefore, one cannot say that meaning is communicated or conveyed as a static reference via a sign (Kramer, 2004a).

A Brief Look at Peircean Semiotics

According to Peirce (1931, 1958), a mere correlation or correspondence between a sign and its reference does not in itself produce a meaning. Meaning requires a triadic production of what Peirce (1931, 1958) calls the *interpretant*, a relation in which the sign (*representamen*) bears some variety of correspondence to its referent via the immediate object of the sign (*ground*); an idea corresponding to the object not in all its respects but only in certain ways. The meaning of a sign is embedded within a relational triad of representation, in which an *object* is represented by a *representamen* either in or during an *interpretant*. For Peirce (1931, 1958), a sign assumes the presence of an engaged interpretant, a sense-making perception (itself a type of sign) that realizes (takes notice of) the sign. Thus, a sign comprises both sign-action (semiosis) and sign-object (representamen). Semiosis (or sign-action) is a conscious effort when a representamen or sign-object is opaque to the interpretant and a completely normalized, blind process when the representamen is transparent (Merrell, 1995a, 1997). Meaning is thus generated from the opacity or transparency of the representamen through semiosis. No sign can ever represent all aspects of an object to an interpretant, and meaning within the interpretant is a matter of perception and experience. Hence, a sign must be recognized, experienced, and/or perceived as a sign in a context supporting interpretation to be interpreted. This is true of all sign relationships, including ones between statistical values and what they purport to measure or derive. As with other signs, statistics must be interpreted, and one must *learn* how to do so in order to find agreement with the most conventional understandings of them.

But even convention is not enough, for as Searle (1980, 1984) claims, understanding a sign or message requires more background knowledge than merely conforming to conventional usage, that is, more than simply matching signs with referents (objects) in the most conventional way. To illustrate his point, Searle (1980, 1984) notes that a person could be taught to match Chinese characters with German words and could become so proficient at doing this that he or she need no longer refer to a dictionary, for the matching has become a matter of memory. However, unless at least one of the languages is already understood, the person will not understand the messages being matched even as he or she translates them without error. Knowing merely the convention and function of a sign is not sufficient for meaning (Searle, 1980, 1984). As Peirce's (1931, 1958) triadic relationship of representation shows, meaning is a dynamic human action that requires embodied experience, not the automatic derivative of a mechanistic process of reduction and substitution.

Structuralism and Semiotics

While Peirce (1931, 1958) posits meaning as fluctuating and relational, other semiotic theorists adhere to the dualistic position of meaning as fixed within a pre-determined binary system of sign and interpretation. Arguing that binary opposition marks the locus of meaning, structuralist semioticians such as Levi-Strauss (e.g., 1964 Fr./1983 Eng., 1978/2001) consider meaning to be a given that exists in self-presence and seek to identify the grammar (or the binary structure of a system of signs) in a message. Structuralist research is based on the assumption that because texts do have meaning, there must be a system within which meaning is made. According to this rather mechanistic view of semiosis, there is a strict relationship between the structure of a text and its meaning. Sheriff (1989) describes this as the "fate of meaning." In this view, meaning is fixed and singular, so long as the structure of the text endures; only if the structure of a text changes can its meaning change. By reducing meaning to a single structural origin, structuralist semioticians hope to eliminate the problem of conflicts of interpretation. Indeed, Levi-Strauss (1978) even calls for the eventual computerization of the process of interpretation.

However, the concept of a text having inherent, indubitable meaning has been challenged by several theorists who recognize that meaning is not stable and fixed in the text, but rather meaning is instead dynamic and contingent on the process of embodied perception of and interaction with the text (Culler, 1982; Finlay, 1990; Kramer, 1988; Seung, 1982). Structuralism does not explain or even recognize the proliferation of multiple and/or competing interpretations that a text may provoke. Because meaning is not a thing with set, self-contained limits as structuralists presume, the "problem" of interpretation cannot be brought to a final solution. Efforts at finding the locus of meaning have proven to be less than illuminating (Culler, 1982). It is clear that identifying the system of codes responsible for a conventionally accepted meaning amounts to little more than a rationale for and defense of that conventional interpretation.

Despite structuralist desires for essential meaning, essence does not exist "objectively." Hence, no semiotic search can "uncover" the essential codes of meaning. To claim that a particular attribute is an essential characteristic of something, one must draw a line dividing essential and non-essential characteristics. This line is determined by the categories one implicitly applies to the object prior to conceptualizing, perceiving, and understanding it. What is considered essential varies as categorical terms change, so there can never be a characteristic that is essential "in itself" — it is context dependent. The lack of objectivistically essential characteristics for meaning applies to all signs, including those of human purpose and human classification (Foucault, 1972 Fr./1980 Eng., 1969 Fr./1972 Eng.). Although complex, Peirce's (1931, 1958) version of semiotics shows that without human involvement — either purposefully or in unconscious conformity to socially imposed classifications — there cannot be any signified characteristics (essential or non-essential) in the world. In this sense, Peircean (1931, 1958) semiotics presents no crisis of representation of essential meaning (as there is in structuralism) because representation is only one aspect of the multifaceted, interrelational semiotic process (Oehler, 1995).

Bracketing Objectivistic Bias

The structuralist error lies in its metaphysical assumption that meaning exists in a fixed form independent of users, as an object — the objectivistic bias. In contrast, Peirce's (1931, 1958) rigorous, systematic exploration of meaning and sign reflects a critical awareness of the prejudice of metaphysical schools like empiricism (positivism) and materialism that restrict investigation to only phenomena with spatial extension. As discussed in Chapters 8, 9, and 10, much of our meaningful experience (mood, fear, ambition, calculation, etc.) is without spatial extension and is non-empirical in nature. As Husserl (1954 Ger./1970 Eng.) — whose doctoral degree was in integral calculus, not philosophy — notes, the metaphysical tunnel vision displayed by the various scientific "isms" makes even the study of mathematics and logic illegitimate, as these are non-empirical phenomena. The reduction of all things to materialism is not required in order to make their existence real (Husserl, 1954 Ger./1970 Eng.). If empirical objects are the only "real ones," then how can empiricism, which is a metaphysical *concept* (and school of thought), exist to be discussed in any meaningful sense? Because it is a metaphysical concept, we must therefore conclude that empiricism is as much a cultural perspective as is Buddhism or communism.

Attempts to force emotions, motives, logic, and other non-empirical phenomena into spatial parameters by turning them into operationalized measurements miss the basic nature of these phenomena. Awareness is not a material object (just as the concept of "color" has no color and "empiricism" is not an empirical thing). Similarly, it makes no sense to ask how much "language" weighs or how long (in either the sense of distance or time duration) "meaning" is. The concept of "space" is not a spatial object among other objects, nor does spatialization take up physical space. Even "operationalization" and "measurement" are not measurements per se and are not expressed as such (Schutz, 1953/1997).

With relation to this study, one premise should be stressed: Non-empirical existential classes (phenomena) *are* real. As Peirce (1931) points out, "a mere possibility may be quite real" (4.580).[1] To avoid the self-contradicting patterns of empiricism that define not only themselves but consciousness and meaning out of existence, the present investigation follows (what we deem to be more logically sound) paths of inquiry generated by post-metaphysical investigators, including Peirce (1931, 1958), Husserl (1954 Ger./1970 Eng.), Gebser (1949 Ger./1985 Eng.), and Kramer (1992, 1997). The metaphysics of materialism and empiricism are bracketed in favor of direct investigation of phenomena (including how they show themselves and regardless of how they show themselves)—that is, without metaphysical judgment. This approach opens all human experience to legitimate exploration.

Bracketing metaphysical presumptions is not a retreat into subjective solipsism. Empiricists employ a rhetorical (rather than an analytical) device when they charge that only "objective" claims can be transcendent of individual egos. But it is not Husserl's (1954 Ger./1970 Eng.) personal bias or prejudice that leads him to claim that empiricism's self-contradictory propositions and unwarranted limitation of fields of inquiry effectively deny the existence of most experience, including the experience of the concept of empiricism. That empiricism defines itself as non-existent and that Husserl (1954 Ger./1970 Eng.) points this out as an absurdity is not his *fault* nor is it merely his interpretation or perspective. Rather, Husserl (1954 Ger./1970 Eng.) analytically demonstrates this when he compares the premises of empiricism with the claims and behaviors of empiricists.

Peirce (1931) notes, "The real . . . is that which, sooner or later, information and reasoning would finally result in, and which is therefore independent of the vagaries of me and you" (4.580). Such post-metaphysical conceptions of the real recognize thought as a continuous temporal process subject to public, communal testing—something that an independent, fixed empirical object cannot be. Peirce's (1931, 1958) understanding of this is a major reason that the present investigation uses his semiotics to explore Gebserian consciousness structures. As Feuerstein (1987) has described, our everyday consciousness consists of the interplay of these structures; they are continually engaged with each other. Thus, every single day, our consciousness completes a cycle of movement through different stages—from waking to dreaming (or reverie), to sleep, and finally to deep sleep. More important, throughout the day, we thematize the four structures (magic, mythic, mental-rational, and integral) through interaction with other people and in response to our environment. We spend far less time than we like to believe in the mental struc-

---

[1]Concerning quotes from *The Collected Papers of Charles Sanders Peirce Vols. 1-8,* the reader should note that the number to the left of the period indicates the volume and the numbers to the right of the period indicate the paragraph number. For instance, 4.580 indicates volume four, paragraph 580.

ture of consciousness. We are not the strictly rational animals of Aristotlean philosophy; we operate with consciousnesses in transition, with constantly shifting emotional and cognitive states and intensities. Our thoughts about reality and science change because reality and science are not empirical, immutable objects, utterly independent of human volition and entirely "disinterested." Rather, science is a repository of intense interests and narrow paths of deep exploration, a record of curiosity about reality. It is a discursive, uniquely human process and product that is alive and mutable.

By bracketing the objectivistic metaphysics of empiricism and material-ism, we can explore technologization, technization, and technics as aspects of experience that are not the same things as specific empirical objects (i.e., machines and tools that are already more than mere objects by embodying expectations, design, planning, and use-value). Just as computerization is not the same thing as a box with a motherboard, hard disk, power supply, and so forth, so too technologization is not technology. It is instead a consequence of technology, a set of expectations, motives, beliefs, and values that manifest in human interaction with technology. Studies that explore the relationships among technology, humans, and environment cannot be reduced to empirical premises (operationalized). Cartesian dualism and traditional communication approaches that adhere to it (including various structuralist approaches) are limited in their explanatory value. They lack the ability to capture meaning-ful experience because the communication process posited by such approach-es is too abstracted—that is, too dissociated from the lifeworld. In contrast, Kramer's (1992, 1997) theory of dimensional accrual/dissociation brackets objectivism to reveal how the interaction of consciousness structures occurs in human experience and how this shapes perceptions and semiosis.

THE THEORY OF DIMENSIONAL ACCRUAL/DISSOCIATION (DAD)

In order to understand differences in semiosis—the different ways people act (and react), communicate significance, and speak of reality—we must take into account differences in spatio-temporal orientations. Gebser (1949 Ger./1985 Eng.) notes that the perception of space and time varies among the magic, mythic, and mental consciousness structures. Kramer (1992, 1997, 2013; Kramer & Ikeda, 1998) claims it is demonstrable that these three spa-tio-temporal orientations manifest in specific modes of expression or artic-ulation (i.e., in recognizable *kinds* of communication/comportment). The various articulations correlate with the dimensions of consciousness struc-tures and form a continuum of semiotic dissociation: Magic communication is one-dimensional (idolic), mythic is two-dimensional (symbolic), and the perspectival world of the mental is self-articulating in a three-dimensional (signalic) way (Kramer, 1992, 1997, 2013; Kramer & Ikeda, 1998). According to Kramer (1997, 2013), as one moves from idolic to symbolic to signalic ways of being and communicating, one becomes more and more dissociated from the world. Language increasingly becomes an arbitrary system of labels, a mere medium of code rather than a magical source of being (Kramer, 1992, 1997, 2013; Kramer & Ikeda, 1998). An example would be computer code versus holy communion.

Bringing together Gebser's (1949 Ger./1985 Eng.) notion of integral transparency and Mumford's (1934/1963) idea of dissociation, Kramer's (1992, 2013; Kramer & Ikeda, 1998) theory of dimensional accrual/dissociation (DAD) explores the variety of human communication behaviors by considering them at the fundamental level of space, time, and attitude or mood (Kramer, 1997; Kramer & Ikeda, 1998). The theory of dimensional accrual/dissociation states that as one moves from the magic univalent to the mythic bivalent and on to the perspectival trivalent world, dimensional awareness accrues or increases. This does not mean, however, that awareness becomes better, more sophisticated, or more evolved, for no transcendental evaluative criteria are assumed. As Kramer and Ikeda (1998) point out:

> History demonstrates that none [of the consciousness structures] are inherently superior to any of the others. Such a valuation is dependent upon the criteria used for comparison and there are no known "transcendental" criteria outside of each world orientation that could be applied to each one independently. (p. 43)

Nor is accrual a form of "progress" because no final goal or *telos* is assumed. In DAD, no linear progressivism is presupposed. Rather, all previous spatio-temporal orientations are present in the later, more complex ones (Kramer, 1992, 1997, 2013; Kramer & Ikeda, 1998).

Still, modern dissociation tends to mask the presence of magic univalent and mythic bivalent experience. As dissociation occurs, people come to see themselves as separate from the larger environment, including other human beings. Emotional involvement wanes and spiritual interests fade in favor of rational division and predictive control. Consider the differences between mythic and mental modes of time-telling. In mythic societies, time is not reckoned abstractly; it is not fragmented into discrete categories of invariable units—minutes and hours that reduce to predictable quanta. Instead, time is grounded in natural cycles, experienced as a constantly varying flux. For example, each day is directly experienced as having different lengths of light and dark than every other day; the time of an hour varies according to the diurnal and nocturnal rhythms of the seasons (Kramer & Ikeda, 1998).[2]

---

[2]Prior to clock time, hours and days were longer in summer than in winter. A day's work was measured not by hours but by what needed to be done (Landes, 1983). The first mechanical clocks were designed in the thirteenth century, as was the abstract

In mental societies, especially mental-rational ones, people are dissociated from nature and its temporal rhythms. Instead of attuning themselves to the daily variance in the length of daylight, they generate spatialized temporal models that seek to tame the natural world. Time is abstracted from nature, creating a second-order world, a simulacrum that serves the purpose of power and predictability (Baudrillard, 1981 Fr./1994 Eng.; Kramer & Ikeda, 1998); in other words, the meaning of *time* changes.

Using the ideas of dimensional accrual and dissociation helps explain changes in semiosis. Objectivism (or subjectivism) is impossible in the magic and mythic worlds; they have no dissociated subject that can dichotomize and objectify alterity. In turn, the semiotic division of the sign into a signifier and a signified is a mental (Cartesian) construal that cannot explain or even understand magic communication because magic messages have an uninterpretable (indecipherable) vital unity. In the modern perspectival world, idolic communicative forms such as incantation and oath-taking (which assume the one-dimensional unity of the magic structure's vital nexus) have little relevance. In keeping with the vast litany of perspectival dichotomies (such as subject/object, form/content, and case/category), language is considered a totally arbitrary system of object/signified and linguistic construction/signifier. The mental-rational world is spatialized and, as such, is linear, so signifier points directly to signified and a thing can have only one meaning at a time (Kramer, 1997, 2013). Synthesis may mix two meanings (as in the popular notion of cultural hybridization), but this still implies a fixed border and a dichotomy. Kramer (2000b) rejects this in favor of cultural fusion—that is, the recognition that many cultural artifacts freely fuse meanings and expressions drawn from far more than one or two isolated cultures.

Communication theories that posit a dualistic sign-object relationship (as structuralism does) are grounded in the dissociation of perspectivism that diminishes their explanatory power. Because the semiotics of Peirce (1931, 1958) emphasizes meaning as dynamic and relational, it is a useful way to explore the communicative diversity wrought by the dimensional accrual/dissociation of the consciousness structures.

---

grid of 60-minute hours and 60-second minutes (Mumford, 1934/1963). Clock time equalized the days and fixed the working hours. It introduced precision, replacing midmorning with 10:30 a.m. And it made the implicit rhythm of life's daily round evident and surveyable. The employment of clock time also shows that the ability to see things in a new way can lead to ordering them in a new way as well.

A DEEPER LOOK AT PEIRCEAN SEMIOTICS

The extreme complexity of Peirce's (1931, 1958) work is notorious. Interpreting his general philosophy of language is a demanding task largely because his complicated semiotic trichotomies do not reduce to mechanistic data in an easily discernible hierarchy of meaning. In Peircean semiotics, to name a sign (i.e., to identify it) does not solve the problem of the way it acts in semiosis. Peirce's (1931, 1958) emphasis on interpretation (as opposed to conception) suggests that meanings are to be explained ultimately in terms of the human context in which they are interpreted. A sign can only be conceived of and interpreted within the spectrum of a specific semiotic event (in Wittgenstein's [1953] terminology, according to use).[3] Therefore, it is important to understand the integral nature of the components of semiosis.

Semiosis and Its Components

Semiosis is an experience that everyone has at every moment of life. Semiotics, the theory of this experience, is another name for logic—"the quasi-necessary, or formal, doctrine of sign" (Peirce, 1931, 2.227; see also Sebeok, 1994). As previously mentioned, the formal constituents of semiosis are the representamen (sign), the interpretant (a sense-making perception), and the object. Peirce (1931, 1958) refers to this object within the semiotic process as the *immediate object* to discriminate it from the object outside of semiosis that he calls the *dynamical object*. Peirce's (1931, 1958) tripartite division is not an aggregate of disconnected categories because the constituents have no separate existence of their own. It must be remembered that for Peirce (1931, 1958), semiosis is an indecomposable triadic sign process. Insofar as meaning is coherent even as one follows its mode of changing, the three components (representamen, interpretant, and object) are evident and integral.

Yet the components are not fixed; representamen, object, and interpretant refer to contingent relationships rather than preset things. For example,

---

[3]In place of the traditional view that appoints mind and meaning as agents of thought and conceives of language as the medium of expression for meanings, Wittgenstein (1953) draws attention to our factual use of signs in concrete situations of action. The philosophical question then no longer reads, "What does this sign *mean*?" but "How is this sign *used*? What does it *do*?" Rorty (1961) points out the similarities between Wittgenstein's (1953) *Philosophical Investigations* and the philosophical framework of Peirce (1931, 1958). The view suggested by Rorty (1961) is that Peirce had envisaged and repudiated positivistic empiricism 50 years earlier than Wittgenstein and had developed a set of insights and a philosophical mood similar to those of contemporary philosophers working under the influence of the later Wittgenstein.

something that is an interpretant in one semiosis may be a representamen in another semiosis. Therefore, it is the analysis of a *particular* semiosis, not the formal analysis of the semiotic triad, that tells us the nature of its constituents. The formal rigor of Peirce's (1931, 1958) definitions should not be confused with mechanistic empirical descriptions.[4] Because semiosis is experienced, it cannot analyze itself without destroying itself. Semiosis, as with any communicative act it is used to analyze, can be subjected to a semiotic analysis. However, that analysis must be a phenomenological rather than a metaphysical one. At the point one attempts to define the true nature of semiotics (just as if one attempted to define deconstruction), one has moved against the spirit of the method. An experienced semiosis is a pure transaction in which specific terms, experiences, and/or ideas cannot be distinguished from one another (or from the transaction). It is a temporally transitive experience, not a spatialized substantive one (Deledalle, 2000; Merrell, 1995b).

Trichotomies of Sign

According to Peirce (1931, 1958), before becoming an object of formal analysis, semiosis is an experienced inference that cannot be other than triadic. Peirce divides the triad of representamen, object, and interpretant into the further triads of signs of nature (representamen), signs of humans (object), and signs of culture (interpretant). The signs of nature are qualisign, sinsign, and legisign. The signs of humans are icon, index, and symbol. And the signs of culture are rheme, dicent or dicisign, and argument (see Table 12.1). Theoretically dividing the sign trichotomies enables a better understanding of semiosis. Concerning this conceptualization, Peirce (1931) writes:

> Signs are divisible by three trichotomies; first, according as the sign in itself is a mere quality, is an actual existent, or is a general law; secondly, according as the relation of the sign to its object consists in the sign's having some character in itself, or in some existential relation to that object, or in its relation to an interpretant; thirdly, according as its interpretant represents it as a sign of possibility or as a sign of fact or a sign of reason. (2.243)

---

[4]According to Wittgenstein (1953), many philosophical confusions, especially the confusion concerning language, can be unmasked by bringing into view the concrete use we make of certain words and propositions within the framework of different "language-games" (p. 5). What Wittgenstein means by language games are contexts of action that contain "both linguistic and extra-linguistic" elements and are embedded in inclusive forms of life (Wittgenstein, 1953, p. 11).

Peirce (1931, 1958) describes representamen, object, and interpretant as being characterized by firstness, secondness, and thirdness (see Table 12.1). This numeration is not a linear measurement, preset sequence, or hierarchy; rather, it reflects Peirce's (1931, 1958) principle that semiosis is triadic and serves to explicate the roles of the three trichotomies. The firstness of the representamen is its potential, its possibility for meaning. The secondness of the object is its power to actualize through the object-representamen relation. The thirdness of the interpretant is its pragmatic anticipation of conventionalities in semiotic relations and interpretations. Similarly, firstness, secondness, and thirdness also characterize the sign triads of nature/representamen (qualisign first, sinsign second, legisign third), humans/object (icon first, index second, symbol third), and culture/interpretant (rheme first, dicent second, argument third).

The first of the three semiotic trichotomies, the representamen, is the representing sign; as first, it is possibility of meaning. The first trichotomy consists of nonsigns (i.e., signs that do not relate to anything). As potential, though, they form the basis for the creation of meaning. It can be confusing to refer to nonsign as sign; however, Peirce is aware of the problem of explaining something that by nature is unexplainable.[5] The relationship among the representamen triad of qualisign, sinsign, and legisign is that these signs exist within themselves, monadically and as nonsigns (Merrell, 1995a, 1997). The first of the representamen, the qualisign, is a quality of a sign. Before the manifestation of a given sign, the qualisign must carry its meaning as a possibility. Because a quality is positive and valid within itself, a qualisign can only distinguish a particular object on the basis of some kind of resemblance to it or an element shared with it. Hence, a qualisign necessarily has to be an icon as well, as icons are human signs that bear some natural or cultural likeness to their objects (and icons, like qualisigns, are firsts; see below for more detail on icons).

When a quality is a logical possibility (rather than a present actuality), the qualisign is also a rheme, the cultural first sign of possible conventional meaning (see below for more detail on rhemes). An example of a qualisign is the experience of the color red. The color red will, of course, be carried by some thing or event; in order to be interpreted as red, however, there must be a qualisign for the possibility of redness. An actual red cloth is an example of a sinsign: the cloth carries the quality of redness (established with a qualisign) and can be interpreted as being red. As second, a sinsign actualizes; it is an existent thing or event as a sign. The sinsign exists only through

---

[5]For the same reason, Wittgenstein (1966) writes in the *Tractatus*, "Anyone who understands me eventually recognizes them [*sic*] as nonsensical. . . . He [*sic*] must, so to speak, throw away the ladder after he [*sic*] has climbed up it" (¶6.54). And he writes, "What we cannot speak about we must pass over in silence" (Wittgenstein, 1966, ¶7.0).

its qualities; therefore, it contains or carries several qualisigns (so the terms red, square, hemmed, and dirty are qualisigns, and the term cloth is the sin-sign). The third representamen, the legisign, is a conventionalized sign. Peirce (1931, 1958) describes the legisign as a law that is a sign. At the same time, the legisign is a general type and not a particular object. Its convention-ality is a matter of communicative application: The lawfulness of legisign is defined and determined by the users.[6]

The second of the three semiotic trichotomies is the object, consisting of icon, index, and symbol. It is important to note that this trichotomy describes the dyadic relation between representamen and object without any interpretation. In semiosis, interpretation occurs, so this dyadic relation becomes the familiar triadic one of representamen-object-interpretant. For instance, to say that a picture of a person is an icon is only partly correct in the Peircean sense. The relation between the figure in the picture and the fig-ure in reality is dyadic; however, this is not how we interpret it. If we inter-pret the person in the picture as an iconic relation—if we recognize the pic-ture as the image of the person—a dyadic relation no longer exists; it becomes a triadic relation consisting of the person, the picture, and the relationship between the person and the picture. In keeping with the idea of a representa-men-object dyad, instead of saying the picture is an icon (which invariably assumes interpretation), it would be more correct to say that the picture con-tains iconical features. The secondness expressed in the object (or more prop-erly, in the representamen-object relation) is what actualizes a sign, what real-izes the possibility set up by the firstness of the representamen.

As the first of the triad of object signs, the icon carries potentiality with-in its actualization. The icon is a sign that shares a likeness with the object it represents. The qualities of the icon resemble the qualities of the object, and, through that resemblance, a similar sense is evoked in those who see the rela-tion as a resemblance. This possibility of meaningful resemblance is an expression of firstness in the icon. Common examples of iconic signs are photographs, as they resemble the object (i.e., the model they depict).

The second class of object signs (the index) comprises signs that make a direct reference to an object through a causal relationship. Rather than a potential resemblance to something, as an expression of secondness, the index is an actual reference to something. The index is *physically connected* to the object, yet the interpreter has no influence on the relationship between the index and its object other than noticing the relation after it has been established. An index describes its object by virtue of a relationship in which the sign is caused by the object: smoke is an index of fire, the result of a medical thermometer is an index of body temperature, and so forth.

---

[6]In this study, the law of the legisign is understood as (different) consciousness struc-tures in the Gebserian (1949 Ger./1985 Eng.) sense or as a language game in the Wittgensteinean (1953, 1966) sense.

Like footsteps indicate a person walking past (another index), an index sign points to its object.

The third class of object signs, the symbol, denotes an object by virtue of a law—that is, through an association of common ideas (a law may be considered the same as a Wittgensteinian language-game and the Gebserian integral consciousness structure). Characterized by thirdness, the symbol has meaning based solely on rules and conventions. A sign being conventionalized means that there is an agreement among users on the meaning of the sign. This common association means that the symbol will be semiotically interpreted as (spatially) pointing to the object. Letters, words, and numbers are examples of symbolic signs. As Peirce (1931) writes:

> Any ordinary word, as "give," "bird," "marriage," is an example of a symbol. It is applicable to whatever may be found to realize the idea connected with the word; it does not, in itself, identify those things. It does not show us a bird, nor enact before our eyes a giving or a marriage, but supposes that we are able to imagine those things, and have associated the word with them. (¶2.298)

Thus, symbol refers to its object through the realization of meaning based on common understandings or conventions—things are what they are to the extent that we agree about what they are. Because of its complexity, a symbol integrally contains iconic and indexical features. Peirce (1931) uses the concept *to love* as an example:

> A Symbol is a sign naturally fit to declare that the set of objects which is denoted by whatever set of indices may be in certain ways attached to it is represented by an icon associated with it. To show what this complicated definition means, let us take as an example of a symbol, the word "loveth." Associated with this word is an idea, which is the mental icon of one person loving another. Now we are to understand that "loveth" occurs in a sentence; for what it may mean by itself, if it means anything, is not the question. Let the sentence, then, be "Ezekiel loveth Huldah." Ezekiel and Huldah must, then, be or contain indices; for without indices it is impossible to designate what one is talking about. Any mere description would leave it uncertain whether they were not mere characters in a ballad; but whether they be so or not, indices can designate them. Now the effect of the word "loveth" is that the pair of objects denoted by the pair of indices Ezekiel and Huldah is represented by the icon, or the image we have in our minds of a lover and his beloved. (¶2.295)

The symbol emanates from the icon and the index. The interaction among the symbol, index, and icon connects the idea to the symbol.

The third sign, trichotomy, describes the relation between the sign and the interpretant. Expressing thirdness, the interpretant is the pragmatic interpretation of a sign in regard to convention. It is a misunderstanding to claim that the thirdness of the interpretant makes it possible to understand the relation between firstness and secondness. The interpretant is not independent of the representamen and the object; meaning requires the semiotic interconnection of first, second, and third. Also, whereas interpretation is an embodied perceptual process, the interpretant is not a human being per se but rather a trichotomy of signs denoting the sense-making relation of sign and interpretant.

The interpretant consists of rheme, dicisign or dicent sign, and argument. As the interpretant signs expressing firstness, rhemes refer to possible objects. Nouns are examples of rhemes, as they clearly refer to possible objects. Since a rheme represents only possible existence, it can be used to lie. Eco (1976) notes that signs are prerequisites for lying, as the object does not have to be present at the same moment as the representamen. Dicisigns (the second interpretant class) are signs of actual existence (although of course they may be deceitful). A dicent sign must contain a rheme to describe the object that the sign is interpreted as referring to. The secondness of the dicisign is expressed in its actualization of the rheme's possibility. An example of a dicent sign is a sentence; sentences convey meaning by representing something and thus actualizing its existence as meaningful. Note that because a dicent sign represents existence, it cannot be an icon—icons resemble their objects, they do not represent them, and therefore do not provide an opportunity for interpretation (the iconic resemblance is either noticed or not). The third interpretant, the argument, represents the object in its capacity as a sign; the argument states something about the sign. Using rhemes and dicent signs, an argument is a set of meaning relations based on convention or law. Whole passages of text (i.e., meaningful links of dicent signs) exemplify an argument. Because it is a conventionalized sign (characterized by thirdness), the argument is also a legisign.

As the preceding shows, Peirce (1931, 1958) created not only a rigorous system describing semiosis but also a complex one that assumes the interdependency of semiotic constituents. Every part of a sign is in itself a sign, and it is constructed by different kinds of signs with different natures. Although the system exists in wholeness, parsing it enables closer examination. Table 12.1 summarizes the signs discussed above.

The representamen is the horizontal firstness trichotomy in Table 12.1. The semiosis of the representamen triad could be called the semiosis of natural signs. The qualisign is the sign that expresses firstness the most in this trichotomy; it is the representamen. The sinsign is the object that is the sign carrying the qualisign. Because the sinsign is an actual thing or event, in order to be manifested, the qualisign must be embodied in the sinsign. The legisign connects qualisign and sinsign; it is the interpretant. When the qual-

Table 12.1 The Components of Semiosis

	Firstness	Secondness	Thirdness
Representamen: (That which represents) *possibility* (Largely the nature of firstness)	**Qualisign** quality, timbre, or color	**Sinsign** particular item or event	**Legisign** conventional representation
Object: Relation of representation to object (Ground of representation) *Actualizes signs* (Largely the nature of secondness)	**Icon** likeness to some object (naturally or by convention)	**Index** causal connection to the object	**Symbol** conventionally stipulated relation (most words)
Interpretant: Anticipated relation of sign to object and interpretation (Pragmatic status of interpretation) Conventional signs (Largely the nature of thirdness)	**Rheme** sign of possibility (terms or words)	**Dicent sign (Dicisign)** sign of an actual occurrence (propositions/sentences)	**Argument** sign of a set of stipulated relations (texts)

isign is manifested in the sinsign through the legisign, some kind of convention or lawfulness occurs. Peirce (1931) calls the law of this relation "force of habit" (¶2.243-2.246). In this case, semiosis is monadic; there is no intelligent interpretation behind semiosis.

The object is the secondness trichotomy. A dyadic relationship exists between the firstness and secondness trichotomies. The secondness trichotomy is triggered by the semiosis occurring in the firstness trichotomy. Because of this relationship, icon, index, and symbol all contain elements from the firstness trichotomy (Peirce, 1931).

The interpretant is the thirdness trichotomy (Peirce, 1931). These signs are pure triads (i.e., genuine signs) because the interpretant forms the equivalent of a more developed sign in semiosis. The rheme, dicent sign, and argument all express lawfulness or convention. Peirce (1931, 1958) has primarily worked with this trichotomy when developing his logic of sign relations. The relation among the rheme, the dicent sign, and the argument is the same as that of a logical inference: the rheme is the predicate, the dicent sign is the premise, and the argument is the conclusion. In this way, the conclusion mediates the predicate and the premise; during this process, a sign occurs. A consequence of the logic within the interpretant is the human ability to make judgments and to draw conclusions based on an innate logic. This is not the logic of the natural sciences or classical empiricism; rather, it is a symbolic logic—a logic that evolves (Peirce, 1931, 1958).

Ten Classes of Signs

The vertical columns of Table 12.1 also track firstness, secondness, and thirdness across signs. The first of these trichotomies is qualisign, icon, and rheme; all three sign types refer to firstness and thus to possibility and quality. The basic sign is the qualisign, on which both the icon and the rheme are constructed. Peirce (1931) writes, "Since a quality is whatever it is positively in itself, a quality can only denote an object by virtue of some common ingredient or similarity" (¶2.254). The need for similarity means that a manifested qualisign must be an icon. The rheme mediates between the qualisign and the icon: the rheme is the logical possibility of whether a qualisign's iconic resemblance to an object is noticeable by convention. The movement from the qualisign to the icon through the rheme constitutes the lawfulness within firstness (Peirce, 1931).

The secondness sign types of sinsign, index, and dicisign all denote signs of actual existence. They act as objects, and (because of the dyadic representamen/first-object/second relation) they all carry qualities from firstness. Within the dicent sign is the rheme, in the sinsign there are one or more qualisigns, and in the index is the icon. The dicent sign actualizes the manifestation of the particular object designated by the sinsign and causally connected by the index (Peirce, 1931).

Characterized by thirdness, the third trichotomy of legisign, symbol, and argument denotes lawfulness and conventionality. The legisign expresses a conventionalized sign and denotes lawfulness in nature. The symbol is also a conventionalized sign; it denotes lawfulness as a dyadic relation between nature and human. As a dyad, this relation is not yet interpreted. The argument creates the triadic connection that brings lawful interpretation to the legisign-symbol dyad. The argument is the sign manifesting thirdness the most. Within the argument are the legisign consisting of qualisign and sinsign and the symbol consisting of qualisign, sinsign, legisign, icon, and index. Also within the argument are the rheme and dicisign. Thus, the argument is the most degenerate sign in the sense that it is the sign furthest from firstness (Peirce, 1931). For Nietzsche (1887 Ger./1974 Eng.), it would be the most abstracted sign, and for Kramer (1997; Kramer & Ikeda, 1998), it would be the most dissociated sign.

As shown in Table 12.2, Peirce (1931) distinguishes 10 classes of signs from the nine sign types of the three trichotomies discussed above (¶2.254-2.265): (a) rhematic iconic qualisigns, (b) rhematic iconic sinsigns, (c) rhematic indexical sinsigns, (d) dicent indexical sinsigns, (e) rhematic iconic legisigns, (f) rhematic indexical legisigns, (g) dicent indexical legisigns, (h) rhematic symbolic legisigns, (i) argument symbolic legisigns, and (j) dicent symbolic legisigns. Each class of sign is logically exclusive and can be characterized by a familiar term and a technical expression, as shown in Table 12.2 (Peirce, 1931).

Table 12.2. Ten Types of Signs

Type of Sign	Familiar Term	Technical Expression
Rhematic iconic qualisign	Feeling	R1O1I1
Rhematic iconic sinsign	Imaging	R1O1I2
Rhematic indexical sinsign	Sensing	R1O2I2
Dicent indexical sinsign	Awaring	R2O2I2
Rhematic iconic legisign	Scheming	R1O1I3
Rhematic indexical legisign	Impressing-saying	R1O2I3
Dicent indexical legisign	Looking-saying	R2O2I3
Rhematic symbolic legisign	Seeing-saying	R1O3I3
Dicent symbolic legisign	Perceiving-saying	R2O3I3
Argument symbolic legisign	Realizing	R3O3I3

It is important to understand that these sign types are ideal, basic analytical classifications that we seldom see in the lifeworld in pure form. The classifications assume specific sign relations: a qualisign will always be a rhematic iconical sign, a symbol will always be a legisign, an argument will always be a symbolic legisign, and so forth. Even in idealized form, such divisions do not mean that the firstness trichotomy does not exist in the thirdness trichotomy of culture signs, that is, in the intellectual signs of rheme, dicent sign, and argument. Firstness does indeed exist in intellectual signs as a displacement; in Gebserian (1949 Ger./1985 Eng.) terms, it is a plus-mutation.

In a sense, Peirce's (1931) sign system presupposes the process of plus-mutation because it posits sign classes as ever-present. Thus, all 10 sign classes refer to the thirdness trichotomy, indicating they are rooted in culture. Without cultural context, semiosis could not be completed. Peirce (1931) stresses that thirdness is a category of habits that tend to become subconscious. This tendency provides a crucial point of Peircean semiosis for the present study: As habits gradually become more and more subconscious, thirdness begins to shift into firstness. This is the point at which Cartesian dualism, empiricist causality, and positivism collapse. To Peirce (1931, 1958), no sign is exclusively of the body or the mind, and semiosis requires the intermingling of constituent trichotomies for sense-making to occur.

13

Embodiment and Technology

As discussed in Chapters 10 and 11, Gebser (1949 Ger./1985 Eng.), Mumford (1934/1963, 1970), and Ellul (1954 Fr./1964 Eng.) indicate transformation in the nature of the technological milieu. Modern technology and modern science continually shape new objects to be seen and new ways of seeing these objects.[1] The quest for positivity in objectivistic scientific research finds its impetus in this ongoing production. However, for rationalist scholars such as Feinberg (1977), science is not so much a question of discovering new objects and ideas but rather of improving and refining what is already possessed and understood. New entities will continue to appear; however, their forms will follow the strict lines established earlier in the already established perception. According to the objectivist viewpoint, this notion of science exists because modern perception is not only perfectible but also self-reliant and self-evident. Such technically inspired positivism attempts to annihilate meaning, destroying semiosis by limiting its conception of communication to simple linear information processing. The reduc-

---

[1]Some approaches oriented toward an acting agent (i.e., a researcher), such as Kuhn's (1962) work that explains revolutions in research paradigms through the use of historical factors, overlook something fundamental concerning the emergence and domination of the modern Newtonian scientific view: The mutation of modern science is perceptual and technical as much as intellectual. In other words, mutation does not come from merely the constitutional process of a subject (researcher). Rather it comes from the institutionalizing processes of human and world. Accordingly, making sense of a form of scientific dominance is driven in large part by perceptual and technical commitments or convictions (Kuhn, 1962).

tion of communication to calculation diverts meaningful communication and fosters the time anxiety that plagues modernity (Gebser 1949 Ger./1985 Eng.); these manifestations will be explored in Chapters 14 and 15. This crisis in the contemporary attitude concerning the nature of communication stems from the dehistoricization of appearance and perception via technicization. The relentless focus on method and/or quantification instead of on deep sense-making, and the emphasis on following empty rules instead of working toward fuller understandings, impoverishes our understanding not only of perception and appearance but also of language and history (Husserl, 1954 Ger./1970 Eng.).

Contrary to the modern perspectival depiction, perception differs depending on the perceiving subject and the perceived object. Perception as a dichotomous arrangement between a spatialized subject and object suffers from the fact that the object of positivistic research recedes as questioning advances. Heidegger (1927 Ger./1962 Eng.) argues, "[T]he character of Being which belongs to the ready-to-hand is just such an involvement. If something has an involvement, this implies letting it be involved in something" (p. 115). Perception is thoroughly dialogical and hermeneutical. Accordingly, perception occurs when there is a context formed for a perceiver *and* a perceived, a context of mutual involvement or implication. In other words, perception *is* the very process of context-formation, as well as the activity that takes place within it — both process and result.

To assume that the perceiver gives rise to the perceived (or vice versa) is to overlook the shared context of the emergent nature of reality. Merleau-Ponty (1945 Fr./1962 Eng.) and Husserl (1954 Ger./1970 Eng.) indicate that subjectivism and objectivism hold this oversight of perceptual context in common. Merleau-Ponty (1945 Fr./1962 Eng.) claims primordial experience engenders the contextual possibility of any given perception, although it also limits the perceptual domain of clarity insofar as this primordial experience (the ability to perceive) cannot be rendered completely visible. Merleau-Ponty (1945 Fr./1962 Eng.) notes, "Between my sensation and me always lies an obscure thickness of a primordial experience which prevents my experience being clear [even] to myself" (p. 250). The clarity of the perceptual horizon is a matter of spatio-temporal orientation. Husserl (1954 Ger./1970 Eng.), criticizing Kant (1781 Ger./1929 Eng.), recognizes the temporal structure of perception and further explores the constitutive characteristic of consciousness in terms of his schema of protention and retention.[2] Continuing in this vein, Merleau-Ponty (1945 Fr./1962 Eng.) posits the per-

---

[2]To Kant (1781 Ger./1929 Eng.), temporality, for better or worse, is not something beyond the human perceptual scheme, although the quest for it is any temptation of metaphysical desire of human intelligence. Temporality for Kant (1781 Ger./1929 Eng.) is a transcendental form of all sensibility. The objectivistically biased paradigm regards time primarily as a barometer for external changes. Kant (1781 Ger./1929

ceptual horizon as necessarily both spatial and temporal. Merleau-Ponty (1945 Fr./1962 Eng.) asserts that "the synthesis of horizons [past, present and future] is only a presumptive synthesis, it operates with certainty and precision only in the object's immediate vicinity" (p. 58; see also Merleau-Ponty, 1964 Fr./1968 Eng.). The meaning of Merleau-Ponty's (1945 Fr./1962 Eng.) notion "open and unfinished object" is clearly explained. Object perception is constantly constituted and much is implied. So, for instance, as I walk around a table, I can never see the "other side," but that implied, yet empirically invisible, quality of the table is essential to its meaning as a complete whole that I call "table." In our technological milieu, much of my behavior is based on the implicature that computer chips are in my devices and working, that satellites are flying overhead conveying my messages, that the pill I took will prevent pregnancy, and so forth. We live in a mundane reality that we largely do not understand, do not see, yet take for granted. In this sense, the modern is far less empirically rooted in her world than the so-called primitive who lives in a Paleolithic hamlet. In this way, we have become dissociated from our environment and even our own bodies as we work at them with cosmetics, exercise, dieting, and so on, as if they were a medium for our egos rather than the basis of our being.

Merleau-Ponty's (1945 Fr./1962 Eng.) notion of the body, together with Peirce's (1931) notion of habit, provide new ways to understand perception and technology. The central theme in Merleau-Ponty's (1945 Fr./1962 Eng.) investigation is the body as an anchoring point for perception and communication. The chiasm between the words-as-gestures having sedimented meaning-in-the-world (not as my private meaning) and words as existential meanings marks the place of dissociation. As the subject and object become increasingly fragmented in the modern world, language becomes increasingly perceived as utterly arbitrary, and the sign too is fragmented into the signifier and the signified. As a result, signs become less rooted, less motivated. Meaning becomes increasingly indeterminate. This makes relationships and institutions increasingly interpretable. This is essential to the objectivist bias, which by implicature gives birth to the modern subject (Merleau-Ponty, 1964 Fr./1968 Eng.). The notion of embodiment facilitates bracketing the objectivistic bias and thus provides the ability to more easily grasp the relationship between technology and semiosis. For Merleau-Ponty, one forms habits and inhabits the world as embodied (1945 Fr./1962 Eng., p. 153). As the world technologizes, so my habitus changes.

Eng.), in contrast, shifts the thematic focus from time to time-experience. Husserl's (1954 Ger./1970 Eng.) term *retention* refers to the unified totality of horizon-consciousness against which the present stands out and in which recollection is a particular mode of consciousness, the focal point of which is a certain past event. Thus, retention is part of an ongoing experience; it remains continuous with the present. The consciousness of present always involves retention as the consciousness (horizon) "background."

Embodiment corresponds to Peirce's (1931) notion of habit. Habit for Peirce (1931) is not that described in behavioral psychology; rather, it involves engendering meanings for signs. Habit entails the activity that mind and body engage in according to dispositions entrenched by use, individual experience, social customs, and cultural rules of conduct. Rather than being judged as true or false, habits are considered in terms of their degree of contextual validity. A habit is valid to the degree that it applies to the other contextual fields of habit that position it; it may be invalid in other contexts and, hence, does not possess a universal or inherent truth-value (Peirce, 1931).

Peirce's (1931) notion of habit provides a semiotic correlate to the physics term *potentia*, which Heisenberg (1958) coined to speak of reality in relation to the results of experiments in quantum mechanics. Reconciling the disparities between the results of traditional physics experiments and the results of quantum mechanics experiments requires an interpretation of reality different from the interpretation provided by objectivism. Experimental outcomes in quantum research do not necessarily fit the objectivistic natural laws of Newtonian physics. For example, in Newtonian physics, particles have specific, fixed properties; something that is a particle exhibits these properties and no others in predictable behavioral patterns that exist independent of any observation. Quantum experiments with light, however, reveal that light displays properties of both particles and waves depending on experimental conditions. Hence, the reality of the tendency of light to behave as a particle with certain other properties when acted on in experiment is *potentia*, a correlate of a possible union of subject and object in the act of observation or interpretation under certain conditions.

For another example, if energy is a characteristic of a particular physical milieu, *potentia* is the possible types of energy systems and processes permitted in that context of experimentation and interpretation. Hence, the reality of potential—as opposed to the traditional physics or noumenal reality—is not a representation of reality in itself; rather, *potentia* describes an interactive production/presentation of reality, an embodied grasp of the world (Heisenberg, 1958).

In traditional Newtonian physics, results of experimental observation of physical objects are conceived of as idealized normative abstract objects or as real effects. This conception supports the rationalist idea of reality as a predictable, lawful object-world completely independent of experimental observer or method of observation. The dynamic results of quantum mechanics experiments repudiate this idea of reality in favor of *potentia* because they demonstrate that reality exists only in relation to the act of observation. The seminal works of Heisenberg (1958) and Heelan (1965) suggest that while observations of time-space and causality can temporarily halt the flux of movement to isolate a given quantity of energy and measure it, these results do not refer to anything other than points of observation. An experimental observation is an embodied perspective that produces a moment of stability (a snapshot of a moment in time, rather than a motion-capturing film). This stability is not an ideal revelation of a fixed, objective reality but is instead a product of the momentary interaction of (a) the researcher, (b) the apparatus doing the measuring, and (c) the object being measured. The focal object of a study is unknowable except in, through, and as an experimentally measured or interpreted entity. Reality is thus the mutually engaged presence of knowing subject and object to be known. With reality as *potentia*, the Newtonian universal laws of nature are transformed into laws of the possible relationships between subject and object (Peirce, 1931).

By regarding or viewing reality as a relational process between the embodied subject and the lifeworld (or as simply the infinite expression of being-in-the-world), the concept of *potentia* offers a way of interpreting experimental results and conceptualizing reality as one of many potential results of interaction. Heelan (1965) notes that, "[S]cience, the atomic physics, is but a link in the infinite chain of [human] argument with nature and that it cannot simply speak of nature 'in itself'" (p. 152). Therefore, "[T]he true object of quantum mechanics [is] not nature but [human] relationships with nature" (Heelan, 1965, p. 54). Accordingly, if science produces particular experimental results or certain formulae, these do not represent a noumenal reality of pure nature and independent empirical objects. Rather, they present potential configurations that may be actualized—or that probably will be actualized given the instituted rules of the scientific language game. Hence, truth (and/or meaning) exists as potential. An experimental result has no absolute truth, only validity. Therefore, laws of various kinds are more or less applicable to certain well-defined domains of experience; their validity is contextually delimited and conventionally presupposed (Heelan, 1965).

Potentia refers to the possibility of producing laws or models of objects in and through experimentation and interpretation; it is neither a pure idea nor an actual event, neither a transcendental category nor a particular substance, neither an object nor an interpretation (Heisenberg, 1958). The relational nature of *potentia* corresponds with Husserl's (1954 Ger./1970 Eng.) assertion that any phenomenon represented by a model is actually the interaction of knowing subject and object to be known, as well as the traces left by both. According to Heelan (1965):

> The elementary particle, on the one hand, is not phenomenally real; for it has "no color, no smell, no taste; . . . and the concepts of geometry and kinematics, like shape or motion in space, cannot be applied to it consistently." On the other hand, it is not a pure idea, for it can be "converted from potency to act," by the process of measurement and observation. *Heisenberg called it real but potential.* (p. 154; italics added)

Human beings have no "direct" knowledge of an object as brute independent reality (sensory data). Apart from the symbols and/or traces produced by their encounters with the particular conditions of experiment (i.e.,
within a particular context), researchers know nothing about the object of
an experiment (Heelan, 1965). One can know possible results only of the
observational event and only as the interaction of the empirical behavior of
the world, already formed thoughts and/or instruments, and semiosis
(Heelan, 1965).

Potentia does not mean our knowledge of reality is any less "real"; it
changes the limits and definitions of the type of reality we can know. With
potentia, Heisenberg (1958) has perhaps found a solution to the problem of
the impossibility of Kantian transcendentals or Aristotelian pure experiences, epitomized in the crisis of modern science. For Nietzsche (1887
Ger./1974 Eng.), the crisis is the nihilistic boredom that arises from positivity rendering a single absolute interpretation intolerant of any other possible worlds. For Husserl (1954 Ger./1970 Eng.), at least in part because of the
fascism he witnessed firsthand (a fascism that Nietzsche [1901 Ger./1967
Eng.] prophesied), the ultimate scientific crisis is its dehistoricizing and
dehumanizing determinism. With potential-as-reality, science deconstructs
the problems of its own classical materialism by recognizing that models are
reflections of perspectives rather than reality (Heelan, 1965).

Potentia is both the result of the dialectical interaction of subject and
object as well as the process. Potentia does not stem from a one-sided idealism abandoned to subjectivity any more than it arises from objectivistic
empiricism. The notion of potentia describes reality as an interrelational
constitution (co-constitution) without absoluteness or universality claimed
by those embracing the objectivistic viewpoint (Heisenberg, 1958). With
emphasis on possibility and validation, as well as its embodiment, potentia
corresponds to Peirce's (1931) concept of habit as a conventionalized series
of possible experimental results—only certain answers are possible, and
only certain answers mean anything (i.e., statistical significance).

PEIRCE'S NOTION OF HABIT

Peirce (1931) proposes habit as the solution to the discrepancy of reality
containing ordered patterns and the continuous, dynamic, chance-generat-
ed, uncertain fields of sign-relations. Because habit enables one to fix sign-
relations and find regularity in them, Peirce (1931) asserts, "[I]t is clear that
. . . a principle of habit . . . is the only bridge that can span the chasm between
the chance medley of chaos and the cosmos of order and law" (¶6.262).
Meaning is determined by the habits of past sign-relationships in connection
with the interpreter. For Peirce, then, "[T]here remains only habit, as the

essence of the logical interpretation" (¶5.486). Habit may be considered semiotic code, although to Peirce (1931), code is not a connective medium that links meaning with object (i.e., a dyadic semantic transfer mechanism). Rather, habit-as-code must be understood as a triadic communicative inter-relationship among interpretant, object, and representamen. Habit is a reg-ularity (normalization) of transformations among objects, persons, and signs (Peirce, 1931).

Therefore, habit is a temporary limitation of possibilities or relations largely pre-established by the perceiver's sociocultural conventions (inter-pretant). Convention may temporarily and contingently isolate possible meaning configurations that are the interaction of sign-functional habits. Triadicity, relativity, relationality, conventionality, and communication are all developed within habit, which engenders them to the interaction involved in knowing objects. Hence, a habit is an embodied regularity of semiotic procedures. The perception of object and representamen (as an interpretant effect) depends on previous interpretant-habits of perception that are stored in what Peirce (1931) calls "associations in memory." For Peirce, this type of memory is more social than individual, acting as a cul-tural-historical repository of habits (customs and ways of being).

Habit, then, is a configuration of temporarily isolated sign-relations that are contextualized historically in order to be completely (although not ade-quately) interpreted. Accordingly, habits are neither fixed laws nor parts of mechanical models, neither absolutes nor exempt from variation by chance. In short, habit bears the epistemological flux, interrelativity, and possibility of *potentia*. As manifestations of *potentia*, the acquisition of interpretant-habits and their interpretation are subject to growth, mutation, and alter-ation (Peirce, 1931).

Peirce (1931) proposes the notion of sign-field (or *phaneron*) to explain the configurations generated by sign-habits. According to Peirce, "[S]igns are irreducibly triadic—they function in relation to other elements of the triad in that they are situated in a field—ground—*phaneron*" (¶2.228). For Peirce (1931), "[F]ield is synonymous for relation of signs" (¶1.286). The sign-field describes the sign-habits present to the interpreter at the time of the reception of a particular sign-relation, a presence that necessarily gov-erns the reception and contextualization of the particular sign-relation (Peirce, 1931).

Hence, for Peirce (1931), the phaneron is the organization of sign-rela-tions in a particular time and space that governs the functions of any new perception of sign-relations. Therefore, the phaneron is the "[C]ollective totality of all that is present to the mind no matter what manner or sense, and *without worrying at all whether it corresponds or not to any real thing*" (Peirce, 1931, ¶1.285; italics added). As *potentia*, the reality of a semiotic configuration lies in the contextual validity of its phaneron—understandable within a certain field of relations. For Peirce (1931), truth and meaning depend on neither a singular habit nor on the habits of the idiosyncratic self, but rather on the consensus of the community. As noted in Chapter 12, in the lifeworld, the real is that which, sooner or later, information and reasoning would finally *result in*, and which is, therefore, independent of the whims of you and me (Peirce, 1931, 1958). This conception of reality essentially involves the notion of community as historical consciousness without definite or commonly held limits (Peirce, 1931).

MERLEAU-PONTY'S HABIT-BODY

Merleau-Ponty (1945 Fr./1962 Eng.) uses a concept of habit similar to that of Peirce (1931) to emphasize the situated nature of the body. Merleau-Ponty claims, "Prior to stimuli and sensory contents, we must recognize a kind of inner diaphragm which determines, infinitely more than the stimuli and sensory contents do, what our reflexes and perceptions will be able to aim at in the world, the area of possible operations, the scope of our life" (p. 79). Being-in-the-world, he concludes, is a pre-objective and pre-subjective *perception* that serves to "anchor" the subject-body within a definite (although not fixed) environment. Being-in-the-world is "an intention of our whole being" caught up in the dynamics of a "definite involvement" (Merleau-Ponty, 1945 Fr./1962 Eng., p. 82). Hence, the body, in Merleau-Ponty's account, is "the unperceived term in the center of the world toward which all objects turn their face" (p. 82). Further, Merleau-Ponty (1960 Fr./1964 Eng.) suggests that there must be another layer to the body's nature, another layer besides that of "the body at this moment," which is the "flesh-body" (p. 16; see also Merleau-Ponty, 1945 Fr./1962 Eng., pp. 67-134, 175-199). Merleau-Ponty (1945 Fr./1962 Eng.) calls this second dimension the "habit-body" (p. 94). Together, the flesh-body and the habit-body constitute the situatedness of the body (Merleau-Ponty, 1945 Fr./1962 Eng.). I in-habit my body not as an object but as the foundation of all my ability to perceive.

The habit-body is an "anonymous" realm of bodily orientation, a horizon of sedimented "manipulatory movements," or "axes" and "vectors" (Merleau-Ponty, 1964 Fr./1968 Eng., pp. 220-222) through which the body participates in the spectacle of involvement that is being-in-the-world. The habit-body serves to foundationally situate the existential subject within a context of possibilities that then induce the actions and anticipations of the lived-body (the flesh-body). The habit-body, therefore, serves to initiate the existential subject into a range of possible themes that constitute the framing or orientation for the lifeworld (Merleau-Ponty, 1945 Fr./1962 Eng., 1964 Fr./1968 Eng.).

"Beneath intelligence as beneath perception," Merleau-Ponty (1945 Fr./1962 Eng.) remarks, "[W]e discover a more fundamental function" that orients us "within a particular world," or "within a situation" (p. 135). Merleau-Ponty (1945 Fr./1962 Eng.) calls this function the "intentional arc," stating that "Intentional arc projects us our past, our future, our human setting, our physical, ideological and moral situation, or rather, . . . results in our being situated in all these respects" (p. 136). The intentional arc integrates different dimensions and points of view into the unity of a personal core of being that is then capable of responding to both familiar and unfamiliar sorts of situations. The intentional arc, thus, supplies people with a foundational unity that is not a synthesis of aspects (our physical, ideological, and moral situations), but is rather the basis for synthesis and integration. It is the origin of the attitude of synthetic and integral trajectories (Merleau-Ponty, 1945 Fr./1962 Eng.).

Walking upright on two legs is a good example. In placing one foot in front of another, my intentional arc unifies each step into a rhythmic cadence we call balanced and constantly balancing gate. If I fragment walking temporally, spatially, if I think or intellectualize it, then I become clumsy and walking becomes effortful. In fact, I may fall because since I fragmented the whole into objective parts, I may not be able to think somatically fast enough to keep upright. Walking and running are constitutive wholes that are presumed and assumed ensembles of motion fused into one continuous, flowing movement. Trying to walk by putting discrete fragments of motion together is nearly impossible, and that is why stroke victims and engineers of walking robots have such a difficult time doing what most of us take for granted.

The foundational unity wrought by the intentional arc is bodily intentionality, which manifests itself in experience, a sort of performatory knowledge.[3] Merleau-Ponty (1945 Fr./1962 Eng.) states, "[I]t is never an objective body that we move, but our phenomenal body, and there is no mystery in that, since *our body, as the potentiality* of this or that part of the world, surges toward objects to be grasped and perceives them" (pp. 105–106; italics added). Merleau-Ponty (1945 Fr./1962 Eng.) concludes there is a bodily possession of space that is more primordial than a perspectival possession of "objective" space. This pre-objective spatial existence is the "primary condi-

---

[3]Pierre Bourdieu's (1972 Fr./1977 Eng., 1990 Fr./1990 Eng.) sociological approach offers many similar points to Merleau-Ponty's (1945 Fr./1962 Eng.) notions of embodiment and the intentional arc. In a sense, Bourdieu's (1972 Fr./1977 Eng., 1990 Fr./1990 Eng.) works can be regarded as the application of Merleau-Ponty's (1945 Fr./1962 Eng.) philosophical explorations. Both thinkers share the conceptualization of lived body as the dissolution of the subject and object dichotomy. Bourdieu (1972 Fr./1977 Eng., 1990 Fr./1990 Eng.) clearly focuses on the visible—or what is seen— more than on the invisible. In contrast, Merleau-Ponty (1945 Fr./1962 Eng.) focuses on the potentiality or possibility of "motility"—the "I can."

tion of all living perception" (Merleau-Ponty, 1945 Fr./1962 Eng., p. 109). In other words, actual bodily movement is more primordial than the *thought* of bodily movement (Merleau-Ponty, 1945 Fr./1962 Eng.).

Merleau-Ponty (1945 Fr./1962 Eng.), following Husserl (1954 Ger./ 1970 Eng.), emphasizes, "[C]onsciousness is in the first place not a matter of 'I think' but of '*I can*'" (p. 137). The body *inhabits* the world even as it is a point of view *on* the world. Through the perceptual habits of the body, we "come into possession" of the world, setting "boundaries to our field of vision and our field of action" (Merleau-Ponty, 1945 Fr./1962 Eng., p. 152). In this vein, Merleau-Ponty (1945 Fr./1962 Eng.) posits the intertwined nature of body and existence:

> The body expresses total existence, not because it is an external accompaniment to that existence, but because existence comes into its own in the body. . . . Understanding in this way, the relation of experience to thing expressed, or of sign to meaning is not a one-way relationship like that between original text and translation. Neither body *nor existence* can be regarded as the original of the human being, since they presuppose each other. (p. 166)

Through the body's initial capacity to enter a field, the world first becomes a world and the subject becomes a worldly being. Hence, the body is "the initial upsurge of meaning, the basis of all possible truth, of all rationality" (Madison, 1981, p. 65). Stated differently, "[T]o have lost one's voice is not to keep silence: one keeps silence only when one can speak" (Merleau-Ponty, 1945 Fr./1962 Eng., p. 161). To keep silent is an intentional self-censorship. To lose the power of speech is to lose the power to selectively and willfully keep silent.

Merleau-Ponty's Body and Technology

For Merleau-Ponty (1945 Fr./1962 Eng.), perception as embodied consciousness is the primal point of contact between existence and the world. The body is never an object among other objects, either natural or artificial, in the world; the body as the subject of the sensorium belongs to the human being—as Merleau-Ponty states, "I am not in front of my body, I am in it, or rather I am it" (p. 150). Merleau-Ponty (1945 Fr./1962 Eng., 1964 Fr./1968 Eng.) attacks naïve empiricism and positivism with its emphasis on body-objects and insists that my body and, by implication, the body of an authentic Other is not an object but rather a medium, an organization, a continually integrated and constituted act of consciousness. As such, the body is my being, my access to the world. It is the vehicle of communication with the world.

> The body is our general medium for having a world. Sometimes it is restricted to the actions necessary for the conservation of life, and accordingly it posits around us a biological world; at other times, elaborating upon these primary actions and moving from their literal to a figurative meaning, it manifests through them a core of new significance: this is true of motor habits such as dancing. Sometimes, finally, the meaning aimed at cannot be achieved by the body's natural means; it must then build itself an instrument, and it projects thereby around itself a cultural world. . . . Habit is merely a form of this fundamental power. (Merleau-Ponty, 1945 Fr./1962 Eng., p. 146)

For Merleau-Ponty (1945 Fr./1962 Eng., 1964 Fr./1968 Eng.), the flesh-body connects inner and outer reality. Merleau-Ponty (1964 Fr./1968 Eng.) illustrates this fact with the synergic operation of the two eyes. Binocular vision is not composed of two monocular visions operating in parallel, nor is it as an association, assemblage, or aggregate of two separate visual entities. Rather, the experience of binocular vision is one sole unitary vision. Touch, too, is an interlacing of the movement that touches and the movement that is touched. In a handshake, for example, we are touching and being touched at the same time (Merleau-Ponty, 1964 Fr./1968 Eng.). The body is inexorably bound to the world; the body is within the world, and the world is within the body.

Incarnate consciousness, embodied perception, applies to all aspects of the environment, including the instruments humanity has fashioned as extensions of the senses. Modern technology is no longer limited to simple machines for basic tasks; today the extension of the body makes the world a technological complex (Ellul, 1954 Fr./1964 Eng.; Mumford, 1934/1963). Technology is not simply part of the visible realm; it is the embodiment of a way of seeing, of the visible itself (Mumford, 1934/1963). Consciousness has become technologized.

Embodiment and Institution

According to Descartes (1641 Lat./1647 Fr./1901 Eng.), it is not perceptibility but intelligibility that dominates (and largely constitutes) the essence of bodies; this exaltation of cognitive consciousness permeates all subsequent manifestations of the Cartesian objectivistic bias in what Gebser (1949 Ger./1985 Eng.) classifies as the deficient rationality of the mental consciousness structure. However, Merleau-Ponty (1968 Fr./1970 Eng.) is reluctant to grant a primary constitutive power to Cartesian consciousness. The Cartesian objectivistic view of perception remains derivative and overlooks the source of its possibility of self-certainty: embodiment. As discussed in Chapters 9 and 10, Cartesian constitution cannot account for the world. For Merleau-Ponty (1968 Fr./1970 Eng.), the primordial movement of appearance is not so much a case of constitution as it is one of "institu-tion." To perceive is not to constitute a meaningful, sensible situation; rather, to perceive is to find oneself in the midst of an appearance that institutes the possibilities of meaning. As institution, perception precludes any simple notion of beginnings; it arrived ahead of itself. Merleau-Ponty (1968 Fr./1970 Eng.) argues,

> If the subject were not taken as a constituting but an instituting subject, it might be understood that the subject does not exist instantaneously and that the other person does not exist simply as a negative of myself . . . an instituting subject could coexist with another because the one instituted is not the immediate reflection of the activity of the former and can be regained by [the self] or by others without involving any-thing like a total recreation. Thus the instituted subject exists between others and myself, between me and myself, like a hinge, the conse-quence and the guarantee of our belonging to a common world. (p. 40)

Things (objects) are not subordinate to some unilaterally productive power of conscious constitution; they are caught in the play of institutional forces along with consciousness itself. If consciousness does play the role of institutor or quasi-agent, it is only with the support and collaboration of things-in-the-world and only within the context of movement of institu-tions always already at work (Merleau-Ponty, 1968 Fr./1970 Eng.).[4]

In a sense, every perception has the characteristic of ever-present origin (Gebser, 1949 Ger./1985 Eng.) because a world of things is always and unavoidably already there before we arrive. Hence, a thing has its own right in the establishment of the institution of perception. In contrast, "for [rational] consciousness there are only the objects which it has itself consti-tuted" (Merleau-Ponty, 1968 Fr./1970 Eng., p. 39). With perception as insti-tution, when we perceive something, we are engaging what has come before us by taking up an institution of perception as our own. The conventions of perceptual institution are not transcendental absolutes. Instead, institution accounts for the relationality of perceiving and perceived, and (as things are invested with this relationality) they precede any personal perception as well as cognitive constitution (see Merleau-Ponty, 1945 Fr./1962 Eng., on "The Body as Expression, and Speech," especially p. 197). The institution of lan-

---

[4]Kramer (1993b, 1997) indicates the same point in terms of co-constitutional process. However, Kramer's term *co-constitution* still provides the subject or acting agent with the primary constitutional power, although tacitly. Kramer (1993b, 1997), like Husserl (1954 Ger./1970 Eng.), fully recognizes the eloquence of things (i.e., things-in-the-world) and clearly insists on that point in his argument. However, the usage of the term *co-constitution* reveals a subject-oriented tendency with constitution positioned as the action of an agent.

guage is a perfect example of this relationality that precedes us. We are born into language and come to mean through it.

TECHNOLOGY AND PERCEPTION

The institution of technology into perception is established with the human talent for extending itself beyond its physical boundaries. In *The Primacy of Perception*, Merleau-Ponty (1947, 1955, 1964 Fr./1964 Eng.) emphasizes "the lived body is not where it is nor what it is" (p. 72). To Merleau-Ponty (1947, 1955, 1964 Fr./1964 Eng.), all technique with all kinds of instrumentation is "technique of body" (p. 168) in that it represents and amplifies the metaphysical structure of our flesh. As discussed in Chapters 10 and 12, when a blind person's cane becomes an extension of the sense of touch, the cane becomes invisible as cane and visible as *body* (Merleau-Ponty, 1945 Fr./1962 Eng., p. 152). "Once the stick has become a familiar instrument, the world of feelable things recedes and now begins, not at the outer skin of the hand, but at the end of the stick. . . . It is a bodily auxiliary, an extension of bodily synthesis" (Merleau-Ponty, 1945 Fr./1962 Eng.). This is the assimilation of instrument into the field of the live-body. All technology comes to be a "habit formation," which becomes invisible yet influential in the formation of reality, the habitation of our lived-body-consciousness. Technology becomes an integral part of us and our world. There are countless examples such as false teeth, the familiarity of one's automobile, chopsticks, a bow and arrow . . . how a master pianist comes to inhabit and to be inhabited by the keyboard in such a manner that it seems to be an extension of the player's hands, with which he or she makes music (Merleau-Ponty, 1945 Fr./1962 Eng.). In fact it becomes a seamless part of awareness. Or we might add the remote control of a TV or the keyboard on your computer or cellular phone.

Hence, from Merleau-Ponty's (1947, 1955, 1964 Fr./1964 Eng., 1964 Fr./1968 Eng.) perspective, the question concerning the place of technology is the question of how a technical body insinuates itself and becomes instilled (and/or installed) into the flesh-body.

Merleau-Ponty (1947, 1955, 1964 Fr./1964 Eng.) explores the relationship between body and technology by noting how mirrors symbolize the way in which (seemingly) technology plays a representational role in human life. With improvements in mirrors (and more generally improvements in technology), the flesh-body is reflected more and more accurately (i.e., MRIs, CT scans, etc.). However, this increasing accuracy of reflection has occurred only because the body already held the possibility of existing in two senses, as "seeing body" and "visible body." The mirror (technology) and the human body imply and provoke each other's latent qualities of the body as double body (the visible-seer) and of the mirror as the transparent medium that encourages this doubling aspect of the body. The mirror is but one of the virtually unlimited number of technical and perceptual relationships that constitute the modern technological milieu. As Merleau-Ponty (1964 Fr./1968 Eng.) writes of the representation of body to itself by technology, "[T]he visible-seer (for me, for the others) is . . . not a psychic something, nor a behavior of vision, but a perspective, or better, the world itself with a certain coherent deformation" (p. 262).

For Merleau-Ponty (1947, 1955, 1964 Fr./1964 Eng., 1964 Fr./1968 Eng.), it is crucial to understand how the human flesh-body and the technical body (the body extended by technology) provoke and sustain one another, as well as how together they amplify one another to exceed the potential of either alone. However, Merleau-Ponty (1947, 1955, 1964 Fr./1964 Eng.) also recognizes that the technical amplification of the body has a price. All such amplification is, in fact, deformation or transformation. Implicit in transformation is the privileging of a certain form of perception (e.g., Euclidean geometry) and the accompanying forgetting or masking of other possibilities.[5] Euclidean geometry, as a typical example of the co-occurrence of transformation and deformation, is an embrace not only of some particular perspectival technique but also of the revelatory spirit of the Renaissance perspective. The perceptual power of modern science stems from its unconditional embrace of this historical possibility, not the technique per se (on faith, not fact) (Carey, 1989; see also footnote 5 in Chapter 11).

Ihde (1979) insists, "Modern technological embodiment lies in our technology and its relation to polymorphic perception" (p. 99). By using the term *polymorphic*, Ihde is asserting the role of previously constructed meanings from our cultural perspectives, previous encounters, and so on that influence our construction of current meanings. In other words, when we encounter new technologies, we come to these encounters with pre-conceptions already formed about them based on the already existing meanings derived from our cultures and previous experiences (Ihde, 1979). Three theoretical depictions are used in the analysis of the relation between technology and perception (i.e., technological embodiment): technology as outside the body, exemplified by the claims of Dreyfus (1972); technology as inside the body, as considered by Heelan (1983); and technology as neither inside nor outside, as posited by Ihde (1998) in accordance with Merleau-Ponty's (1945 Fr./1962 Eng., 1947, 1955, 1964 Fr./1964 Eng.) emphasis on the interrelated and co-constitutive nature of perceiver and perceived. We recognize that these theoretical depictions may be considered to be dated by some

---

[5]Gebser (1949 Ger./1985 Eng.) makes a similar point, indicating the privileging of a certain form is "a gain as well as a loss" (p. 12). When consciousness mutation occurs, some aspects gain manifestation, some aspects become latent. Kramer (1997) argues this point in his theory of dimensional accrual/dissociation (DAD).

based on their original usages. However, these same frameworks can also be seen in more current critical/analytical works on technology and perception and are therefore still relevant to the ongoing conversation (e.g., Postman, 1992; Vanderburg, 2005).

First, in his discussion about what computers cannot do, Dreyfus (1972) concludes that the computer cannot be intelligent because it does not have a human body. In a sense, of course, the computer does have a body; however, there are differences between electronic and flesh bodies. For Dreyfus, computers do not think differently than humans; they do not "think" at all. Their materiality can neither perceive, nor move, nor act. The computer remains outside the realm of embodiment, an alien presence that only through philosophic illusion (metaphor) becomes similar to the human (Dreyfus, 1972).

In contrast, the second theoretical depiction of technology and perception, shown in the work of Heelan (1983), comes close to humanizing the computer. Insofar as an instrument enters into an extended human embodiment, it becomes virtually transparent. For example, Heelan claims that reading a thermometer is equivalent to a direct perception. However, Heelan collapses his conceptualization of "readable technologies" too much into unique measuring perceptions of a particularly trained, as well as a technologically extended, human body. In this respect, Heelan's technologies are taken *inside* the body, whereas Dreyfus (1972) leaves the technology *outside* the body.

For the third depiction of the perception-technology relation, exemplified by Ihde's (1998) expansion on Merleau-Ponty (1947, 1955, 1964 Fr./1964 Eng.), technologies are neither outside nor inside. Technologies do not reveal themselves directly but rather indirectly or reflexively—in a phenomenological way. Ihde (1998) insists that interpretation of technology is a distinctively *relativistic* act. In a sense, this is analogous to Heisenberg's (1958) notion of *potentia*, in that the perspective of technology must account for *what* is observed and simultaneously depends on the situation or position of the observer: The object does not simply reveal itself, particularly not objectivistically. In this phenomenological, relativistic framework, the co-constitutionality (or institutionality) of the body and technology is crucial (Ihde, 1998). Thus, phenomenological exploration examines human-technology relations not the technology or the human alone.

Considering technologies as artifacts, Ihde (1990) notes that it is possible to use any material entity technologically. Ihde insists that taking up an artifact in some human-directed or referential praxis toward the world (e.g., picking up a stone and throwing it) is to accomplish at least some minimal technical modification of the artifact before putting it into use. In the spectrum of such relations, as Heidegger (1927 Ger./1962 Eng.) observes through the hammer example, our uses of artifacts are such that the artifacts do not stand out; indeed, when they do stand out, they are no longer functioning in the world-related way through which we experience them. When I must consciously foreground my use of the hammer (when I am first learning to use it or I am learning to use it in a new way), it no longer seamlessly integrates into my understanding of the world. Intricate care must be taken when first mastering a new device, be it a hammer, a Blackberry, or a fishing rod.

Ihde (1998) suggests technological mediatedness is a central feature of the human-technology relationship. He describes a mediated situation:

> In the mediated situation, my "reach" is extended or "magnified"—I can do more than I could do in my naked body position. But, simultaneously, at least during the actual use of the technology, my experience of apple is "reduced." This latter point is often overlooked in favor of the former magnificational point—but for example, I do not feel the fleshiness of the apple, nor tactilely sense as fully its state of ripeness, etc. . . . The mediated situation, then, is one in which both what is experienced and how one experiences the object are changed. Technologies transform our experience of the objects in the world non-neutrally. (Ihde, 1998, p. 47)

Borrowing Ihde's (1982, 1990) notion of the interrelated human-technology-world yields configurations of the embodiment of technology given in Tables 13.1-13.3). Because the present investigation considers technology from two viewpoints (as a tool/instrument and as a mode of revealing), *medium* is a more appropriate term than *technology* for the three configurations. Medium expresses a specific technological apparatus and technological mode, as well as a specific point in time and space.

Configuration 1 illustrates the unperspectival world in terms of embodiment, technological or otherwise. Because there is no clear distinction between world and human in unperspectival consciousness, there is no intentional directionality in the perception of things-in-the-world; rather, human and world are components of an ambivalent whole (Gebser, 1949 Ger./1985 Eng.). This is shown in Configuration 1 by the arrows connecting human to world and world to human, as well as the parentheses enclosing human and world as a set. Because the unperspectival human has not cre-

Table 13.1. Modes of Being

Configuration 1	(Human ⟷ World)	Unperspectival consciousness
Configuration 2	Human ⟶ World	Perspectival consciousness

ated a schism between nature and culture, both human and world inform the other's identity (and there isn't anything—internal or external—that the unperspectival human would recognize as technology in the way modern humans do).

Configuration 2 indicates the typical form of the mental, perspectival world. This configuration is an expression of the Cartesian objectivistic-biased paradigm. The parenthesis have disappeared because perspectival human has stepped out of the mythic circle as an individuated ego into the empty space of the world in order to conquer it with directed thinking (indicated by the arrow only pointing toward the world). As discussed in previous chapters, this perspective objectifies things in the world, including other human beings and technology. This configuration illustrates the Cartesian view that the world is waiting to be discovered and perceived (i.e., interpreted and labeled) by cogito, as indicated by the directional arrow connecting human to world.

Technology is a purely perspectival phenomenon because humans cannot perceive technology until the split between nature and culture comes with the emergence of the perspectival consciousness/dimension. In the perspectival world, there are two orientations toward the mediated world. Ihde (1990, 1998) describes these two situations in Table 13.2.

Table 13.2. Technology and Embodiment

Configuration 3	(I ----- Technology) ——➤ World		Embodied Relation
Configuration 4	I ——➤ (Technology ----- World)		Hermeneutic Relation

In embodied relations, Ihde (1990) notes, "[W]hat allows the partial symbiosis of myself and the technology is the capacity of technology to become perceptually *transparent*" (p. 86; italics original). In Configuration 3, if embodied relations are empowered in perception, the medium becomes another aspect of the co-constitutional process. The parentheses denote how human and technology are conceptualized as part of the same being, although the lack of arrows between them indicates that it is not a conscious polar-ambivalent identity-creating relationship as in the unperspectival. Once people objectify themselves as the mechanism or process of technicization, not merely the knowledge or usage of technological apparatus or skill, the configuration may be regarded as an expression of the deficient mental-rational consciousness structure (i.e., as the extreme extension of Cartesian dualism). Within this configuration, as Dreyfus (1972) points out, unattainable ambitions, such as artificial intelligence (AI), arise. This argument is discussed in relation to semiosis/communication in Chapter 12.

In Configuration 4 (the hermeneutic relationship), technology is understood as altering the nature of the world, which in turn alters technology. However, both are treated as neutral tools to be acted on by humans—humans who are not influenced by the tools they choose to use, only by the intentions brought to their use.

The aperspectival modality is not egocentric. Consequently it is not dualistic. Therefore technology is not perceived or grasped as a disembodied manifold for will-power-drive and as merely an instrument for expressing desire and dominance display. Merleau-Ponty's (1964 Fr./1968 Eng.) notion of institutional embodiment of technology is illustrated in Table 13.3.

Table 13.3. Aperspectival Integration

Configuration 5	{[Human/World) ---- Medium] ---- World	Aperspectival

According to Merleau-Ponty (1964 Fr./1968 Eng.), "The world seen is not 'in' my body, and my body is not 'in' the visible world ultimately" (p. 138). Therefore,

> [W]e must not think the flesh starting from substance, from body and spirit—for then it would be the union of contradictories—but we must think it, as we said, as an element, as a concrete ensemble of a general manner of being. (Merleau-Ponty, 1964 Fr./1968 Eng., p. 147)

Embodiment cannot be explained with substance, but it can be understood through the concept of *potentia* or possibility as a general element of existence. Merleau-Ponty (1964 Fr./1968 Eng.) clarifies this point:

> To designate it [the flesh], we should need the old term "element", in the sense it was used to speak of water, air, earth, and fire, that is in the sense of a *general thing*, midway between the spatio-temporal individual and idea, a sort of incarnate principle that brings a style of being wherever there is a fragment of being. The flesh is in this sense an "element" of Being. Not a fact or sum of facts, and yet adherent to *location* and to the now. (pp. 139-140)

Merleau-Ponty's (1964 Fr./1968 Eng.) notion of embodiment as related to Ihde's (1990, 1998) mediated context of technology in { [(Human/World) --- Medium] --- World} is illustrated in Figure 13.4.

Unlike the previous configurations, Merleau-Ponty's (1964 Fr./1968 Eng.) notion of embodiment is aperspectival because it awares a diaphanous

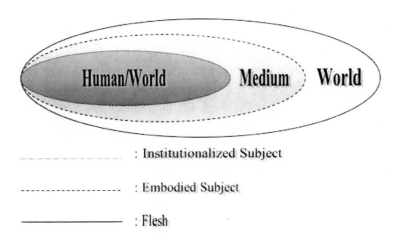

: Institutionalized Subject

: Embodied Subject

: Flesh

Fig. 13.4. Relationship between technology and embodiment

relationship among human, world, and medium. The relationship between human and world affects the medium, which in turn affects the world, which affects the human, which affects the medium, and so on. All are connected as integral parts of a diaphanous whole in which the origin is ever-present (Gebser, 1949 Ger./1985 Eng.).

Technologies are culturally embodied; that is, any given technology is culturally relative. The cultural embodiment of technology can explain why there is no such thing as a simple technology transfer; there is only a culture-technology transfer, for all technologies have a cultural network of assignment. For Merleau-Ponty (1964 Fr./1968 Eng.), it is precisely in relation to cultural factors that perception becomes enigmatic, even tautological. Merleau-Ponty (1964 Fr./1968 Eng.) states, "[W]hat I maintain is that: there is an informing of perception by culture which enables us to say that culture is perceived" (p. 212). Cultural embeddedness is a matter of technology-in-a-context, where technology is and *what* it is have meaning only contextually. The enigmatic notion of technological embodiment and its relationship to communication is presented in detail in the next chapter through the exploration of vision.

14

Visiocentrism and Overdetermination

This chapter includes a discussion of the transformation or mutation of visualism as a typical and fundamental realization of consciousness structures and perception. The exploration of the mutation of perspectivism (or vision) serves as a good example of the characteristic differences among the pre-perspectival, the unperspectival, the perspectival, and Merleau-Ponty's (1968 Fr./1970 Eng., 1964 Fr./1968 Eng.) embodied perspective (or embodied vision). The implications of embodied vision with regard to semiosis and communication are investigated in this chapter through the notion of overdetermination.

With the advent of the modern perspective, technology has come to represent the means by which people, objects, and works are judged. Technology is taken as *the* model entity, the being against which all beings can be evaluated. For example, we sort the world into developed, developing, and underdeveloped nation-entities largely based on technological capacity. This paradigmatic status facilitates and intensifies the modern faith in sensory perception, especially vision. Seeing is the directed scan of a spatial extension. With its stress on space and directionality, the mental consciousness structure distinguishes the eye as the chief source of information for the other organ of emphasis, the brain. Trust in the power and truth of the visual perspective differentiates modernity from mythic and magic worldviews (Gebser, 1949 Ger./1985 Eng.). Since the invention of the telescope, eyeglasses, and the microscope, *seeing* is believing. And the augmentation of seeing (the technological expansion of the eye) to the previously

279

unseen realms of the cosmos and micro-cosmos is a major ambition of the modern project (Mumford, 1934/1963).

Modern faith in and obsession with enhancing vision has been termed "visiocentrism" (e.g., Kramer, 1988, 1993c, 1997; Kramer & Ikeda, 1998, 2000). Derrida (1972 Fr./1981 Eng. b) claims that the metaphysics of presence, which marks logocentric[1] modernity, places sensory emphasis on the ear—phonocentrism—as opposed to visiocentrism. However, according to Kramer (1988, 1997, 2013), phonocentrism is a magic potency (not a mental one, and definitely not a mental-rational one). Obsessed with the eye and its perceptual product of vision, modern logocentrism reduces auditory data to unreliable hearsay[2] and inflates visual data to unequivocable truth, promoting the visiocentric belief in sight as the most reliable sense. Hence, production and utility become the dominant ontological motifs of the modern perceptual faith, and, as such, the essence of objects is cast in the light of purposefulness and availability. In Heidegger's (1952, 1954, 1962 Ger./1977 Eng.) terminology, *poeisis* (bringing forth) gives way to a sort of fundamental instrumentalism that finally declares the human being capable and indeed obliged to do anything desired, just as God does (as shown in Chapter 10, Feinberg [1977] falls prey to such instrumentalism). The modern god does not so much hear all as see all and know all. To see is to know, to know is to see. Therefore, it is not a mere coincidence that instrumentalism is reflected in the ubiquitous references to God as clockmaker and cosmic draftsman/ engineer, not to mention giver of sight and all that is seen. The modern world is a built world, a world to be made, not inherited or simply given (Deloria, 1999).

As laid out in Chapters 1 to 6, this glorification of instrumentation makes sense because the inaugural writers of the modern ambition were predominantly mathematicians and engineers, including social and economic engineers. Thus, the modernist cosmology is a product of an engineer's image-ination. Beginning in the Renaissance, the modern world liberated itself from medieval stories (hearsay) fixated on good versus evil to pursue pragmatic *visions* of utopia. Utopia came to be conceived in the language of machines: What is utopian is what works, what produces efficiently. The

---

[1]Logocentrism is Western modernity's search to locate the (a singular) truth at the center of a text.

[2]Kramer (1988, 1993c, 1997) stresses the danger of logocentrism (what Derrida indicates in his concern with metaphysics and violence) as moderns place so much faith in what they see. As any slight-of-hand artist knows, the eye is rather easily fooled. With current technologies of digital manipulation, faith in visual evidence—often counted as solid proof of a state of affairs (historical fact)—leaves the true believer in the precarious position of being utterly fooled. While moderns distrust hearsay, they tend to be gullible about what they see with their own eyes (Kramer, 1988, 1993c, 1997).

mechanical becomes conflated with the rational. New rational orders are envisioned and pursued; thus, we have the age of revolutions—personal, public, entrepreneurial, sexual, social, and political. Change, progress, and evolution are expressed as linear movements. Ratio and proportion are conceived as visual phenomena and institutionalized in Renaissance geometric proofs for proper perspective as even art reverts to the classical Greek ideals of mechanical drafting (Mumford, 1934/1963). The modern cosmos is conceptualized as a gigantic clockwork, in which reason is manifested as precise movement guided by eternal law. Plato's dream in the *Timaeus* of the celestial city is reborn but articulated in the way of a specific culture. And the specific culture that adopted Plato's eternal form as reasonable and like the celestial movement was Renaissance Europe. This modern adaptation is mechanical, which is to say mathematized (technological), for mathematics is a precise language of functions that interacts according to transcendental requirements beyond the mere opinions of individual mathematicians, entirely unambiguous and unbiased (Bailly & Longo, 2010).

The mystery of creation, posited by magic peoples as pure will and mythic discourse in the form of good versus evil, becomes "intelligent design" in the modern mental-rational perspective. "Intelligent design" is used here not in the sense it is used in current debates about the theory of evolution, but in the sense that the orderliness of the universe was evidence of God's righteousness and that divinity was synonymous with reason. For Emerson, the visual order of the age, such as ships moving with regularity, had a cosmic divinity to it (Mumford, 1934/1963). In modern discourse, it is common for natural and biological scientists to refer to plants, animals, the orbits of planets—in fact everything—as being engineered, designed, and ordered. However, this engineering is mechanical, not moral: Mythic good and evil are replaced by a design that is logical or illogical. Rationality becomes the good and irrationality the bad (Schlag, 1998). What follows is just one of endless examples that may be culled from any scientific periodical, scholarly or popular. This one is from the front material section "Geographica" of the December 2002 *National Geographic* magazine.

> Namibia's *Stenocara* beetle, whose bumpy back gathers moisture from fog, is teaching architects in arid lands to build better roofs. Oxford biologist Andrew Parker has discovered that the slightly flattened peaks on the bug's back attract water. Droplets then run into waxy, water-repellent valleys and are channeled into the mouth. With physicist Chris Lawrence, Parker has duplicated and enlarged this design for tents and rooftops, increasing fog-harvesting efficiency. "Animals are master engineers, so we copy them," says Parker, who has also modeled a nonreflective plastic after the eye of a 45-million-year old fossil fly. (Steinberg, 2002, p. 25)

Parker is suggesting that animals are not "master engineers" but are masterly engineered by either God or the process of evolution. In either case, unbreakable laws dictate the most efficient solutions to the design process at work. The entire universe is conceived from the engineering perspective as a problem to be resolved (Bailly & Longo, 2010).

The success of the Newtonian appropriation of appearance (which manifests as visiocentric technophilia) profits from the Baconian view of objects as already primordially technical. In the Baconian view, God provides humanity with technical inspiration from the beginning; the nature of all things, natural or not, follows this divine model of production (Koyre, 1965). In other words, what had been for Descartes (1641 Lat./1647 Fr./1901 Eng.) a necessarily direct appeal to God's creative power in the attempt to ground the essential origin of objects or things in a truth of rectitude is no longer necessary. The appeal to gods is no longer necessarily direct; rather, it flows through a quasi-technical constitution of the real (Koyre, 1965).

The irrepressible force of Aristotle fused with Christian theology to effect this mathematization of God and creation. Under the influence of a rising mutational tide of perspectival rationality signaling the end of European Medievalism, Adelard of Bath (1075-1160) launched the dawn of modern technical science with his book *Quaestiones Naturales*. Several decades later, Robert Grosseteste (1168-1253), the Bishop of Lincoln and one of the first chancellors of Oxford, founded experimental science, insisting on the use of quantitative measurement that was not related to some worldly entity, such as relying on a day as a measurement of time. At about the same time, Albertus Magnus (1200-1280) taught Thomas Aquinas that God is a logician, while the Benedictians installed the usage of the mechanical clock to mark God's temporal syncretism. Furthering the quest for precision, the Late Medieval philosopher and Aristotlean scholar Jean Buridan (1295-1318) inspired his pupil, the Bishop of Liseux, Nicolas Orseme (1323-1382), to invent the x and y axes that set the stage for the Cartesian coordinate system. Also, those who artistically depicted the Bible—most notably Giotto (1266-1337) and Ambrogio Lorenzetti (1290-1348)—began to formulate geometric perspective in painting.

The point is that the inception of the mental-rational attitude is clearly present in these medieval works as it reinterprets religion. It took almost two more centuries before Nicolaus Copernicus (1473-1543) bluntly announced that the book of creation is written in mathematics. Finally, with this declaration, God was judged to be "intelligent" according to modern mental-rational, even mathematical standards (Koyre, 1965). As Husserl (1954 Ger./1970 Eng.) discusses, the new Galilean mathematizing science emerges wherein number is all. In this numeric theism, the discursive formation of God's intellect is an engineering logic (Husserl, 1954 Ger./1970 Eng.).

•

The clearest example of this mathematicization is found in the high point of modernism, Hegel's (1812, 1813, 1816 Ger./1969 Eng.) Absolute Logic, which has had a profound effect on society, from the massive wars between the Left and Right Hegelians to the notion of economic determinism. The Market—the deified abstraction of economics—is logical. Working with clockwork precision and determination, market forces are inescapably omniscient, omnipresent, and indifferent. They impact all human behavior equally and without remorse. The Market blindly adjudicates human effort. The Market is pure logic, pure divinity. It destroys any values that cannot be translated into its own (such as sacred lands), and its failures are usually blamed on its practitioners and their lack of faith in the free market system (Cox, 1999). Prayer is replaced by consumer/economic research. It makes perfect sense that the U.S. dollar bill would have the Masonic pyramidial eye on it with the Latin phrases *Annuit Cœptis* ("He [God] has favored our undertakings") and *Novus Ordo Seclorum* ("A new order of the ages"; translations from the U.S. Department of the Treasury, 2009, p. 13). The Market is the new order of divine favor.

The all-seeing eye atop the Egyptian pyramid illustrates that the association between divinity and vision has existed since ancient times. Considering the fusion of Aristotle's profound faith in mathematical reason with medieval Christianity during the Renaissance, we can, for the reader's sake, conditionally acknowledge Carpenter and McLuhan's (1960) claim that there is, in Descartes (1641 Lat./1647 Fr./1901 Eng.), a unique correspondence between "eye culture" and "I-culture."[3] Descartes comes on the scene during the seventeenth century with his philosophical visualism. Descartes (1641 Lat./1647 Fr./1901 Eng.) culminates the modern subjectivism/individualism of the Renaissance seen especially with Leonardo da Vinci, who was very much influenced by the works of Buridan (Hughes, 1982).

The "I" of the Cartesian *cogito* or human subjectivity is the center of thought from which the "I-viewpoint" and subjectivism of modernity originates. The hypertrophy of the "I" in Cartesian subjectivism and the objectivistic configuration of space and vision are inseparable; they are two faces of the same phenomenon. With technical developments that fix observations without bodily agency (and that distance previously direct bodily activities from their original contexts), actual embodied seeing is replaced by techno-

---

[3]We say here for the reader's sake because many current students of this correspondence unfortunately hold the rather simplistic claims of the Toronto School to be authoritative on this matter. While the Toronto School and its followers lack rigor and precedence since Nietzsche (1887 Ger./1974 Eng., 1901 Ger./1967 Eng.) and Gebser (1949 Ger./1985 Eng.) each had published extensive explications of the visual bias of Western modernity well before McLuhan (1964) or Foucault (1969 Fr./1972 Eng.,1972/1980) for that matter), they are not entirely wrong about Descartes.

logical constructivism that allows vision to be mechanically stabilized. In this vein, the Greek metaphysical preference for the eternally fixed remains (in the Galilean/Newtonian configuration of the world) as operating under absolute laws of time and space. As God becomes an engineer, the machine becomes the epitome of modern perspectival metaphysics (Husserl, 1954 Ger./1970 Eng.).

As Mumford (1934/1963) and Gebser (1949 Ger./1985 Eng.) indicate, the emergence of new technologies, such as optical devices and precision timepieces that institute measurement, was as much an outcome of the modern scientific impulse as it was a result of some innate human volition to master the material world. The emergence of modern technology accompanies the emergence of modern perception. This technical and perceptual thrust shapes a world so radically different (from previous perceptions of the world) as to retrospectively render all previous worldly precedents unthinkable and imperceptible in its mental-rational purview. The world as perceived—its shapes and contours, its durations and periodicities—changes dramatically with this new age of discovery.

SCALE AND THE FIXATION OF SPACE

The spatial preoccupation of modernity is expressed by ever-greater precision, which requires ever-more diminutive subdividing of the world. These subdivisions are then arranged in hierarchical schema, supposed to operate automatically, methodically, and (ironically) *naturally*. Autonomy of method is an attempt to ensure objectivity and freedom from awareness (i.e., subject-consciousness or bias). Automation is unthinking for thinking involves consideration, interpretation, and assessment. Fixity in the form of standardization enables the fulfillment of the desire for unthinking action (Husserl, 1954 Ger./1970 Eng.).

Modernity presumes—and through discursive means establishes and maintains—a consistent version of a fixed, measurable, and systematic universe. The modern world is unitized into discrete bits that are essentially identical and infinitely divisible. Unitization enables precision and efficiency (i.e., conformity, standardization), which heralds the awakening of temporal anxiety in the modern world. Moreover, unitization empowers manipulation (and manipulators). As Gebser (1949 Ger./1985 Eng.) indicates, this fundamental way of looking at the world enables technology to reconstitute and remake the world on a grand scale. Far from being objective, engineering is desire inscribing the material world—rearranging it to meet the wishes of a particular group (or market ideology, science, etc). *Technology is making, not describing.* Hence, there is often an unexamined sense of justice and right versus wrong way to do things presumed by every utopian social engineer and futurist from Karl Marx to Ray Kurzweil. The danger is the positivistic self-righteousness found in all dictatorships, from that of the proletariat to that of genetic and technological determinism. Utopianism has a nasty tendency to limit freedom.

The domestication of space/time is the central problem of visiocentrism: to render all experience as visual/spatial (Kramer, 1992, 1994a, 1994b, 1997). Schematics, flow charts, and graphs are attempts to create visual representations of organizations and activities to aid in our conceptual understanding. Visiocentrism privileges the eye-brain, which is its strength as well as its weakness. The more faith in the veracity of mediated information grows, the more the faithful become vulnerable to the power of the medium because seeing is believing. Seeing is "real"; hence, although scales of unit measurement are social constructs having power/value only so long as convention holds, scales become real because they visually track spatialized data (Kramer, 1992). The structure of a scale enables relativization of one point to another, which institutionalizes subjective judgment within the structure of the scale itself. Once institutionalized, a scale is inoculated from reflection, and it becomes presumed as indifferent, as objective. But by plotting one point as relative to others, the *supposedly objective* scale presets judgment to create a picture of reality that is pure interest. For example, when the arrow goes down on the graph of a stock, that is *bad* for the investor. Or when a plot of temperatures goes up, today is hotter than yesterday (and when an upward trend or pattern appears, it indicates an undesirable heat wave).

Graphic displays structure how things are seen relative to other constructed points or values. Scales orient the world spatially, including invisible phenomena such as opinions, so these phenomena can be made visible and thereby grasped (understood or made to become "real"). But as Ihde (1990, 1998) illustrates through the example of a map, scales do more than simply orient things spatially. The graphed relationships in maps are materialized as spatial extensions; that is, relationships are reduced to ratios. The map not only orients a point but also shows this point as farther than another one (Ihde, 1990, 1998). As scales transform things into spatial quantities, they become real. As we look at these scales in making our decisions, that reality shapes our actions. In this sense of making reality, scales are manifestations of magic consciousness. As magical phenomena, ratios are seen as things-in-themselves, as if the numbers are independent of human action. For the modern scientist, measures constitute the thing itself. But the process of transforming a thing into quantified operational units introduces subjective perspective (Ihde, 1990, 1998).

Operationalizations contain the essentially modern prejudice that the phenomenon defined is conceived as being measurable. This is the modern metaphysics of idealism, of "pure mathematics." For anything to be real, it must be essentially divisible into quanta. Things are presumed to be fixed as spatial and unitary. As Kramer (1997) observes, "[O]perational definitions include *a priori*, the means of *creating the phenomenon as measurement*. . . . By this operation, the world becomes a mathematical product" (p. 115; italics in original). The world becomes a construction, the product of operations, of human *qua* perspectival agency.

Much of modernity is founded on the belief that God (or gods) made the universe logically and mathematically; the representational epistemology of discovery amounts to human beings retro-engineering the universe. In discovering the mathematical relationships of the universe and dutifully recording a second-order mimetic universe in the form of numerical modeling, human beings forget that mathematics exists nowhere in nature; that it is a language, a discursive language-game. The ontological distinction between the scientific article and the thing it describes—the fact that they bear no actual resemblance to each other whatsoever—is lost. Thus, scientists who work in the mathematizing Galilean style of science fail to recognize that they are living the linguisticality of *Dasein*, just as Heidegger (1927 Ger./1962 Eng.) argued. While objectivism rejects ontological and linguistic contingencies such as those described by the Sapir-Whorf hypothesis (Whorf, 1956) as irrational relativism, this hypothesis describes mathematization well. Mathematics (for rationalists) is not a mere contingent language among other languages; it is the undisputed best way to ponder and articulate the universe—and (for many rationalists) the only authentic, legitimate way of knowing. The fetishization of language (in this case, mathematics) is complete when scientists proclaim that the universe is inherently logical, that the "book of creation" is written in mathematics. Their language is *the real*. This is pure linguisticality, and their metaphysical prejudice is just as strong as the prejudices of those who claim that one must read the Quran in Arabic and the Torah in Hebrew, or that one must speak a magical spell exactly as it originated, without translation or modification, or it will not work.

To summarize, the identities, values, and patterns that scales generate are mythical when they are assumed to exist before human intervention and are represented, or rather revealed, by measurement. Mythically, measurement is not seen as identical with what it measures; however, the numerical values are not wholly arbitrary either. There is an emotional association between the two. Insofar as a thing is defined as—or by—its measures, numerical scale structure reveals its magical identification.

PERSPECTIVISM AND MODERN TECHNOLOGICAL PERCEPTION

The development of three-dimensional perspective is one of the major hallmarks of mental consciousness. Gebser (1949 Ger./1985 Eng.), Ihde (1990), and Koyre (1965) indicate that "establishment of the laws of perspective is significant in that it made technical drafting feasible and thereby initiated the technological age" (Gebser, 1949 Ger./1985 Eng., p. 19). Still, while the reality created by the advent of perspectivalism has affected great expansions in human knowledge and works, it has also affected great reductions. Gebser (1949 Ger./1985 Eng.) asserts, "Perspectival vision and thought confine us within spatial limitations. . . . The positive result is a concretion of [human] and space; the negative result is the restriction of [human] to a limited segment where [the individual] perceives only one sector of reality" (p. 18). By virtue of the perspectival human's increased ability to sharpen focus, the world becomes increasingly narrow. Vision becomes "sectorized by the blinders of the perspectival worldview," and "the deeper and farther [humans] extend [their] view into space, the narrower is the sector of [their] visual pyramid" (Gebser, 1949 Ger./1985 Eng., p. 23).

As humans become materialists (i.e., the more they reject the existence of non-spatial things), their perceptual and perhaps even conceptual horizons narrow. Vast domains of human experience become illegitimate for rational discussion when objects in the world can be considered only if they can be spatialized and operationalized (Gebser, 1949 Ger./1985 Eng.).

The basic concern of perspective is "to 'look through' space and thereby to perceive and grasp space rationally" (Gebser, 1949 Ger./1985 Eng., p. 19). With its detached objectivism, the development of perspective is a triumph of the rationalist sense of reality as well as a triumph of human ambition for power with its negation of distances (and of uncertainty). Modernity is dedicated to friction-free speed in spatial and calculative mobility. Progress is measured in how fast things can be moved and problems can be solved. With modern technology, this desire reaches the final point—the vanishing point, or what Heidegger (1952, 1954, 1962 Ger./1977 Eng.) calls "distantlessness." Gebser (1949 Ger./1985 Eng.) asserts that this tendency can be seen as a process of establishing and systematizing the external world and the concurrent expansion of the ego sphere.

Gebser (1949 Ger./1985 Eng.) provides two important remarks regarding perspectivism. The first contains one of da Vinci's earliest general definitions of perspective: "Perspective is a proof or test, confirmed by our experience, that all things project their images toward the eye in pyramidal lines" (as quoted in Gebser, 1949 Ger./1985 Eng., p. 20). "The eye" is *my eye*, and thus we have the spatial objective world inextricably presupposing the hypertrophic subject. Objectivity is extrapolated from subjectivity.

For Gebser (1949 Ger./1985 Eng.), the ultimate achievement of perspectivity is the operationalization of "aerial perspective," perfected in the god's eye view of Leonardo da Vinci's *Last Supper*.

In line with the rise of inductive epistemology, categorical truths are derived from multiple, contingent observations. Like Galileo, this attitude expresses da Vinci's combination of "Platonic, even pre-Platonic animism with Aristotelian empiricism as 'all things project their images toward the eye' and the eye does not perceive but rather, suffers or endures" (Gebser, 1949 Ger./1985 Eng., p. 20). This formulation is held to be an essential truth about all contingent perceptions. For da Vinci, his formulation of aerial perspective is true for all possible vision. His way of rendering perspective *is the one correct way*. For Gebser (1949 Ger./1985 Eng.), "[T]his creates an unusual and even disquieting tension between the two parts of the [above quoted] sentence, since the purely Aristotelian notion of the first part [i.e., 'perspective is a proof or test,'] not only speaks of proof but indeed proceeds from the 'experience' of early science" (p. 20) as not merely a perspective among countless others but as the one and only rational and accurate perspective; hence, calling it "God's eye view."

Da Vinci's struggle within himself reflects "the transitional situation between the unperspectival and the perspectival worlds" (Gebser, 1949 Ger./1985 Eng., p. 20) (see Figure 14.1). The source of the tension is the fear of relativism and contingency. Objectivity makes sense only if seeing—the eye and all media—is considered passive and inert, the eye as enduring impressions rather than structuring them. Hence, the radicality of the Kantian-Copernican inversion of Locke (Kant, 1781 Ger./1929 Eng.; Locke, 1690/1996)—only much later and less rigorously than many of their predecessors (e.g., McLuhan's [1964] argument that the medium [the human body in the case of empiricism] is not passive but influential, and Üexkull's [1957] observation that human eyeballs behold a different empirical reality than fly or owl or cat eyeballs). This is where Merleau-Ponty's (1945 Fr./1962 Eng.) notion of the sensical body comes in. Without the structuring transducing activity of the body, there can be no sensation (Kramer, 2000a).

The second note on perspective is illustrative of da Vinci's complete dissociation from the dominant unperspectival structure of ancient and early medieval consciousness. In its measurements, perspective employs two counter-posed pyramids. One has its vertex in the eye and its base on the horizon. The second has its base resting against the eye and its vertex at the horizon (see Figure 14.1). Da Vinci explains these two pyramids: "The first pyramid is the more general perspective since it encompasses all dimensions of an object facing the eye . . . while the second refers to a specific position . . . and this second perspective results from the first" (as quoted in Gebser, 1949 Ger./1985 Eng., p. 20). Gebser (1949 Ger./1985 Eng.) continues to explain da Vinci's definition of perspective:

> These remarks express the change from a *participation inconsciente* to what we may call a *relation consciente*, or conscious relationship. Leonardo was able to place the vanishing point in space (on the horizon) in opposition to the passive or "enduring" point of the eye, the receptor of the stream of object impressions and thus, realized the close interrelationship between the two. (p. 20)

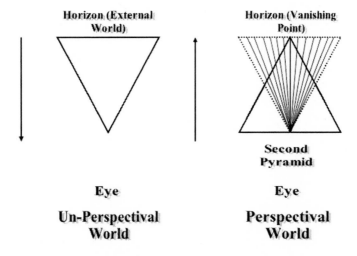

Fig. 14.1. Perspective from pre-perspectival to perspectival world

Gebser (1949 Ger./1985 Eng.) argues that in the second pyramid:

The emphasis has shifted to the eye of the subject, the eye that has realized space, and, as such has established an equilibrium between the ego
world (of the eye) and the external world (the horizon). The statement
by Leonardo also represents a conceptual realization or actualization of
perspective, a realization that has logically, geometrically, and fixedly
determined the Western image of the world ever since. (p. 20)

Correct seeing is (ironically) essentially perspectival. Thus, the pre- and
unperspectival magic and mythic ways of being are discredited as invalid.

The growing emphasis on perspective results in a growing fixation on
one's position in the world as the source of perspective. Gebser (1949
Ger./1985 Eng.) argues,

The magnification of space and spatiality that increases with every century since 1500 is at once the greatness as well as the weakness of perspectival humanity. Their maximization of the "objectively" external, a
consequence of an excessively visual orientation, leads not only to
rationalization but also, to an unavoidable hypertrophy of the "I,"
which is in confrontation with the external world. This exaggeration of

the "I" amounts to what may be called an ego-hypertrophy: the "I" must be increasingly emphasized, indeed, over-emphasized, in order for it to be adequate to the ever-expanding discovery of space. (p. 22)

Gebser's (1949 Ger./1985 Eng.) argument nicely summarizes two results of the modern objectivistic paradigm that is expressed as the form of the hypertrophic "I." First, he indicates:

The expansion of space brings on the gradual expansion, and consequent disintegration of the "I" on the one hand, preparing favorable circumstances for collectivism. On the other hand, the haptification of space rigidifies and encapsulates the "I," with the resultant possibility of isolation evident in egocentrism. (p. 22)[4]

Following Gebser's (1949 Ger./1985 Eng.) configuration, perspective changed from ambiguous mythic to an objective-deterministic mental-rational consciousness structure. In other words, nothing less than a mutation in consciousness and perception occurred.

As a consequence, increasing precision as quantification replaced concern for qualities as the dominant theme of the time. However; this replacement is not a putting aside, but rather a penetration and fusion—or in Gebser's (1949 Ger./1985 Eng.) term, "plus-mutation." In this way, the pre-perspectival quotidian form of perception—with its tendency to grant the qualitative and the imprecise—is dominated by the new, more radically appropriating rational perceptual form.

With regard to this perceptual mutation, Ihde (1990, 1998) and Heelan (1983) explain that the disappearance of non-Euclidean space in conjunction with the appearance of the Renaissance technique of perspective was exemplified by da Vinci's perspectivism and offers a striking example of the way in which a specific transformation of the everyday realm paves the way for the advent of early modern science. The appearance of modern science involves not only the transformation of perception but also the new science's bold claim that it is entirely self-motivated and thoroughly clear about—and in control of—its own aims.

However, according to Ihde (1998), modern technology precedes modern science insofar as modern technology plays a central role in the perceptual mutation that embodies the legacy without which modern science could not arise. The innumerable aspects of technological utopianism—such as

---

[4]Uniquely Modern collectivism or "mass society," as opposed to pre-modern community, is not only closely related to the expansion of space, the consequence "being lost" in space, the alienation of the individual, but it is also conditioned by a temporal-psychic component.

Feinberg's (1977) position—imply the increasing indispensability and invisibility of technology. In other words, various technologies gather intimacy and thus become more and more familiar to the ways of our seeing and speaking in everyday life. They also take on the sense of being logical but, as such, inevitable. To paint correctly is to submit to the dictates of geometric proof. Painting becomes "by the numbers" (Kramer, 1997, p. 113). Painting and technical drafting converge.

The dominance of the mechanical paradigm in early modern science offers a direct yet subtle formulation of a new light and an order that was provided by the then new technical horizon. As Descartes demonstrates the limitations of empiricism, he shows how both body and world must, according to the Lockean (Locke, 1690/1996) doctrine, necessarily function according to strictly mechanical laws. The human body comes to be viewed as an "automata," as a robot or thing like a candle sitting on a desk.

> We say, for example, that we see the same wax when it is before us, and not that we judge it to be the same from its retaining the same color and figure: I should therefore be disposed to conclude that the wax is known by the act of sight, and not by the intuition of the mind alone, were it not for the analogous instance of human being passing on in the street below, as observed from a window. In this case I do not fail to say that I see the men themselves, just as I say that I see the wax; and yet what do I see from the window beyond hats and cloaks that might cover artificial machines, whose motions might be determined by springs? (Descartes, 1641 Lat./1647 Fr./1901 Eng., ¶13)

However, with the advent of the Newtonian denial of Cartesianism, Newtonians do not call the mechanical paradigm entirely into question. Instead, the questioning is selective, leaving the paradigm in unbroken form in terms of the operations of sense perception (Koyre, 1965, pp. 54-56). In fact, this is the Lockean model with little revision as one can see when reading *An Essay Concerning Human Understanding* (Locke, 1690/1996). If the mechanistic approach gradually loses its popularity, it is only because it does not faithfully follow the driving force of an already transformed technological tendency, a tendency that tries to *incarnate* technology into human perception (Ellul, 1954 Fr./1964 Eng., 1977 Fr./1980 Eng.; Mumford, 1934/1963). In the end, the earlier layers of integration suspect that not all is well with Frankenstein.

Contrary to (so-called) objectivistically biased science, our perception is neither a fixed nor an ahistorical structure. People have not always seen the world quite the way modern—especially Western—people do. As Kramer (1997) indicates, "[S]ome cultures present an atomistic, fragmentary mode of being, while others present a more animistic and fluid world" (p. x). It is becoming increasingly evident that our post-Renaissance perspective stems from a historical formation that has manifested itself within the last 500 years. According to Kramer (1997),

> Some cultures qualify, or establish a quantifiable type of space and time, while other cultures establish (through their expressions) spaces and times that are qualitatively different. Leonardo da Vinci did not "discover" three-dimensional depth-space, as if it were somewhere or somewhen else. Rather, he established it by articulating it. (p. x)

Therefore, this unique historical mode of perception (i.e., da Vinci's vision) characterizes early modern science. Koyre (1968) indicates that the destruction of the *Kosmos* and this emergence of a universe of homogeneity in its place is a direct and profound result of seeing the world in a radically new manner (see also Ramo, 1999). From this historical point on, modern science began to pronounce itself to be an ahistorical institution—God's view. According to the modern scientific viewpoint, everything obscure is declared unthinkable and imperceptible, and, therefore, is necessarily *unreal.* Clarity becomes the prime parameter of the real and the perceivable. In this configuration, that which does not make itself manifested to consciousness as qualitatively clear in thought and vision is regarded as fictitious.

Modern people finally find in the new geometric approach of the Renaissance perspective, a new "true" form of revelation, a new world possibility. However, as Merleau-Ponty (1964 Fr./1968 Eng.) recognizes, it is no "infallible" gimmick. It is only "a particular case, a date, a moment in the poetic information of the world which continues after it" (p. 175). In other words, perspective is never "instituted by nature"; rather, "it is to be made and remade over and over again" (p. 175). Merleau-Ponty (1964 Fr./1968 Eng.) recognizes the way in which technical perception covers up its own status as a perceptual form. The transformation of perception by technology holds, at its most negative, the danger of entirely forgetting itself as perception, as just a historical possibility. However, "our perception is cultural-historical," and therefore "the perception of the world is formed in the world" (Merleau-Ponty, 1964 Fr./1968 Eng., p. 253). As Roland Barthes (1973 Fr./1975 Eng.) declares, the denial of history is a basic tenet of myth-making. This point would be the common emphasis for every phenomenology discussed heretofore. Meanwhile, McLuhan (1964) also seems to understand the relation between the transformation of perception and technology, although he has critical shortcomings in understanding the nature of that transformation from the phenomenological standpoint; he gets closer to the point of "overemphasis on visual sensorium" (Kramer, 1993c, p. 107; see also Kramer, 1993a) yet fails to understand the concept of "embodied vision."

MCLUHAN'S SENSORIUM: A TRUNCATED ECOLOGY

The Body of the Television Set

For McLuhan (1964), like Innis (1951), the medium of communication shapes and controls the structures of the human sensorium and association. The message is contentless. The most important aspect of McLuhan's thought is what he says about the effects of the medium on the sensorium. According to McLuhan (1964), a change in the medium changes the ratio mixture or rationality of the senses. In this vein, McLuhan (1964) declares, "[I]n the electronic age, we wear all mankind [*sic*] as our skin" (p. 47).[5]

According to Carpenter and McLuhan (1960), the typographic period is characterized by the preeminence of the space-binding power of the eye over the time-binding power of the ear. Speaking of typographic culture as "eye culture," McLuhan says, "Truth, we think, must be observed by the 'eye,' and judged by the 'I' . . . most of our thinking is done in terms of visual models, even when an auditory one might prove more efficient" (Carpenter & McLuhan, 1960, p. 66). By associating television with tactility, as opposed to vision, McLuhan contrives to heighten the sense of a union between human and the medium as technology. For McLuhan (1964), tactility represents the utmost intimacy of human with technology. Whereas sight is the least intimate sense, when touch predominates within the sensorium, it is the most intimate relationship between the human and the environment.

Ong (1977) also orders the sensorium in this manner: Touch—Taste—Smell—Hearing—Sight. The sensory direction from touch to sight indicates the movement toward greater distance, abstraction, formalization, objectification, and idealization, whereas the opposite direction indicates greater proximity, concreteness, potency, subjectivity, and actual existence. As discussed in Chapter 11, this ordering of the sensorium can be found in the order of signs in Peirce's configuration of his semiotics. According to his theory of dimensional accrual and dissociation, Kramer (1997) also tends to agree with this relative dissociation among the senses; however, he also argues for a more complex neo-Kantian notion of manifold as including moods, memories, habits, beliefs, and emotions. Kramer (1997), not unlike Peirce's (1931, 1958) configuration, suggests that the ordering of the sensorium is not hierarchical. While Peirce (1931, 1958) suggests degrees of dissociation, Kramer (1997) speaks in terms of intensities so that even the perspectival tendency to posit spatial extension can also be discussed in terms of intensity.

---

[5]The elevation of the role of media in McLuhan (1964) is more thoroughly criticized by Mumford (1970) for its technological determinism and other over-generalizations. Mumford's critique on McLuhan's position is more meticulous than those of more recent efforts by others, such as Meyrowitz (1985) and Mosco (1989).

McLuhan's (1964) idea of the tactility of electronic technology or television is an incredible proposition that is (at least phenomenologically) untenable and inadmissible. This is because McLuhan's (1964) configuration contains a fundamental confusion between two ontological categories: the human and the technological. As Kramer (2004a) has noted in his discussion of synthetes, technology is not essential to the integration of the sensorium, nor of the overall manifold, which includes far more than sensory input. Harkening back to Kant (1781 Ger./1929 Eng.), the categorical a priori of space and time are not technological functions. Space (as a dimension) is not a spatial thing among other things, nor is time (as a dimension) a product of measurement, be it historical or chronographic. They are not organizing principles; rather, they are part of the world. Stated differently, McLuhan (1964) replaces the primacy of the sensing subject (body) where transcendence, including the invisible, is rescendent (not transcendent) with that of the sensed medium. McLuhan (1964) offers a sort of hyper-behaviorism or sensationalism abstracting an epiphenomenal sensorium into transcendence and thus neglecting the lived body. That is, McLuhan (1964) treats the message as a totalizing experience. For him, when we watch television, the image on the screen is all that we see and experience, as if it were projected directly into our brains, rather than a message that we incorporate into the larger embodied experience that we live out. Such an understanding of technology as transparent falls under Ihde's (1990, 1998) embodied relation and treats the human being as technicization.

Television viewing or watching belongs to what Wittgenstein (1953) categorizes as "seeing as," or seeing a "picture-object" *essentially*.[6] This has to do with the body of the television set as an object within the world and met there by my embodied awareness. The rules of the game are given in various examples of games—even as they are not contingent content but structures that enable sense making. Such is also the case of the structure of the television set as it is encountered by the lived-body and the relationship between the visible and the invisible. The television embodies prejudices and, as such, projects its own horizon that structures seeing, thus limiting the romantic sense of unlimited Sartrean freedom that Merleau-Ponty (1945 Fr./1962 Eng.) recognized as phenomenologically false. One need only think of the initially disorienting experience of watching a musical performed live on stage after years of strictly television and movies. With no clearly guided focus from the director (as in television), one is consciously aware of the need to choose where to look. The television set, as a body, is evident when

---

[6]Wittgenstein (1953) makes a distinction between "seeing" and "seeing as," that is, seeing a real object and seeing it as a picture or an image. For Wittgenstein, there is the "categorical difference" between seeing a real object and seeing a picture-object: the latter or "the flashing of an aspect on us seems half visual experience, half thought" (p. 197).

one breaks concentration from its images long enough to ponder its existence as a piece of furniture like others within a living space. Such a deconstruction of its privileged position within lived experience exposes its incredible finitude and, thus, the myth of its extension. The flesh can be reversed, exposing our attentiveness to the television set to be an expression of our own curiosity. No doubt the television set within one's living room is often beheld as special, as unique among the objects there, but it can be seen otherwise.

McLuhan's (1964) association of the television viewing experience with tactility confuses the visual with the tactile and masks or redirects us away from seeing it as both a tactile object and therefore an assemblage of prejudices. Our way of seeing thus remains structured by it. By associating television with tactility, McLuhan (1964) instantly and romantically homogenizes human and machine. McLuhan's conception of the medium as technology merely places the human body as the natural mediator between human and the world. The human body is no longer regarded as the anchor point of perception, as having the ability to look away or shift our attitude toward the television set as an object. Rather (McLuhan reduces), the human body is surrendered to the medium of communication called television. From the phenomenological standpoint, at least from Merleau-Ponty's (1945 Fr./1962 Eng., 1960 Fr./1964 Eng., 1964 Fr./1968 Eng.) position, to understand the carnal source of tactility means to understand the notion of embodiment, to understand the "flesh" of the body as Being-in-the-World. This includes the television set as an embodied projection.

Critiquing McLuhan's Mixed Metaphors

Ihde (1979) opposes McLuhan's presentation of the shift from one (vision) to another dominant sensory form (hearing), insisting, "[T]he reduction of early modern scientific culture was *not* so much a reduction *to* vision as the McLuhanites hold, but *a reduction of vision*. What is needed is a re-evaluation of the full range of possibilities within sensory experience" (p. 99; italics added). Consequently, Ihde proposes a fully phenomenological restoration of vision along the path already opened by Merleau-Ponty (as previously discussed in Chapters 12 and 13). Merleau-Ponty (1968 Fr./1970 Eng.) has understood more profoundly that "perception itself is polymorphic and that if it becomes Euclidian, this is because it allows itself to be oriented by a system" (p. 212). Accordingly, in the technological milieu, if vision and hearing become attuned to the potentials of technology, it is because our perceptions are concretely situated within a newly orienting system.

Television as a "reproducing" medium of communication is preeminently visual and auditory. McLuhan's metaphor of tactility for television deceptively conceals its visualness. So too does the Internet and almost all

computer-mediated media. McLuhan (1964) conceals the fact that our existence, channeled by television, is a visual enframing. That is to say, McLuhan
(1964) neglects the fact that television processes, programs, focuses, skews,
selects, edits, and so on. It is not a medium so much as a maker of a style of
seeing. In essence, the casting of both its visual image and sound is all
enframed. Television, therefore, disconnects rather than integrates the operative senses of vision and hearing, which creates a sensory schizophrenia. We
believe only half of what we hear but all of what we see. Hearsay is trumped
by personal observation.

In television, the natural informational balance between aural and visual has been shattered. Information that we take in with the visual sense cannot be used to modify or help the information from the aural sense because
they have each been isolated from the other and reconstructed according to
the structure of the apparatus, which includes more than merely the physical biases concretized in the television set. Thus, for Heim (1993), as well as
for other virtual reality (VR) theorists and critics, VR may be an exciting
new medium of representation; but like all imitations, it must always be distinguished from and grounded in a clear sense of reality. Going beyond the
modern representational metaphysic, television is no more a mirror than it
is a window. What television presents is *itself*. What one sees "on" television
has no correlate in reality, as if it were an innocent and transparent window
onto the world. Television is both a producer and product at once. But
because of the modern visocentric bias, we are vulnerable to confusing it
with seeing some postulated reality "out there," brought into our living
rooms via some mechanical and simple extension of our optic nerve. When
one watches television, one is not seeing "the world out there" as though it
were merely a window, merely an extension. Rather, television (like all technologies) is a projection of our already extant prejudices. We like it because
it "agrees" with us. It is not a reflection of the modern world; instead, it is
an expression of it. Television is (as the Frankfurt theorists understood) a
means of cultural production.

Mass image technologies also lack depth. Technologies focus, increase,
and project desires and wants. Simplification is a form of elimination of context and intensification. Technologies (including television) are thus "reductive" when compared to plenary, constant, and active or full sensory experience. Imaging technologies are neither virtual nor actual. They are as real, as
culturally artifactual, as other phenomena, and as such they are substitutable
(Kramer, 1993a). Within the multiple uses of scientific imaging, there is a
spectrum that runs from partial isomorphism to variations upon isomorphism that move away from the "literal" (or copy) form and toward a certain kind of "fictive" (or technologically enhanced) variation. But after the
Cartesian metaphysical bias has been bracketed as a cultural prejudice, modern technological seeing exists as no more or less real than so-called "natu-

ral" vision (seeing in the lifeworld). The problem comes when the essential differences are lost and one form of vision substitutes for (or even "improves on") the other. Television is indeed different from other forms of seeing, and this difference has real consequences for culture and society and its members. Although the intent of television (especially televised news broadcasts) is to reveal, to highlight "real" phenomena, the complex journalistic story-telling techniques employed have consequences similar to the positivistic fixing function that can be done through digitally enhanced photography—an ethical issue in journalistic contexts today (Kramer, 1994a, 1994b). Because seeing is believing for moderns, such techniques have not only epistemological but also ethical implications in social science as well as in journalism. Digital photography manipulation forces us to recall (to openly discuss, meta-analytically) the difference between reality and fiction. While none of the imaging described mimics old-fashioned notions of copy-epistemology, it does, through variational means, refer to "real effects." Without a negative, there is no way to trace back to any source of representational truth. Digital photography manipulation can lead (some would perhaps argue that it *has led*) this visual culture into the crisis of being unable to trust any image.

MERLEAU-PONTY'S THEORY OF EMBODIED VISION

The body as expression lies at the center of Merleau-Ponty's concerns. He sees this as being the essence of the body as an open and appropriative structure. Therefore, the question of embodiment is obviously a major theme of Merleau-Ponty's work. However, it would be hasty to say that Merleau-Ponty reifies the "lived body" above all else. If the "lived body" (*corps proper*) stands at the center of his ongoing exploration of incarnation, it will only be so in the more broad sense of the term the "proper body" as articulated in the notion of "flesh." What Merleau-Ponty's (1947, 1955, 1964 Fr./1964 Eng.) account of the lived body and flesh introduces is the possibility of a world in which essential form stems from neither a constant and ever-lasting objective presence nor the interpretations or expressivity of a thinking subject. Merleau-Ponty (1947, 1955, 1964 Fr./1964 Eng.) criticizes the scientific vision of Cartesian objectivistic bias that holds the contemporary technicization of the body as objective body. What is missing, Merleau-Ponty argues, is the realization that such a body is a product, and the process that yields that particular sense of the body is technicization. Heidegger (1927 Ger./1962 Eng.) succinctly makes this point: "The kind of Being which belongs to entities within-the-world is something which they themselves might have been permitted to present; but Descartes does not let them do so" (p. 129). Hence, the confinement of the status of objects (including the body) to a realm of simple existence is untenable in itself. It is possible only within the modern, biased configuration of clear-cut subject and object dualism.

McLuhan (1964) misunderstands Merleau-Ponty's argument concerning vision. It is a mistake to conclude that Merleau-Ponty places vision in a privileged position within the hierarchical order of senses. Rather, for Merleau-Ponty (1968 Fr./1970 Eng.), *visibility is a generality of the sensible*, an exemplar sensible, or one variant of the variations of the sensorium, as the flesh of the body, or, as Being-in-the-World. As "there is the visible seer," so too exists "the audible hearer" and "the tangible toucher" (pp. 254-260). Therefore, there is just a circular interplay of senses; the senses are interlaced or intertwined. Accordingly, Merleau-Ponty (1964 Fr./1968 Eng.) is cautious about the modern seduction of "a fundamental narcissism of all vision" (p. 139). Based on this narcissistic tendency for the visual, the idea that "seeing is believing" is endemic to television viewers (or, perhaps more accurately, television consumers, as we do so much more than view television programming). As Merleau-Ponty (1964 Fr./1968 Eng.) illustrates, the fact that people *must learn to see* the world means that there is also a will to believe in what people see, even though what people see on the screen is enframed, reproduced as pictures. Television images are more than mere reproduction. As a projection of the flesh, television (including its prejudices) produces a *way* of seeing in addition to what is seen.[7]

Merleau-Ponty (1964 Fr./1968 Eng.) provides a new understanding of seeing or vision, what he calls "embodied vision":

> It is an idea not of a slice of the objective world between me and the horizon, and not of an objective ensemble organized synthetically (under an idea), but of an axis of equivalencies — of an axis upon which all the perceptions that can be met with there are equivalent, not with respect to the objective conclusion they authorize (for in this respect they are quite different), but in that they are all under the power of my vision of the moment. Elementary example: *all the perceptions are implicated in my actual I can—*.

---

[7]Mander (1978) indicates the lack of people's learning to see the nature of a framed world fully and points out the bias toward naïve belief about what people are seeing. He argues, "Without the human bias toward belief, the media could not exist. What's more, because the bias is so automatic and unnoticed, the media, all media, are in a position to exploit the belief, to encourage you to believe in their questionable sensory information. . . . The media, all media but particularly moving-image media, which present data so nearly natural, effectively convert our naïve and automatic trust in the reliability of images into their own authority" (pp. 249-250).

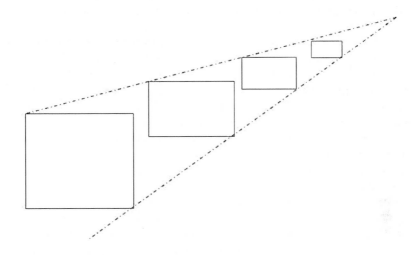

Fig. 14.2. Apparent shapes via perspective

What is seen (in one of my perceptions) can be an object near and small or large and far-off. . . . The ray of the world is neither this series of logical possibilities, nor the law that defines them—(interobjective relation)—It is the gaze within which they are all simultaneous, *fruits of my I can*—It is the very vision of depth. . . . The "ray of the world" is *not a synthesis* and *not* "*reception*," but, *segregation* i.e., implies that one is already *in the world* or *in being*. One carves in a being that remains in its place, of which one does not make a *synopsis*—and which is not in itself. (pp. 241-242; italics added)

Here, Merleau-Ponty appreciates that before the voice of reason there is the voice of things, and the ability, or rather, the pre-institutionalized possibility, of the authentic Other—on their own terms—the subject. This includes nature and the environment, including our built environment, which has become our habitat, the world that is co-constituted (Kramer, 1993a, 1995, 2004a, 2013). It shapes us as we shape it. Here we can begin to see television as subject rather than as object and begin to realize that we experience television in terms of (in the arena of) interpersonal communication rather than mass communication. It is part of our synthesized body, of our vision, just as the cane is for the blind person. It alters the way we see. How often now do we hear eye witnesses describe an event by saying, "it was just like a movie." Merleau-Ponty's (1964 Fr./1968 Eng.) explanation enables us to emphasize the co-constitutive process of seeing between world and institutionalized body—how television, radio, stereos, the computer interact with us, and how we are affected by the encounters.

Gebser's (1949 Ger./1985 Eng.) explanation of Georges Braque (i.e., *Man with Guitar*, 1911-1912) and Pablo Picasso's efforts (i.e., shadows moving across rooftops in *Maisons sur la colline—Horta de Ebro*, 1909) to paint time and three-dimensional space on canvas illustrates the synthetic concretization across duration that Merleau-Ponty describes. We add here the insights of Cézanne (i.e., *Mont Sainte-Victoire*, 1887), which taught Braque and Picasso so much, as well as one more example of temporal synthesis expressed in Marcel Duchamp's equally illustrative *Nude Descending a Staircase No. 2* (1912). The reader can see in these exactly what is meant.

All of these, as well as the explosion of relativism in all fields from physics to literature, illustrate the concretization Merleau-Ponty (1945 Fr./1962 Eng.) was explaining in terms of bodily synthesis including motility, space, and time. According to Gebser (1949 Ger./1985 Eng.), "[W]e accord to the present, for both space and time exist for the perceptual capacities of our body only in the present via presentiation" (pp. 25-26). The presentation or making present evident in Picasso's drawing was possible only after he was able to *actualize* (i.e., bring to consciousness) all of the temporal *structures of the past latent* in himself (in other words, those structures that are *institutionalized* in him). Only where time emerges as pure present, and time is no longer divided into its three phases of past, present, and future, can it be said to be concrete. To the extent that Picasso from the outset reached out beyond the present, incorporating the future into the present of his work, he was able to presentiate (or make present) the past.

Stated from the phenomenological standpoint, relational distance is the intentional distance that must include both the referent object and the perceiving, perspectival "lived" body; however, not in the same way as in Cartesian-Newtonian frames. Therefore, what must be avoided is the ideal observer (or god's eye) as simultaneous sight. Merleau-Ponty's embodied vision provides the way to overcome the tendencies toward the Cartesian-Newtonian objectivistic bias (positivism).

For Merleau-Ponty, the Cartesian-Newtonian ideal perspective is impossible. As Merleau-Ponty (1964 Fr./1968 Eng.) insists:

> In short, there is no essence, no idea that does not adhere to a domain of history and of geography. Not that it is *confined* there and inaccessible for the other, but because, like that of nature, the space or time of culture is not surveyable from above, and because the communication from one constituted culture to another occurs through the wild region wherein they all have originated. (p. 115; italics added)

Hence, for Merleau-Ponty (1945 Fr./1962 Eng., 1964 Fr./1968 Eng.), there can be no pure objects (things) of vision because there is no pure or omniscient visibility. This is the myth of television. Television is a strong expression of the perspectival consciousness structure as it inflates what is actually a narrow slice of vision (e.g., giving marginal groups mainstream coverage). The more people attend to this tiny slice, the more cultural streamlining occurs, including a particular way of seeing, and seeing that particular way as *the best/only way* (without seeing that we're seeing that). But it can be revaluated as just another noise-making appliance among other appliances, de-privileged, decentered. We can redirect our gaze toward it (i.e., by turning it off and watching it anyway), opening a space for reflection rather than consumption, thereby escaping its structuring tyranny. One can literally look away and refocus intentionality, making of it one thing among other things in the room. As Merleau-Ponty (1964 Fr./1968 Eng.) argues, even the future and past are caught up in the cohesion that is visibility. But this structure of the flesh can be reversed so that the visible is re-historicized, re-contextualized—in a word, demythologized.

Following Merleau-Ponty (1964 Fr./1968 Eng.), the regularities we devoutly seek (as well as the unmanageable differences that offend our sense of conformity) spring from the fact that objects are not isolable and interchangeable individual things permanently fixed in an objective time and space (so absolutism/ideal forms are wrong). Certainly regularities exist— even lawful structures—but this does not permit us to assume that the world is laid out before us as a detailed topographical map. Rather, the world is inhabited with beings, *each possessing a certain manner of managing the domain of space and time* over which it has competence to pronounce judgment and articulate. In other words, people should understand that such a map is not a depiction of a fixed entity but rather a product of catching up and structuring time and space. Once this is realized, then, as Nietzsche (1887 Ger./1974 Eng.) argues, an infinity of possibilities appears.[8] Life, as potential, can reemerge.

The following illustration helps elucidate Merleau-Ponty's (1964 Fr./1968 Eng.) embodied vision concept more clearly. Let's suppose a situa-

---

[8]In the same vein, Dreyfus and Rabinow (1983) indicate that Foucault "should be seen not as a historian but as a new kind of map-maker—maps made for use, not to mirror the terrain" (p. 128). Dreyfus and Rabinow suggest that Foucault's genealogical approach to the past reflects Foucault's awareness of the contingent character of every historical truth, his recognition that knowledge is moved by pragmatic concerns. "Genealogy," a term Foucault borrows from Nietzsche (1887 Ger./1974 Eng.), acknowledges the interpreter's involvement in the activity of sense making. For Foucault, the correspondence theory of reality is dead. Therefore, Foucault cannot claim to give us a true history, one that is adequate to the past, that represents it correctly, that gets the (or more of the) whole picture. The history of the present explicitly and self-reflectively begins with a diagnosis of the current situation.

tion in which both the still photographer and the motion picture camera-person working on a film decide how much time the recording should take. There is an important difference between them concerning the perception of time. The motion picture cameraperson has to pay attention to time while the cameras "work." This is a way of paying attention to time that is irrele-vant to and not experienced by the still photographer. This sense-difference between these two interpretations of time becomes clearer when we try to imagine the conditions of recordings.

In order to do this, one can imagine someone recording a short film showing only one room, nothing changing in it, just a desk, a chair, and a lamp. The movie would show no change, just a static picture. Now notice that the audience will become impatient with this far faster than if it were considering a still photo. This is because the audience also (not just the pro-ducers of the image) has different temporal expectations between consum-ing a still photograph and a movie. Let's imagine that for technical reasons, the photographer has to look through the viewfinder as long as it takes to take the shot, this time being as long as the cameraperson would use to pro-duce his or her static film. Even though the two seem to do exactly the same thing (showing a static view of a room), there is an important difference. The cameraperson, while filming his or her movie, has to pay attention to the duration of what he or she sees, whereas the photographer has to pay atten-tion only to the measurable time necessary to take a still photograph (the time it takes to frame, focus, and click, plus the shutter speed). In the first form of interaction, the duration of the perceived process is communicated, which is not the case in the second one. Even though they seem to be the "same" picture, the embodied viewing is notably different. The difference stems from the context of "I can" and "I would like to."

Overdetermination and Communication (Semiosis)

With relation to the notion of embodied vision, the concept of "overde-termination" illustrates a characteristic principle of communication (i.e., the co-constituting process of communication). As Merleau-Ponty (1945 Fr./1962 Eng.) indicates, no pure, singular, ideal forms of vision exist. Communication, always and already, implies non-comprehension and non-clarity. The whole of one's attention sways between two rather fuzzy cate-gories, focal and subsidiary. Therefore, Bennington (1994) insists, "Communication takes place, if at all, in a fundamental and irreducible uncertainty as to the very fact and possibility of communication" (p. 2).

Focal attention, the term coined by Polanyi (1958), is conscious aware-ness (or perception), such as concentrating on a book one is reading. Individuals are subsidiarily or relatively unconsciously aware of other processes in their surroundings. Subsidiary and focal attention can be switched as an individual's field of interest and practical needs dictate. What was previously one's focal attention becomes, over time, subsidiary attention and vice versa.

Merleau-Ponty (1945 Fr./1962 Eng., 1947, 1955, 1964 Fr./1964 Eng.) states that the unity of a thing is exhibited in the perceptual grasp of the thing as showing itself through a given perspective. The thing is not built from perspectival viewings; rather, it is *evident* to us. However, it is never empirically "given exhaustively" in these showings. Merleau-Ponty (1947, 1955, 1964 Fr./1964 Eng.) concludes from this that there is "a paradox of immanence and transcendence" in perception (p. 17). Perception (or, in another word, vision) is "immanence, because the perceived object cannot be foreign to the one who perceives; transcendence, because the thing always contains something more than what is actually given" (p. 16). From this paradox, Merleau-Ponty draws the concept of *overdetermination*.

Given that people see *things*, and not mere sensory profiles, it must be the case that perception "asserts more than it grasps" (Merleau-Ponty, 1945 Fr./1962 Eng., p. 361). That is, it "overdetermines" the showing given to any particular bodily point of view (Merleau-Ponty, 1964 Fr./1968 Eng., p. 240). Merleau-Ponty (1945 Fr./1962 Eng.) provides the following as an example of overdetermination:

> When I say that I see the ash-tray over there, I suppose as completed an unfolding of experience which could go on ad infinitum, and I commit a whole perceptual future. Similarly, when I say that I know and like someone, I aim, beyond his [*sic*] qualities, at an inexhaustible ground which may one day shatter the image that I have formed of him [*sic*]. (p. 361)

Merleau-Ponty (1945 Fr./1962 Eng.) concludes, "It is, thus, of the essence of the thing and of the world to present themselves as 'open,' to send us beyond their determinate manifestations, to promise us always 'something else to see'. . . there is nothing to be seen beyond our horizons, but other landscapes and still other horizons, and nothing inside the thing but other smaller things" (p. 333).

In fact, the mystery of things solicits the overdetermination inherent in our perceptual experience. Merleau-Ponty (1945 Fr./1962 Eng.) insists that conscious life, which is taken to be "the seat of clear thinking," is contrarily "the very abode of ambiguity" (p. 332). Therefore, Merleau-Ponty (1964 Fr./1968 Eng.) proclaims, "[T]here is no vision without the screen" (p. 150). Not surprisingly, Peirce (1931, 1958) makes almost identical points.

Peirce (1931) offers a conception of semiosis based on habit that disrupts the notion of referentiality. In the same vein, it unsettles the objectivistic bias. From the standpoint of Peirce's (1931) notion of habit, meaning is not *attached* to a sign by a habit (what we call intersubjective agreement). Rather, meaning *is* the relation itself. Meaning is the habit, just as the result of a quantum mechanics experiment *is* the interactional relation of object, instrument, and observer. Hence, meaning is never permanent and fixed, but in flux with a past, present, and future embodied in every relation to it. Peirce (1931) indicates, "[T]he whole function of thought is to produce habit of action. . . . To develop its meaning, we have therefore, simply to determine what habits it produces, for what a thing means is simply what habits it involves" (¶5.400). Habit refers to more than the one-to-one relationship that holds between a signifier and signified. Habit, as institutionalized body, what Merleau-Ponty (1964 Fr./1968 Eng.) calls *habit-body*, leads the way toward a conception of communication/semiosis as inter-actional, as a concretization, and as a production of relations.

At a given time and space, what is considered to be true might actually be false from the perspective of another time and space or from different consciousness structures. For instance, to call a (medical or mental) symptom the presence of a demon would be false in the view of modern medicine. Yet few doctors openly discourage their patients from praying. In this manner, within the sphere of pure possibilities of overdetermination, contradictory interpretations can quite easily live in peaceful coexistence with one another, so the classical principle of contradiction does not necessarily apply. These spheres of overdetermination, where the signs are exceedingly vague, exist as a complement to the sphere of underdetermination, consisting of signs of generality, which is chiefly the nature of what Peirce (1931, 1958) calls *Thirdness*. As what was previously neither true nor false can emerge as an underdetermined sign; the classical principle of excluded middle need not be necessarily regarded as an unbreakable law or principle.

In short, a thing is never given simply "on its own." It is impossible to remove the screen of vision so as to gain an unbiased and "all-seeing" point of view (i.e., a god's eye view, a transcendent reality). In a similar vein, were people to remove the screen of vision, people would lose their access to the world, so that instead of seeing all, people would in fact see *nothing*.

People do not first constitute a sense through which the world and things are given "as existing." Rather, Merleau-Ponty (1964 Fr./1968 Eng.) seems to argue that people are first in reality; only then do they try to make sense of their environment. But this is only an apparent notion born of a cursory reading. For the world is neither taken nor given except as a perspective. Sense is not the same as meaning, and this is why Merleau-Ponty (1945 Fr./1962 Eng.) responded to Sartre's claim that we are condemned to freedom with his alternative claim that we are condemned to meaning and all meaning is an inscription of the flesh. In addition, what people are trying to make sense of is not the thing (i.e., not the world) but rather the "mark" or "trace" that the thing and world have made on them (Merleau-Ponty,

1964 Fr./1968 Eng., p. 194). Hence, the constituting activity is always already a situated activity, always already my activity, the activity of a being whose insertion in the commonsense world is already a point of view. According to Merleau-Ponty (1945 Fr./1962 Eng.), the constituting life of transcendental subjectivity is thus already a particular subject's way of "taking up" the world, of "taking note" of facts, or of "taking in" the spectacle of the world as flesh (p. 395). For Merleau-Ponty, our primary initiation to meaning comes in the world in the contact between the flesh of my body and the flesh (objects, other's flesh, etc.) of the world. Similarly, and as discussed earlier, Heidegger (1952, 1954, 1962 Ger./1977 Eng.) insists that the modern technological modality is not objective but rather a particular perspective, a way of making sense of the world as a field of resources available for conquest, manipulation, and consumption—a technical-mechanical world.

My knowledge of the world, even my scientific knowledge, is gained from my own particular point of view. Given this fact, Merleau-Ponty (1945 Fr./1962 Eng.) argues, "We must begin by reawakening the basic experience of the world of which science is a second order expression" (p. viii). In this vein, Merleau-Ponty (1964 Fr./1968 Eng.) acknowledges that "[W]e do not see, do not hear the ideas, and yet they are there, behind the sounds, or between them" (p. 151). Merleau-Ponty (1964 Fr./1968 Eng.) stresses that people are neither pure spectators standing before pure objectivity nor absolutely active beings capable of bringing about the detachment necessary for the emergence of objectivity that might result from people "changing into their meaning" (p. 108). Merleau-Ponty (1947, 1955, 1964 Fr./1964 Eng.) says, "Do I not know that there is a life of ideas, as there is a meaning of everything I experience, and that every one of my most convincing thoughts will need additions and then will be, not destroyed, but at least integrated into a new unity? This is the only conception of knowledge that is scientific and not mythological" (p. 20).

In this vein, the more people have learned about language, the less its structures have come to look like portraits of the speaker or pictures of reality (Pinker, 1994). When language informs people about reality, it does not picture what is remote in time, space, or conception, but reminds people of the *eloquence* of things or prompts people to imagine their voice.

Although such eloquence emerges from the physical structure of persons and things, it does so in contingent and unforethinkable ways. In this sense, signs are not mere vehicles but rather *vectors*. By the nature of physical and consciousness structures, perspectivism is inevitable. The meaning things embody directs how a thing is for us. Things are a part of institutionalizing (or co-constituting) reality, of the ever-present vision of the world; of a structuring of time, and of a transformation of space. All structuring is a restructuring, and this is what transformation reveals. No ground or final solution is available (or possible). The morphological aspect of language is apparent only through the difference that duration enables. But even time itself, as a mode of being, is mutable. Duration changes pace, intensity, and thickness. Change requires the retentive aspect of memory that abides (not over or under, but) through mutation, through mutability and contingency. Change posits differences, even oppositional or contradicting ones, simultaneously.

Thus, we have the transparency of integral understanding. Change—which presumes difference—lives in the in-between, which separates positive features and enables identity. For example, when a new feature emerges with relative force within the ecology of thought and/or culture (such as a new technology), it disrupts and restructures all previous relationships. Thus, all that *is* suddenly becomes *what was*. In this way, we have the movement of obsolescence not only in machines but in ideas and the identities of those who work with them and think them and who are thought by them, as Foucault (1969 Fr./1972 Eng.) would argue. This is how the old and out-of-date become *antiquated*.

The vectoring of language shapes how a thing, idea, or person is grasped, understood, and experienced. How the things that are "not me" are grasped also changes how I grasp myself. Am I obsolete or cutting-edge? Am I catching on or falling behind? Am I capable or incapable? Technological development has changed our sense of time, making of it a measurement of progress that has had profound implications for how individuals and entire societies are understood. Thus, in the modern age, societies are described as "developing," "underdeveloped," "developed," and so on. All such identities are relative and vulnerable to mutation, to morphogenesis (Kramer, 1997, 2003a).

The meaning or vectoring of this mutation is technologically accented. Time and history have become technicized, operationalized, reduced to being chronicles of measured technical progress, of the material expression of will-power-drive. This drive is often articulated as war prowess and economic competition. A good example is the rise of various colonial powers that rely on their advanced technologies and the rapid rebuilding of postwar economies. National and personal pride are often expressed as technical manifestations, from the space race to colossal building projects, and economies that "run like dynamos."

Not all obsolescence is bad. For instance, to become a "classic" means to be old yet appreciated—and often valued more highly than a similar contemporary object. Thus, we have the museum of selected machines that have become presumed and built on, machines that embody salient virtues and desires. The perfect example is the Smithsonian National Air and Space Museum, which has one of the largest attendance numbers of any museum on Earth (Zongker, 2007). It is not unlike a cathedral where hordes of visitors cross the threshold and pause in awe at its initial impact before delving deeper into its exhibits. On the centennial anniversary of the Wright

Brothers' first powered flight, the romance of technological power perceived as a liberating force—technology as hero in both fiction (Hollywood movies) and industrial and military realities—was celebrated around the world. Ironically, at the same historical moment, the United States mourned the destruction of the World Trade Towers in New York City by impact from two modern jet airplanes. In this case, the force of ideology was expressed through relatively primitive technology. Box cutters proved effective in forcing the world's last superpower to alter its sense of civil liberties in the contradictory effort to secure those liberties.

The goal of securing freedom has been confronted with the technological prowess of weapons of mass destruction so that security has come to rival and replace freedom. Security (i.e., surveillance technology) is increasingly no longer utilized in the service of protecting civil rights and personal freedoms; instead, civil rights and freedoms are being eroded (through the use of technology) in the interest of security. Military technological balance, tantamount to fighting fire with fire, has been precariously maintained through the chilling history of the cold war, for example.

The world, including the most intimate aspects of private life, is being not merely impacted by technology (which is Cartesian thinking) but is shaped by technology. While transportation technology has a huge impact, communications technology proves even more powerful, especially in primary aspects of culture such as values, beliefs, motives, and expectations that fundamentally direct which material and organizing artifacts will be pursued, researched, and manufactured.

REFERENTIALITY OF SIGN: A BROKEN ARROW

Referentiality or the representational theory of sign is a typical form of objectivistic bias, one that has broadly influenced communication theories. However, if people and things are intimate and active participants in a world-structure that undergoes continual transformation as a result of its essential openness, then it is absurd to insist that language remain a representational structure when what it supposedly represents is no longer taken as more than half made-up. Hence, if perception does not capture the visible "print" of things, then it seems that language is not entirely willing to co-constitute with perception. This is what the notion *overdetermination* indicates.

For Merleau-Ponty (1945 Fr./1962 Eng.), signs, as the bodies of language, do not simply "stand for" (or straightforwardly "stand in for") the objects they signify, any more than perceptual things are entirely accessible and fathomable by the observer's gaze. According to Merleau-Ponty (1945 Fr./1962 Eng.):

> If the body expresses at each moment the modalities of existence, we
> shall see that it is not like stripes signifying rank or like a number desig-
> nates a house. The sign in question here does not merely indicate what
> it signifies, it is inhabited by it. (p. 188)

In other words, "[T]he meaning is not on the phrase like the butter on
the bread" (Merleau-Ponty, 1964 Fr./1968 Eng., p. 155) because, in sign
action or semiosis, the situation is complicated by an essential property of
embodiment, a property of embodiment that differs in the shape it takes,
such as written sign, speech, human body, and so on, while remaining
nonetheless essentially a bodily phenomenon. In the same vein, Heidegger
(1927 Ger./1962 Eng.) claims:

> A sign is not a Thing which stands in for another Thing in the relation-
> ship of indicating. . . . A sign to mark something indicates what one is
> "at" at any time. Signs always indicate primarily "wherein" one lives,
> where one's concern dwells, what sort of involvement there is with
> something. (pp. 110-111)

Accordingly, signs point to our preoccupations and concerns; not as
simple, artificial indicators, but rather as intimate participants in when and
where we live.

Semiosis (or communication), then, is not proper linguistic speaking,
but rather is the general interpretive activity (i.e., inter-subjective agreement)
that makes language possible. Accordingly, in a sense, language (e.g.,
"Argument," "$R_3O_3I_3$" in Peirce's semiotic analysis, previously described in
Chapter 12) is the most abstracted form (structure) of semiosis. For
Merleau-Ponty (1945 Fr./1962 Eng.), the question of language is primarily
investigated in terms of the body's nascent *potential* of expression. This is
different from the idea that expression stems from intentional power, which
is the property of the subject and the subject alone. The semiotic/communi-
cating subject is not a subject at all, at least not in the sense of the Cartesian
"thinking subject" (Descartes, 1641 Lat./1647 Fr./1901 Eng.).

The visibility or opaqueness of an object is determined by the movement of things-in-the-world, actions that are already underway. From this
standpoint, to render objects thoroughly transparent and consistent is, paradoxically, to obscure their most proper possibility and make the nature of
the object thoroughly inaccessible. Stated differently, to make objects
unquestionably visible is to make them unquestionably opaque. From this
observation, a crucial point appears. The Cartesian objectivistic bias has
actually paved the way to the annihilation of our ability to ascertain and
think about communication and semiosis. As Kramer (1997) indicates, the
inclination to the obvious transparency and reliability of tools and instru-

ments coincides with the emergence of modern perceptual authority as the Cartesian notion of presence. It is the tendency in which tools come to have an intermediate or intervening status between objects and works, indicating the advent of modern (scientific) perception. The entire world is thus fragmented. What is lost in this "progress" away from other modalities is the magical identity relationship among tool, process, producer, product, and consumer. For instance, in the magic world, all production/consumption is a sacred activity—from agriculture to building a dwelling or a boat to utensils for cooking and adornments for the body. Another example is the preparation of food and its consumptive import, including who eats it, when, how, why, and with whom. Holy Communion is another example, as are adornments for the home (also saturated with identity)—Persian rugs were originally created during years of effort by girls in preparation for marriage as part of their dowries. If the girl failed to marry, these complex creations were not sold but instead placed in mosques. The product cannot be separated from the producer or the consumer. As Karl Marx (1962/2000) noted, the fragmenting process of separating the product from the producer and/or consumer, which marks modern economics, is alienating and dissociating.

In summary, following Merleau-Ponty (1945 Fr./1962 Eng., 1964 Fr./ 1968 Eng.), when we perceive something—bringing it into perceptual focus—other things must remain in the background. But the background is integral to the overall view. To be put in the background does not mean to be eliminated; background is a necessary, integral component of foreground. To perceive something is to valuate other things as relatively secondary, even if these other things are physically in front of us. Perception involves not only what is behind and before us literally, but also what is "before" us in the historical sense of the word. This historical sense of "before" describes the way in which our perception always begins in the middle of things. As Gadamer (1960 Ger./1975 Eng.) and Dilthy (1883 Ger./1988 Eng.)—prior to Merleau-Ponty—argued, we stand within an always already operant history.

Merleau-Ponty (1945 Fr./1962 Eng., 1947, 1955, 1964 Fr./1964 Eng., 1960 Fr./1964 Eng., 1964 Fr./1968 Eng., 1968 Fr./1970 Eng.) struggles to show that the world is not filled with a collection of objects that are radically distinct from consciousness. Instead, the world is an open-ended domain in which sensible and invisible things, bodies, and ideas arise. However, such ideas (or the world) are not regarded as pure or absolute essence. According to Merleau-Ponty (1945 Fr./1962 Eng., 1964 Fr./1968 Eng.), perception not only engenders our capacity for revealing, it also (conversely) limits that capacity. Because of the openness of things in the world, people find themselves in a typical perception that is threatened by other possibilities. This is why Gadamer (1960 Ger./1975 Eng.) similarly insists that perception and conception are necessarily prejudicial.

This tension between the typical perceptual form that people adhere to faithfully and the other forms that threaten it engenders perceptual power. This is the nature of perception and semiosis: overdetermination. Stated differently, things provide more than the raw material for some thoroughly and precisely (monolithic) constructive subject; they lend themselves to endeavors that people call their own, but always in a provocative, even appropriative manner. When people act as if things present themselves in a simple and unambiguous manner, the participation with the things surrounding us is distinctly—and imperceptibly—repressed (limited). Thus, people face the "distantlessness" between themselves and things in the environment. People assume that the work they are pursuing stems from them and them alone; everything around them merely serves like furniture or implements. For instance, it is naïvely believed that the introduction of a new thing, a machine like the computer, the automobile, or the airplane, is simply there to be used by us in our a priori interests. But the computer, the automobile, the airplane, and other technologies change our culture, our modality of perceiving and conceiving, our expectations, beliefs, aspirations, and the structure of the world. Technology opens new possibilities even as it limits others. The computer, typical thing that it is, is not the exception. This is not a kind of embodiment of technology or embodied vision for technology, but rather it is the *technicization* of human beings. This is so because these machines change our prejudices; the very structure of our consciousness is changed, enabling us—even compelling us—to reevaluate ourselves, our world, the past (as obsolete), and the future. Therefore, only people who have embodied technological vision *can* see (or perceive) the distance between technology and themselves.

SUMMARY

This chapter explored how the modern technological milieu elevates the importance of vision in culture and how technology also changes the nature of vision. The spatial preoccupation of the perspectival human called for greater precision, which contributed to new methods of measurement and observation: the microscope, the telescope, and so on. The new abilities these instruments of observation enabled elevated the measurable to a seat of prime importance, as *the* unarguable reality. A similar narrowing is going on in the study of technology, as exemplified by McLuhan's studies. Studies of the medium that disregard the lived body elevate the medium to the same totalizing reality that visiocentric quantification can create; they also technicize the human experience as the move to quantification relegated the qualitative to fictional status. Such an overdetermined approach can only be corrected by attending to how technology (e.g., television) produces a way of seeing in relation to our embodied perception. Any attempt to capture the total picture of the process repeats the Cartesian mistake, failing to attend to the open nature of being in embodied perception. We must remain constantly aware of how the act of foregrounding through our perception affects the background, including ourselves—the human background.

15

Our Sense Within the Technological Milieu

Any advance in technology is both a gain and a loss. Just as Gebser's (1949 Ger./1985 Eng.) mutations of consciousness suggest that a dominant mode of living is lost, so too a change in technology turns us off one avenue of living and guides us toward another. The complaints and occasional hysteria that power outages provoke in today's world seem overblown compared to the relative stoicism with which people of previous centuries confronted the prospect of a night without air conditioning or television. While mirrors give us the freedom to confirm that our hair is in place, they also compel us to take a quick look before going out the door to make sure we're "presentable." Parents today cite the use of Internet gaming to placate their children as "necessary" to allow them the freedom to prepare dinner, despite the fact that households have had children and dinners for millennia without the aid of even VHS tapes (Brand & Chadwick, 2007). We've put ourselves in the situation of requiring two incomes (or more—many parents have two jobs) to have *things* that make us socially presentable. Previous generations of families didn't need such placations because a parent could stay home, and we had grandparents and neighbors we actually knew and trusted. When we change the technology we use, our everyday life (and our expectations for that life) changes also.

We tend to focus exclusively on how we use the technology (the foreground) and don't attend to what we no longer do or what we do differently (the background, what is in place before it arrives) because of it. Mumford (1934/1963) explains that the steam engine was initially measured purely in terms of the power it could produce. Raw output was the only concern, without consideration of the fuel efficiency, maintenance costs, environmental pollution, or danger to workers involved in operation and production. With an incomplete ledger sheet, total cost cannot be calculated. Likewise, Mumford (1934/1963) argues, Venetian glass-makers' mass production of mirrors produced revolutionary growth in self-consciousness and introspection once the bourgeois had the ability to see themselves (to a certain, limited extent) as others did. Technology is both a tool and much more than a tool—a tool that shapes us often as much as we use it to shape our world. Descriptions of technology that do not keep this possibility in mind are dangerous for two reasons: They conceal and even exacerbate the hidden costs of technology, and they can lead to incomplete or distorted definitions of what it means to be (a successful) human. Hence, we accept increased time away from our families as a normal, necessary condition for success; we also re-define success from meaning familial contributions (in interaction) to meaning the possession of (technological) *things*.

A study that focuses only on the "noise" of technology, and not its "silence," runs the risk of producing an incomplete understanding of that technology. For example, studies of social networking sites (Boyd & Ellison, 2007; Ellison, Steinfield, & Lampe, 2007) focus on describing how individuals use sites such as Facebook and MySpace (not how to *use* them but how they are *used* socially). These approaches describe the use of these sites in relation to "the formation and maintenance of social capital" (Ellison, Steinfield, & Lampe, 2007, p. 1143). Using economic metaphors to describe a social phenomenon forces that phenomenon to resemble the market just as tracking the movement of the stars with the assumption that the Earth is the center of the universe shapes the patterns we trace. If we start describing something in economic terms, we're likely to describe it as a market, and that description is likely to be most useful to marketers. Past experiences suggest that early adopters shape the future use of technology (e.g., Bijker, Hughes, & Pinch, 1987; MacKenzie & Wajcman, 2002; Pemberton, 1936; Rogers, 1962). If the only data social scientists are producing are demographic and usage surveys, and if they are casting this data in terms of a market, then they are merely expediting the commodification of that technology, reducing it to its ability to move merchandise. Hence, the accusation that uncritical (i.e., positivistic) social science is actually market research (Kramer, 1997); it is somewhat akin to studying the possibility of splitting the atom without considering the consequences of doing so.

A study that comes close to the approach of this book, but falls critically short, is Lee Humphreys's (2007) study of the use of the Dodgeball mobile social network system in the *Journal of Computer Mediated Communication Studies*. Dodgeball is software that allows people to send multiple text messages to members of a social group to make them aware of their location and actions. A member can "check in" at a given location, and other members can either "check in" from their location or perhaps join other members at a given physical location. The system allows individuals to quickly make large numbers of people aware of (and/or allow them to congregate to) their location at a given time. The system can lead to what Humphreys (2007) calls "social molecularization" (p. 353), in which:

> Informants both experience and move about through the city in a collective manner. This is not to say that people did not experience urban public space socially before Dodgeball; however, the social molecularization encouraged by Dodgeball seems different in two particular ways. First, rather than having to discuss places or venues explicitly, Dodgeball allows users to communicate indirectly about public places. That is, people do not necessarily have to tell a friend they went to a new bar, but they can indirectly alert him or her by checking in to a new venue. Second, the exchange of social and locational information is accelerated, because it can occur in real time and, thus, allow users to make decisions about their physical movements based on the social and spatial information available to them. (p. 353)

Although Humphreys (2007) acknowledges that public spaces are experienced differently, there is no exploration of what the totality of that difference might be. Users acknowledge that one user checking in will prompt them to check in from their location and that multiple check-ins from the same place can create peer pressure to join the group (Humphreys, 2007), but there is no exploration of how this alters their previous relationships with public spaces. As Mumford (1934/1963) points out, we don't get ready to go out in public the same way once we have a mirror in our house; a network like Dodgeball also changes our most basic orientations to public places. Once I have the ability to link to my friends instantaneously, can I experience sitting quietly in a coffee shop alone as I had before? What motivation do I have to attempt to strike up a conversation with a total stranger in my immediate presence? Other authors have argued that the proliferation of communication and transportation technologies has (for example) fundamentally altered the experience of going away to college (Gardner, 2006). A heavy Dodgeball user facing the prospect of an evening without the network may be like someone who has grown accustomed to the speed of broadband Internet dealing with a 56k modem. The ability of these networks to presentiate space not only makes us aware of where we and others are, it also makes us much more aware of where we are not (and who is there rather than here).

If a couple broke up, it may be awkward if they bump into each other at a future point after the break-up. Now, thanks to networks like Facebook, an individual may be assaulted with constant reminders of their ex. With GPS being placed into phones, it is becoming possible to create a visual real-time cyber-social network (Humphreys, 2007; Townsend, 2000). Although these systems may allow us to coordinate activities as never before, the tightening of the network noose is also making it exceedingly harder to "live off the grid" while remaining socially viable (Kramer, 1997). Just as perspectival vision sought to see through and grasp all at once (Gebser, 1949 Ger./1985 Eng.), social network systems are moving to make socialization slicker and faster on the way to creating an all-encompassing system. We "know" an ever-growing number of people a little bit and very few people very well. The more "friends" you have on Facebook, the better (professional) you are. Facebook and similar computer-mediated communication technologies allow us to have written EVIDENCE of what was said, when (and where) it was said, and who said it. In the past, "we had he said, she said" issues, but now we don't have to recall (or debate) what was said; we can produce a copy, and we can even cut and paste it and circulate it to others online globally and instantaneously.

We can see a similar process at work in the classroom. Studies show that exposure to television at a young age adversely affects attention spans and language acquisition (Christakis, Zimmerman, DiGiuseppe, & McCarty, 2004). Network television has also been identified as retarding children's abilities to attend to educational tasks (Geist & Gibson, 2000). Education theorists are now attempting to compensate for this by breaking up class periods so that they resemble the length of television programs, even taking "commercial breaks" so classes require shorter durations of sustained concentration from students. We also don't teach kids to write in cursive any longer; they can't read it because it's not the penmanship of the computer. Telling time on a clock with a traditional clock face (with hands to indicate time increments) is also becoming extinct in favor of digital-face timepieces. Television is accepted as an inevitable force to which we must adapt our social-institutional behaviors. This is not only an example of our tools tooling us; it raises the unsettling question of where such adaptation leads us. As HDTV technology spreads and TV screens become brighter, shinier, prettier, bigger, and omnipresent, the over-stimulation that already retards childhood development (Geist & Gibson, 2000; Postman, 1992) and raises expectations that education be entertaining—creating "edutainment"—increases. Even the tactile satisfaction some of us get from holding a book is diminishing; increasingly, books are read on screens too (i.e., Kindles and Nooks). Adapting our classrooms to this reality encourages a "race to the bottom" in terms of attention span. In this acquiescence, the technicization (Husserl, 1954 Ger./1970 Eng.) of human beings is complete.

The study of technologized communication can be dangerous, not only in how it explains the use of technology but also in how it describes humans.

Sociologists are now beginning to use social network sites to gather sociological data (Rosenbloom, 2007, ¶8). The obvious problem is that scholars are attempting to use a particular mediated behavior to draw broad conclusions about human behavior. These social network sites encourage users to create profiles that allow one to "type oneself into being" (Boyd & Ellison, 2007, p. 3).

Profiles allow individuals to strike a highly manipulated and easily "corrected" or adjusted pose to accommodate other people's posts and profiles (and even changes in the lifeworld). I can carefully select the movies, books, quotes, and so on that I want to use to represent myself and put them on display for others to see. Even though the profile can be changed, it approaches a form of permanence (in the sense of creating a presence that is unconstrained both geographically and temporally—virtual immortality) that an embodied being cannot match.

A flesh-embodied person cannot forever list his or her favorite bands or meticulously tend to and change his or her image as one can by choosing profile pictures. Online profiles are, in a way, an eternal mirror. While we may check our appearance in the mirror of the material world, we eventually must forget about how we look and start doing other things. In contrast, the maintenance of an online profile promotes (even demands) near-continual conscious attendance to one's image (and now we have a new image to protect: our cyber-image joins our self-image and our image in the eyes of those who are actually looking at us in the world, rather than on a screen). Even users of more abstract systems such as Dodgeball will import their check-ins to a Google map to create a visual map of their evening or to catalogue the day's events (Humphreys, 2007). This desire for concrete, visiocentric representations of self and time speaks to the desire for permanence embedded in modernity.

Online avatars are not living beings. They are attempts to create a Cartesian self. Humans think (i.e., type, key, keyboard—whichever term for computer-related activity is in vogue at a given time) themselves into existence. The deficient mode of rationality takes over as thinking precedes existence, and being becomes dependent on thinking (Gebser, 1949 Ger./1985 Eng.). There is not the openness that Merleau-Ponty (1947, 1955, 1964 Fr./1964 Eng.) points out is critical to embodied perception. However, sociologists from leading universities such as Harvard, UCLA, Northwestern, Carnegie Mellon, and the University of Texas are using these profiles to see whether mutual taste or friendship comes first or to test Simmel's theory of triadic closure (Rosenbloom, 2007).

One need only ask the tenants of the Pruit-Igoe projects (Rainwater & Pittman, 1967), patients who received electroshock therapy for homosexuality (McConaghy, Armstrong, & Blaszczynski, 1981), or the parents of children who have committed suicide because of cyber-bullying (Hinduja &

Patchin, 2010) about the dangers of acting with an inaccurate understanding of human nature.

Although concerns exist about the demographic representativeness of these online groups, there is no concern about the representativenss of the medium. Social scientists appear perfectly comfortable decontextualizing the findings of these mediated (and complex) behaviors. Decontextualizing variables in pursuit of theory is hypertrophic perspectivism. Those who decontextualize do not consider (bracket) that in a given cause-and-effect relationship, the cause is also an effect and that the effect is also a cause of another effect, and so on (except as they consider it overcome-able by "controlling" for variables and throwing out results that don't meet a numerical criterion). If car A rear ends car B, then we ask what caused car A to run into car B, and we realize that car B may now ram into the car ahead of it. However, those questions are often not examined in the positivistic social science tradition. In an attempt to replicate the serendipity (and gain the same level of respect) of Archimedes's and Pythagoras's geometric proofs, positivists are pursuing a kind of human geometry (trying to earn physical science/mathematics street cred and failing to do much besides eroding their own contributions). To do this, they attempt to identify the basic postulates. Hence, the academy separates into what Husserl (1954 Ger./1970 Eng.) calls "regional ontologies" with the proliferation of biologism, pyschologism, and a whole host of other "isms" in an attempt to "explain it all" (Kramer, 1997). Unfortunately, none of these postulates has proven satisfactory for explaining human behavior. Regardless of near boundless evidence to the contrary, social science (in the positivistic vein) continues the postulate pursuit in an attempt to find the frame (a single grand narrative) for understanding human behavior. The fact that a single frame does not exist does not stop their vigorous pursuit of it.

Pierre Schlag (1998) describes the larger problem these attempts (and self-view) point to as the struggle between rational frame construction and critical reflexivity. Studies of social phenomena are commonly attempts to build a rational frame to both approach the particular phenomenon and ultimately explain what is going on in the larger context. The obvious problem with constructing a frame is that while it allows one to focus on a certain sector, it doesn't allow seeing the larger picture or the vital meanings that exist outside the frame (and, of course, what we care about is neither of these but that relationship between the particular and the general).

Bracketing is illusory—as are operationalizations and, to a lesser extent perhaps, generalizations. In this case, the positivist (i.e., dominant) approach to the technological milieu is scrambling to create frames with little concern for their accuracy or benefit. Frames must be called into question (which requires that they must first be seen), and critical reflection allows one to locate and dislodge frames, to see the invisible. However, critical reflection can devolve into a form of rational frame construction of its own in its unending search for "a context of genesis" (Schlag, 1998, p. 64).

This infinite regression is the problem Husserl (1954 Ger./1970 Eng.) identified in the bickering between the "regional ontologies." For example, we name our courses based on where we are and who owns which words—"leadership" belongs to the business college, so it can't be taught in the interpersonal communication program; those in other disciplines can't name a course "Sources and Discourses of Power" because the English department owns the word "discourse" and isn't willing to sell or lease it. To avoid this problem, we must adopt a frame of inquiry that casts the widest net over the most direct observations of human experience (e.g., observation vs. recollection on a survey, or an original vs. a secondary source in journalism) while retaining a usable frame. That solution is attending to how time and space, the fundamental media of human consciousness (Kramer, 1997), are experienced through an embodied perception that is the heart of human reality (Merleau-Ponty, 1964 Fr./1968 Eng.).

Attending to how a technology affects time and space (and how we embody those media)—rather than simply examining how a given technology works—allows us to employ a rational frame that speaks to the most basic elements of the human condition. This creates a more fully formed picture of how that technology affects us (how it works in the lifeworld) rather than simply how it is being used. It is the drive to discover what that technology is doing to *us* rather than only considering what we are doing *with* that technology.

Historically, technology has been a means. Technological innovation was slow to develop as people were only likely to invent solutions when a problem became severe enough to warrant the time, thought, and effort to render and then argue/promote and finally execute a solution. The water mill met the needs of those using it, so it remained virtually unchanged for hundreds of years. Similarly, the primary form of intellectual property was trade secrets that guilds vigilantly protected as their own (Mumford, 1934/1963), much like current trade secrets such as the formulae for Kentucky Fried Chicken, Coca-Cola, and other powerful proprietary products.

However, with the growth of chartered companies and/or franchises (and the advent of patents), technology became a commodity. This radically changed the focus of the economy from local to global and vice versa as well as from maintaining the skill, experience, and knowledge of the past—departing from it to claim an exclusive and elusive new monopoly (Mumford, 1934/1963). In the developed world, inventions became worth exponentially more once people could lay exclusive claim to a design, an idea, a piece of art, and so on and charge others for its use. Invention allowed individuals to escape their social class and become fabulously rich as a result of a flash of (licensable) inspiration.

This contributes to an increasingly technological society as entrepreneurs rush to identify (or, in some cases, create) needs they can invent solutions to and thereby produce profit. Flipping through late-night television will bring a host of commercials and infomercials touting the benefits of everything from juicers, to abdominal exercisers, to hot-dog cookers, to electric scissors (all of which beg the question as to why people watching television at such an hour would need these "time-saving" devices regardless of price). With this wave of products comes an advertising blitz designed to assault our satisfaction levels (creating a perceived need) and get us to pony up the three easy installments of $19.95 (right now because operators are standing by and this offer won't last long!).

For better and worse, our society (and, more specifically, our economy) has grown increasingly technological. As people increasingly use technology, the market for it grows, and more entrepreneurs move to meet the created demand. This entrepreneurial drive means that technology also becomes increasingly defined by capital (Mumford, 1934/1963), and the market is becoming increasingly technological.

But it is not only the market that is becoming increasingly technological in nature; technology is also expanding the market by offering more and more options—faster and faster—to more and more consumers (not to mention apps that make technology more technical—it technologizes more and more of our tasks). Broadcast television's four networks did not provide as many consumers with as many options; times were tough before we had 400 kinds of shampoo and 178 kinds of Campbell's Soup. If Steve Allen wanted to have an hour-long discussion with Hemingway or Picasso, Americans didn't have many other viewing options. Now some cable television packages offer viewers more than 400 different channels as well as movies and programs "on demand." We now have 400 channels of little or nothing to watch, but because it's there, we lower our bar for what we consider entertaining, informative, worth watching, and so on. With online video sites such as YouTube, an individual can instantaneously access videos of anything—Bob Dylan's 1965 San Francisco press conference, Secretariat's win in the Belmont Stakes, a fish jumping into a boat and hitting a man in the genitals—there really is something for everyone! Media technology is moving toward giving consumers the broadest spectrum of options possible.

The broader the spectrum grows, the less definitive direction and consistency and commonality there is in public media consumption. Sloterdijk (1983 Ger./1988 Eng.) identified what this lack of direction does when he observed magazines that had stories of starvation in the undeveloped world opposite full-page ads for expensive champagne or reports of torture placed between perfume ads. There is no distinction between foreground and background, important or unimportant: the "and" of the media becomes an "is equal to" (Sloterdijk, 1988, p. 313). Just as the magazines Sloterdijk discussed didn't differentiate between the importance of actual human suffering and advertisements for luxury goods (they *ignored* the difference, which is even worse), YouTube doesn't tell viewers whether JFK's "man on the moon" speech is any more historically significant than a video of a monkey drinking its own urine. The television doesn't tell viewers whether a presidential primary debate or a celebrity weight loss program is more vital to the future of the nation (and, worse, too many don't care to find out). This move toward absolute freedom means that individuals are become increasingly atomized, and experiences that bind us as a nation, a culture, or a family are becoming increasingly abstract and ethereal. This cultural diaspora means that there are fewer and fewer collective myths that tell us who we are and who we should be. Joseph Campbell (1988) argues that this lack of myth is why there is so much juvenility in contemporary culture. If we have no larger cultural forces telling us what an adult should be, then it is hard for individuals to figure it out on their own.

The diffusion of entertainment is not only affecting consumers, it is in turn affecting the market as well. As YouTube, TiVo, and iTunes allow individuals to entertain themselves without commercial interruption, advertisers must find new ways to create and raise product awareness. Hence, we see the advent of viral commercials and increasing product placement in television and movies, and of course the marketing *coup de grace*, when commercials are entertainment—for example, we wait all year to watch Superbowl commercials. People can now create "virtual bookshelves" on Facebook to show their friends books they have read or are currently reading (or aspire to read, or aspire to convince others they have read). Soon (but not soon enough some would argue), one realizes the bookshelves provide direct links to purchase the book on Amazon.com. The move to maximize profit means that it is becoming increasingly difficult to have personal (i.e., private) interaction free of market interests. Marketers can infiltrate any firewall or secure link, it appears.

Technology moves as the market (via consumers) directs it. There is more money in treating a disease than curing it or in combustion engines than electric cars. Planned obsolescence is the economic future, the blood of producers. So we have a nation that consumes more medication and gasoline than ever before. Not because we must; rather because we have little direct incentive to do anything about our own health or that of the planet—we are just too busy making money. The continuing expansion and commercialization of technology in our everyday lives increasingly defines our lives. We are money-earning spenders; even in times of war and savagery, we are coaxed to go shopping as part of our responsibility to our democracy. The question increasingly moves from "What is good?", "What does somebody need?", or "Do those who need it (or who can be convinced that they do), have the money to pay for it?" to "What will sell?" Marketers and producers of goods and/or services see everything as commodity, from the "burial grounds to the cove of the local fertility sprite" (Cox, 1999, p. 20). In the technological milieu, even human beings are commodities. We are the sum of our incomes, our computer searches, the hits we produce, and the dollars we spend. The benefit of consumers to the market is measured by how much they consume, not how happy or healthy they are. As technology and the market continue to converge and increasingly shape our lives, then our lives, and our idea of what it means to be a human being, will be further defined by them. So, until we are willing to take up the task of attending to what is human again, we will be increasingly beholden to what technology decides we should be.

16

Conclusion

It is worthwhile to actively inquire about the processes and events that have sustained or reinforced the development—and, crucially, how development is defined—during the past four centuries that have preceded the tendency toward the annihilation of time and space and, consequently, annihilation of communication and semiosis in the contemporary world. As Gebser (1949 Ger./1985 Eng.), Mumford (1963, 1970), Ellul (1954 Fr./1964 Eng., 1977 Fr./1980 Eng.), and Heidegger (1952, 1954, 1962 Ger./1977 Eng.) commonly indicate, answers can be found in the notion of technology that brought about the age of the machine with the aid of perspectival, technical drafting; in the notion of progress that spawned the various abstractions that represent contemporary time: the age of progress, the information age, the digital age, and so on.

The theoretical abstractions of limitless power, profit, and prestige are inherent in the myth that technological abundance guarantees the "good" and prolonged life (and, of course, the more significant question is about how the "good life" is defined). These abstractions are inherent in the magic that technology presumably can produce without the limitations of time and/or space. The concept of time and space as boundaries of social interaction is countered by the concept of place as an abstract or metric space and moment (the reality of cyber-space) in the form of time-anxiety as a socially desirable relational position from which to relate the world and realize the modern-rational discrete (i.e., individual) self.

Where and when one dwells shapes and frames the world that one claims as one's own. What makes the modern person's world characteristically his or her *own* is the manner in which the person situates him or her-self—leading to a reconstitution of the world through the metric and topo-graphic perspectives of technological apparatuses and prosthetic amplifica-tion of select capacities. Technological enframing disembodies human capac-ities, ignoring some while vastly amplifying others, intensifying particular interests, and thus skewing perspective. Enframing also creates a world with the characteristic that one is "in the world" rather than co-constitutive of it. Perception that had always been intimately linked to the human talent for manipulation—or what Merleau-Ponty (1945 Fr./1962 Eng.) calls motility—of the world around us—has come to be defined as the capacity to train our "projectors" (sensory receivers) in all directions, inside and out. Perception, under this new definition, is the process of *situating ourselves* in the world and is characterized by a dominating technetronic and mechanistic modali-ty qualifying the technological milieu as legitimate, *as that which must be accommodated*. The promise and dangers of modern technology include the sterilization of space, the myth of technical progress, and the process of making space and time perceptually absolute. In detaching facets of reality from their (meaning-laden) contexts and setting them afloat in cyberspace, information technology allows for trivialization and glamorization, as well as blurring of the line between fact and fiction. The ambiguity of cyber-space dissolves the subtle contours of facts, the uniqueness of persons, and the nuance of place. As a consequence, humans lose the flesh or incarnate horizon of their perception and the embodied ground of meaning.

Regardless of how large, fine-grained, three-dimensional, and photo-realistic images may become, no matter how universally accessible and smoothly integrated every imaginable piece of information may become, the rule of simple desire, having conceived of flying carpets, genies in bottles, and magic wands, has *always* and *already* preempted the most sophisticated feats of technology. Hence, reality as being-in-the-world remains inescapable and enigmatic. The world as "flesh" is the ground on which the de-contextualization of technological information can be rehabilitated and its fragilities repaired.

At the initial stage of research, students are told that the scientist devel-ops a hypothesis and then performs some experiment(s) to check it out; if the hypothesis can withstand the "test" of experimental verification, then support for the hypothesis can be claimed. At risk of over-simplification, we are told that a theory is a good theory only if the experiment can be repeat-ed in different places and render the same result. This attitude is a legacy of Newtonian science, the view that makes experimentation the faithful assis-tant of theory. However, as many scientists already recognize, this is a naïve story. As Heelan (1983) and Ihde (1998) illustrate, scientific theory and sci-entific phenomena generally emerge together at the end of scientific inquiry. Expressed differently, Hacking (1983) states that experimentation need not be taken as simply blind, on the one hand, or completely theory-laden, on the other. Rather, experimentation and theory are interdependent. Together they "create" new scientific phenomena. A crack in the veneer of the neat, linear notion of classical Aristotelian thinking is apparent. Variables may be both dependent and independent at the same time. Likewise, theory and research are integral, not discrete, cogs in a research machine. The laboratory, according to Latour (1993), is not only the place where scientists work; it is where inscriptions are produced. The instruments of science, while producing the visual display, are not visible, nor are they in the forefront. The tendency to see new "scientific" phenomena as waiting to be discovered stems from an objectivistic bias and theory-dominated philosophy.

Contrary to the pre-supposed maxim of objectivism/positivism, Max Planck's quantum theory suggests that nature makes leaps, effectively demolishing our prevailing view of time (Jaeckel, 2007). Our world is not constructed continuously or, with respect to time, as a constant, as the mechanistic view of classical physics holds. Rather, the world displays discontinuities that thwart often gallant (not to mention expensive) efforts at prediction. This implies that a perception from physics reveals the complexity of what has been hidden "behind" the concept of time. An example is probability theory. Probability theory has undergone substantial refinement and resurgence and is progressing into all of the sciences on its triumphal remodeling of the classic world-image (i.e., the world) dominated by laws into an (unbiased) "statistical world-image" in which there is no certainty but only "degrees of probability."

The invention of photography can be seen as a genuine technological breakthrough. Technologies as perception-transforming devices not only magnify (and reduce) referent phenomena but also—often radically—change parameters either barely noted or not noted at all. It is the dramatic appearance of a transformation of *time* that photography brought into our world in general and to the horizon of scientists. The freezing of time produced a repeatable image of a thing that can be analytically observed and returned to time and again. Virtual reality (VR) audaciously insists it can "make" time (yet virtually). However, the hallmark of virtual reality is escape and seclusion from the actual social world or lifeworld. VR is already defined and further pre-designed or programmed in detail.

The more a program meticulously defines a virtual world, the more it *looks like* the actual world, the further it moves from the embodied world. This claim can be applied to CD music, for instance. A CD tends to have a preternatural purity and perfection that makes live performances sound rough and flawed. Similarly, the space we traverse in virtual flight promises to have more captivating shapes and more saturated colors than anything in the actual world.

All forms of abstract rationality (including VR) are actually substantiated by the lifeworld. In this sense, rationality is thought to be a social product as instituted consciousness rather than a prescriptive logic. Time is a fabulous example and (at the same time) a crucial theme for overcoming objectivistic bias. For Gebser (1949 Ger./1985 Eng.), the mental/rational, three-dimensional world is ordered temporally, yet each dimension is thought to possess its own temporal ratio. Therefore, time is basically autonomous or anonymous—each moment of time is mutually exclusive of each other moment, and the entire temporal system is thought to possess its own organizational principles, laws, and/or structure.

The modern objectivistic notion of the world as a matrix of mechanical dependencies might best exemplify this three-dimensional world. Each component in this temporal system is self-contained and dualistically removed from every other. Most important is the fact that the individual is thought to exist *in* time and, therefore, to be moved by its basic direction. As Gebser (1949 Ger./1985 Eng.) illustrates, the consequences of the perspectivalization of the world evident in the isolation and mass phenomena of the present day (alongside the isolation in the form of thinking) deceptively dazzles with premature judgments and hypertrophic abstraction devoid of connection to the lifeworld. It is the same with mass phenomena—overproduction, inflation, rampant technology, and atomization in all forms.

In the integral world, on the other hand, the organizing principle is not the system, but *systasis*. This understanding of the world as the product of integration processes announces a new conception of time. As Gebser (1949 Ger./1985 Eng.) says, it actually dissolves time but does not renounce it. Rather, time comes to be viewed as "time-freedom" rather than "time-location." History is no longer understood to be in time, as if time merely labors to connect discrete historical episodes. In terms of social action, the individual is not comprehended as existing *in* time; rather, the individual is believed to upsurge as the temporal capacity to structure the dimensions of existence because of human ability (or inability) to allow conception of time to structure existence. This new realization enables us to see temporal moments as not consigned to a status of mutual exclusivity and the individual social actor as subsisting in a manner that is categorically removed from the world. Daylight and dark cycles no longer inhibit us, with technology of artificial light, and so make it appear that we are further and further removed from the natural world. As Gebser (1949 Ger./1985 Eng.) says, the integral world is a world without opposites (e.g., there is no inside or outside, no night and day, etc.).

What Gebser advances with this notion of a systatically integrated world is what might be called—in Merleau-Ponty's terminology—a "fleshy" transcendental. What this means is that the world and the constitutional acts of human consciousness are to be understood as intimate correlates.

Accordingly, the world can no longer be perceived only as an empirical referent that provides the social world with its required organizational principle. What is important here is that the world does not possess an autonomous status; rather it must be understood to be subtended by embodiment.

The purity of mathematical structures is a reflection of signs that do not refer to "things" but to "structures"; simply put, mathematical structures refer to lawful relations whose objects are free of empirical or causal contingency. As Borgmann (1999) illustrates, mathematical structures can be applied to music or cosmology; however, they do not of themselves encapsulate the essence of a cantata or the universe. An organist (as well as a listener) will enjoy the performance of Bach's music—even if the performer and the audience are quite familiar with the piece. Nevertheless, it is doubtful that many mathematicians would once more go through the proof of the Pythagorean theorem just for the enjoyment of it. Because concretization based on spontaneity makes music delightful, we ask, what is different about the process of proofing the Pythagorean theorem? It is crucial to a piece of music that it be *realized* as embodied, integral, and fluxing manifold. Each performance is different. It has a new interpretation, even if one is listening to a recording of it. This is the endless dynamism of the hermeneutic cycle of dialogue that Gadamer (1960 Ger./1975 Eng.) explores. Each encounter changes the possibilities (as potential) for the next one. And, the interpretation of music also occurs on the side of the performer. Variance, and therefore novelty (creativity and innovation), compounds as the performer (not only the audience) takes something from each performance, manifesting experience in future performances (or exposure in the case of the audience member).

In jazz music and oral poetry, the composition is the performance. McLuhan (1964)—in paradox to his notion of technology—indicates this point. If jazz is considered a break with mechanism in the direction of the discontinuous, it can also be seen as a return to a sort of oral poetry in which performance is both creation and composition. It is a truism among jazz performers that recorded jazz is "as stale as yesterday's newspaper." Jazz is alive, like conversation, and as with conversation, it depends on a repertory of available themes. In this way, performance is composition.

For a (classical) musical score to become real, it requires its proper place and time and a communal tradition of extraordinary discipline and training as well. Classical musicians need to struggle with the recalcitrance of things (their instruments) and the awkwardness of their bodies before proficient music-making erupts from them. Once they are trained, musicians manifest an ever-variegated voice.

From this standpoint, the first prerequisite for our continued survival (as humans) is a revolution in our thinking. As questioning is the piety of thinking, and as it makes a way for change, our survival depends on the questioning of technology as enframing. Skepticism is *not* cynicism. Quite the contrary, to question is the opening of horizon rather than the close-mindedness of dogmatic faith. The ability to preserve our humanity comes with recognizing the danger of technology as the metaphysics of the present technological milieu. As Gebser (1949 Ger./1985 Eng.) indicates, the world is currently undergoing a mutation—a mutation that embodies what Gebser (1949 Ger./1985 Eng.) refers to as the integral or diaphanous world. When technology ceases to act as language (i.e., forming our path to being while establishing the limitation of the possible), and when we stop struggling to adapt the world to the clock and other technologies, technology will become transparent to us. The structures that manifestly constitute technology—that form the values, beliefs, and motives that it articulates and the expectations that it engenders—will be seen as mutable and, as such, transparent. Technological limitation (somewhat ironically and paradoxically) will lead to solutions that are not restricted to technological "fixes." Human development and value will not be limited to the archaic realm of *Homo Habilis* ("handyman") that technological magic amplifies. Futures freed from the (mythic) tyranny of the calendar, modern mechanical time, and cause-effect notions of progress become liberated and conceivable. A life of new potentialities becomes conceivable. Such a world is not really a new world but rather incorporates the recognition of an ever-present origin that subtends all worlds, providing them with dimensional prerequisites not seen before.

However, as Gebser (1949 Ger./1985 Eng.) cautions, acceptance of what is "new" regularly meets with fierce resistance because it demands the overthrow of what has been handed down (i.e., various objectivistic biases that are acquired, entrenched, and painfully secured). Also, new situations pose threats arising from our inability to understand them because we are still too enmeshed in the old structure of awareness or structural habits. This is why what is "new" looks as though it is beyond the real (as though it is, perhaps, supernatural). Further, the new not only appears that way—when considered on the basis of structured awareness, it *transcends* the reality to which people are accustomed. The usual way to the new is an attempt to accommodate the new to the old. In so doing, the new loses its genuineness. In attempting to explain the new by concepts rooted in tradition, misunderstandings, misinterpretations, and misconstrued presumptions are bound to arise. To avoid these misconstructions while doing justice to the originality of the new, we must realize that the novelty of a situation must be appreciated if it is not to be hopelessly wasted (or watered down) in its adjustment to living reality. Likewise, Merleau-Ponty (1947, 1955, 1964 Fr./1964 Eng.) insists in his notion of "embodied vision" that change can be accomplished only if or when people are clear in their own minds about what has gone before. That is why Gebser's (1949 Ger./1985 Eng.) brilliant articulation of the mutational unfolding of human consciousness is crucial for this study.

Peirce (1931, 1958) uses the term *semiosis* with respect to the general phenomenon of sign process. The very idea of semiosis challenges the objectivistic, biased view of sign—that signs are relatively static instrumental tools used to describe (and thus "mirror") the world. Semiosis, rather, is a dynamic process in which sign users may exercise only *limited* control. In other words, the conception of language as an abstract and static mechanical system devised for communication is untenable and inaccurate. As Peirce (1931, 1958) explores the infinite production of signs and the infinite expansion of sign-fields, he acknowledges that permanent fixation, even in a partial context, is impossible. Any interpretation of signs must admit bias (and, therefore, a lack of equifinality for all receivers/interpreters of a sign) and acknowledge the eventuality of being surpassed or relativized by yet other interpretative moments from different contexts.

Meaning, truth, and "reality" are relative (i.e., "related to"). Meaning, truth, and reality are related products of a triadic process of Object-Representamen-Interpretant; they, in turn, relate to other triadic fields or contexts. Meaning and knowledge must be conceived of as products of the interrelationship of signs. The only way to study semiosis is to identify certain contexts for examination while also taking into account people's own critical-interpretative contexts. However, it is clearly impossible to pose fixed and absolute laws of semiosis.

The continuous interaction of sign-relations is the communicative procedure of allowing many voices and perspectives to coexist and interact without reducing or subsuming one to the other. The attempt to fixate is a typical characteristic of modern rational consciousness in terms of language and other symbols and signs. Fixation (the symptom of hypertrophic perspectivism) ignores or relegates to the background signs of indexical and iconic nature. Fixation ignores potentia and latency that are essential to seeing real yet invisible phenomena.

As Gebser (1949 Ger./1985 Eng.) and Ellul (1954 Fr./1964 Eng.) warn, communication (political or cultural) is threatened by an ultimate loss of quality in that people are threatened by submergence into autonomous masses and consequent atomization. In everyday life, few are aware that the mechanization and technicization, which impose quantitative conditions on human beings, are leading to an immeasurable loss of freedom; the atomization of the human being is the ultimate divide-and-conquer strategy. The manner of enframing and operationalizing that characterizes modern perspectival positivism qualifies existence as a reactionary adapter rather than a creative actor.

We are assured by technophiles that we should have no fears about automation. McLuhan (1964) assures us that, in the end, electronic technology as synesthetic tactility promises to confer on us a "global embrace" and "perpetuity of collective harmony and peace" (p. 359). Because "electronic technology does not need words any more than the digital computer needs numbers . . . computers hold out the promise of a means of instant translation of *any* code or language into *any other* code or language" (McLuhan, 1964, p. 80). In this regard, McLuhan cannot escape criticism from an ideologue of technology (or a technophile). If McLuhan's world can be realized, it means the end of communication. The pursuit of perfect efficiency and ultimate profitability leaves us with only calculation by pre-programmed computers.

With technological changes—from the oral tradition, through the era of the printing press, to the current era of the computer—come shifts in language and thinking. What is occurring now is a shift in the language of technology and in the exploration of philosophical inquiry from the analysis of conversation to that of text and, most recently, to the metaphoric analysis of communication as a program or algorithm manifested in a system of technologies and practices (Carey, 1989). In other words, currently the discourse is one of an irresistible moment metaphorically represented by the symbol of the computer as the defining (if not determining) technology of contemporary cultural (and interactional) change.

The computer as a communication technology connects, controls, and organizes all other communication technologies and their content (Mosco, 1989). Mosco means *all* interconnected appliances and systems, including television, telephone, and telecommunication networks, as well as text and talk. The computer is (so far at least) the ultimate refinement of the machine in form and function. It serves to challenge modern technology as the focal point of power (McLuhan & Powers, 1989; Mumford, 1970). This constitutes not just a mutation in power but in thinking too; and, of course, that's where REAL power lives—in making us think we like things as they are. The computer, the mediating organizer of the machine that is the totality of the technological complex, will absorb the modern technological milieu, usurping its manifold functions and forms of social intercourse.

Like language, the computer is not a transparent, innocent, or objective medium. It can become transparent—the transparency we are talking about is not a transparency of mediation, but rather the realization and acknowledgment that it is a medium with structural biases. Its enabling, blinding, and limiting constructs can become clear to us as such, opening a new and potentially more beneficial way of interacting with technology. Just as Gadamer (1960 Ger./1975 Eng.) examines the dialogical encounter one has with a work of art, so too we must come to understand our encounter with technology, virtual reality, and computerization. Technology is neither transparently objective (value-free or bias-free), nor does it escape the fundamentally hermeneutic quality of life; it is shaped by and shapes the lifeworld.

Space, in a global network of computers, is a "fuzzy" concept when compared to the "place" defined by the modern technological milieu. Many communication theorists, including de Sola Pool (1990), theorize about technologies of communication as being "without boundaries." This implies, therefore, a world without boundaries. Hence, Utopia becomes a frictionless existence without limits (emancipating), meaning (nihilistic), or life (impossible). From this typical technophile viewpoint that manifests a mental-rational attitude, we can recognize "time-anxiety" as a characteristic of the computerized/clocked world and the desire to conquer space and transcend time. The love of (and blind faith in) technology as savior becomes a kind of piety.

In the case of technologies of communication, their deconstruction coincides with their internalization. This social and consensual process alters a group's (or an individual's) consciousness of culture as that which is taken in as part of the social organism providing constructs that define the individual in terms of interaction. This dynamic of social interaction is formed by, and formative of, communication technology. The materialization of technology and the internalization of practice, for example, are symbolic exchanges that dramatically represent the Utopian project of preserving and bettering the quality of life in the present—here and concrete, in both *form* and *function*. To McLuhan, electronic technology culminates in "automation" (or "cyber-nation") in which an invisible tactile contact is made between human and technology (McLuhan, 1964; McLuhan & Quentin, 1967). Cyber-nation is a retribalization, a return of the synesthetic interplay of the senses as central to human experience. The fact that people today continue to think in terms of a spatial, fixed, three-dimensional world of conceptuality is an obstacle to our realization of the more complex significance of the world (or technology). As Gebser (1949 Ger./1985 Eng.) and Husserl (1954 Ger./1970 Eng.) argue, time is a much more complex phenomenon than the mere instrumentality (the grammar or inflection) or accidence of chronological time. In this sense, the topological aspect of modern communication technology such as generated by the Internet (i.e., Facebook use) has many implications, such as what counts as social capital and friendship, which have been poorly understood thus far.

There are still unsuspected developments within the realm of communication, although many are one-sided technological, dehumanizing ones (although "progressive" to the positivist). If the destructive power of positivism's (or contemporary forms of positivism's) "progress" is not weakened—as Ellul (1954 Fr./1964 Eng.) and Heidegger (1952, 1954, 1962 Ger./1977 Eng.) significantly warned—these developments (specifically their tendency toward enframing the world) will occupy the place of "lawgiver," of dictator. As we've become slaves to the clock, so will we continue in becoming slaves to technology without the kinds of understandings rendered by the approaches advocated in this study. As Gebser (1949 Ger./1985 Eng.) argues, if we are soberly prepared for this new transparency—this new understanding of technology—then there is nothing terrifying about it.

We do not offer a solution to the technological paradox; instead, we offer (hopefully, and with hope) a new understanding of it and its central importance. People are not doomed to calculate with each other in the pale and pure glow of the computer monitor, in the objectified technological world. This study is an attempt to provide an understanding of various aspects of the objectified technological attitude that has become naturalized, institutionalized, and invisible. This study focuses on this objectified technological attitude and attempts to penetrate it, to get to the straightforward pursuit of one's own theoretical or other life interests. From the phenomenological standpoint, we can attempt to go back to being as before but never *exactly* as before. We can never again achieve the old naiveté. But we *must* understand it. Potentia is open horizon, not merely expanding old structures. It means the joy one finds in the invisible. Not just feeling anxiety in the face of the unknown, which encourages a reactionary retreat into familiar technological constructs and habits.

About the Authors

Eric Mark Kramer, Ph.D., is Associates Second Century Presidential Professor of Communication at the University of Oklahoma. Dr. Kramer has published several books and journal articles and is currently Associate Editor of the *Journal of Intercultural Communication Research*. He has written extensively about technology, globalization, forced assimilation, and cultural and biological extinction.

Gabriel Adkins, Ph.D., is Assistant Professor of Communication at Arkansas Tech University. He is Director of the Center for Increased Responsiveness in Emergency Networks (C.I.R.E.N.) at ATU. His research interests and publications include examinations of Organizational Communication, Crisis and Emergency Management Communication, and Communication Technology.

Sang Ho Kim is Associate Professor at Kyungpook National University, Korea. He has written extensively on the human-technology interface and the social implications of globalism. He focuses on how technology impacts our sense of identity, space, and time.

Greg Miller, J.D., M.A., is currently a law clerk to Chief Judge Ed Carnes of the U.S. Court of Appeals for the Eleventh Circuit. He received his Juris Doctor degree from the University of California at Berkeley Law School, where he was elected to the Order of the Coif. He received his Master's degree in communication from the University of Oklahoma and his

Bachelor's degree in English literature from Rice University. He has written extensively about concepts of law, justice, and honor across cultures.l

References

Abbot, J. (2010). *Overschooled but undereducated: How the crisis in education is jeopardizing our adolescents.* New York: Continuum.

American Beauty. (1999). (A. Ball, writer; S. Mendes, director). Los Angeles: Dream Works.

Arendt, H. (1963/1968). *Eichmann in Jerusalem: A report on the banality of evil.* New York: Viking.

Aristotle. (1991). *On rhetoric: A theory of civic discourse* (G. Kennedy, Trans.). New York: Oxford University Press.

Assadourian, E. (2013). *State of the world 2013: Is sustainability still possible?* Washington, DC: Worldwatch Island Press.

Assange, J., & Appelbaum, J. (2012). *Cyberpunks: Freedom and the future of the Internet.* OR Books.

Bagdikian, G. (2004). *The new media monopoly.* Boston: Beacon Press.

Bailey, R. (August, 2004). Transhumanism: The most dangerous idea? *Reason*.com. Available at http://reason.com/archives/2004/08/25/transhumanism-the-most-dangerous-idea

Bailly, F., & Longo, G. (2010). *Mathematics and the natural sciences: The physical singularity of life.* London: Imperial College Press.

Barrat, J. (2013). *Our final invention: Artificial intelligence and the end of the human era.* New York: St. Martin's Press.

Barringer, F. (June 21, 2013). Pot growers in California starting to see environmental consequences. *New York Times.* Available at http://www.bendbulletin.com/apps/pbcs.dll/article?AID=/20130621/NEWS0107/306210406/&template=print

Barthes, R. (1957 Fr./1972 Eng.). *Mythologies* (A. Lavers, Trans.). London: Jonathan Cape.

Barthes, R. (1973 Fr./1975 Eng.). *The pleasure of the text* (R. Miller, Trans.). New York: Hill and Wang.

Baudrillard, J. (1981 Fr./1994 Eng.). *Simulacra and simulation* (S. Glaser, Trans.). Ann Arbor, MI: University of Michigan Press.

Baudrillard, J. (1983). *Simulations* (P. Foss, P. Patton & P. Beitchman, Trans.). New York: Semiotext(e), Inc.

Baudrillard, J. (1995). *The Gulf war did not take place* (P. Patton, Trans.). Bloomington, IN: Indiana University Press.

Bauerlein, M. (2009). *The dumbest generation: How the digital age stupefies young Americans and jeopardizes our future*. New York: Jeremy P. Tarcher/Penguin.

BBC News. (1986, November 1). *Chemical spill turns Rhine red*. Available at http://news.bbc.co.uk/onthisday/hi/dates/stories/november/1/newsid-467900 0/469789.stm

BBC News. (2005, November 24). *Chinese papers condemn Harbin lies*. Available at http://news.bbc.co.uk/2/hi/asia-pacific/4465712.stm

BBC News. (2005, December 16). *Toxic leak reaches Russian River*. Available at http://news.bbc.co.uk/2/hi/europe/4534542.stm

Becker, E. (1973, 1997). *Denial of death*. New York: The Free Press.

Bell, D. (1973). *The coming of the post-industrial society*. New York: Basic Books.

Bell, D. (1976). *The cultural contradictory of capitalism*. New York: Basic Books.

Bellah, R., & Madsen, R. (2007). *Habits of the heart: Individualism and commitment in American life*. Berkeley, CA: University of California Press.

Benjamin, W. (1936, 1961 Ger./1969 Eng.).The work of art in the age of mechanical reproduction (H. Zohn, Trans.). In H. Arendt (Ed.), *Illuminations: Essays and reflections* (pp. 217-252). New York: Harcourt Brace Jovanovich.

Benjamin, W., Arendt, H., & Zohn, H. (1955 Ger./1969 Eng.). *Illuminations: Essays and reflections* (H. Arendt, Ed., W. Benjamin, Trans.). New York; Random House/Schoken.

Bennington, G. (1994). *Legislations: The politics of deconstruction*. New York: Verso.

Berdayes, V., & Murphy, J. (2000). *Computers, human interaction, and organizations: Critical issues*. Westport, CT: Praeger.

Berkeley, G. (1710/2008). *Treatise concerning the principles of human knowledge*. Rockville, MD: Manor.

Berkeley, G. (1713/2007). *Three dialogues between Hylas and Philonous* (M. B. Mathias & D. Kolack, Eds.). New York: Pearson.

Bernstein, R. (1983). *Beyond objectivism and relativism: Science, hermeneutics, and praxis*. Philadelphia, PA: University of Pennsylvania Press.

Bijker, W. E., Hughes, T. P., & Pinch, T. J. (Eds.). (1987). *The social construction of technological systems: New directions in the sociology and history of technology*. Cambridge, MA: MIT Press.

Binfield, K. (2004). *Writings of the Luddites*. Baltimore: Johns Hopkins University Press.

Birdwhistell, R. L. (1973). *Kinesics and context: Essays on body-motion communication*. Harmondsworth: Penguin.

Bireda, M. (2011). *Schooling poor minority children: New segregation in the post-Brown era*. New York: Rowman & Littlefield.

Boorstin, D. (1993). *The creators* (3 Vols.). New York: Vintage.

Borgmann, A. (1984). *Technology and the character of contemporary life: A philosophical inquiry.* Chicago, IL: University of Chicago Press.

Borgmann, A. (1999). *Holding onto reality.* Chicago, IL: University of Chicago Press.

Bostrom, N. (2005, April). A history of transhumanist thought. *Journal of Evolution and Technology, 14*(1), 20–44. Available at http://www.nickbostrom.com/papers/history.pdf.

Bostrom, N. (2011). *Existential risk reduction as the most important task of humanity.* The Future of Humanity Institute, Oxford University. A free PDF is available at http://www.existential-risk.org/concept.pdf

Bourdieu, P. (1977 Fr./1991 Eng.). *Language and symbolic power* (G. Raymond & M. Adamson, Trans.). Cambridge, MA: Harvard University Press.

Bourdieu, P. (1972 Fr./1977 Eng.). *Outline of a theory of practice* (R. Rice, Trans.). Cambridge: Cambridge University Press.

Bourdieu, P. (1990 Fr./1990 Eng.). *The logic of practice* (R. Nice, Trans.). Stanford, CA: Stanford University Press.

Boyd, D. M., & Ellison, N. B. (2007). Social network sites: Definition, history, and scholarship. *Journal of Computer-Mediated Communication, 13*(1), article 11. Available at http://jcmc.indiana.edu/vol13/issue1/boyd.ellison.html

Brand, M., & Chadwick, A. (Hosts). (2007, August 7). *Day to day* [Radio broadcast]. Washington, DC: National Public Radio. Retrieved January 12, 2008, from http://www.npr.org/templates/story/story.php?storyId=12560124

Braverman, H. (1974). *Labor and monopoly capital: The degradation of work in the twentieth century.* New York: Monthly Review Press.

Brzezinski, Z. (1970). *Between two ages: America's role in the technetronic era.* New York: Viking Press.

Bultmann, P. (2001). *Environmental warfare: 1991 Persian Gulf War.* Albany, NY: SUNY Press.

Burke, J. (2007). *Connections.* New York: Simon & Schuster.

Caldicott, H. (1986). *Missile envy: The arms race and nuclear war.* New York: Bantam Doubleday Dell.

Campbell, J., with Moyers, W. (1988). *The power of myth.* New York: Bantam/Doubleday.

Carey, J. W. (1975). A cultural approach to communication. *Communication, 2*, 1-22.

Carey, J. W. (1981). McLuhan and Mumford: The roots of modern media analysis. *Journal of Communication, 31*, 162–178.

Carey, J. W. (1988). *Communication as culture: Essays on media and society.* Boston: Unwin Hyman.

Carey, J. W. (1990). The language of technology: Talk, text, and template as metaphors of communication. In M. J. Medhurst, A. Gonzalez, & T. R. Peterson (Eds.), *Communication and the culture of technology* (pp. 43–62). New York: Pullman/Washington State University.

Carey, J. W., & Quirk, J. (1992). The mythos of the electronic revolution. In J. W. Carey (Ed.), *Communication as culture: Essays on media and society* (pp. 113–141). New York: Routledge.

Carlsmith, J., Collins, B., & Helmreich, R. (1966). Studies in forced compliance: I. The effect of pressure for compliance on attitude change produced by face-to-face role playing and anonymous essay writing. *Journal of Personality and Social Psychology, 4*, 1-13.

Carnap, R. (1928 Ger./2003 Eng.). *The logical structure of the world and pseudoproblems in philosophy* (R. George, Trans.). New York: Open Court.

Carnap, R. (1932 Ger./1934/2011 Eng.). *The unity of science* (M. Black, Trans.). London: Kegan Paul, Trench, Trubner & Co.

Carpenter, E., & McLuhan, M. (1960). Acoustic space. In E. Carpenter & M. McLuhan (Eds.), *Explorations in communication: An anthology* (pp. 65–70). Boston: Beacon Press.

Carr, D. (1970). Husserl's problematic concept of the life-world. *American Philosophical Quarterly, 7*(4), 331–339.

Carr, D. (1977). Husserl's problematic concept of the life-world. In F. Ellison & P. McCormick (Eds.), *Husserl: Expositions and appraisals* (pp. 202-212). Notre Dame, IN: University of Notre Dame Press.

Carr, N. (2011). *The shallows: What the Internet is doing to our brains.* New York: W. W. Norton.

Cascio, J. (2010). *The singularity needs you.* Self-published online.

Caspian Environment Programme. (2013). *Caspian Sea.* Available at http://www.caspianenvironment.org/newsite/Caspian-EnvironmentalIssues.htm

Chabris, C., & Simons, D. (2010). *The invisible gorilla.* New York: Crown/Random House.

Chang, B. (1996). *Deconstructing communication.* Minneapolis, MN: University of Minnesota Press.

Changeux, J.-P., & Ricoeur, P. (2002). *What makes us think: A neuroscientist and a philosopher argue about ethics, human nature, and the brain* (M. DeBevoise, Trans.). Princeton, NJ: Princeton University Press.

Chester, R. (2000). *Marine geochemistry.* Oxford, UK: Blackwell Science.

China.Org.CN. (2007, November 13). *Bengal tiger pelts seized in Qingdao.* Available at http://www.china.org.cn/english/China/231752.htm

China News Agency/*Taipei Times*. (2012, May 1). *Formosan leopard extinct.* Available at http://www.taipeitimes.com/News/taiwan/archives/2013/05/01/2003561173

Chipty, T. (2007, June 24). *FCC media ownership study #5: Station ownership and programming in radio.* Available at http://transition.fcc.gov/ownership/studies.html

Christakis, D. A., Zimmerman, F. J., DiGiuseppe, D. L., & McCarty, C. A. (2004). Early television exposure and subsequent attentional problems in children. *Pediatrics, 113*(4), 708–713.

Chuang Tzu. (1961). *Inner chapters-Chuang Tzu* (H. A. Giles, Trans.). London: Ruskin House.

Cibelli, J., Wilmut, I., Jaenisch, R., Gurdon, J., Lanza, R., West, M., & Cambell, K. (Eds.). (2013). *Principles of cloning* (2nd ed.). London: Academic Press/Elsevier.

Comte, A. (1830–1842 Fr./1853 Eng.). *Course of positive philosophy* (6 Vols.). (H. Martineau, Trans.). London: J. Chapman.

Comte, A. (1851–1854 Fr./1875-1877 Eng.). *System of positive polity* (4 Vols.). London: Longmans, Green and Co.

Comte, A. (1852 Fr./2012 Eng.). *The catechism of positive religion* (R. Congreve, Trans.). New York: Ulan Press.

Comte, A. (1975). *Auguste Comte and positivism* (G. Lenzer, Ed.). New York: Harper.

Covey, S. (1990). *The 7 habits of highly effective people.* New York: Free Press.

Cox, H. (1999). The market as god. *The Atlantic Monthly, 283*(3), 18–23.

Cross, T., & Carr, G. (2012, March 31-April 6). Bees and insecticides: Subtle poison. *The Economist,* p. 38.

Crutzen, P., & Stoermer, E. (2000). The "Anthropocene." *Global Change Newsletter, 41,* 17–18.

Crutzen, P. J. (2002). Geology of mankind. *Nature, 415*(6867), 23.

Culler, J. (1976). *Ferdinand de Saussure.* Middlesex: Penguin.

Culler, J. (1982). *On deconstruction, theory, and criticism after structuralism.* Ithaca, NY: Cornell University Press.

Dalton, P., & Kramer, E. (2012). *Coarseness in public communication.* Florham, NJ: Fairleigh Dickinson University Press.

Davis, W. (2007). *Light at the edge of the world: A journey through the realm of vanishing cultures* (4th ed.). Vancouver: Douglas & McIntyre.

Davis, W. (2009). *The wayfinders: Why ancient wisdom matters in the modern world.* Toronto: House of Anansi Press.

Davis, W. (2010). *Shadows in the sun: Travels to landscapes of spirit and desire.* South Beach, OR: Shearwater.

Day, K. (2005). *China's environment and the challenge of sustainable development.* Armonk, NY: M. E. Sharpe.

Deledalle, G. (2000). *Charles S. Peirce's philosophy of signs.* Bloomington, IN: Indiana University Press.

Deloria, V., Jr. (1999). *For this land.* New York: Routledge.

Derrida, J. (1967 Fr./1976 Eng.). *Of grammatology* (G. C. Spivak, Trans.). Baltimore: Johns Hopkins University Press.

Derrida, J. (1972 Fr./1981 Eng. a). *Dissemination* (B. Johnson, Trans.). Chicago: University of Chicago Press.

Derrida, J. (1972 Fr./1981 Eng. b). *Positions* (A. Bass, Trans.). Chicago: University of Chicago Press.

Derrida, J. (1977 Fr./1988 Eng.). *Limited Inc* (S. Weber, Trans.). Baltimore: Johns Hopkins University Press.

Descartes, R. (1641 Lat./1647 Fr./1901 Eng.). *Meditations on first philosophy* (J. Veitch, Trans.). New York: Anchor Books.

De Sola Pool, I. (1990). *Technologies without boundaries: On telecommunications in a global age.* Cambridge, MA: Harvard University Press.

Diamond, J. (1999). *Guns, germs, and steel: The fates of human societies.* New York: W. W. Norton.

Diamond, J. (2004). *Collapse: How societies choose to fail or succeed.* New York: Viking.

Diamond, J. (2006). *The third chimpanzee: The evolution and future of the human animal.* New York: HarperPerennial.

Dickie, M. (2008, February 2). Google faces lawsuit from Chinese dissident. *Financial Times,* p. 8.

Dilthey, W. (1883 Ger./1988 Eng.). *Introduction to the human sciences: An attempt to lay a foundation for the study of society and history* (R. Betanzos, Trans.). Detroit: Wayne State University Press.

Drew, J., Lyons, W., & Svehla, L. (2010). *Sound-Bite saboteurs: Public discourse, education, and the state of democratic deliberation.* Albany, NY: SUNY Press.

Drexler, K. (1985). *Engines of creation: The coming era of nanotechnology.* London: Fourth Estate.

Drexler, K. (1992). *Nanosystems: Molecular machinery, manufacturing, and computation.* New York: Wiley.

Drexler, K. (2013). *Radical abundance: How a revolution in nanotechnology will change civilization.* New York: Public Affairs.

Dreyfus, H. (1972). *What computers can't do: A critique of artificial reason.* New York: Harper & Row.

Dreyfus, H. (1995). Heidegger on gaining a free relation to technology. In A Feenberg & A. Hannay (Eds.), *Technology and the politics of knowledge* (pp. 99–107). Bloomington, IN: Indiana University Press.

Dreyfus, H. (2001). *On the internet.* London: Routledge.

Dreyfus, H., & Rabinow, P. (1983). *Michel Foucault: Beyond structuralism and hermeneutics.* Chicago, IL: University of Chicago Press.

Driscoll, S., Bozzo, A., Gray, L., Robock, A., & Stenchikov, G. (2012). Coupled model intercomparison Project 5 simulations of climate following volcanic eruptions. *Journal of Geophysical Research: Atmospheres, 117*(D17), 1984–2012.

Du Bois, W. (1903, 2013). *The souls of Black folk.* New York: Bantam Classic, Eucalyptus Press. Available at http://www.bartleby.com/114/1.html.

Dulvy, N., Baum, J., Clarke, S., Compagno, L., Cortés, E., Domingo, A., . . . Valenti, S. (2007). *Global status of oceanic pelagic sharks and rays.* IUCN-World Conservation Union, Washington, DC. Available at http://www.iucnssg.org/ tl–files/Assets/pdf/Reports/Lenfest%20RS%20Sharks%20final.pdf

Durkheim, E. (1893 Fr./1997 Eng.). *Division of labor in society* (L. Coser, Trans.). New York: The Free Press/Simon & Schuster.

Durkheim, E. (1897 Fr./1979 Eng.). *Suicide.* New York: The Free Press/Simon & Schuster.

Dusek, V., & Scharff, R. (Eds.). (2003). *Philosophy of technology: The technological condition.* Oxford, UK: Blackwell.

Eco, U. (1976). *A theory of semiotics.* Bloomington, IN: Indiana University Press.

Economy, E. (2010). *The river runs black: The environmental challenge to China's future.* Ithaca, NY: Cornell University Press.

Eliade, M. (1957 Ger./1987 Eng.). *The sacred and the profane.* New York: Harcourt, Inc.

Eliot, T. (1932). *Selected essays.* New York: Harcourt Brace & Company.

Ellison, N. B., Steinfield, C., & Lampe, C. (2007). The benefits of Facebook "friends": Social capital and college students' use of online social network sites. *Journal of Computer-Mediated Communication, 12*(4), article 1. Available at http://jcmc.indiana.edu/vol12/issue4/ellison.html

Ellul, J. (1954 Fr./1964 Eng.) *The technological society* (J. Wilkinson, Trans.). New York: Alfred A. Knopf.

Ellul, J. (1963 Fr./1972 Eng.). *False presence of the kingdom* (C. E. Hopkin, Trans.). New York: Seabury.

Ellul, J. (1977 Fr./1980 Eng.). *The technological system* (J. Neugroschel, Trans.). New York: Continuum.

Engstrom, T., Shaffer, H., & McCord, W. (2002). Phylogenetic diversity of endangered and critically endangered Southeast Asian softshell turtles. *Biological Conservation, 104(2)*, 173–179.

Ettinger, R. (1972). *Man into superman: The startling potential of human evolution — and how to be part of it.* New York: St. Martin's Press.

Farrell, K. (2011). *Berserk style in American culture.* New York: Macmillan.

Federal Communications Commission. (2013). *Overview.* Available at http://www.fcc.gov/osp/inc-report/INoC-Footnotes-Master.pdf

Feenberg, A. (1991). *Critical theory of technology.* New York: Oxford University Press.

Feinberg, G. (1977). *Consequences of growth: Prospects for a limited future.* New York: Seabury Press.

Festinger, L., & Carlsmith, J. (1959). Cognitive consequences of forced compliance. *Journal of Abnormal and Social Psychology, 58*, 203–210.

Feuerstein, G. (1987). *Structures of consciousness: The genius of Jean Gebser.* Lower Lake, CA: Integral Publishing.

Feynman, R. (2005). *The pleasure of finding things out: The best short works of Richard P. Feynman* (J. Robbins, Ed.). New York: Basic Books.

Finlay, M. (1990). *The potential of modern discourse.* Bloomington, IN: Indiana University Press.

Foucault, M. (1969 Fr./1972 Eng.). *The archaeology of knowledge and the discourse on language* (S. Smith, Trans.). New York: Pantheon Books.

Foucault, M. (1972 Fr./1980 Eng.). *Power/knowledge: Selected interviews and other writings.* New York: Harvester Press.

Foucault, M. (1975 Fr./1977 Eng.). *Discipline and punish* (A. Sheridan, Trans.). New York: Pantheon Books.

Fromm, E. (1968/2010). *The revolution of hope: Toward a humanized technology.* New York: Harper & Row/American Mental Health Foundation.

Fromm, E. (1976, 2013). *To have or to be.* New York: Bloomsbury Academic.

Fry, E. (2012, September 28). *The Oklahoman* distributes a hit piece on Obama. *Columbia Journalism Review.* Available at http://www.cjr.org/ united–states–project/the–oklahoman–distributes–a–hi.php?page=all

Fukuyama, F. (2004, September/October). The world's most dangerous ideas: Transhumanism (reprint). *Foreign Policy, 144*, 42–43. Available at http://www.foreignpolicy.com/articles/2004/09/01/transhumanism

Gadamer, H.-G. (1960 Ger./1975 Eng.). *Truth and method* (J. Weinsheimer & D. Marshall, Trans.). London: Continuum International Publishing.

Gadamer, H.-G. (1976 Ger./1981 Eng.). *Reason in the age of science* (F. G. Lawrence, Trans.). Cambridge, MA: MIT Press.

Gans, H. (1991). *Middle American individualism.* New York: Oxford University Press.

Gardner, R. (2006, December 14). In college, you can go home again and again. *New York Times.* Retrieved December 28, 2007, from www.nytimes.com

Gebser, J. (1949 Ger./1985 Eng.). *The ever-present origin* (N. Barstad & A. Mickunas, Trans.). Athens, OH: Ohio University Press.

Geddes, P. (1915). *Cities in evolution: An introduction to the town planning movement and to the study of civics.* London: Williams.

Geist, E. A., & Gibson, M. (2000). The effect of network and public television programs on four and five year olds' ability to attend to educational tasks. *Journal of Instructional Psychology, 27*(4), 250–261.

Gelles, D. (2009). Immortality 2.0: A Silicon Valley insider looks at California's transhumanist movement. *The Futurist.* Available at http://ce399eugenics.wordpress.com/2010/06/19/immortality-2-0-a-silicon-valleyinsider-looks-at-californias-transhumanist-movement/

George, J., Bada, J., Zeh, J., Scott, L., Brown, S., O'Hara, T., & Suydam, R. (1999). Age and growth estimates of bowhead whales (Balaena mysticetus) via aspartic acid racemization. *Canadian Journal of Zoology, 77*(4), 571–580.

Gergen, K. J. (1994). *Realities and relationships: Soundings in social construction.* Cambridge, MA: Harvard University Press.

Gibson, J. (1950). *The perception of the visual world.* Boston: Houghton Mifflin.

Glazebrook, T. (2000). *Heidegger's philosophy of science.* New York: Fordham University Press.

Godwin, M. (2003). *Cyber rights.* Cambridge, MA: MIT Press.

Goldsmith, J., & Wu, T. (2006). *Who controls the Internet? Illusions of a borderless world.* New York: Oxford University Press.

Goldstein, E. (2012, July 16). The strange neuroscience of immortality. *The Chronicle of Higher Education.* Available at http://chronicle.com/article/The-Strange-Neuroscience-of/132819/

Gould, S. (2006). *The richness of life: The essential Stephen Jay Gould* (P. McGarr & S. Rose, Eds.). London: Jonathan Cape.

Gouldner, A. (1976/1982). *The dialectic of ideology and technology.* Oxford, UK: Oxford University Press.

Gramsci, A. (1952 It./2011 Eng.). *Prison notebooks* (3 Vols.). (J. Buttigieg, Trans.). New York: Columbia University Press.

Greider, W. (1997). *One world ready or not: The manic logic of global capitalism.* New York: Touchstone/Simon & Schuster.

Gudykunst, W., & Kim, Y. (2003). *Communicating with strangers: An approach to intercultural communication* (4th ed.). New York: McGraw-Hill.

Gurwitsch, A. (1966). *Studies in phenomenology and psychology.* Evanston, IL: Northwestern University Press.

Gurwitsch, A. (1974). *Phenomenology and the theory of science.* Evanston, IL: Northwestern University Press.

Habermas, J. (1968 Ger./1972 Eng.). *Knowledge and human interests* (J. Shapiro, Trans.). Boston: Beacon.

Habermas, J. (1968, 1971 Ger./1973 Eng.). *Theory and practice* (J. Viertel, Trans.). Boston: Beacon.

Habermas, J. (1995). Peirce and communication. In K. L. Kenneth (Ed.), *Peirce and contemporary thought* (pp. 243–266). New York: Fordham University Press.

Hacking, I. (1983). *Representing and intervening: Introductory topics in the philosophy of natural science.* New York: Cambridge University Press.

Hall, E. (1959). *The silent language.* Garden City, NY: Doubleday & Company.

Hall, E. (1966). *The hidden dimension.* New York: Anchor Books.

Hall, E. (1983). *The dance of life.* New York: Anchor Books.

Hannon, T. S., Rao, G., & Arslanian, S. A. (2005). Childhood obesity and type II diabetes mellitus. *Pediatrics, 116*(2), 473–480.

Hawking, S. (1998). *A brief history of time.* New York: Bantam Books.

Hayworth, K. (2012a, July). Can we resurrect the dead? *Through the Wormhole with Morgan Freeman,* Season 3, Episode 6.

Hayworth, K. (2012b). Electron imaging technology for whole brain neural circuit mapping. *International Journal of Machine Consciousness. 4*(1) 87-108. Available at http://www.worldscientific.com/doi/pdf/10.1142/S1793843012400057

Hayworth, K. (2013). *Ken Hayworth — the connectome — neuroscience part 2 with Adam Ford.* YouTube interview. Available at http://www.youtube.com/watch?v=Z63tKv6xcKM

Heelan, P. (1965). *Quantum mechanics and objectivity.* The Hague: Martinus Nijhoff.

Heelan, P. (1983). *Space-perception and the philosophy of science.* Berkeley: University of California Press.

Hegel, G. W. (1812, 1813, 1816 Ger./1969 Eng.). *Hegel's science of logic* (A. V. Miller, Trans.). London: Allen and Unwin.

Hegel, G. W. (1807 Ger./1977 Eng.). *Phenomenology of spirit* (A. Miller, Trans.). New York: Oxford University Press.

Hegel, G. W. (1820 Ger./2002 Eng.). *The philosophy of right* (A. White, Trans.). Newburyport, MA: Focus Publishing.

Heidegger, M. (1927 Ger./1962 Eng.). *Being and time* (J. Macquarrie & E. Robinson, Trans.). New York: Harper & Row.

Heidegger, M. (1925 Ger./2009 Eng.). *History of the concept of time: Prolegomena* (T. Kisiel, Trans.). Bloomington, IN: Indiana University Press.

Heidegger, M. (1952, 1954, 1962 Ger./1977 Eng.). *The question concerning technology and other essays* (W. Lovitt, Trans.). New York: Harper & Row.

Heim, M. (1993). *The metaphysics of virtual reality.* New York: Oxford University Press.

Heisenberg, W. (1958). *Physics and philosophy: The revolution in modern science.* New York: Harper.

Hemingway, E. (1933, March). A clean, well-lighted place. *Scribner's Magazine.*

Henry, J. (1963). *Culture against man.* New York: Random House.

Hess, S., & Kalb, M. (Eds.). (2003). *The media and the war on terrorism.* Washington, DC: The Brookings Institution.

Heyns, C. (2013, June 7). *A call for a moratorium on the development and use of lethal autonomous robots.* Office of the High Commissioner for Human Rights. Available at http://www.ohchr.org/EN/NewsEvents/Pages/ Acallfor amoratoriumonthedevelopmentrobots.aspx

Hiltz, R., & Turoff, M. (1993). *The network nation.* Cambridge, MA: MIT Press.

Hinduja, S., & Patchin, J. W. (2010). Bullying, cyberbullying, and suicide. *Archives of Suicide Research, 14*(3), 206–s221.

Hiscock, G. (2012). *Earth wars: The battle for global resources.* New York: Wiley.

Hoffmann, M., Hilton-Taylor, C., Angulo, A., Böhm, M., Brooks, T., Butchart, S., . . . Stuart, S. (2010). The impact of conservation on the status of the world's vertebrates. *Science, 330,* 1503–1509.

Hofstadter, R. (1966). *Anti-intellectualism in American life.* New York: Vintage.

Hofstede, G. (1991). *Cultures and organizations*. London: McGraw-Hill.

Homans, G. (1958). Social behavior as exchange. *American Journal of Sociology, 63*, 597–606.

Hönisch, B., Ridgwell, A., Schmidt, D., Thomas, E., Gibbs, S., Sluijs, A., . . . Williams, B. (2012). The geological record of ocean acidification. *Science, 335*, 1058–1063.

Hovland, C., Janis, I., & Kelley, H. (1953). *Communication and persuasion: Psychological studies of opinion change*. New Haven, CT: Yale University Press.

Hughes, G. E. (Ed. & Trans.). (1982). *John Burdian on self-reference: Chapter eight of Burdian's "Sophismata," an edition and translation with an introduction and philosophical commentary*. New York: Cambridge University Press.

Hughes, J. (2004). *Citizen cyborg: Why democratic societies must respond to the redesigned human of the future*. Cambridge, MA: Westview Press.

Hume, D. (1739/1973). *A treatise of human nature*. Oxford, UK: Oxford University Press.

Humphreys, L. (2007). Mobile social networks and social practice: A case study of dodgeball. *Journal of Computer-Mediated Communication, 13*(1), article 17. Available at http://jcmc.indiana.edu/vol13/issue1/humphreys.html

Hunnicutt, B., & Hunnicutt, B. K. (1996). *Kellogg's six-hour day*. Philadelphia: Temple University Press.

Husserl, E. (1905–1910 Ger./1964 Eng.). *The phenomenology of internal time-consciousness* (M. Heidegger Ed., J. Churchill, Trans.). Bloomington, IN: Indiana University Press.

Husserl, E. (1913 Ger./1982 Eng.). *Ideas pertaining to a pure phenomenology and to a phenomenological philosophy* (Vol. 1) (F. Kersten, Trans.). Dordrecht, The Netherlands: Kluwer Academic Publishers.

Husserl, E. (1952 Ger./1989 Eng.). *Ideas pertaining to a pure phenomenology and to a phenomenological philosophy: Vol. 2. Studies in the phenomenology of constitution* (R. Rojcewicz & A. Schuwer, Trans.). Dordrecht, The Netherlands: Kluwer Academic Publishers.

Husserl, E. (1952 Ger./1980 Eng.). *Ideas pertaining to a pure phenomenology and to a phenomenological philosophy: Vol. 3. Phenomenology and the foundations of the sciences* (T. Klein & W. Pohl, Trans.). The Hague: Martinus Nijhoff.

Husserl, E. (1917/1928 Ger./2009 Eng.). *On the phenomenology of the consciousness of internal time (1893-1917)* (E. Stein & R. Boehm, Eds., J. Brough, Trans.). Dordrecht, The Netherlands: Kluwer Academic Publishers.

Husserl, E. (1954 Ger./1970 Eng.). *The crisis of European sciences and transcendental phenomenology: An introduction to phenomenological philosophy* (D. Carr, Trans.). Evanston, IL: Northwestern University Press.

Huxley, J. (1927). *Religion without revelation*. London: E. Benn.

Hylton, H. (2007, May 8). Keeping U.S. turtles out of China. *Time Magazine*. Available at http://www.time.com/time/health/article/0,8599,1618565,00.html

Ihde, D. (1967). Some parallels between analysis and phenomenology. *Philosophy and Phenomenological Research, 27*, 577–586.

Ihde, D. (1979). *Technics and praxis*. Boston: D. Reidel Publishing Company.

Ihde, D. (1982). The technological embodiment of media. In M. J. Hyde (Ed.), *Communication philosophy and the technology age*. Tuscaloosa, AL: University of Alabama Press.

Ihde, D. (1990). *Technology and the lifeworld: From garden to earth.* Bloomington, IN: Indiana University Press.

Ihde, D. (1998). *Expanding hermeneutics: Visualism in science.* Evanston, IL: Northwestern University Press.

Ikeda, R. (1997). History of communication theory: A Gebserian analysis. *SIETAR, 1,* 35–55.

Ikeda, R., & Kramer, E. M. (1998). The Enola Gay: The transformation of an airplane into an icon and the ownership of history. *Keio Communication Review, 20,* 49–73.

Innis, H. (1951). *The bias of communication.* Toronto: University of Toronto Press.

IUCN. (2013, July). *Pelagic chondrichthyans.* Shark specialist group. Available at http://www.iucnssg.org/pelagic-chondrichthyans

Iyer, V. (2002). Embodied mind, situated cognition, and expressive microtiming in African-American music. *Music Perception: An Interdisciplinary Journal, 19*(3), 387–414.

Jackson, M. (1983). Knowledge of body. *Man, 18,* 327–345.

Jackson. M. (2008). *Distracted: The erosion of attention and the coming dark age.* New York: Prometheus.

Jacoby, S. (2009). *The age of American unreason.* New York: Vintage.

Jaeckel, T. (2007). *The God particle: The discovery and modeling of the ultimate prime particle.* Boca Raton, FL: Universal Publishers.

Janis, I. (1968). *Personality: Dynamics, development, assessment.* New York: Harcourt, Brace & World.

Janis, I. (1972). *Victims of groupthink: A psychological study of foreign-policy decisions and fiascoes.* Boston: Houghton, Mifflin.

Jaspers, K. (1931 Ger.). *Man in the modern age* (E. Paul & C. Paul, Trans.). London: Routledge.

Jaspers, K. (1938 Ger./1971 Eng.). *Philosophy of existence* (R. Grabau, Trans.). Philadelphia: University of Pennsylvania Press.

Johnson, A. (1978, September). In search of the affluent society. *Human Nature,* pp. 50–59.

Jones, C. (2010, June 16). Frank Fenner sees no hope for humans. *The Australian.* Available at http://www.theaustralian.com.au/higher-education/frank-fenner-sees-no-hope-for-humans/story-e6frgcjx-1225880091722.

Kafka, F. (1925 Ger./1998 Eng.). *The trial* (B. Mitchell, Trans.). New York: Schocken/Random House.

Kafka, F. (1926 Ger./2009 Eng.). *The castle* (A. Bell, Trans.). London: Oxford University Press.

Kamalipour, Y., & Snow, E. (Eds.). (2004). *War, media, and propaganda.* Oxford, UK: Rowman & Littlefield Publishers.

Kant, I. (1781 Ger./1929 Eng.). *Critique of pure reason* (N. Smith, Trans.). New York: Macmillan.

Kasthuri, N., & Lichtman, J. (2010). Neurocartography. *Neuropsychopharmacology, 35,* 342–343.

Kaufmann, W. (1975). *Nietzsche: Philosopher, psychologist, Antichrist.* Princeton, NJ: Princeton University Press.

Kaufmann, W. (1992). *Nietzsche, Heidegger, and Buber: Discovering the mind* (Vol. 2). New York: Transaction Publishers.

Kearney, R. (1984). *Dialogues with contemporary continental thinkers.* Manchester, UK: Manchester University Press.

Keynes, J. M. (1971/1989). *The collected writings of John Maynard Keynes.* New York: St. Martin's Press.

Khordagui, H., & Al-Ajmi, D. (1993). Environmental impact of the Gulf War: An integrated preliminary assessment. *Environmental Management, 17*(4), 557–562. Available at http://dx.doi.org/10.1007%2FBF02394670

Kierkegaard, S. (1843 Danish/2006 Eng.). *Fear and trembling* (S. Walsh, Trans.). Cambridge, UK: Cambridge University Press.

Kiester, A., & Olson, D. (2011). Prime time for turtle conservation. *Herpetological Reviews, 42*(2), 198–204.

Kirn, W. (2007, August 5). Vacation, all I never wanted. *New York Times.* Retrieved January 7, 2008, from www.nytimes.com

Klare, M. (2001). *Resource wars: The new landscape of global conflict.* New York: Holt.

Klare, M. (2012). *The race for what's left: The global scramble for the world's last resources.* New York: Metropolitan.

Klemens, M. (2000). *Turtle conservation.* Washington, DC: Smithsonian.

Kolbert, E. (2011). The acid sea. *National Geographic Magazine.* Available at http://ngm.nationalgeographic.com/2011/04/ocean-acidification/kolbert-text

Koestler, A. (1940 Ger./1984 Eng.). *Darkness at noon* (D. Hardy, Trans.). New York: Bantam.

Koyre, A. (1965). *Newtonian studies.* Cambridge, MA: Harvard University Press.

Koyre, A. (1968). *Metaphysics and measurement: Essays in scientific revolution.* Cambridge, MA: Harvard University Press.

Kozol, J. (2006). *The shame of the nation: The restoration of apartheid schooling in America.* New York: Broadway Books.

Kramer, E. M. (1988). *Television criticism and the problem of ground: Interpretation after deconstruction.* Unpublished doctoral dissertation, Ohio University.

Kramer, E. M. (1991). Terrorizing discourses and dissident courage. *Journal of Communication Theory, 1*(4), 336–347.

Kramer, E. M. (1992). Gebser and culture. In E. M. Kramer (Ed.), *Consciousness and culture: An introduction to the thought of Jean Gebser* (pp. 1–60). Westport, CT: Greenwood.

Kramer, E. M. (1993a). The origin of television as civilizational expression. In K. Haworth, J. Deely, & T. Prewitt (Eds.), *Semiotics 1990: Sources in semiotics* (Vol. XI, pp. 28–37). New York: University Press of America.

Kramer, E. M. (1993b). Understanding co-constitutional genesis. *Integrative Explorations: Journal of Culture and Consciousness, 1,* 41–47.

Kramer, E. M. (1993c, June 24). *Videocentrism.* Delivered at the 25th annual Husserl Circle Conference, DePaul University, Chicago.

Kramer, E. M. (1994a). *A prolegomena to an ethic for digital deception: Rationale for an ethic for new technologies of ontogenesis: Modernity and visiocentrism.* Authored by request of the Director of American Forces Information Services, Department of Defense, The Pentagon.

Kramer, E. M. (1994b). Making love alone: Videocentrism and the case of modern pornography. In K. Callaghan (Ed.), *Ideals of feminine beauty: Philosophical, social, and cultural dimensions* (pp. 78–98). Westport, CT: Greenwood.

Kramer, E. M. (1994c). *Ethic concerning digital information manipulation.* Authored by request of the Director of American Forces Information Services, Department of Defense, The Pentagon.

Kramer, E. M. (1995). A brief hermeneutic of the co-constitution of nature and culture in the West including some contemporary consequences. *History of European Ideas, 20*(1-3), 649–659.

Kramer, E. M. (1997a). *Modern/postmodern: Off the beaten path of anti-modernism.* Westport, CT: Praeger.

Kramer, E. M. (1997b). The spiders of truth. In E. M. Kramer (Ed.), *Postmodernism and race* (pp. 1–15). Westport, CT: Praeger.

Kramer, E. M. (2000a). Contemptus mundi: Reality as disease. In V. Berdayes & J. Murphy (Eds.), *Computers, human interaction, and organizations.* Westport, CT: Praeger.

Kramer, E. M. (2000b). Cultural fusion and the defense of difference. In M. K. Asante & J. E. Min (Eds.), *Socio-cultural conflict between African and Korean Americans* (pp. 182–223). New York: University Press of America.

Kramer, E. M. (2000c). Ressentiment and racism. In M. K. Asante & E. Min (Eds.), *Socio-cultural conflict between African and Korean Americans* (pp. 35–70). New York: University Press of America.

Kramer, E. M. (2003a). Cosmopoly: Occidentalism and the new world order. In E. M. Kramer (Ed.), *The emerging monoculture: Assimilation and the "model minority"* (pp. 234–291). Westport, CT: Praeger.

Kramer, E. M. (2003b). Gaiatsu and cultural judo. In E. M. Kramer (Ed.), *The emerging monoculture: Assimilation and the "model minority"* (pp. 1–32). Westport, CT: Praeger.

Kramer, E. M. (2004a). The body in communication. In V. Berdayes, L. Esposito, & J. Murphy (Eds.), *The body in human inquiry: Interdisciplinary explorations of embodiment* (pp. 51–86). Cresskill, NJ: Hampton Press.

Kramer, E. M. (2004b). Vanishing meaning, the ideology of value-addition, and the diffusion of broadband information technology. In J. M. Choi, J. W. Murphy, & M. J. Caro (Eds.), *Globalization with a human face* (pp. 87–108). Westport, CT: Praeger.

Kramer, E. M. (2008). Theoretical reflections on intercultural studies: Preface. In S. Croucher (Ed.), *Looking beyond the hijab* (pp. ix–xxxix). Cresskill, NJ: Hampton Press.

Kramer, E. M. (2010). Immigration. In R. L. Jackson II (Ed.), *Encyclopedia of identity* (pp. 384–389). Thousand Oaks, CA: Sage.

Kramer, E. M. (2011). Preface. In S. Croucher & D. Cronn-Mills (Eds.), *Religious misperceptions: The case of Muslims and Christians in France and Britain* (pp. vii–xxxii). Cresskill, NJ: Hampton Press.

Kramer, E. M. (2012). Addressing the grand omission: A brief explanation of the pragmatics of intercultural communication in terms of spiritual systems–A taxonomic approach. In S. M. Croucher & T. M. Harris (Eds.), *Religion and communication: An anthology of extensions in theory, research, and method* (pp. 189–221). New York: Peter Lang.

Kramer, E. M. (2013). Dimensional accrual and dissociation: An introduction. In J. Grace & E. M. Kramer (Eds.), *Communication, comparative cultures, and civilizations* (Vol. 3, pp. 123–184). Cresskill, NJ: Hampton Press.

Kramer, E. M., Callahan, C., & Zuckerman, D. (2013). *Intercultural communication and global integration.* Dubuque, IA: Kendall Hunt.

Kramer, E. M., & Hsieh, E. (2012). Anti-culture and aging. In S. Arxer & J. Murphy (Eds.), *The symbolism of globalization, development, and aging* (pp. 135–156). New York: Springer.

Kramer, E. M., & Ikeda, R. (1998). Understanding different worlds: The theory of dimensional accrual/dissociation. *Journal of Intercultural Communication, 1*(2), 37–51.

Kramer, E. M., & Ikeda, R. (2000). The changing faces of reality. *Keio Communication Review, 22,* 3–32.

Kramer, E. M., & Ikeda, R. (2001). Standardization and loss of identity through globalism. *Journal of Intercultural Communication, 4*(1), 1–13.

Kramer, E. M., & Ikeda, R. (2002). Japanese clocks: Semiotic evidence of the perspectival mutation. *The American Journal of Semiotics, 17*(2), 71–137.

Kramer, E. M., & Isa, M. (2003). Adopting the Caucasian "look": Reorganizing the minority face. In E. Kramer (Ed.), *The emerging monoculture: Assimilation and the "model minority"* (pp. 41–74). Westport, CT: Praeger.

Kramer, E. M., & Kim, T. (2009). The global network of players. In J. M. Choi & J. W. Murphy (Eds.), *Globalisation and the prospects for critical reflection* (pp. 183–211). Delhi, India: Aakar.

Kuhn, T. (1962). *The structure of scientific revolutions.* Chicago, IL: University of Chicago Press.

Kurzweil, R. (2000). *The age of spiritual machines: When computers exceed human intelligence.* New York: Penguin.

Kurzweil, R. (2005). *The singularity is near: When humans transcend biology.* New York: Viking Adult.

Kurzweil, R. (2013). *How to create a mind: The secret of human thought revealed.* New York: Penguin.

Laing, R. D. (1969). *Politics of the family.* Toronto: CBC.

Lakoff, G., & Núñez, R. (2001). *Where mathematics comes from: How the embodied mind brings mathematics into being.* New York: Basic Books.

Landes, D. S. (1983). *Revolution in time: Clocks and the making of the modern world.* Cambridge, MA: Harvard University Press.

Langer, M. (1989). *Merleau-Ponty's phenomenology of perception: A guide and commentary.* Tallahassee, FL: The Florida University Press.

Langrebe, L. (1981). *The phenomenology of Edmund Husserl* (D. Welton, Ed.). Ithaca, NY: Cornell University Press.

Lanier, J. (2013). *Who owns the future?* New York: Simon & Schuster.

Lanza, R., & Berman, B. (2010). *Biocentrism: How life and consciousness are the keys to understanding the true nature of the universe.* Dallas, TX: BenBella Books.

Latour, B. (1993). *We have never been modern.* Cambridge, MA: Harvard University Press.

Leigh, D., & Harding, L. (2011). *Wikileaks: Inside Julian Assange's war on secrecy.* London: Guardian Press.

Lerner, D. (1965). *The passing of traditional society.* New York: The Free Press.

Lessig, L. (1999). *The limits in Open Code: Regulatory standards and the future of the net.* Berkeley, CA: University of California Press.

Lessig, L. (2008). Foreword. In J. Zittrain (Ed.), *The future of the Internet and how to stop it* (pp. vii–viii). New Haven, CT: Yale University Press.

Levinas, E. (1961 Fr./1969 Eng.). *Totality and infinity: Essays on exteriority* (A. Lingus, Trans.). Pittsburgh, PA: Duquesne University Press.

Levinas, E. (1948 Fr./1987 Eng.). *Time and the other: And additional essays* (R. Cohen, Trans.). Pittsburgh: Duquesne University Press.

Levinas, E. (1972 Fr./2005 Eng.). *Humanism of the other* (N. Poller, Trans.). Champaign, IL: University of Illinois Press.

Levine, R. (1998). *The geography of time: The temporal misadventures of a social psychologist.* New York: Basic Books.

Levi-Strauss, C. (1964 Fr./1983 Eng.). *The raw and the cooked: Introduction to a science of mythology* (Vol. 1) (J. Weightman & D. Weightman, Trans.). Chicago: University of Chicago Press.

Levi-Strauss, C. (1978/2001). *Myth and meaning: Cracking the code of culture (Massey Lectures on CBC)* (W. Doniger, Trans.). London: Taylor & Francis.

Lewin K. (1943). Defining the "field at a given time." *Psychological Review, 50,* 292–310 (Republished in *Resolving Social Conflicts & Field Theory in Social Science,* Washington, DC: American Psychological Association, 1997).

Lifton, R. (1999). *Destroying the world to save it.* New York: Henry Holt.

Lippmann, W. (1955). *The public philosophy.* New York: Transaction Books.

Locke, J. (1690/1996). *An essay concerning human understanding* (K. P. Winkler, Ed.). Indianapolis, IN: Hackett Publishing.

Loon, J. (2003). *Risk and technological culture: Towards a sociology of virulence.* London: Routledge.

Lovekin, D. (1977). Jacques Ellul and the logic of technology. *Man and World, 10,* 251–272.

Lovekin, D. (1980). Technology as the sacred order. *Research in Philosophy and Technology, 3,* 203–222.

Lovekin, D. (1990). Technology and the denial of mystery: The sacralization of the familiar. In G. L. Ormiston (Ed.), *From artifact to habitat: Studies in the critical engagement of technology* (pp. 74–98). London: Associated University Press.

Lovekin, D. (1991). *Technique, discourse, and consciousness: An introduction to the philosophy of Jacques Ellul.* Bethlehem, PA: Lehigh University Press.

Lovelock, J. (1972, August). Gaia as seen through the atmosphere. *Atmospheric Environment, 6*(8), 579–580.

Lovelock, J., & Margulis, L. (1974, February). Atmospheric homeostasis by and for the biosphere: The Gaia hypothesis. *Tellus* (Series A: Stockholm: International Meteorological Institute), *26*(1–2), 2–10.

Low, D. (2000). *Merleau-Ponty's last vision.* Evanston, IL: Northwestern University Press.

Lu, C., Warchol, K., & Callahan, R. (2012). In situ replication of honey bee colony collapse disorder. *Bulletin of Insectology, 65*(1).

Lukács, G. (1957 Ger./1963 Eng.). *The meaning of contemporary realism* (J. Mander & N. Mander, Trans.). London: Merlin Press.

Luo, S., Kim, J., Johnson, W., Van Der Walt, J., Martenson, J., Yuhki, N., Miquelle, D., Uphyrkina, O., & O'Brien, S. (2004). Phylogeography and genetic ancestry of tigers (Panthera tigris). *PLoS Biology, 2,* 2275–2293.

Lutz, A. (2012, June 14). These 6 corporations control 90% of the media in America. *Business Insider.* Available at http://www.businessinsider.com/these-6-corporations-control-90-of-the-media-in-america-2012-6

Lyotard, J.-F. (1979 Fr./1984 Eng.). *The postmodern condition: A report on knowledge* (G. Bennington & B. Massumi, Trans.). Minneapolis: University of Minnesota Press.

Macedo, D. (2006). *Literacies of power: What Americans are not allowed to know.* Boulder, CO: Westview.

Mack, A., & Rock, I. (2000). *Inattentional blindness.* Cambridge, MA: MIT Press.

MacKay, D. (2009). *Sustainable energy—without the hot air.* Cambridge, UK: MIT Cambridge.

MacKenzie, D., & Wajcman, J. (2002). *The social shaping of technology* (2nd ed.). Buckingham, UK: Open University Press.

Madison, G. (1981). *The phenomenology of Merleau-Ponty.* Athens, OH: Ohio University Press.

Mahr, K. (2010, August 9). Shark-fin soup and the conservation challenge. *Time Magazine.* Available at http://www.time.com/time/magazine/article/0,9171,2021071,00.html

Malone, M. (2011). *Over-incarcerated and undereducated: The impact of California's prison proliferation on Los Angeles urban high schools.* Ann Arbor, MI: Proquest, UMI Dissertation Publishing.

Mander, J. (1978). *Four arguments for the elimination of television.* New York: Morrow.

Mannheim, K. (1936 Ger./1985 Eng.). *Ideology and utopia* (L. Wirth, Trans.). New York: Harvest.

Marcel, G. (1950–1951Ger./2001 Eng.). *The mystery of being* (2 Vols.). South Bend, IN: St. Augustine's Press.

Marcuse, H. (1964). *One dimensional man: Studies in the ideology of advanced industrial society.* Boston: Beacon Press.

Martin, P. (2007). *Twilight of the mammoths: Ice Age extinctions and the rewilding of America.* Berkeley, CA: University of California Press.

Marx, K. (1962/2000). *Karl Marx: Selected writings* (D. McLellan, Ed.). Oxford: Oxford University Press.

Marx, K., & Engels, F. (1845/1932 Ger./1998 Eng.). *The German ideology, including Theses on Feuerbach* (Unknown, Trans.). Amherst, NY: Prometheus.

Matthews, E. (1999). Temporality, subjectivity and history in Merleau Ponty's phenomenology. *Philosophical Inquiry, 21,* 87–98.

Mauss, M. (1934 Fr./2006 Eng.). *Techniques, technology and civilization* (N. Schlanger, Trans.). New York: Berhahn Books.

Mauss, M. (1925 Fr./1990 Eng.). *The gift: The form and reason for exchange in archaic societies* (W. Halls, Trans.). London: Routledge.

McCarthy, A. (2010). *The citizen machine: Governing by television in 1950s America.* New York: The New Press.

McChesney, R. (2013). *Digital disconnect: How capitalism is turning the Internet against democracy.* New York: The New Press.

McConaghy, N., Armstrong, M. S., & Blaszczynski, A. (1981). Controlled comparison of aversive therapy and covert sensitization in compulsive homosexuality. *Behavior Research and Therapy, 19*(5), 425–434.

McCord, W., & Iverson, J. (1991). A new box turtle of the genus cuora (testudines: emydidae) with taxonomic notes and a key to the species. *Herpetologica, 47*(4), 407–420.

McLuhan, M. (1962). *The Gutenberg galaxy: The making of typographic man* (1st ed.). Toronto: University of Toronto Press.

McLuhan, M. (1964). *Understanding media: The extension of man.* New York: Sphere Books.

McLuhan, M., & Powers, B. (1989). *The global village: Transformations in world life and media in the 21st century.* New York: Oxford University Press.

McLuhan, M., & Quentin, F. (1967). *The medium is the massage: An inventory of effects.* New York: Random House.

Merleau-Ponty, M. (1945 Fr./1962 Eng.). *Phenomenology of perception* (C. Smith, Trans.). New York: Humanities Press.

Merleau-Ponty, M. (1947, 1955, 1964 Fr./1964 Eng.). *The primacy of perception: And other essays on phenomenological psychology, the philosophy of art, history and politics* (J. M. Edie, Ed.; W. Cobb, Trans.). Evanston, IL: Northwestern University Press.

Merleau-Ponty, M. (1960 Fr./1964 Eng.). *Signs* (R. C. McCleary, Trans.). Evanston, IL: Northwestern University Press.

Merleau-Ponty, M. (1964 Fr./1968 Eng.). *The visible and invisible: Followed by working notes* (J. O'Neil, Trans.). Evanston, IL: Northwestern University Press.

Merleau-Ponty, M. (1968 Fr./1970 Eng.). *Themes from the lectures at the College de France 1952–1960* (J. O'Neil, Trans.). Evanston, IL: Northwestern University Press.

Merrell, F. (1995a). *Peirce's semiotics now: A primer.* Toronto: Canadian Scholar's Press.

Merrell, F. (1995b). *Semiosis in the postmodern age.* West Lafayette, IN: Purdue University Press.

Merrell, F. (1997). *Peirce, signs, and meaning.* Toronto: University of Toronto Press.

Meyrowitz, J. (1985). *No sense of place: The impact of electronic media on social behavior.* New York: Oxford University Press.

Michelakis, E., Webster, L., & Mackey, J. (2008). Dicholoroacetate (DCA) as a potential metabolic-targeting therapy for cancer. *British Journal of Cancer, 99*, 989–994.

Mickunas, A. (1986). Technological culture. In J. W. Murphy, A. Mickunas, & J. J. Pilotta (Eds.), *The underside of high-tech: Technology and the deformation of human sensibilities* (pp. 1–14). Westport, CT: Greenwood Press.

Mickunas, A. (1998). Permanence and flux. In B. C. Hopkins (Ed.), *Phenomenology: Japanese and American perspectives* (pp. 253–272). Dordrecht, The Netherlands: Kluwer Academic Publishers.

Mickunas, A., & Pilotta, J. (1997). *Technocracy vs. democracy: Issues in the politics of communication.* Cresskill, NJ: Hampton Press.

Mill, J.S. (1843/2014). A system of logic: Ratiocinative and inductive. In *Collected works of John Stuart Mill* (J. Robson, Ed.). London: Routledge.

Miller, J. H. (2009). *For Derrida*. New York: Fordham University Press.

Minsky, M. (1994, October). Will robots inherit the earth? *Scientific American, 271*, 108–113. Available at http://web.media.mit.edu/~minsky/papers/sciam.inherit.html

Mishima, Y. (1953). Death in midsummer. In Y. Mishima (Ed.), *Death in midsummer and other stories* (E. Seidensticker, Trans.) (pp. 1–29). New York: New Directions.

Mitcham, C., & Mackey, R. (1971). Jacques Ellul and the technological society. *Philosophy Today, 15*, 102–121.

Mitnic, K. (2012). *Ghost in the wires: My adventures as the world's most wanted hacker*. Boston: Back Bay Books.

Molnar, A. (2005). *School commercialism: From democratic ideal to market commodity*. New York: Routledge.

Moravec, H. (1988). *Mind children: The future of robot and human intelligence*. Cambridge, MA: Harvard University Press.

More, M., & Vita-More, N. (Eds.). (2013). *The transhumanism reader*. West Sussex, England: Wiley Blackwell.

Moriarty, S. E. (1996). Abduction: A theory of visual interpretation. *Communication Theory, 6*(2), 167–187.

Morris, D. (1969). *The human zoo*. New York: Kodansha International.

Mosco, V. (1989). *The pay-per society: Computers and communication in the information age*. Norwood, NJ: Ablex.

Mozingo, J. (2012, December 23). Pot farms take dirty toll. *Los Angles Times*. Available at http://articles.latimes.com/2012/dec/23/local/la-me-pot-enviro-20121223

MSN News. (2005, November 5). *The world's worst manmade environmental disasters*. Available at http://news.uk.msn.com/environment/wildlife/photos.aspx?cp-documentid=153204440&page=21#image=2

Mumford, L. (1934/1963/2010). *Technics and civilization*. New York: Harcourt, Brace & World/Chicago: University of Chicago Press.

Mumford, L. (1967). *The myth of the machine: Technics and human development*. New York: Harcourt, Brace & Jovanovich.

Mumford, L. (1970). *The myth of the machine: The pentagon of power*. New York: Harcourt, Brace & Jovanovich.

Murphy, J., Mickunas, A., & Pilotta, J. (1986). *The underside of high-tech: Technology and the deformation of human sensibilities*. Westport, CT: Greenwood Press.

Nagel, T. (2012). *Mind and cosmos: Why the materialist neo-Darwinian conception of nature is almost certainly false*. New York: Oxford University Press.

National Geographic. (2013, July 18). *Filmmakers for conservation: Richard Fitzpatrick*. Available at http://www.filmmakersforconservation.org/featured-filmmakers/91-richarfitzpatrick.html

Negroponte, N. (1995). *Being digital*. New York: Alfred A. Knopf.

Nelson, C. (1985). Poststructuralism and communication. *Journal of Communication Inquiry, 9*, 2–15.

New York Times. (1985, January 31). A great industry in danger; the fish supply of Lake Erie likely to be exhausted unless the state of Ohio takes action. Available at http://query.nytimes.com/gst/abstract.html?res=F20913F8395911738DDDA80B 94D9405B8585F0D3

Newitz, A. (2013, May 6). Can humans survive? *Newsweek.* Available at http://www.thedailybeast.com/newsweek/2013/05/06/the-sixth-mass-extinctionis-upon-us-can-humans-survive.html

Newitz, A. (2013). *Scatter, adapt, and remember: How humans will survive the mass extinction.* New York: Doubleday.

Nietzsche, F. (1895 Ger./1990 Eng.). *The antichrist* (R. Hollingdale, Trans.). New York: Penguin.

Nietzsche, F. (1887 Ger./1989 Eng.). *On the genealogy of morals* (W. Kaufmann, Trans.). New York: Vintage.

Nietzsche, F. (1887 Ger./1974 Eng.). *The gay science* (W. Kaufmann, Trans.). New York: Vintage.

Nietzsche, F. (1901 Ger./1967 Eng.). *The will to power* (W. Kaufmann & R. J. Hollingdale, Trans.). New York: Random House.

Nuttin, J. (1969). Attitude change after rewarded dissonant and consonant "forced compliance." In A. C. Elms (Ed.), *Role playing, reward. and attitude change* (pp. 52–73). New York: Van Nostrand Rheinhold.

Nuttin, J. (1996). *The illusion of attitude change: Towards a response contagion theory of persuasion.* Leuven, The Netherlands: Leuven University Press.

Oehler, K. (1995). A response to Habermas. In K. L. Kenneth (Ed.), *Peirce and contemporary thought* (pp. 267–271). New York: Fordham University Press.

Olson, P. (2013). *We are Anonymous: Inside the hacker world of LulzSec, Anonymous, and the global cyber insurgency.* Boston: Back Bay Books.

Ong, W. J. (1977). *Interfaces of the word: Studies in the evolution of consciousness and culture.* Ithaca, NY: Cornell University Press.

Ong, W. J. (1982). *Orality and literacy: The technologizing of the word.* New York: Routledge.

Ophir, E., Nass, C., & Wagner, A. (2009). Cognitive control in media multitaskers. *Proceeding of the National Academy of Sciences of the United States, 106*(37) 15583–15587.

Orr, J., Fabry, V., Aumont, O., Bopp, L., Doney, S., Feely, R., . . . Yool, A.(2005). Anthropogenic ocean acidification over the twenty-first century and its impact on calcifying organisms. *Nature, 437,* 681–686.

Orwell, G. (1949, 2013). *1984.* Available at http://www.dmoz.org/Arts/ Literature/Authors/O/Orwell,–George/1984/

Packard, V. (1972). *A nation of strangers.* New York: David McKay.

Packard, V. (1957/2007). *The hidden persuaders.* New York: Ig Publishing.

Packard, V. (1964). *The pyramid climbers.* New York: Crest.

Packard, V. (1969). *The status seekers.* New York: Pocket.

Packard, V. (1960/2011). *The waste makers.* New York: Ig Publishing.

Parsons, T. (1964, 2007). *Social structure and personality.* New York: Free Press.

Paterniti, M. (2001). *Driving Mr. Albert: A trip across America with Einstein's brain.* New York: Dial Press/Random House.

Pearce, F. (2007). *When the rivers run dry: Water—the defining crisis of the twenty-first century*. Boston: Beacon.

Pearce, F. (2012). *The land grabbers: The new fight over who owns the Earth*. Boston: Beacon Press.

Pearlstein, M. (2011). *From family collapse to America's decline: The educational, economic, and social costs of family fragmentation*. New York: Rowman & Littlefield.

Peirce, C. S. (1931). *Collected papers of Charles Sanders Peirce* (Vols. 1–6). Cambridge, MA: Harvard University Press.

Peirce, C. S. (1958). *Collected papers of Charles Sanders Peirce* (Vols. 7–8) (C. Hartshorne, P. Weiss, & A. W. Burks, Eds.). Cambridge, MA: Harvard University Press.

Pemberton, H. E. (1936). The curve of culture diffusion rate. *American Sociological Review, 1*(4), 547–556.

People's Daily News. (2005, November 15). *Five dead, one missing, nearly 70 injured in chemical plant blasts*. Available at http://english.people.com.cn/200511/15/eng20051115-221428.html

Pilkington, E. (2013, May 29). "Killer robots" pose threat to peace and should be banned, UN warned. *The Guardian*. Available at http://www.theguardian.com/science/2013/may/29/killer-robots-ban-un-warning

Pilotta, J. J., & Widman, T. L. (1986). Overcoming communicative incompetence in the global communication order: The case of technology transfer. In J. W. Murphy, A. Mickunas, & J. J. Pilotta (Eds.), *The underside of high-tech: Technology and the deformation of human sensibilities* (pp. 159–176). Westport, CT: Greenwood Press.

Pinker, S. (1994). *The language instinct*. New York: W. Morrow Co.

Plato. (1998). *Phaedrus* (J. Nichols, Trans.). Ithaca, NY: Cornell University Press.

Plato. (1998). *Gorgias* (J. Nichols, Trans.). Ithaca, NY: Cornell University Press.

Platt, J. (2012, September 5). Extinction countdown: Japanese River Otter declared extinct. *Scientific American*. Available at http://blogs.scientificamerican.com/extinction-countdown/2012/09/05/japanese-river-otter-declared-extinct/

Polanyi, M. (1958). *Personal knowledge: Toward post-critical philosophy*. Chicago, IL: University of Chicago Press.

Polkinghorne, D. (1983). *Methodology for human science: Systems of inquiry*. Albany, NY: State University of New York Press.

Pool, I. (1983). *Technologies of freedom: Free speech in the electronic age*. Cambridge, MA: Belknap/Harvard University Press.

Popper, K. (1934 Ger./2002 Eng.). *The logic of scientific discovery*. New York: Routledge.

Pospisil, L. J. (1978). *The ethnology of law*. Menlo Park, CA: Cummings Publishing Company.

Postman, N. (1985/2005). *Amusing ourselves to death*. New York. Penguin.

Postman, N. (1992). *Technopoly: The surrender of culture to technology*. New York: Random House.

Postman, N. (1996). *The end of education: Redefining the value of school*. New York: Vintage.

Postman, N., & Weingartner, C. (1969). *Teaching as a subversive activity.* New York: Dell.

Pozner, J. (2010). *Reality bites back: The troubling truth about guilty pleasure TV.* Berkeley, CA: Perseus/Seal Press.

Predicts. (2013). Imperial College London, United Nations Environmental Programme World Conservation Monitoring Centre, University College London, University of Sussex, Microsoft Research. Available at http://www.predicts.org.uk/links.html

Prud'homme, A. (2011). *The ripple effect: The fate of fresh water in the twenty-first century.* New York: Scribner.

Putnam, R. (2000). *Bowling alone: The collapse and revival of American community.* New York: Simon & Schuster.

Quine, W. (1960/2013). *Word and object* (new ed.). Cambridge, MA: MIT Press.

Rainwater, L., & Pittman, D. J. (1967). Ethical problems in studying a politically sensitive and deviant community. *Social Problems, 14*(4), 357–366.

Rainwater-McClure, R., Reed, W., & Kramer, E. (2003). A world of cookie-cutter faces. In E. Kramer (Ed.), *The emerging monoculture: Assimilation and the "model minority"* (pp. 221–233). Westport, CT: Praeger.

Ramo, H. (1999). An Aristotelian human time-space manifold: From Chronochora to Kairotopos. *Time and Society, 8,* 309–332.

Rees, M. (2003). *Our final hour: A scientist's warning: How terror, error, and environmental disaster threaten humankind's future in this century—On earth and beyond.* New York: Basic Books.

Reidenberg, J. (1998). Lex informatica: The formulation of information policy rules through technology. *Texas Law Review, 76,* 553.

Rheingold, H. (1993). *The virtual community.* Reading, MA: Addison-Wesley.

Ricoeur, P. (1950 Fr./1966 Eng.). *Freedom and nature: The voluntary and the involuntary* (E. Kohak, Trans.). Evanston, IL: Northwestern University Press.

Ricoeur, P. (1955 Fr./1965 Eng.). *History and truth* (C. Kelbley, Trans.). Evanston, IL: Northwestern University Press.

Ricoeur, P. (1965 Fr./1970 Eng.). *Freud & philosophy: An essay on interpretation* (D. Savage, Trans.). New Haven, CT: Yale University Press.

Ricoeur, P. (1969 Fr./1974 Eng.). *Conflict of interpretations: Essays in hermeneutics* (W. Domingo, Trans.). Evanston, IL: Northwestern University Press.

Ricoeur, P. (1975). Phenomenology and hermeneutics. *Nous, 9,* 85–102.

Ricoeur, P. (1976). *Interpretation theory: Discourse and the surplus of meaning.* Fort Worth: Texas Christian Press.

Riesman, D., Glazer, N., & Denney, R. (1950, 2001). *The lonely crowd: A study of the changing American character.* New Haven, CT: Yale University Press.

Rifkin, J. (2009). *The empathic civilization: The race to global consciousness in a world in crisis.* New York: Tarcher/Penguin Group.

Rifkin, J. (2004). *The European dream.* New York: Jeremy P. Tarcher/Penguin.

Rifkin, J. (1989). *Time wars: The primary conflict in human history.* New York: Touchstone.

Roberts, D. F., & Foehr, U. G. (2008). Trends in media use. *The Future of Children, 18*(1), 11–37.

Roberts, K. (2010). *Cyber junkie: Escape the gaming and Internet trap.* Center City, MN: Hazelden.

Roberts, S., Frenette, J., & Stearns, D. (2002). A comparison of media outlets and owners for ten selected markets (1960, 1980, 2000). *Federal Communications Commission.* Available at http://transition.fcc.gov/mb/mbpapers.html

Robock, A., Oman, L., & Stenchikov, G. (2008, August 16). Regional climate responses to geoengineering with tropical and Arctic SO2 injections. *Journal of Geophysical Research: Atmospheres, 113*(D16), 1984–2012.

Rogers, E. (1962). *Diffusion of innovations.* New York: The Free Press.

Rokeach, M. (1968). *Beliefs, attitudes and values: A theory of organization and change.* New York: Jossey-Bass/Wiley.

Rokeach, M. (1973). *The nature of human values.* New York: Free Press.

Rorty, R. (1961). Pragmatism, categories, and language. *Philosophical Review, 70*(2), 197–223.

Rorty, R. (1989). *Contingency, irony and solidarity.* New York: Cambridge University Press.

Rosenbloom, S. (2007, December 17). On Facebook, scholars link up with data. *New York Times.* Retrieved January 10, 2008, from www.nytimes.com

Rostow, W. (1960). *The stages of economic growth: A non-communist manifesto.* Cambridge, UK: Cambridge University Press.

Rozell, N. (2001, February). *Alaska science forum: Bowhead whales may be the world's oldest mammals* (Article No. 1529). Geophysical Institute, University of Alaska Fairbanks. Available at http://www2.gi.alaska.edu/ScienceForum/ASF15/1529.html

Ruesch, J., & Bateson, G. (1951/2006). *Communication: The social matrix of psychiatry.* New York: W. W. Norton & Company/New York: Transaction Books.

Sagan, C. (1996). *The demon-haunted world: Science as a candle in the dark.* New York: Ballantine.

Samways, M. (1999, June). Translocating fauna to foreign lands: Here comes the Homogenocene. *Journal of Insect Conservation, 3*(2), 65–66.

Sartre, J.-P. (1943 Fr./1984 Eng.). *Being and nothingness* (H. Barnes, Trans.). New York: Washington Square Press.

Schiller, H. I. (1989). *Culture, Inc.: The corporate takeover of public expression.* New York: Oxford University Press.

Schlag, P. (1998). *The enchantment of reason.* Durham, NC: Duke University Press.

Schor, J. (1993). *Overworked America: The unexpected decline of leisure.* New York: Basic Books.

Schumacher, E. (1973). *Small is beautiful: A study of economics as if people mattered.* New York: Harper & Row.

Schutz, A. (1945 Ger./1970 Eng.). Indirect social realities. In H. Wagner (Trans., Ed.) *Alfred Schutz on phenomenology and social relations* (pp. 200–235). Chicago: University of Chicago Press.

Schutz, A. (1945). On multiple realities. *Philosophy and Phenomenological Research, 5,* 533–576.

Schutz, A. (1953/1997). Positivistic philosophy and the actual approach of interpretive social science: An ineditum of Alfred Schutz from spring 1953 (L. Embree, Ed.). *Husserl Studies, 14,* 123–149.

Searle, J. (1980). Mind, brains, and programs. *Behavior and Brain Sciences, 3,* 417–457.

Searle, J. (1984). *Minds, brains, and science.* Cambridge, MA: Harvard University Press.

Sebeok, T. A. (1976). *Contributions to the doctrine of signs.* Bloomington, IN: Indiana University Press.

Sebeok, T. A. (1994). *An introduction to semiotics.* Toronto: University of Toronto Press.

Seidensticker, J., Christie, S., & Jackson, P. (1999). *Riding the tiger: Tiger conservation in human-dominated landscapes.* Cambridge, UK: Cambridge University Press.

Seigel, J. (1991). A unique way of existing: Merleau-Ponty and the subject. *Journal of History of Philosophy, 29,* 460–482.

Seung, S. (2012). *Connectome: How the brain's wiring makes us who we are.* New York: Houghton Mifflin Harcourt Publishing Company.

Seung, T. K. (1982). *Structuralism and hermeneutics.* New York: Columbia University Press.

Shapiro, J. (2012). *China's environmental challenges.* New York: Polity Press.

Shannon, C. E., & Weaver, W. (1949). *A mathematical theory of communication.* Urbana, IL: University of Illinois Press.

Shelley, M. (1818/2013). *Frankenstein: Or, the modern Prometheus.* New York: Simon & Brown.

Sherif, M., & Hovland, C. (1981). *Social judgment: Assimilation and contrast effects in communication and attitude change.* New Haven, CT: Yale University Press.

Sheriff, J. K. (1989). *The fate of meaning: Charles Peirce, structuralism, and literature.* Princeton: Princeton University Press.

Shettleworth, S. J. (2009). *Cognition, evolution, and behavior.* New York: Oxford University Press.

Simmel, G. (1908 Ger./1950 Eng.). *The sociology of Georg Simmel.* New York: The Free Press.

Skinner, B. F. (1999). *Cumulative record: Definitive edition* (V. G. Laties & A. C. Catania, Eds.). Cambridge, MA: B. F. Skinner Foundation.

Sloterdijk, P. (1983 Ger./1988 Eng.). *Critique of cynical reason* (M. Eldred, Trans.). Minneapolis, MN: University of Minnesota Press.

Solomon, S. (2011). *Water: The epic struggle for wealth, power, and civilization.* New York: Harper Perennial.

Spencer, H. (1831, 2013). *Social statics: Or, the conditions essential to happiness specified, and the first of them developed.* London: John Chapman. Available at http://oll.libertyfund.org/index.php?option=com–staticxt&staticfile=show-php%3title=273&layout=html

Spring, U., & Brauch, H. (2011). Coping with global environmental change: Sustainability revolution and sustainable peace. *Hexagon Series on Human and Environmental Security and Peace, 5,* 1487–1503.

Star Trek: The Next Generation. (G. Roddenberry, creator and producer). (1987–1994). Los Angeles: CBS Studios.

Steinberg, J. (2002, December). A mist opportunity. *National Geographic Magazine,* p. 199.

Steinberg, S., Kincheloe, J., & McLaren, P. (2006). *Literacies of power: What Americans are not allowed to know*. New York: Westview.

Stigliz, J. (2003). *Globalization and its discontents*. New York: Norton.

Stigliz, J., Sen, A., & Fitoussi, J.-P. (2010). *Mismeasuring our lives: Why GDP doesn't add up*. New York: New Press.

Stout, M. (2001). *The feel-good curriculum: The dumbing down of America's kids in the name of self-esteem*. New York: Da Capo/Perseus Books.

Strasberger, V. C., Jordan, A. B., & Donnerstein, E. (2010). Health effects of media on children and adolescents. *Pediatrics, 125*(4), 756–767.

Stuart, B., & Platt, S. (2004). Recent records of turtles and tortoises from Laos, Cambodia, and Vietnam. *Asiatic Herpetological Research, 10*, 129–150.

Sweeney, J., & Nussbaum, K. (1989). *Solutions for the new work force: Policies for a new social contract*. Cabin John, MD: Seven Locks Press.

Swingland, I., & Klemens, M. (Eds.). (1989). *The conservation biology of tortoises*. New York: IUNC–The World Conservation Union.

Sykes, C. (1996). *Dumbing down our kids: Why American children feel good about themselves but can't read, write, or add*. New York: St. Martin's Griffin.

Tilt, B. (2009). *The struggle for sustainability in rural China: Environmental values and civil society*. New York: Columbia University Press.

Time Magazine. (1969, August 1). America's sewage system and the price of optimism. Available at http://www.time.com/time/magazine/article/0,9171,901182,00.html

Toffler, A. (1970). *Future shock*. New York: Random House.

Toffler, A. (1991). *Powershift: Knowledge, wealth, and violence at the edge of the 21st century*. New York: Bantam.

Tönnies, F. (1887 Ger./2001 Eng.). *Community and civil society* (J. Harris, Trans.). Cambridge, UK: Cambridge University Press.

Townsend, A. (2000). Life in the real-time city: Mobile telephones and urban metabolism. *Journal of Urban Technology, 7*(2), 85–104.

TRAFFIC. (2005, August 8). *Nowhere to hide: The trade in Sumatran Tiger*. Available at http://www.traffic.org/sumatranTigers.pdf.

Turkle, S. (1995). *Life on the screen: Identity in the age of the Internet*. New York: Simon & Schuster.

Turkle, S. (1997). Computational technologies and images of the self. *Social Research, 64*, 1093–1112.

Twenge, J. (2007). *Generation me: Why today's young Americans are more confident, assertive, entitled —and more miserable than ever before*. New York: The Free Press/Simon & Schuster.

Twenge, J., & Campbell, W. (2010). *The narcissism epidemic: Living in the age of entitlement*. New York: Atria/Simon & Schuster Books.

Üexkull, von J. (1934 Ger./2010 Eng.). *A foray into the worlds of animals and humans* (J. O'Neil, Trans.). Minneapolis, MN: University of Minnesota Press.

U.S. Department of the Treasury, Bureau of Engraving and Printing. (2009). *Currency notes*. Retrieved July 5, 2013, from http://www.moneyfactory.gov/images/Currency–notes–508.pdf#search="Annuit Coeptis"

Vanderburg, W. H. (2005). *Living in the labyrinth of technology*. Toronto: University of Toronto Press.

Waldman, S., & the Working Group on Information Needs of Communities. (2011, June). The information needs of communities. *Federal Communications Commission.* Available at http://journalistsresource.org/wp-content/uploads/2011/06/57454752-FCC-Report-THE-INFORMATION-NEEDS-OF-COMMUNITIES.pdf

Walston, J., Robinson, J., Bennett, E., Breitenmoser, U., da Fonseca G., Goodrich, J., & Wibisono, H. (2010). Bringing the tiger back from the brink—The six percent solution. *PLoS Biology, 8*(9), e1000485.

Watzlawick, P., Beavin, J., & Jackson, D. (1967/2011). *Pragmatics of human communication: A study of interactional patterns, pathologies and paradoxes.* New York: W. W. Norton & Company.

Weber, M. (1905 Ger./1958 Eng.). *The Protestant ethic and the spirit of capitalism* (T. Parsons, Trans.). New York: Charles Scribner's Sons.

Weinberger, D. (2008). *Everything is miscellaneous: The power of the new digital disorder.* New York: Holt.

Whitehead, A. (1929). *Process and reality.* New York: Macmillan.

Whitehorn, P., O'Connor, S., Wackers, F., & Goulson, D. (2012). Neonicotinoid pesticide reduces bumble bee colony growth and queen production. *Science, 336*(6079), 351–352.

Whorf, B. (1956). *Language, thought, and reality: Selected writings of Benjamin Lee Whorf* (J. B. Carroll, Ed.). Cambridge, MA: MIT Press.

Whyte, W. (1952, March). "Groupthink." *Fortune,* pp. 114–117, 142, 146.

Whyte, W. (1956/2002). *The organization man.* Philadelphia: University of Pennsylvania Press.

Williams, E. (2012). Driven to distraction: How electronic media are affecting the brain and the implications for human resource development in the future. *Advances in Developing Human Resources, 14*(4), 626–639.

Williams, R. (1983). *Keywords.* New York: Oxford University Press.

Williams, R. H. (2002). *Retooling: A historian confronts technological change.* Boston: MIT Press.

Williamson, J. (1994). *Decoding advertisements: Ideology and meaning in advertising.* London: Marion Boyars Publishers.

Wilson, E. (2012). *The social conquest of the earth.* New York: W. W. Norton & Company.

Wilson, E. (2013). *Letters to a young scientist.* New York: W. W. Norton & Company.

Winner, L. (1988). *The whale and the reactor: A search for limits in an age of high technology.* Chicago: University of Chicago Press.

Wittgenstein, L. (1953). *Philosophical investigations* (G. E. M. Anscomb & R. Rhees, Eds.; G. E. M. Anscomb, Trans.). Oxford: Basil Blackwell.

Wittgenstein, L. (1966). *Essays on Wittgenstein's Tractatus* (I. M. Copi & R. W. Beard, Eds.). London: Routledge.

Wittgenstein, L. (1969). *On certainty.* Oxford, England: Blackwell.

Wolff, R. P. (1966). Hume's theory of mental activity. In V. Chappell (Ed.), *Hume* (pp. 95–110). New York: Anchor Books.

Wong, K. (1999). *Funding public schools: Politics and policies.* Lawrence, KS: University of Kansas Press.

Wright, R. (2004). *A short history of progress*. Markham, Ontario, Canada: House of Anansi Press/Stoddart Publishing/Fitzhenry & Whiteside Ltd.

Yoon, C. (1999, May 4). Turtles vanish in black hole: Soup pots and pans of China. *New York Times*. Available at http://www.colorado.edu/Economics/morey/4535/readings/fishing/turtles.html

Zengotita, T. (2006). *Mediated: How the media shapes your world and the way you live in it*. New York: Bloomsbury.

Zielinski, S. (2010, April 27). Updated: The world's worst oil spills. *Smithsonian News*. Available at http://blogs.smithsonianmag.com/science/2010/04/the-worlds-worst-oil-spills/

Zimmerman, M. E. (1975). Heidegger on nihilism and technique. *Man and World, 8*, 394–414.

Zimmerman, M. E. (1979a). Marx and Heidegger on the technological domination of nature. *Philosophy Today, 23*, 99–112.

Zimmerman, M. E. (1979b). Technological culture and the end of philosophy. In P. T. Durbin & C. Mitcham (Eds.), *Research in philosophy and technology* (Vol. II). Westport, CT: JAI Press.

Zimmerman, M. E. (1990). *Heidegger's confrontation with modernity: Technology, politics, art*. Bloomington, IN: Indiana University Press.

Zimmerman, M. E. (1993). Rethinking the Heidegger-deep ecology relationship. *Environmental Ethics, 15*, 195–224.

Zittrain, J. (2008). *The future of the Internet and how to stop it*. New Haven, CT: Yale University Press.

Zongker, B. (2007, August 20). *Smithsonian air and space museum see fewer visitors*. Retrieved January 15, 2008, from www.usatoday.com.

Author Index

Subject Index

CPSIA information can be obtained
at www.ICGtesting.com
Printed in the USA
FFOW03n2134150217
32416FF